Micro-Macro
Political Analysis

Micro-Macro Political Analysis

Accents of Inquiry

Heinz Eulau
Stanford University

ALDINE PUBLISHING COMPANY 1969

First published 1969 by
Aldine Publishing Company
529 South Wabash Avenue
Chicago, Illinois 60605

Library of Congress Catalog Card Number 76–91717
SBN 202–24018
Printed in the United States of America

to

Samuel J. Eldersveld
Robert E. Lane
Dwaine Marvick
Herbert McClosky
Warren E. Miller
John C. Wahlke

workmen all
who
within a standard deviation or two
traveled the same road

Preface

A common theme pervades the essays and studies brought together in this volume: the fascination with the relationship between individual and collective political behavior. I was only dimly aware of this theme when in the middle fifties I worked on "Dimensions of Political Involvement" (chapter 8) and "Identification with Class and Political Role Behavior" (chapter 9). Today, in 1969, the theme is quite explicit. In the introductory essay, "On Units and Levels of Analysis," I try to articulate some of the methodological problems involved in the relationship. And two studies (chapters 15 and 16) are applications of the understanding that evolved only slowly over the years.

As long as the data available came from individuals randomly selected in the population, the problems of relating individual and collective behavior were simply handled verbally by invoking George Herbert Mead's conception of communication as "a taking of the role of the other." Role is neither an exclusively individualistic nor an exclusively collectivistic concept. It is both, and for this reason serves as a "linkage" term. "Dimensions of Political Involvement" was based on the assumption that an individual's "relatedness" to the political process "is largely a function of (1) the degree to which he has internalized his role as a citizen, and (2) the degree to which he evaluates this role as being an efficacious one, in the sense that performance of the role will make a difference in political affairs."

There was more than magic use of the role concept in "Identification with Class and Political Role Behavior." In retrospect this study still seems full of unnecessary mental gymnastics. But they were necessary then because it seemed to me that the consequences of a collective phenomenon such as social class for individual political behavior were more subtle than the rampant social determinism of previous voting research. I did not realize until fairly recently that this genre of research was then in process of developing. Commenting on the study, Hyman and Singer said that I

> reasoned that anticipatory socialization may be an effective means for learning *attitudes,* but not *conduct,* since the aspirant will have had little real opportunity to practice the skills required and to be taught the correct performance of the role.
>
> Eulau, finally, distinguishes between norms that are purely attitudinal in their implications and those that require performance of some sort, hypothesizing that persons who take a non-membership group as a reference group will be more adept at conforming to the former than to the latter. Specifically, he predicts that *self*-identification, in terms of social class, will be more effective in shaping political values, whereas *objective* class situation will be more reliably related to *participation* in politics.[1]

Most of the controversies that raged in the fifties and early sixties over "behavioralism" in political science missed the point that individual behavior and collective political institutions or processes are inevitably intertwined in the manifold of politics. Role analysis seemed to have the virtue of overcoming both the methodological individualism of those who worked primarily with the concepts of clinical psychology and also the methodological holism of those who worked primarily with the concepts of global sociology. When in the late fifties my colleagues and I undertook research in legislative behavior in four states,[2] we had little difficulty, at least intellectually, in bridging the schism between behavioralism and institutionalism in political science. In a paper delivered in 1961, about the time when we readied the research for publication, I wrote:

> The smallest social system, then, involves at least two actors who are related to each other in a structure which is given meaning by mutually complementary roles. But roles are only rarely defined in terms of a single structure alone. In most situations they represent configurations of role orientations and expectations concerning the actors' behavior. These configurations constitute "role systems." We can think, then, of any concrete institution or organization—a legislature, a party, a pressure group, a bureaucracy, and so on—as a role system, and it becomes possible to scrutinize relatively large structures, now conceived as role systems, by studying the role behavior of the individual actors who constitute the structure.[3]

1. Herbert H. Hyman and Eleanor Singer, *Readings in Reference Group Theory and Research* (New York: Free Press, 1968), pp. 11, 324.

2. See John C. Wahlke, Heinz Eulau, William Buchanan, and LeRoy C. Ferguson, *The Legislative System: Explorations in Legislative Behavior* (New York: John Wiley, 1962).

3. "Recent Developments in the Behavioral Study of Politics," 1961 Annual Meeting of the Northern California Political Science Association, p. 36. The paper is no longer available for distribution.

The method suggested here is "reduction"–moving analysis from the level of the institution to the level of the individual actor, and then reconstructing the whole out of its parts. (The strategies of reduction and construction are more fully discussed in the Introduction.)

Role analysis permitted us to come to grips, at least so it seemed, with the intractable problem of representation. In "The Role of the Representative: Some Empirical Observations on the Theory of Edmund Burke" (chapter 10) we distinguished between *style* and *focus* of representational role-taking. Style refers to internalized norms, while focus refers to external targets of the role such as constituencies or interest groups. Once again the role concept was useful in linking individual and collective aspects of political behavior. But several years later, when I had occasion to re-evaluate this body of research in a historical perspective in "Changing Views of Representation" (chapter 3), I had misgivings and concluded that "our conceptions of representation are obsolete."

In more recent research reported in "Political Matrix and Political Representation" (chapter 16), Kenneth Prewitt and I felt that representation must be treated as an "emergent" property of politics rather than as an attribute of individual actors. But how does one study emergent phenomena? As in so many other matters, I found suggestive leads in the work of Harold D. Lasswell, and even though we had to develop our own procedures, Lasswell's ideas, pieced together in "The Maddening Methods of Harold D. Lasswell" (chapter 5), were always in the background.

Two other studies, "Occupational Mobility and Political Career" (chapter 11) and "Political Socialization and Political Roles" (chapter 12), also reflect the influence of role formulations. There has been surprisingly little research on intergenerational occupational mobility as a political variable. By his multiple role-taking the politician mediates between collective demands on government. Establishing linkages does not solve what I consider the problem of the level of analysis, but the problem of establishing linkages deserves attention in its own right.

In "Political Socialization and Political Roles" (chapter 12) we had available something rare in political research–genuinely comparable data collected from different populations. We sought to test the developmental hypothesis that predispositions brought to the adult role from prior experiences account for adult political behavior. The evidence did not support the hypothesis. We therefore speculated that experiences intervening between early socialization and adult conduct, such as those stemming from recruitment and induction into politics, might be more relevant. And we concluded that the institutional setting and interactions occurring in that setting may be more appropriate in explaining individual behavior than socialization. Analysis of individual political behavior can be meaningfully conducted at the level of the group of which the individual is a member.

The transition from role analysis at the individual level to structural analysis is indicated by "The Ecological Basis of Party Systems" (chapter 13). I doubt that today I would phrase the problem of accounting for competition among political parties in the structural-functional requisite terms used in this study. The study is instructive, however, because it uses aggregate census and election data for structural analysis of ecological relationships.

Aggregate data disguise much of the variance characteristic of individual behavior. They are useful when individual data are not vailable for constructing a collective phenomenon. In "Bases of Authority in Legislative Bodies" (chapter 14) authority is conceived as a structural property of organizations. Authority is not an easily reducible group property, but available individual data permitted at least partial construction of authority relationships in eight large legislative bodies. The study demonstrates the viability of observing a group property at the individual level of analysis.

In the early sixties, when this study was done, I was especially sensitive to the dilemmas that the level-of-analysis problem engenders. This is evident in "Comparative Political Analysis" (chapter 6) and even more so in "The Behavioral Treatment of Politics" (chapter 7). In the latter I stuck my neck out arguing that "all problems of interest to political science are potentially susceptible to behavioral treatment"—in other words, that all units are reducible. But I guarded myself by saying that this position is predicated on the condition that "the relationship between macro- and micro-analysis is satisfactorily settled." I was much less confident then than I am now that the level of analysis problem can be solved by appropriate procedures.

Only very slowly did it become clear that it was one thing to do research on the behavior of individuals *in* groups (be they legislatures, organizations, or nations) and another thing to do research on the behavior *of* groups in the political arena. The difficulties involved in using aggregate data, random population samples, or universe data on individuals collected in large institutions led to the conclusion that the problem of the level of analysis could be more effectively tackled in small institutional groups. It seemed to me that all such problems—reduction, construction, imputation, linkage, or impact—could be more easily investigated and subjected to systematic measurement by observing small units of five, seven, or nine members. With a team of ten graduate students, all of them now colleagues spread around the country, I began a study of decision-making in and by small groups in the real world of government, using city councils as research sites and the interview as the research tool. The two analyses reported in Chapters 15 and 16 are preliminary reports of this research.

"Policy Maps of City Councils and Policy Outcomes: A Developmental Analysis" (chapter 15) introduces a number of methodological innovations, of which the use of budget data as indicators of group policy-making in its developmental aspects is not the least inconsequential. As "H. D. Lasswell's Developmental Analysis" (chapter 4) shows, Lasswellian notions again influenced the research design. But more important, perhaps, the study shows how an action unit can be disassembled into its individual parts and then reconstructed to permit analysis at its own level—that is, how correlation of distributive, emergent, and contextual properties is possible.[4]

"Political Matrix and Political Representation" (chapter 16) not only challenges the behavioral research tradition of dealing with representation at the level of the individual, but also shows that procedures other than computation are feasible in order to come to grips with representation as an emergent collective property. Although the article does not describe the procedures in detail, the fact that they yielded meaningful results suggests their validity.[5]

There is often an inverse relationship between theorizing activity and empirical knowledge of what is theorized about. Data, it seems, have a sobering effect on the theorist who has them and an inebriating effect on the theorist who has them not. I am not much devoted to theory that is not grounded in empirical data or at least provides operational leads to empirical data. I am not sure just where "Logics of Rationality in Unanimous Decision-Making" (chapter 1) would fall on the pure-theory-to-pure-data continuum. The article was stimulated by empirical observations, but unanimity in decision-making is an emergent group property, easily measured once it has appeared but most difficult to observe as a process. This, perhaps, explains why the essay took the deductive form it did. Research is certainly needed to distinguish between unanimity and consensus. That each member of a group may agree with every other member (unanimity) is by no means the same thing as group consensus, although the latter is often confused with the former in studies that claim to measure it.

The reader will not, I trust, take "Manifest and Latent Functions in Legislative Politics" (chapter 2) more seriously than it should be taken. What would happen, the essay asks, if the Congress of the United States did in fact correspond to a pristine model of a strong and independent legislature in a system of checks and balances? The analysis shows how policy recommendations deduced from a model may well differ from policy recommendations that are in the nature of *ad hoc* propositions.

"Ideas come when they please," Max Weber once observed, "not when it pleases us." But ideas are also stimulated by others. One writes book reviews to please or displease their authors, to aid others in determining whether to read a book or not, and as a bonus to learn something. "Notes on Power and Personality" (chapter 17) brings together a selection of reviews written in the

4. The interested reader may wish to compare this analysis with another based on individual data in Robert Eyestone and Heinz Eulau, "City Councils and Policy Outcomes: Developmental Profiles," in James Q. Wilson, Ed., *City Politics and Public Policy* (New York: John Wiley, 1968), pp. 37–65.

5. But see footnote 8 of Chapter 16. Of course, we shall describe the procedures in detail in later publications.

last few years that forced me to pay attention to what my colleagues were doing. The reviews are all relevant to my major theme, and for this reason I shall say no more about them.[6]

"From Utopia to Probability: Liberalism and Recent Science" (chapter 18) and "Values and Behavioral Science: Neutrality Revisited" (chapter 19) are responses to some current idiocies pronounced by those who find behavioral science not "relevant" to their own interpretation of what "man" (microman) and the "world" (macro-man) "need." I like to cultivate an inbred distaste for doctrinaires and moralists who think they can tell me what is good for me and the world I live in. For this reason science appeals to me as the method that protects us, as does liberalism, from the stock-in-trade prophesies of the doctrinaires and moralists. Science, like liberalism, the philosopher Morris Cohen said, "is based on a critical attitude to all plausible and self-evident propositions. It seeks not to reject them, but to find out what evidence there is to support them rather than their possible alternatives. . . . Liberalism can move forward, like science, because it embraces self-correcting principles which permit the correction of error and partial truth without an overthrow of the system that makes such correction possible."

Science, then, is anything but "value-free." But because "value neutrality" is neither fact nor attainable goal, it does not follow that as scientists we should not strive to neutralize those biases that stem from our commitment to values, whatever these may be. It seems to me mistaken, therefore, if scientists, and especially social and political scientists, hide what they are or want to be as human beings behind a façade of apparent neutrality and self-imposed impersonality. Science, like art, religion, or politics, is a highly personal enterprise to which one is "called" by inner impulses that make for dedication and creativity. Consciousness of self and of what one is doing is a necessary condition of that value neutralization which, I believe, the scientific enterprise must cultivate. Therefore, in an article about "The Behavioral Movement in Political Science: A Personal Document" (chapter 20), I chose a form of presentation not generally common among scientists.[7] I hope that my friends will forgive me my indiscretions.

I am indebted to many collaborators who co-authored some of the chapters in this volume–to Peter Schneider (chapter 8), to John C. Wahlke, William Buchanan, and LeRoy C. Ferguson (chapter 10), to David Koff (chapter 11), to Betty H. Zisk (chapter 12), to Robert Eyestone (chapter 15), and especially to Kenneth Prewitt (chapters 12 and 16), who has been the "significant other" on the journey from studying individual to studying collective political behavior.

For comment that cleared up several confusions in Chapter 1, I am grate-

6. For other book reviews, see Part V, "Maps for a Science of Politics," in Heinz Eulau, *Journeys in Politics* (Indianapolis: Bobbs-Merrill, 1963), pp. 229–93.

7. For a more formal exposition of behavioralism in political science, see Heinz Eulau, *The Behavioral Persuasion in Politics* (New York: Random House, 1963), and Heinz Eulau, Ed., *Behavioralism in Political Science* (New York: Atherton Press, 1969).

ful to Martin Shapiro, Richard A. Brody, Kenneth Prewitt, and John D. Sprague. For permission to use their data in chapters 8 and 9 I am indebted to the Survey Research Center of the University of Michigan, and for financial support of the research included in these chapters I owe a great deal to the Social Science Research Council. Funding of the research reported in chapters 10, 11, and 13, also came largely from the Social Science Research Council. The research reported in chapters 12, 15 and 16 was made possible by a generous grant from the National Science Foundation.

Research productivity thrives in congenial environments. I spent two summers, in 1954 and 1955, at the Survey Research Center in Ann Arbor, where I had the wise counsel of Angus Campbell and Warren Miller. A year at the Center for Advanced Study in the Behavioral Sciences in 1957–58 made possible the fermentation of many of the ideas that have found their way into this volume. In 1961–62 I spent a year at my alma mater, the University of California in Berkeley, as Visiting Legislative Research Professor and began the research on small decision-making groups reported in chapters 15 and 16. In 1964–65, as a Visiting Professor at the Institute for Advanced Studies in Vienna, Austria, I had occasion to formulate the thoughts found in chapters 2, 3, 5, 18, and 19. Since 1963 I have been a member of the Institute of Political Studies at Stanford University, a facility inspired by Gabriel A. Almond who, as a colleague, has been most supportive along the way.

Contents

Introduction

On Units and Levels of Analysis

Political inquiry is concerned with the actions of and relations between units of greatly varying size and complexity, ranging from individual persons or small groups to large organizations, associations, and inclusive territorial collectives like nation-states. Political science has been singularly free of controversies over the "reality" of groups or collectives in the social process that from time to time have raged in the other social sciences. That collectives as well as individuals are real and can be effective units of political decision or action has always seemed self-evident and common-sensical to political scientists. The institutional tradition of political analysis takes for granted the primary reality of decision-making collectives—nations, governments, parliaments, agencies, courts, parties, interest groups, and so on.

But, in avoiding the nominalist denial of the group as real and the nominalist view of the group as nothing more than "an assemblage of individuals,"[1] institutional analysis has failed to pay more attention to the manifold of inter-individual actions and relationships that make the group what it is.[2] By treat-

1. Bronislaw Malinowski, "The Group and Individual in Functional Analysis," *American Journal of Sociology,* Vol. 44 (May, 1939), p. 938.

2. For linguistic convenience, I shall use the term "group" in referring to any collective of two or more individuals that is an "action unit," i.e. any unit, from the dyad to a nation, that can make a collective decision committing all the members of the unit to a course of action. An action unit is to be distinguished from an "aggregate unit." Like an action unit, an aggregate unit or, simply, an aggregate is an empirical phenomenon whose behavior can be observed. But an aggregate differs from a group in that its "unit character" is an artifact of quantification and not the result of interactions or relationships between its components. Interaction is not a necessary condition of an aggregate's existence. This does not mean that the behavior of an aggregate may not have consequences for the behavior of an action unit. A change of government as a result of changes in the behavior of the electorate (an aggregate) is an obvious example. An aggregate is composed of action units—individuals or groups—with identical or similar properties. We can speak of an aggregate of individuals or of an aggregate of groups.

ing the group as a "whole" or global entity rather than as *also* a set of interacting persons, institutional analysis has not done justice to the internal complexity of the group, its multiple properties, and the multiphasic nature of group behavior.

This approach has changed in recent years. Political scientists now study, both intensively and extensively, the behavior of individuals as members either of organized and institutionalized collectives such as legislatures, or of decision-making aggregates such as electorates. The focus on individual political behavior has increased the range and reach of political research. But as yet it has not contributed as much as we might hope to the analysis of the behavior of collectives and especially of very large collectives (which are as real as individual human actors). As a result, the scientific study of collective phenomena in politics has not achieved the precision and rigor now standard in the analysis of individual political behavior. In the study of international politics where nations are the action units, or in the study of comparative politics where subnational collectives such as parties or parliaments are the action units, research relies either on inferences from the unit's distributive, integral, or contextual properties[3] or on impressionistic accounts of the unit's behavior.[4]

The longstanding reluctance in political science to take its methodological problems seriously led to much conceptual and analytical confusion. Rather than coping methodologically with the problems arising from the fact that political science must deal with both individual and collective actors, the issues were thought soluble by some sort of compromise between behavioral and institutional analysis.[5] A textbook of the late fifties, when the controversy between behavioralists and institutionalists occasioned discomfort among those who had a foot in both camps, was subtitled "an institutional and behavioral approach."[6] Though this work juxtaposed behavioral and institutional statements, it did not come to grips with the methodological problems stemming from the *simultaneity* of individual and collective action.

Let me explicate what I mean when I speak of the simultaneity of individual and collective action. When, after discussion, a committee makes a decision, two sets of decision are in fact made simultaneously. Each member of the

3. See, for instance, Richard L. Merritt and Stein Rokkan, Eds., *Comparing Nations: The Use of Quantitative Data in Cross-National Research* (New Haven: Yale University Press, 1966); or J. David Singer, Ed., *Quantitative International Politics: Insights and Evidence* (New York: The Free Press, 1968).

4. See, for instance, Arthur S. Banks and Robert B. Textor, *A Cross-Polity Survey* (Cambridge, Mass.: MIT Press, 1963).

5. Apropos the behavioral versus institutional controversey, Donald E. Stokes has made this comment: "It is in a way remarkable that the anti-thesis between institutions and behavior should ever have seemed plausible to political scientists. Perhaps it never did to the keenest observers." See his "Analytic Reduction in the Study of Institutions," a paper delivered at the 1966 Annual Meeting of the American Political Science Association in New York, p. 1.

6. Avery Leiserson, *Parties and Politics: An Institutional and Behavioral Approach* (New York: Alfred A. Knopf, 1958).

committee makes a decision about the merits of a proposal and votes one way or another. As each member votes, the group's decision emerges simultaneously as a collective product. It is not that the individuals decide and vote first, and then the group decides. The group's decision is simultaneous with each individual member's decision as votes are being combined into the collective decision. Institutional analysis would be satisfied with knowing the outcome of the decision process, with the decision as an emergent property of the group. It might speculate about how the group decision came about, but having no information on the behavior of the individuals in the group it can only rely on inference.

The methodological problem of "moving" from the level of individual behavior to the level of collective behavior has also not been coped with in the research that has an institutional setting but focuses on the behavior of individuals. These studies deal with the behavior of individuals *in* collectives but not with the behavior *of* collectives. For instance, in their study of four state legislatures John C. Wahlke and his associates treat the attitudes, perceptions, orientations and norms *of* individual legislators and compare the distributions of individual responses *in* the legislatures rather than the structures or behavior patterns *of* the four legislatures as collectives.[7] Similarly, Almond and Verba in their five-nation study of citizen behavior compare the distributions of individual characteristics *in* five nations rather than five nations as collective actors.[8] This is not to minimize the importance of this type of research. Treating individuals *in* groups is a proper task of political science. But it is not the same as dealing with groups as behavioral units in collective decision-making and action.

The reluctance of students of individual behavior to be concerned with the behavior of the units to which individuals invariably belong is understandable. In part the reluctance is a negative reaction to the often rather sweeping statements made by institutionalists. But there are other reasons as well. In particular, there are some familiar fallacies of logical inquiry that are to be avoided. Because these fallacies point up some problems involved in the relationship between individual and collective actors, I shall briefly discuss them.

THE FALLACY OF REASONING BY ANALOGY

Because two units are structurally, functionally, or behaviorally homologous, i.e., there is a real identity or near-identity between them, it does not follow that we can treat them as analogues and assume that statements about one are

7. See John C. Wahlke, Heinz Eulau, William Buchanan, and LeRoy C. Ferguson, *The Legislative System: Explorations in Legislative Behavior* (New York: John Wiley and Sons, 1962). However, it should be pointed out that in chapters 16 and 17 these authors sought to reconstruct the legislature's "role structure" out of the individual data.

8. See Gabriel A. Almond and Sidney Verba, *The Civic Culture: Political Attitudes and Democracy in Five Nations* (Princeton, N.J.: Princeton University Press, 1963).

as good as statements about the other. Because a legislative subcommittee may have properties very similar to the properties of the whole committee, it is erroneous to believe that explanation of subcommittee behavior can be simply applied to committee behavior. The error is aggravated by the assumption that the smaller unit may be a "replica" of the larger unit, in a sampling sense, just as a "representative sample" is a numerically smaller replica of a population universe. To illustrate, let us listen carefully to Robert A. Dahl's justification for studying the politics of New Haven. He studied New Haven, he informs us, because it lay conveniently at hand, but he also made this guarded comment:

> Though no city can claim to represent cities in general, and though certainly none can claim to display the full range of characteristics found in a national political system, New Haven is *in many respects typical* of other cities in the United States.[9]

The issue Dahl here raises is one of New Haven's representativeness in a sampling sense. I have no quarrel with the statement as a matter of logic. Whether New Haven is "typical" of other cities is a soluble empirical question. But, Dahl continues, New Haven is also atypical in certain respects that he finds advantageous to his purposes. One of these is:

> Because, unlike most American cities, it has had a highly competitive two-party system for over a century, it *offers analogies* with national politics that few other cities could provide.[10]

In this sentence Dahl implies that because New Haven has a property—a competitive two-party system just as the nation has such a system—it is feasible to reason *from* the case of New Haven *to* the nation as a whole. In the following paragraph Dahl further justifies the choice of New Haven as a research site as follows:

> If the disadvantages and limitations of studying one city are self-evident, the overwhelming and, I hope, compensating advantage is that the enterprise is reduced to manageable proportions. Many problems that are almost unyielding over a larger area can be relatively easily disposed of on this smaller canvas. It is not, perhaps, wholly accidental that the two political theorists who did the most to develop a descriptive political science were Aristotle and Machiavelli, who, though separated by eighteen centuries, both witnessed politics on the smaller, more human scale of the city-state. Nonetheless, I had better make clear at once that explanations presented in this study are tested only against the evidence furnished in the political system of New Haven.[11]

9. Robert A. Dahl, *Who Governs? Democracy and Power in an American City* (New Haven: Yale University Press, 1961), p.v. Italics added.

10. *Ibid.*, p.v. Italics added.

11. *Ibid.* pp. v–vi.

As his caveats indicate, Dahl is much too sophisticated an investigator to be insensitive to the methodological problems involved in reasoning by analogy. But he nonetheless leaves the impression that his study of New Haven politics tells us something about national politics. And I am not sure what Dahl means when he tells us that Aristotle and Machiavelli witnessed politics "on the smaller, more human scale of the city-state." Applied to the New Haven situation, it means that Dahl is dealing with three types of unit–the good citizens of New Haven, New Haven itself and the nation. Perhaps political science would be better off if it could free itself of notions of politics developed in the small city-state units of Aristotle's and Machiavelli's (and now Dahl's) worlds.

THE FALLACY OF REASONING BY INFERENCE

This fallacy of reasoning by inference takes two forms.[12] First, there is the "fallacy of composition," which is probably more widespread than one might suspect. It involves inference from the properties of subunits to the properties of the unit they compose. For instance, the fact that the members of a collective are "unstable" in their behavior patterns does not permit the conclusion that the group is "unstable." The word "unstable" does not mean the same thing on the two levels of analysis–that of the individual member and that of the group. Applied to the individual, it refers to a personality trait; applied to the group, it refers to the structure of relationships obtaining in the group. One cannot explain or predict the group's structure or behavior from knowledge of its individual parts.

The converse error is the "fallacy of division." Because of the nature of the data with which social scientists are often dealing, it is better known today as the "ecological fallacy." [13] It is most frequently encountered with units whose distributive properties are known but whose subunits cannot be singly identified. The fallacy of division involves inference from the properties of a whole to the properties of its parts. For instance, we may say that the Supreme Court is a "just" body, but this statement does not mean that all judges are just. The administrative inertia that may be characteristic of a bureaucracy does not prove that every bureaucrat in the organization is inert.

The same fallacies arise at other levels of analysis. The committees of a legislature may be well integrated, yet the legislature itself may be poorly integrated. To make inferences about integration from the larger to the smaller unit, or from the smaller to the larger, is fallacious. In fact, it may be that high integration of "lower-level" units (such as families, cliques, tribes, cities, re-

12. See Morris R. Cohen and Ernest Nagel, *An Introduction to Logic and Scientific Method* (New York: Harcourt, Brace, 1934), p. 377.

13. For a highly perceptive discussion of the "ecological fallacy" and some of the relevant literature, see Douglas Price, "Micro- and Macro-politics: Notes on Research Strategy," in Oliver Garceau, Ed., *Political Research and Political Theory* (Cambridge, Mass.: Harvard University Press, 1968), pp. 124–34.

gions, and so on) impedes the integration of "higher-level" units. And the integration of a large unit is no guarantee that its component parts are also similarly integrated.

These fallacies should not be confused with what I think are two viable analytic operations that involve relationships between smaller and larger units. Both create methodological problems of their own, but both are either theoretically or empirically soluble. There is, first, the question of "linkages" between larger and smaller units, regardless of whether the smaller units are parts of or independent of the larger units.[14] Role analysis and reference group theory are propitious approaches to the linkage problems.[15] There is, second, the question of "impact," either of the larger on the smaller unit or of the smaller on the larger unit. The contemporary work on "structural effects" and "breakage effects" seeks to deal with relevant methodological issues.[16] I do not propose to pursue these issues here. For my interest is in the problem of simultaneity–the problem arising from the fact that a larger unit and its smaller subunits are simultaneously involved in political action. The larger unit cannot act unless its constituent subunits also act, but the latter cannot act without implicating the larger unit in the action.

Although the individuals *in* a group and the group as a whole make decisions simultaneously, in the real world of politics where institutionalized groups make decisions and take action, it is the group as a whole and not its individual members that, under given decision rules, is the *effective* decision-maker. The city council, not the individual city councilman, commits the city to a course of action: the Senate of the United States, not Senator Jones, ratifies treaties.

It follows that we may want to say something about the behavior of the group rather than the behavior of its component parts. In that case, the behavior of the individual members may get in our way. This is particularly so if we want to compare the behavior of many groups–say, all the city councils in a metropolitan area, all the committees of the Congress, or all the nations in the world. Yet it is difficult if not impossible to observe the behavior of the group without observing the behavior of the individuals in the group. How can we go about our business of making statements about group behavior without

14. As far as I can tell, Oliver Garceau was the first political scientist to call attention to the task of linking different units of analysis. See his "Research in the Political Process," *American Political Science Review*, Vol. 45 (March, 1951), pp. 69–85. Reprinted in Heinz Eulau, Samuel J. Eldersveld, and Morris Janowitz, Eds., *Political Behavior: A Reader in Theory and Research* (New York: The Free Press, 1956), pp. 42–52.

15. See Bruce J. Biddle and Edwin J. Thomas, Eds., *Role Theory: Concepts and Research* (New York: John Wiley and Sons, 1966); and Herbert H. Hyman and Eleanor Singer, Eds., *Readings in Reference Group Theory and Research* (New York: The Free Press, 1968).

16. Peter Blau, "Structural Effects," *American Sociological Review*, Vol. 25 (1960), pp. 178–93; James A. Davis, "A Technique for Analyzing the Effects of Group Composition," *American Sociological Review*, Vol. 26 (1961), pp. 215–25.

either talking about the individuals in the group or by using analogical and inferential reasoning?

The answer lies, I think, in bringing all of a unit's properties, whether residing in the group as a whole or in its parts, on to the same level of analysis. But what does it mean to "bring properties on to the same level of analysis"? Let me give some examples. For instance, the group's decision rules—its constitution—are integral properties of the group. By an integral property is meant an attribute of the unit as a whole that under no circumstance is an attribute of a subunit. The decision rules are of the group and not of the individuals composing the group. We can find out what the rules are by asking questions of the members, or by reading the rule book, or by observing the group. Plurality voting, majority voting, extraordinary majority voting, or unanimous voting may be required by the rules. The rules as an integral property can tell us a good deal about the behavior of the group as a whole. We need not investigate the individuals in the group to say something about the group's behavior.

But now take the case of a five-member group that has majority rule. This information tells us that there must at least be three members in the majority on every vote. But the rule itself cannot tell us whether a *particular group* has or has not a three-member majority or majority faction. If by inspection of recorded vote divisions we can determine that over many issues there always seems to be the same majority of three and the same minority of two, we are no longer observing the group as a whole but two subunits whose patterned relationship to each other makes for one structural property of the entire group. What we are actually doing is this: we reduce the group to two subunits and then reconstruct it by saying that it has a bipolar structure. The factions are the subunits out of which the group property "bipolarity" is being constructed. In other words, we have brought a relational property initially characteristic of the subunits unto the unit level as a structural property.

But now let us assume that though we know that the group splits along majority and minority lines, we do not know the composition of the two factions. In that case we cannot really say that the group has a bipolar structure. If we did, we would commit the compositional fallacy. The group may, in fact, have a nonpolar structure; that is, different individuals may compose the majority and minority in any *particular vote*. Put differently, the composition of the minority and majority is so unstable that one can hardly speak of factions. Rather than being bipolarized, the group is fragmented. The group's subunits are not factions but individuals or possibly cliques. At this point we must look at the relationships that obtain among all of the group's individual members. If we find no stable relationships among the individuals, that is, if their individual voting patterns appear random rather than regular, we employ the irregular individual voting to characterize the whole group as fragmented or having a nonpolar structure.

We might also discover that whenever three-to-two voting splits occur in the group, it is always the same two individuals in the majority and the same two in the minority, while a fifth member "swings" back and forth. How can we characterize the group in which this behavior occurs? Our subunits are now two dyads, but what gives the group its characteristic property is the presence of a "pivotal" individual as another subunit. The pivotal voter's erratic behavior becomes, at the group level of analysis, a property that characterizes the group as a whole.

All these examples suggest that if we are to discover a group's relational or structural properties, we must reduce the group to the relevant subunits—factions, dyads, or individuals—that compose the group. But having reduced the group to subunits, we must reconstruct it out of the data gathered about the behavior of the subunits.

The procedures I have tried to illustrate by various examples differ significantly from the methods of analogy and inference. Reducing larger units to smaller ones in order to discover group properties "at a lower level" and constructing larger units out of smaller ones to permit comparative or correlational analysis "at a higher level" are operations quite different from making inferences from individual to collective phenomena or from collective to individual phenomena. These operations clearly involve a great deal of methodological contrivance. I shall try in the second part to present them more formally and systematically.

II

The level-of-analysis problem stems from two requirements. First, diverse units can be compared only at the same level of analysis and the properties of diverse units can be correlated only at the same level. And second, a unit's properties may have to be derived from other units at other levels because they are not available at the unit's own level. Only the unit's integral and possibly some of its emergent properties are directly observable. All other properties must be constructed or imputed to the unit as contextual properties. I shall first clarify what is meant by "unit of analysis" and "level of analysis."

Let us distinguish between an "object unit" and a "subject unit" of analysis.

By *object unit* I mean the unit whose behavior is to be explained. The unit whose behavior is to be explained is given by the *research problem*. If we want to explain how voters make up their minds in an election, individual persons are the object units, or simply objects, of analysis. If the Supreme Court's pattern of decisions in a set of cases is to be explained, the Court is the object unit of analysis. If our research problem is to compare the concentration or distribution of power in local communities, our object units are communities. If we are interested in the actions of nation-states in an international crisis, our object units of analysis are nations.

By *subject unit* is meant the unit whose behavior is observed in order to explain the behavior of an object unit. The notion of subject unit is more difficult to explicate than the concept of object unit. It is perhaps best understood in the sense the experimental psychologist uses the word "subject." His subject is the person he brings into the laboratory in order to observe his behavior. But the notion of the person as subject can be extended to collectives. A group, a committee, a party, a state, and so on can be treated as subject units if their behavior is observed.

The distinction between object unit and subject unit is purely conceptual. But since the distinction is conceptual, in empirical reality *an object unit can be the subject unit.* For instance, for the clinical psychologist the individual person is both the object to be explained and the subject to be observed.[17]

The conception of the individual person as object and subject of analysis is simple enough. More complex is the notion that a collective, too, may be both object and subject of analysis. A group as a group is more difficult to observe than is an individual person observed as a person. It involves technical problems of analysis that are by no means easy to solve. But if they can be solved, considering a collective both object and subject of analysis is viable.

The conception of a unit, be it an individual person or a group of varying size, as both object and subject of analysis serves to clarify what is meant by *level of analysis.* For if we say that a unit is both object and subject, we are in effect saying that the behavior of the unit is to be both observed and explained *at its own level.*

By itself the conception of observing and explaining a unit's behavior at its own level is nothing more than a linguistic convention of little practical use. It is simply a shorthand expression. But it is of formal logical use. For it implies, in a logical sense, the possibility of *observing* the unit *at another level,* while *explaining* it *at its own level.* In other words, if our object unit is a group, the notion of level of analysis suggests that it may be observed at its own or at another level. The conception does not tell us automatically at which level the group is to be observed—at a "lower level" in terms of properties inherent in its subunits, which then become the subjects of analysis, at its own level, or at a "higher level," say the level of intergroup relations.

The crucial methodological question then is what subject units are to be chosen as foci of observation in order to explain the behavior of the object unit. David Singer has rightly complained that choice of level is often "ostensibly a mere matter of methodological or conceptual convenience." [18] Speaking of his own discipline of international relations, he writes: "We have, in our texts and elsewhere, roamed up and down the ladder of organizational complexity with remarkable abandon, focusing upon the total system, international organizations, regions, coalitions, extra-national associations, nations,

17. See Ernest R. Hilgard and Daniel Lerner, "The Person: Subject and Object of Science and Policy," in Daniel Lerner and Harold D. Lasswell, Eds., *The Policy Sciences: Recent Developments in Scope and Method* (Stanford, Calif.: Stanford University Press, 1951), pp. 16–43.

18. J. David Singer, "The Level of Analysis Problem in International Relations," *World Politics,* Vol. 14 (October, 1961), p. 77.

domestic pressure groups, social classes, elites, and individuals as the needs of the moment required."[19]

Singer's distress is not exaggerated. If choice of level is a mere matter of convenience, it can lead only to analytic confusion. But, it seems to me, the issue is not "moving up and down" from one level of analysis to another, but failure to distinguish between object and subject units of analysis. If this distinction is not made, it is certainly never clear just which unit's behavior is to be explained and which unit's behavior is to be observed. As I have suggested already, moving from one level, the level of the object unit, to another level, where a subject unit is observed, may be necessary if the object unit cannot be fully observed at its own level–i.e., if it cannot also serve as the subject of analysis. But such movement to another level cannot be a matter of methodological convenience. If we were limited to observing a unit only at its own level, political science would be deprived of a powerful mode of analysis.

Let me illustrate the level of analysis problem by a simple example. John Smith never votes. He reads the sports page of the newspaper but is not interested in political news. When asked why he is not interested in politics and never votes, Smith tells us that he just isn't interested, that he is satisfied with his job, enjoys his family life, and therefore does not find it necessary to vote. He says that he has lived through many administrations in Washington, Democratic and Republican, and that it has made no difference to him. How are we to explain Smith's behavior? Smith is our object of analysis. One way would be intensive treatment of Smith himself, of his personality, his motivations, cognitions, aspirations, and so on. In that case, we would be dealing with Smith as both object and subject at the same level of analysis.[20]

But we might soon discover that dealing with Smith at this level of analysis does not get us very far. Smith has no evident personality defects, he is alert on his job and happy in his personal life. Yet his nonpolitical stance requires explanation. We may decide therefore to shift our observations to another level of analysis, to focus on Smith's social relationships–the groups to which he belongs. Smith remains our object unit. But we decide to observe the groups to which he belongs *because* we suspect that these groups, too, are largely nonpolitical. Indeed, we find Smith belonging to a church group in which talking politics is taboo. Smith also attends the weekly meeting of a poker group. Politics is never discussed by the group. And he belongs to a union that has never asked about his political opinions or made political demands on him.

In other words, the groups to which Smith belongs have become our subject units. It is still Smith's behavior that is to be explained, but we are trying to

19. *Ibid.*, p. 78.

20. For this type of analysis, see Robert E. Lane, *Political Ideology: Why the American Common Man Believes What He Does* (New York: The Free Press, 1962); also M. Brewster Smith, Jerome S. Bruner, and Robert W. White, *Opinions and Personality* (New York: John Wiley & Sons, 1956).

explain it by "moving up" to another level of analysis. The groups themselves do not interest us as objects. For instance, we are not interested in finding out why talking politics in the church group is taboo (it might be that doing so would disrupt the group's harmony). It is sufficient to know that politics is simply not salient in any of the groups to which Smith belongs.

Now, what I did in presenting this example is to smuggle in my *theoretical standpoint as an observer.* I simply advanced the hypothesis that Smith's behavior is *caused* by his social situation. Smith is nonpolitical because he belongs to nonpolitical groups. Shifting from Smith as the object unit to his groups as subject units was not a matter of methodological convenience, but a matter of the observational standpoint I chose to occupy as a theorist. My theory told me to look at properties of Smith's conduct that could be observed only at another level of analysis.

Let me be quite clear about the operation involved. I am not committing the "fallacy of division." I am not inferring Smith's nonpolitical behavior from the behavior of the group to which he belongs. I am not inferring that because the church group is nonpolitical, all its members, including Smith, are nonpolitical. In fact, just the opposite may be true. Politics may be highly salient to the group's members as individuals. Yet precisely because of this the group as a whole may eschew politics. What I am doing is to *impute* a unit property of the whole to one of its parts. Smith is characterized by "membership in non-political groups." The general hypothesis that individual behavior is caused by membership in groups that led me to shift to the group level of analysis may, on investigation, be true or false.[21] But the point to be made here is that level of analysis is determined by the choice of the *subject unit,* and choice of the subject unit is determined by the theoretical standpoint of the observer.[22]

III

Are there limits on the observer's freedom to move from one level of analysis to another? In answering this question, let me emphasize that the language employed in talk about levels of analysis is clearly metaphorical. If I continue in this vein, it is because metaphors can be useful. My concern is whether

21. A research design for testing the hypothesis would require an aggregate of men with membership in nonpolitical groups and a "control" aggregate of men with membership in political groups. The null hypothesis of no difference in the voting behavior of the two aggregates would have to be confirmed in order to reject the original hypothesis. Such rejection would not invalidate the procedure of imputing a group property to an individual.

22. The importance of the "standpoint of the observer" has been a perpetual theme in the writings of Harold D. Lasswell, to whom I am greatly indebted for many insights. See especially his "General Framework: Person, Personality, Group, Culture," in Harold D. Lasswell, *The Analysis of Political Behavior* (New York: Oxford University Press, 1948), pp. 195–234. See also Heinz Eulau, "The Maddening Methods of Harold D. Lasswell: Some Philosophical Underpinnings," *Journal of Politics,* Vol. 30 (February, 1968), pp. 3–24. Reprinted in this volume, Chapter 5.

there is an upper and a lower limit in the hierarchy of levels beyond which one cannot move, no matter how theoretically desirable it might be to do so.

My answer is that there are limits, practical limits, just as a house has a roof and a basement floor. Much as I might want to, I cannot move beyond the roof or below the basement floor. I can possibly build another story on top of the roof, or I can dig a second basement. But while endless building up and digging down is speculatively conceivable, in practice it is not. Sooner or later my house will collapse under the weight of new stories, or I will hit rock bottom as I try to dig new levels below.

In the language of the philosophy of science, what is involved in the choice of levels of analysis is *reduction* and *construction*. I am concerned with reduction and construction as procedures of analysis and not as philosophical issues. Reduction and the strategy of reductionism have been topics of hot controversy in the past. Reductionism as an approach holds that it is desirable, if not necessary, to explain larger units in terms of the smallest units or elements into which they can be decomposed. The assumption underlying reductionism is that events occurring at a "simpler" level of a unit's organization are also more "fundamental." [23] I cannot get particularly excited about this philosophical aspect of reduction because it seems to me it is a metamethodological issue that is not per se soluble, for three reasons.

First, level of analysis—that is, the choice of a subject unit—is determined by the observer's theoretical standpoint and not by methodological considerations. I see no absolute virtue in reducing an object unit to its "ultimate" subject units. How far one wishes to reduce an object unit depends on one's theory.

Second, the object unit may have properties that cannot be reduced. Because an object unit cannot be reduced, it does not follow that it cannot be scientifically investigated.

Third, reduction may not be feasible on practical grounds because though the object unit may be reducible in theory, relevant subject units may simply not be available. For instance, ecological units characterized by aggregate data cannot be reduced to individuals as units.

It was perhaps inevitable that in response to radical reductionism some analysts would insist on observing object units as "wholes." [24] The position that objects can be understood *only* as wholes strikes me as metamethodological as the pure reductionist formula. Intuitively, I will admit, we see wholes before we see parts—the tree before the branches, the branches before the leaves. But when it comes to empirical operations, the advice of the holist is

23. See Ernest Nagel, *The Structure of Science* (New York: Harcourt, Brace, 1961), pp. 345–58, 541–44.

24. For a persuasive recent statement, see Helen M. Lynd, *On Shame and the Search for Identity* (New York: Science Editions, 1958), pp. 74–132. For other aspects of the "part-whole" problem, see Daniel Lerner, Ed., *Parts and Wholes* (New York: The Free Press, 1963).

easier given than carried out. Except for their integral properties, the properties of wholes are not easily observable. They must often be constructed out of subject units that are parts of the whole. Again, whether one wishes to treat object units as wholes or construct them out of component subject elements is not a matter of methodological virtue but of theoretical relevance, again for three reasons.

First, what from one theoretical standpoint may appear to be a part may from another standpoint appear to be a whole. Some students of political behavior have been criticized for being concerned "only" with the individual political actor and for not using their knowledge of individual behavior in saying something about the "larger" political system (although it is rarely made clear just what "system" the critic has in mind). This position seems to me ill-founded. If one wants to study individual political behavior and has good theoretical grounds for doing so, he cannot be criticized for not doing what he does not want to do. In fact, by choosing the individual actor as both object and subject of analysis, he may treat him as a whole very much as the holist would have it. He would be mistaken to hold that only individual political behavior "matters" and that other units do not matter. But I am not aware of anyone who takes this position.

Second, whether a unit is to be treated as a whole, either directly in terms of its integral properties or indirectly through construction from subunit properties, depends on whether it is a collective actor. Whether or not it is a collective actor depends on whether the unit is a genuinely "behavioral system" or an artifact of aggregation. No one will deny that the Supreme Court, or the U.S. Senate, or the Corps of Engineers are not collective actors. Collective actors are of intrinsic scientific interest just as individual actors are, and statements about them as units describe some behavioral reality. By way of contrast, aggregates are artificial wholes. An electoral unit like a precinct does not act as a whole. Precincts may be treated *as if* they were wholes. For instance, they are treated as wholes in correlational analysis because other subject unit data are not available. If they were, correlational analysis would be based on individual data precisely because the precinct is not a collective actor. Similarly, an aggregate of foreign-born in a population is not a collective actor. Foreign-born citizens may combine into an ethnic association that becomes a collective actor and may be studied at the level of the individuals composing it.

Third, as in the case of reduction, there are practical limits to construction. At some point construction may have to cease if the edifice is not to look absurd. I sometimes sense an absurdity when I read the more imaginary constructions of theoretical-system builders whose edifices defy our powers of empirical observation and construction. More often than not the systems erected in theory become reified as if they corresponded to something "real" in the real world of politics.

I am not denying that philosophical issues are involved in the procedures of reduction and construction. But it seems to me that in addition to theoretical considerations the choice of level of analysis should be guided by practical exigencies and not by counsels of methodological perfection. There are simple practical reasons for following the strategy of reduction in some research situations and for following the strategy of construction in others. Stokes has suggested that analytic reduction of institutional phenomena of politics to the level of the individual has at least these advantages: (*a*) it allows us to generalize the phenomenon under review; (*b*) it increases our power to predict or explain variations of gross phenomena; and (*c*) it permits observations at a lower level of analysis, which may be more generous in a sampling sense.[25] This attitude makes good sense if the object unit is in fact reducible and if there are good theoretical reasons for doing so. But once we have reduced an object unit and observed its properties at a lower level of analysis, it is desirable to reconstruct the object unit, especially if it also contains nonreducible properties and is besides a significant collective actor in the political arena.

The notion of levels of analysis does not preclude treatment of the object unit on only one level other than its own. Several subject units may be inspected at different levels, some higher and some lower than the object unit level. We may want to explain the behavior of the subcommittees of the House Appropriations Committee. We have, minimally, three options that stem from the subcommittees' location in the hierarchy of levels.

First, we can deal with the subcommittees at their own level of analysis, that is, we can treat them as both objects and subjects of analysis. We might correlate such integral properties of the subcommittees as their size, their jurisdiction, their budget estimates, their partisan division, and so on.

Second, we can deal with the subcommittees at the level of the individual members who sit on them. We can identify the proportion of liberals and conservatives on each subcommittee and characterize each subcommittee accordingly. We can ascertain each subcommittee's median tenure. We can determine each member's attitudes on budget cutting and construct the subcommittee's collective orientation in this respect. The subcommittees are still our objects of analysis, but our subject units are now examined at the lower level of the subcommittee's individual members.

Third, we can move to the higher level of the whole Appropriations Committee. We may impute certain characteristics of the whole Committee, such as its goals or norms, to the subcommittees. We might wish to compare Appropriations subcommittees with Agriculture subcommittees, and so on. Again, the subcommittees remain the object units of analysis, but they are now attributed contextual properties characteristic of the larger committee of which they are parts.

This example of a three-level analysis is not fanciful. It formalizes in part the mode of analysis pursued by Richard F. Fenno in his study of congres-

25. Stokes, *op. cit.*, pp. 5–6.

sional appropriations politics.[26] Fenno's work is an outstanding case study of how moving up and down from one level of analysis to another can enrich our understanding of the political process. Fenno uses levels of analysis to good effect in dealing with questions of linkage and impact.

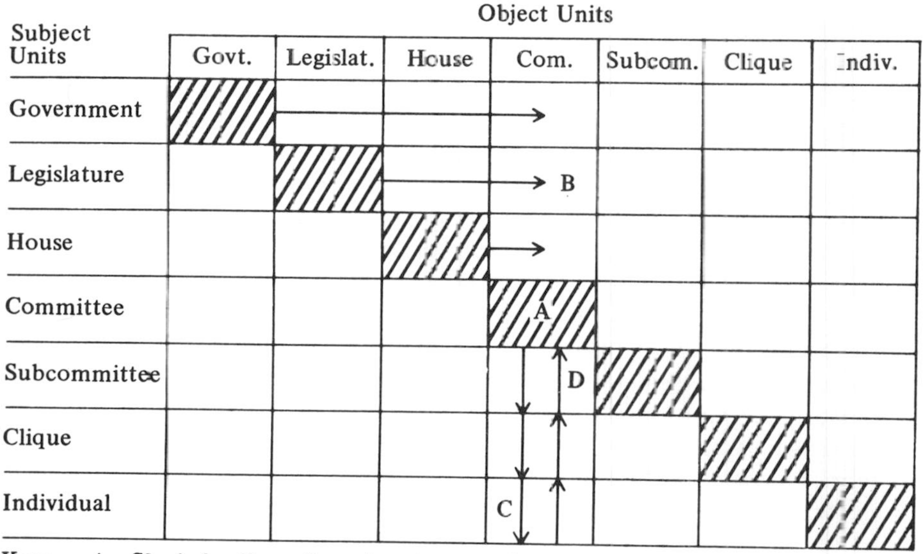

Object Units

Subject Units	Govt.	Legislat.	House	Com.	Subcom.	Clique	Indiv.
Government							
Legislature				B			
House							
Committee				A			
Subcommittee				D			
Clique							
Individual				C			

Key: A Shaded cell: unit analyzed at own level
B Horizontal arrow: unit property imputed from context
C Vertical arrow down: unit properties reduced to lower level
D Vertical arrow up: unit properties constructed from lower level unit

DIAGRAM 1. Units and Levels of Analysis

I shall follow the notion of multiple levels of analysis by way of an illustrative diagram. The matrix columns in Diagram 1 refer to the object units of analysis—the units whose behavior is to be explained. Seven object units, all conceivably real decision-makers, ranging from an individual actor to the large collective actor called "government," are introduced. The matrix rows refer to the corresponding subject units of analysis—the units whose behavior is being observed. Level of analysis is defined by the intersections of the columns and rows. The shaded cells represent the levels where object unit and subject unit are the same, where the unit is observed and explained at its own level. Reductive and constructive operations are indicated by the vertical arrows. Arrows pointing downward suggest the possibility of reduction. Arrows pointing up-

26. Richard F. Fenno, Jr., *The Power of the Purse: Appropriations Politics in Congress* (Boston: Little, Brown, 1966), pp. 127–90.

ward suggest the possibility of construction. The cells to the right of the shaded diagonal cells represent the conditions under which a subject unit provides the context the object unit is located in. The horizontal arrow denotes that some of the subject unit's properties may be imputed to the object unit as the latter's own contextual properties. The smaller the object unit, the greater the number of subject units that may provide relevant contextual properties.

Let me take the case of the committee as the object unit. We can observe and explain the committee at its own level in terms of its integral properties. We can reduce the committee to three types of subject unit: subcommittees, cliques, and individuals. We can ascertain characteristic properties of these subject units and reconstruct the committee by appropriate procedures. For instance, from study of individual roles we can construct the committee's role structure. From study of cliques and interpersonal relations we can construct the committee's degree of integration. From study of subcommittee functions we can ascertain the committee's division of labor.

Analysis may of course proceed on several levels at once. Individuals take roles in networks of interpersonal relations that are a property of the whole. Cliques function within and across subcommittees, and as they do they constitute the interpersonal networks within which individual roles are taken. The organized complexity of a unit such as a committee makes for simultaneous actions, reactions, interactions, and transactions of the different subject actors who, for one theoretical reason or another, are selected to serve as foci of observation.

The contextual properties that may be imputed to the committee have their origin in the subject units that constitute the committee's environment. The committee is located in a house, the house in a legislature, and the legislature in the government. Characteristics of these subject units–whether the government is partisan or nonpartisan, whether the legislature is urban or rural, whether the house is apportioned or not–may be imputed to the object unit as contextual properties.

Reduction, construction, and imputation make possible comparison and correlation of unit properties that otherwise could not be compared or correlated. We cannot correlate the properties of individuals and the properties of a group. Either the properties of individuals must be constructed into group properties, if the object unit is the group, or group properties must be reduced to individual properties, if the object unit is the individual. Similarly, we cannot correlate the properties of an object unit, say, a city council, with the properties of the city environment, say, whether it is urban or rural. But we can impute a characteristic of the environment to the council as a contextual property and speak of "urban councils" or "rural councils." We can then correlate the imputed contextual property with some other council property at the same level of analysis.

IV

Throughout this discussion I have avoided using the concepts *micro* and *macro*, chiefly because I believe that they are not particularly useful in dealing with the problems of levels of analysis. And they may actually confuse the issues involved. Their use is least harmful, but also not very informative, if micro is simply applied to individual political behavior and macro to all collective political behavior. If usage is so restricted, the terms themselves add nothing to our understanding.[27]

Yet if it is not fashionable the micro-macro terminology is prestigious, largely because it is used in economics, the most "advanced" in explanatory or predictive power of the social sciences. I am not impressed by this reason for using the terms, but their usage in economics may be instructive. Economists speak of "micro-economics" if the unit of analysis to be explained is not further reducible *according to economic theory*. Consumers (individuals) and firms (collectives), for instance, are treated by economic theory as nonreducible units. By "macro-economics" economists refer to units that in practice are reducible but which for theoretical reasons are treated as wholes, such as gross national product, national income, and so on. This usage is very close to one I prefer, for I have insisted throughout that level of analysis is a matter of theoretical determination. In any case, economists do not restrict the term "micro" to individuals alone, but to any unit that is theoretically not reducible.

The economist, it appears, has no trouble with identifying a unit as either micro or macro because he maintains a rather fixed theoretical standpoint. This is not the case in political science. Precisely because much analysis in political science is concerned with the linkage between different types of units and with the impact of one unit on another, the observer's theoretical standpoint may change as he seeks to explain the behavior of different object units. As a result, what is micro and what is macro also changes with changing theoretical standpoints. Moreover, we are dealing in politics with a great variety of actors whose unit properties are both nonreducible and reducible, depending on the theoretical standpoint of the observer.

Rather than thinking of micro and macro in dichotomous terms, the political scientist is better off if he thinks of a "micro-macro continuum." What in this continuum is micro and what is macro depends on the point on the micro-macro scale where the observer "dips in," where he fixes his object unit of analysis. If his object unit is the legislative committee and his subject units are the subcommittees or individuals composing the committee, his procedure is micro-analysis. If his object unit is still the committee but his subject units are

27. See, for instance, Stein Rokkan, "The Comparative Study of Political Participation," in Austin Ranney, Ed., *Essays in the Behavioral Study of Politics* (Urbana: University of Illinois Press, 1962), p. 48 where "micropolitics" is defined as "the analysis of the individual citizens' reactions to the political events and alternatives in their communities."

the committee itself or those units that constitute the committee's environment from which derive its contextual properties (the house or the legislature in which the committee is located), his procedure is macro-analysis.

If we envisage, as in Diagram 2, a micro-macro continuum and fix the observer's standpoint, it is apparent that as he moves toward the *micro pole,* he *adds* empirical referents to his analysis. And as he moves toward the *macro pole,* he *subtracts* empirical referents.

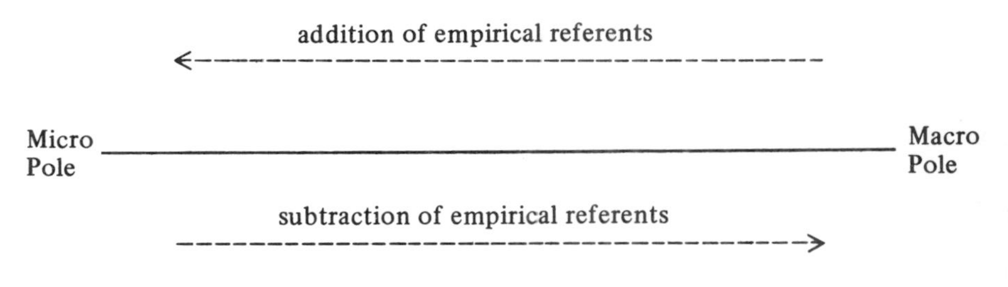

DIAGRAM 2. The Micro-Macro Continuum

In other words, it is not the absolute size of a unit that makes it micro or macro. A nation of millions and the Supreme Court composed of nine justices differ enormously in size. Both may be thought of as subjects of micro analysis if they are decomposed through reductive procedures, that is, through the addition of empirical referents. Or both may be subjected to macro analysis by treatment in terms of their own integral properties or contextual properties.

Let me give another example. There are 50 state legislatures in the United States. We can deal with these 50 legislatures as both objects and subjects of macro-analysis. But we can also reduce them by moving to the micro pole of the continuum. If we were to select legislative chambers as subjects, 99 units would be available for analysis (as Nebraska has only one house). If we were to concentrate on party delegations, the number of subject units would increase to perhaps 198 (on the assumption that there are two delegations per chamber or four per legislature). If committees were to serve as subject units, data on perhaps more than 2,000 units would serve our analysis. If individual legislators were chosen as subjects, we would have several thousand cases available for analysis.

Many of the arguments in political science about "triviality" and "significance" have probably something to do with the observer's movement toward or away from the poles of the micro-macro continuum. The analyst who moves toward the micro pole adds empirical data that make for greater validity and reliability, but he possibly sacrifices significance; the analyst who moves toward the macro pole deprives himself of data, loses in validity and reliability, but possibly gains in significance. I am not convinced by this argument, however. It seems to me that the critical issue is the level-of-analysis problem, regardless of the judgments of validity, reliability, or significance. And this problem, I have suggested, consists in manipulating data in such a way that the properties of various subject units, whatever their level, can be made to serve analysis of an object unit at that unit's own level.

Part I

Accent on Theory

Chapter 1

Logics of Rationality in Unanimous Decision-Making

My starting point is an empirical observation: the tendency of much democratic decision-making to terminate in unanimous or near-unanimous voting.[1] My problem is elusive: Does unanimity in democratic decision-making satisfy criteria of rationality? [2]

Originally published in Carl J. Friedrich, Ed., *Rational Decision*. Reprinted by permission of the Publishers, Atherton Press, Inc.

1. "Democratic" here simply means that there must not be in the decision-making situation external structural constraints which make free choice impossible, as in dictatorship (where only the dictator has free choice). There may be, of course, other constraints—and I shall mention some of them later on. But whatever other conditions may be specified for democratic decision-making, I only require of the situation that it contain a *potential* for free choice. I shall leave the adjective "near-unanimous" operationally undefined and, subsequently, absorb it into the unanimous category. For, conceptually, it makes little difference whether unanimity is fully achieved or not. Where unanimity is not a constitutional decision rule there is always the bitter-end intransigent or the unpredictable maverick whose behavior defies the tendency towards unanimity. This may be an empirically interesting phenomenon. But the quantitative deviations from the norm that are permissible in order to speak of "near-unanimous" decision need not be defined for the theoretical purposes of this paper.

2. There are numerous models of rational behavior. Most prominent are the "means-ends" model often encountered in theories of formal organization, the "maximization" model of economic theories, the "minimax" model of game theory, and the "adaptive behavior" models found in psychology. All of these models make behavioral assumptions that present advantages and difficulties. My discussion of rationality in unanimous decision-making does not require that I systematically explicate various models or choose between them. I shall invoke one or the other as the discussion of one or another type of unanimity may suggest. For my purposes the only requirements of rationality that must be met, whatever assumptions are made or whatever other conditions are specified, are that there be a free choice among alternatives and that the choice be consciously made. Nevertheless, I should acknowledge that my thinking in the matter has been greatly influenced by Herbert A. Simon's discussions of rationality. See his *Administrative Behavior* (2nd ed.; 1957), pp. 61–78. Also "A Behavioral Model of Rational Choice," in *Models of Man* (1957), pp. 241–260; and "Some Strategic Considerations in the Construction of Social Science Models," in *Mathematical Thinking in the Social Sciences*, Ed. Paul F. Lazarsfeld (1954), pp. 388–415.

In order to deal with the problem, I shall first try to show that the frequency with which unanimity occurs in democratic decision-making does, indeed, represent a "problematic situation" that deserves serious inquiry (Section I). I shall then briefly review the institutional arrangement where unanimity is a formal rule of decision-making, and I shall touch upon the principle of rationality involved in constitutional unanimity (Section II). Then, in order to develop a typology of unanimity that can be used to order empirical situations, I shall introduce two dimensions of unanimity—first, what I shall call "ways of decision-handling" (Section III), and second, what I shall call "ways of interest articulation" (Section IV). Once the typology has been elaborated and illustrated by reference to empirical examples (Section V), I shall examine each type of unanimity in terms of whatever criterion of rationality would seem to be useful (Section VI). I shall conclude that certain types of unanimity are not necessarily dysfunctional or symptomatic of a breakdown of the democratic decision-making process (Section VII).

I

Democratic decision-making is most readily observable in legislative bodies.[3] The great amount of unanimous or near-unanimous decision-making in the final stage of the legislative process is a matter of record.[4] Many of these decisions are made, of course, by the formal rule of "unanimous consent" or on private-bill calendars which prohibit passage if a single member objects or requests that the bill be delayed for further consideration.[5] Most of these actions lie outside the arena of political warfare or any other lines of cleavage. But others involve subjects of real importance for individuals or groups.[6]

3. The emphasis here is on "observable." Although, for certain theoretical purposes, the electorate can be conceived as a "committee," the secrecy of the electoral process and its aggregate character make observation impossible. Similarly, the decision-making process in juries escapes direct observation. It is for this reason that I shall deal, at least initially, with decision-making in legislative bodies, though here, too, much of what occurs remains hidden.

4. See V. O. Key, Jr., *Politics, Parties, and Pressure Groups* (1958), pp. 727–731; and Avery Leiserson, *Parties and Politics* (1958), pp. 339–344.

5. These constraints are external to the decision-making process, as are dictatorial constraints, and therefore not within the purview of this discussion, which assumes the potential for free choice among alternatives.

6. William J. Keefe, in a study of the 1951 Pennsylvania legislature, for instance, found many unanimous or near-unanimous votes on such matters as mental health, the training of the physically handicapped, increased aid to the blind, the local department of health operations, stream clearance, control over narcotics, absentee voting for military electors, sabotage control, retirement systems, school-district and school-board elections, merit-system extensions, and improvement of state institutions. See "Comparative Study of the Role of Political Parties in State Legislatures," in *Political Behavior,* Ed. Heinz Eulau, Samuel J. Eldersveld, and Morris Janowitz (1956), p. 315; and "Parties, Partisanship, and Public Policy in the Pennsylvania Legislature," *American Political Science Review,* XLVIII (1954), 452, 461–462.

Some of these have the endorsement of all interested parties, thus making for unanimity or near-unanimity, but others do not. This set of decisions—where one should expect division on substantive grounds of divided interests, but where it does not occur—makes unanimity a puzzling affair. For there is no overt evidence as to why it should occur—no logrolling, no leadership instructions, no purposive "engineering of consent." There has been, as I shall point out in Section V, some empirical speculation about the possible dynamics of the legislative process when it culminates in this kind of unanticipated unanimity, but real empirical evidence is scarce.[7]

Unanimity or near-unanimity may occur, then, in vital as well as minor policy matters. However, in democratic political systems differences over issues of public policy between political actors and conflicts between them are generally expected. The democratic system is, by definition, a contrivance designed to institutionalize conflicts and facilitate the clarification, crystallization, and resolution of political differences. A democratic legislature is an institution composed of opposed sides, and, the more the lines of division follow predictable lines, the more rational would the legislative process seem to be. If predicted divisions do not occur, the rationality of legislative decision-making becomes problematical. Regardless, therefore, of whether issues of high policy significance are involved or not, the fact that many legislative actions where controversy might be expected are consummated by unanimity poses a problem for political theory. This is not to imply that in every case of legislative action division is thought desirable. In crisis situations, notably war and economic emergencies threatening community survival, unanimity rather than division is the preferred decison norm and celebrated as a political achievement.[8]

II

In order to come to grips with the problem, I shall briefly turn to the institutional arrangements, where unanimity is a formal, constitutional requirement of decision-making, for two reasons—one theoretical, the other methodological. In the first place, there has been a good deal of explicit theoretical concern with the constitutional unanimity rule from the standpoint of its rationality. And second, it would seem that constitutional unanimity, with its imputed

7. In part, this lack of evidence is probably due to prevailing research strategies. Studies of legislative decision-making by way of roll-call votes are usually limited to the relatively few situations in which legislatures are divided. The criteria used to determine whether a roll call is to be considered controversial vary, and different research methods employed by different students have led to divergent findings about the importance of one or another factor that is assumed to make for division.

8. In other words, crisis situations may be considered as introducing constraints of an environmental character which make for self-imposed structural constraints. Again, the potential for free choice is severely restricted. Actually, the choice in these situations has already been made elsewhere, and the final decision is not really a matter of choice but rather of promulgation.

rationality, may serve as a kind of "ideal type."[9] Treated as an ideal-type model, rational constitutional unanimity provides a criterion for appraising the rationality of the several situations where unanimity emerges as an empirical phenomenon. As Weber put it,

> by comparison with this [ideal type] it is possible to understand the ways in which actual action is influenced by irrational factors of all sorts, such as affects and errors, in that they account for the deviation from the line of conduct which would be expected on the hypothesis that the action were purely rational.[10]

The most familiar case of constitutional unanimity is found today in an international decision-making body such as the Security Council of the United Nations. Here unanimity among the permanent members is a requirement for any substantive decision to be made. The empirical reasons for the rule are well known: On the one hand, the area of potential disagreement between nations is so large, and, on the other hand, its "interests" are considered so "vital" by each participating nation, that, in order to win support for and acceptance of a decision, unanimity rather than another voting rule is made the formal and effective requirement.[11]

Unanimity as a voting requirement is a rule of long standing. Indeed, unanimity did not give way to majority voting until certain conditions—as just those characteristic of international decision-making today—had given way to other conditions. Gierke reports that in the political life of the early Germanic tribes unanimous consent was sought for decisions precisely because a strong feeling of individuality made for the recognition that what could not be done unanimously would not be done at all.[12] In other words, unanimity appeared as the only decision rule which, if each participant was to be guaranteed membership in the decisive group, facilitated the replacement of private by collective action.

On the other hand, unanimity may serve to prevent collective action. Simmel discusses the dysfunctional consequences of the unanimity rule in the Polish Diet and the Aragonese Cortes, but of interest here are the conditions which made for maintaining the rule—among them the inequality in status and power of the participants, insufficient rules for deliberation, resistance of the constituent members to a feeble executive authority, and others.[13] If, in the

9. See Talcott Parsons' interpretation in *The Structure of Social Action* (2nd ed.; 1949), pp. 604–605.

10. Max Weber, *The Theory of Social and Economic Organization* (1947), p. 92.

11. For a mathematical formulation of the constitutional unanimity rule in international bodies, see Duncan Black, *The Theory of Committees and Elections* (1958), pp. 140–155.

12. Otto von Gierke, "Ueber die Geschichte des Majoritaetsprinzips," in *Essays in Legal History*, Ed. Sir Paul Vinogradoff (1913), pp. 312–335.

13. Georg Simmel, "The Phenomenon of Outvoting," in *The Sociology of Georg Simmel*, Ed. and Trans. Kurt H. Wolff (1950), pp. 240–241.

case of the Germanic tribes, each participant was to be guaranteed membership in the decisive group because all participants were deemed equal, in the cases described by Simmel, membership in the decisive group was to be guaranteed because the participants were unequal in status and power.

Unanimity, it seems, can be the preferred decision rule in two quite different, indeed polar, situations. On the one hand, it may facilitate the transition from private to collective action among equals who recognize that the advantages to be gained from collective action for each participant will be greater than the advantages to be gained from private action. The unanimity rule, then, is the only decision rule capable of resolving deadlock—which means that neither collective nor private action is possible.[14] For under any other rule—majority voting or dictatorship, for instance—each partner would not have a guarantee of being in the decisive group and, therefore, would prefer deadlock. But precisely because each participant is thought to be equal to every other participant and because the advantages to be derived from collective action are greater than those from private action, unanimity must be considered the rational decision rule in this situation.

This explication does not take account, of course, of the costs of decision-making that may be involved in unanimity. It is concerned only with the utilities for each actor that he may anticipate from collective as against private action. But as, in this case of collective action by equals, the costs of unanimity can be assumed to be less than the costs of deadlock, rational actors who are equal will be willing to pay the costs of unanimity.[15]

On the other hand, unanimity may be preferred as the constitutional decision rule in situations where it is the objective of unequal participants to block collective action, not because private action is preferred, but because deadlock is preferred to both private and collective action. Again, unanimity alone guarantees each participant to be in the decisive group, but unanimity is the chosen decision rule not because it resolves deadlock, but because it institutionalizes it. The costs involved may be considerable and, in the long run, as has often been pointed out, dysfunctional for the individual participants as well as for the collectivity because it makes for constitutional anarchy. Unanimity ration-

14. This definition of deadlock differs from that of Robert A. Dahl when he writes that "if the deadlock solution is followed, then no governmental action is taken; but if no governmental action is taken, then in fact x is government policy." See *A Preface to Democratic Theory* (1956), p. 41. The situation to which Dahl's statement refers, and quite accurately, is one where the choice is between one collective action as against another, not, as is the situation here, where the choice is between collective action and private action, but where private action will also not be taken.

15. It seems to me that this aspect of the cost problem involved in unanimous decision-making has been neglected by those who only compare the decision costs of unanimity with the decision costs of majority voting or dictatorship. That, among equals, deadlock in a situation which calls for collective action (because private action is not the alternative) may be more expensive than unanimity that makes collective action possible has been neglected. See, for instance, James M. Buchanan and Gordon Tullock, *The Calculus of Consent: Logical Foundations of Constitutional Democracy* (1962), pp. 85–116.

al in the short run may contain, therefore, the seeds of irrationality in the long run.

The discussion suggests that, under specified conditions, unanimity may be more rational than other formal decision rules. This may come as a startling conclusion, for common sense and experience would seem to prove otherwise. But it is startling only if one fails to specify the conditions. Let me repeat them as a paradigm:

1. Each participant in the decisional situation is equal in status and power to every other participant.
2. Each participant in the decisional situation is guaranteed membership in the decisive group.
3. Each participant expects greater advantages for himself from collective than from private action.
4. The costs of unanimous decision-making for collective action are less than the costs of deadlock.

The explication suggests that, under the conditions specified, the constitutional unanimity rule appears as the "ideal-rational" decision rule, whereas other decision rules appear as variants which become relevant only if the conditions for unanimity are not met.[16] The conditions are, of course, extremely strict and not likely to be found in the real world of politics. This is precisely the reason why the constitutional unanimity rule, however rational it may be, has to yield to behaviorally more viable rules like majority voting or dictatorship.

Implicit in the model of constitutional unanimity is the assumption that unanimity is rational if, upon their merits, all possible alternatives among decision rules—such as exceptional majority voting, bare majority voting, plurality voting, decisional dictatorship (arbitration), or even anarchy—have been considered. The availability of alternate rules, then, is a necessary condition of rationality in the choice of a rule, but it is not a sufficient condition. A second condition is that the decision of how to make decisions involve conscious selection of the rule to be followed in preference to other rules. In other words, if unanimity occurs in a voting situation without alternate decisional possibilities having been consciously contemplated, the unanimous decision cannot be considered as prima facie rational. Now, it is evident that the rationality criterion, so interpreted, pertains to constitutional unanimity, for it is the only situation in which unanimity as a decision rule is consciously selected and institutionalized as against other rules.

But what of situations where unanimity occurs, but where it is not a constitutional rule of decision-making? For instance, if a city council unanimously adopts a measure, even though individual members may be reluctant at first to support it, because it believes that a split decision would undermine its authority in the community, and if the alternatives of unanimous versus split decision

16. *Ibid.*, p. 96, comes to the same conclusion, if by a very different theoretical route.

have been consciously considered, the decision is rational, given the group's values. On the other hand, if the relationship between the group's perception of its authority in the community and its voting pattern is not consciously invoked, and if it has consequences that were not consciously anticipated, then the unanimous decision must be explained on another than its rational basis. Consciousness, then, has to be postulated as an important ingredient of rationality, for otherwise the behavior involved in a unanimous decision where unanimity is not a formal rule would have to be accepted, ex post facto, as rational.

Whether unanimity in situations where it is not a formal voting requirement is rational or not is, therefore, a matter of empirical determination. I shall come back to various possibilities in Section VI.

III

As already mentioned, the defense of the formal, constitutional unanimity rule must be predicated on certain behavioral assumptions which, however, are not empirically tenable. The rule seems to assume that human beings are invariably rationally calculating, in the sense that they seek to maximize personal benefits by some hedonistic calculus and make choices, including the decision of how to make decisions, in terms of least cost. And it seems to be assumed that men live in some kind of state of nature, very much as that of the social-contract theories. In these theories one individual is related to any other individual in some private way that is assumed to be prior to social bonds of family, friendship, or any other interpersonal link, and which the individual only enters if it suits his own interests.

These assumptions cannot be made if one wishes to develop an empirically relevant typology of situations in the real world, where unanimity is not a formal decision rule but an existential phenomenon. In the first place, decisions in the real world are not made as if they were the decisions of an individual alone. An individual may take the initiative in seeking to achieve his own interests through collective action. But a great deal of collective decision-making is designed to achieve public as well as individual interests. The behavioral assumption must be made that man is, indeed, a social animal, that he always lives in a group and is part of a group. The notion implicit in the individualistic model of rationally calculating man that only individual but not public interests are "natural" cannot be maintained as behaviorally adequate. The conception of the solitary, individual man unrelated to others but by ties of self-interested calculation does not provide a viable model.

It would seem that when unanimity occurs spontaneously in democratic decision-making, it stems from a confluence of two behavioral dimensions—the ways in which decisions are generally handled and the ways in which interests are articulated. I shall deal with the latter in the next section.

Constitutional unanimity has been called a formal decision rule. Taking this as a clue, I would like to suggest that decisions, whatever the constitutional rule for decision-making, may be handled informally as well as formally and that both informal and formal patterns may characterize decisional behavior. In fact, the combination of formal and informal processes seems to be characteristic of the kind of behavior conventionally called "political." Though the range from informal to formal patterns is best thought of as a continuum of decision-handling, I shall, for conceptual brevity, present a trichotomous classification.

Informal-Consensual Decision-Handling

Here the emphasis is on the spontaneously consensual and informal character of the decision process. Because there is much customary consensus on the prerogatives of the actors, decision-making is likely to be characterized by little conflict. Decisions are handled through traditional, interpersonal arrangements that are only weakly institutionalized in the governmental sense, but they are highly stable nevertheless. Not only are the relations of the members of the collectivity easygoing, face to face, and permanent, but the group itself is likely to be held together by strong bonds of solidarity. Conflict, if it occurs, is likely to be settled through the intervention of mediators. The situation here stylized is probably characteristic of primary groups, but it can probably be extended both to modern committees in a generic sense and to larger communal groups which are fairly homogeneous in composition, culturally isolated, and relatively static in development.

Formal-Ministerial Decision-Handling

At the opposite pole of the decision-handling continuum, behavior is thought to be formal-ministerial. As the concept "ministerial" conveys, decisions are handled ex officio, that is, by persons who do what they do by virtue of the official position they occupy in the group. Rather than being spontaneous, decision-handling is routinized and bureaucratized. There is relatively little room for personal intervention. Decisions are made by rules which are highly institutionalized, either by constitution or convention. Maximum value is placed on consistency in decision-handling. Decisions are likely to be functionally specialized, with great attention being paid to impersonal authority rather than to personal opinions. Favoritism is improper. The participants in the decision process are not held together by ties of friendship, but rather by formal arrangements that, if removed, would spell the end of the relationship. Conflicts will be resolved by appeal to higher jurisdiction. The formal-ministerial pattern would seem to be characteristic of courts of law or administrative organizations where the personal attributes of the decision-makers are considered irrelevant, and where the group is likely to be heterogeneous in background and pluralistic in composition.

Political Decision-Handling

This type of decision-handling may be located somewhere in the middle between consensual and ministerial ways of making decisions. In other words, it partakes of both formal and informal, personal and impersonal patterns. On the one hand, there is likely to be some agreement, more or less, on the "rules of the game" that is as deeply ingrained as are the norms of consensual decision-handling.[17] On the other hand, the relations among decision-makers are also regulated by formal constraints as in the ministerial pattern. On the one hand, a good deal of the behavior involved in political decision-handling is personal—there is room for bargaining and trades which, unlike the ministerial process, give the actor fair latitude in negotiations before the decision is made. On the other hand, limits are set to decision-handling, not only by formal rules, but by the whole network of interpersonal relations outside of the decision-making group itself (the political environment). The political decision-handling pattern seeks to cope with conflict not through mediation or other pacifying techniques, as the informal-consensual pattern, or through appeal to jurisdictional authority, routine, or precedent, as the formal-ministerial pattern, but through clarifying and crystallizing the conflict in debate or negotiation in order to arrive at a point where the decision will represent a compromise which is acceptable to both sides. Unlike the consensual pattern, the composition of the group is more heterogeneous, though it is held together by some shared characteristics, such as language, historical background, or common fate.

Although I have referred, for illustrative purposes, to some particular types of human group, such as the primary group or the administrative organization, as being representative of one or another way of decision-handling, the three patterns should be clearly understood as analytic categories and not as concrete processes which can be identified in crystalline purity with particular decision-making structures.[18] Any one pattern of decision-handling can probably be found, with more or less impact, in any one concrete decision-making structure. Whether it will or not is an empirical research question, not a conceptual or definitional problem.[19]

17. For an enlightening discussion of the slippery concept of consensus and the extent of consensus on decision rules in American politics, see James W. Prothro and Charles M. Grigg, "Fundamental Principles of Democracy: Bases of Agreement and Disagreement," *Journal of Politics,* XXII (1960), 276–294.

18. For the distinction between analytic and concrete structures, see Marion J. Levy, Jr., "Some Aspects of 'Structural-Functional' Analysis and Political Science," in *Approaches to the Study of Politics,* Ed. Roland Young (1958), pp. 52–65.

19. See below, footnote 30, where I point out that the Supreme Court's ways of decision-handling have been quite different from time to time. It seems that all three ways of decision-handling here described have been variously employed.

IV

It seems reasonable to assume, for the purposes of this discussion, that men engage in collective political action to advance both their individual interests and those of the group to which they belong. If the group's decision is unanimous, furthermore, it may be assumed that different types of unanimity will result, depending on the ways in which individual and group interests are articulated within the group, as well as depending on the ways of decision-handling that are practiced. These assumptions would seem to be more tenable than individualistic assumptions, for they derive directly from the social nature of man. We can assume that, precisely because every man is inevitably and invariably a member of a group, he will want to realize his group's as well as his own individual interests.[20] It is in the interchange of individual and group articulation of interests that the particular format of decision-making emerges.

It is necessary to explain here why I am using, in a discussion which is to deal with the rationality of unanimous decision-making, the concept of "interest" rather than the concepts of "goal" and "utility" that are usually employed in connection with treatments of rational action. I do so partly in order to disengage the discussion from models of rationality that make individualistic assumptions, as those of economic choice, or from models that make assumptions about the relationship between means and ends, as those of organizational behavior. But there is a positive reason as well for introducing the notion of "interest" as a critical dimension. It is a term more appropriate in models of *political* decision-making. Unlike organizational or economic behavior, political behavior rarely centers in the search for or the achievement of a single goal or a single value. The multi-valued "ends" and the equally diverse "means" of politics are often difficult to disentangle. The objects of political activity are more or less coherent complexes of individual and group demands and their supporting expectations. To these complexes we give the name of "interests." [21] Any particular decision, even though it may relate to a particular end or means of collective action, is invariably embedded in a more-or-less well-articulated configuration of propinquitous demands, expectations, and evaluations that influences not only the content of decisions but also their format. The ways in which interests, so defined, are articulated may help to

20. This is not to deny that, in reality, there will occur pathological deviations from the norm. Criminals, certainly, seek to maximize their personal utilities without regard to the utilities of others or the public costs that are involved. But even within the criminal community there are "public interests" which the individual criminal can disregard only at great risk for himself.

21. This definition is indebted to Harold D. Lasswell: "An interest is a pattern of demands and its supporting expectations." See Harold D. Lasswell and Abraham Kaplan, *Power and Society* (1950), p. 23. "Interest" is admittedly an ambiguous term. Though it is so widely used in political science, it has not been really explicated or operationalized. David B. Truman's definition—"The shared attitudes . . . constitute the interests"—does not seem useful for my purposes. See his *The Governmental Process* (1951), p. 34.

account for particular voting patterns—whether unanimous, majoritarian, or plural.

Moreover, speaking of interests is advantageous in a discussion of political decision-making for another reason. Interests are likely to be characterized by an intrinsic reciprocity precisely because they refer to both public and private spheres. Academic excellence, for instance, is an interest of the university (the group) as a whole because it concerns the university's standing among all universities. But the university's academic excellence is also an interest that affects every individual member of the university—students, faculty, and administration alike. The more specifically academic excellence as an interest is articulated by the group as a whole as well as by its individual members, the more agreement can undoubtedly be achieved in connection with any particular decision that may have to be made.

I have spoken of "interest articulation" without defining it. I mean by it the ways in which individual or group interests are structured in the perceptions and verbalizations of the decision-makers. In order to deal with this structuring most efficiently, I shall dichotomize interests into those which are "specific" and those that are "diffuse." These articulations represent forms of orientations to action which decision-makers bring into the choice situation.[22] From this perspective, both individual interests and group or public interests may be described as being specifically or diffusely articulated.

Interest Diffuseness

Interests may be said to be diffusely articulated if the demands that are made, either by an individual or a group, do not constitute a hierarchy of preferences which would give priority in decision-making to one demand over another. In other words, the decision-maker will promote any demand that is compatible with other demands, whether public or private, without, at least initially, ordering these demands in terms of the values which may be involved. By not committing himself to one demand over another in advance, the decision-maker is likely to be guided in the choices he makes by the exigencies of the decisional situation, and he is likely to respond to the situation in terms of his predispositions at the time of decision-making and the nature of the problem at hand. For instance, a city council is intent on making the city "a better place to live in." It does not quite know what it means by this or how to achieve it. Its interest is diffusely articulated. A proposal to build a community

22. The notion that interest articulation may be specific or diffuse is indebted to Talcott Parsons' conception of "pattern variables," defined as "a dichotomy one side of which must be chosen by an actor before the meaning of a situation is determinate for him, and thus before he can act with respect to that situation." See *Toward a General Theory of Action,* Ed. Talcott Parsons and Edward A. Shils (1951), p. 77. However my own usage, it should be noted, deviates somewhat from the Parsonian explication of the specificity-diffuseness "dilemma." Similar formulations are in *The Politics of the Developing Areas,* Ed. Gabriel A. Almond and James S. Coleman (1960), pp. 33–38.

ball park is made, seconded, and, in due time, voted on, without much attention being given to alternatives.

Interest Specificity

Interests may be said to be specifically articulated if the different demands that are made, either by an individual or a group, can be readily located within some hierarchy of preferences so that the relevance of a demand in regard to other demands, and to the choice problem at hand, can be specifically determined. In other words, the decision-maker will give priority to that one of his demands over all other demands that is immediately relevant to the problematic situation. To put this somewhat differently, the decision-maker confronts the problematic situation in terms of specifically articulated interests and the requirements for their achievement, but this behavior will be compatible with the exclusion, temporary or permanent, of other interests. For instance, a political group decides to support X, who is running for office. The group proceeds to collect money, distribute leaflets, and arrange coffee hours for the candidate. The group's interest in seeing X win is specifically articulated, for in ordering its preferences it presumably concluded that support of this candidate will not preclude advancing and attaining other interests.

It is possible now to suggest ways of collective interest articulation that result when individual and group interests are either specifically or diffusely articulated. The following matrix shows the possibilities:

		Articulation of Member	
		Specific	*Diffuse*
Articulation of Group	*Specific*	(1) Pluralism	(2) Monism
	Diffuse	(3) Dictatorship	(4) Anarchy

In cell one of the matrix, as the interests of every individual in the group as well as of the group itself are specifically articulated, the decisional problem is one of dealing with specific demands of a rather plural character by setting priorities through bargaining. Because of the probably very great number of specific demands that are made, the setting of priorities is never likely to be completed. Decisions are likely to be made through majority voting by shifting coalitions. Collective articulation is essentially plural and democratic.

In cell four, on the other hand, inaction is the likely result, for the diffuseness of interest articulation, by all the members as individuals and by the group as a whole, prevents collective articulation. In fact, the situation has so little empirical viability that the group is likely to disintegrate in view of its inability to articulate individual or group interests. Insofar as there is articulation, it is best conceptualized as anarchic.

The outcome of cell-two articulation is quite different. In a situation in which the group's interest articulation is specific, but the individual's articulation is diffuse, there is likely to be strong pressure to accede to group demands. Unlike the situation in cell one, the individual with diffuse interest articulation will not order his own individual preferences in view of the group's specifically articulated interests. The situation points towards a monistic articulation of group interests with unanimous decision-making as a strong possibility.

Finally, the situation that emerges in cell three suggests dictatorship as the form of interest articulation in decision-making. Because the interest articulation of the group as a whole is diffuse, so that there is no predecisional ordering of group preferences, and because at least some individuals have specifically articulated interests, there is a strong strain, initially, towards conflict. But because, unlike in the plural order, group articulation is diffuse, the conflict is likely to be resolved through dictatorship—that is, one person (or a subgroup like a triumvirate) comes to dictate the terms of collective interest articulation. In some respects, this situation, if reinforced by structural constraints of coercion, points to the kind of pseudounanimity which, as Friedrich and Brzezinski suggest, "makes the totalitarians insist on the complete agreement of the entire population under their control to the measures the regime is launching." [23] But even without coercion, group-diffuse, individual-specific interest articulation is likely to make for some form of dictatorial collective articulation.[24]

My concern in the following will be only with the articulation outcomes suggested by cells two and three, for in these situations some form of unanimity appears as a likely decisional result. The process represented by cell one is of no further interest because, if a unanimous decision emerges at all, we can assume that we are dealing with the genuine article that is eminently rational. Presumably, there has been free choice among alternatives and conscious selection, after specific individual or group demands have been deliberated upon and negotiated. But unanimity is not likely in a situation in which individual and group articulation is specific. Majority voting is sufficient to reach decisions. The process represented by cell four will also be ignored in the following discussion. It refers to a situation in which deadlock seems to be preferred. Neither private nor collective action would be possible.

V

A typology of unanimity has the immediate purpose of locating empiricial situations of or hypotheses concerning unanimous decision-making in a consistent

23. Carl J. Friedrich and Zbigniew K. Brzezinski, *Totalitarian Dictatorship* (1956), p. 132.

24. We may well speak of the "arbitrator" as a dictator in the sense that his decision in a dispute is unanimously accepted, by prearrangement, by both sides to a dispute, as in labor-management relations.

schema. A typology of this kind can be constructed out of the two dimensions that have been discussed—ways of decision-handling and ways of interest articulation.

The behavioral assumption is made, to repeat, that the relationship between individual and group is such that individual and group interests need not conflict, but are both attainable simultaneously through collective action. Unanimity in decisional patterns would then be evidence of the validity of the behavioral assumption. This does not mean that unanimity is the inevitable decisional outcome whenever a certain way of decision-handling and a certain constellation of interest articulation intersect. However, there is a strong presumption that one or another type of unanimity, when it occurs, is ascertainable in terms of the intersection or confluence of the two dimensions.

We can construct a six-cell unanimity matrix. In interpreting the types represented by the cells, it will be assumed that the three ways of decision-handling will intersect with the two critical ways of interest articulation (group-specific/individual-diffuse and group-diffuse/individual-specific) in characteristic fashion. The tendency towards unanimity is assumed to be present, then, when group and individual ways of interest articulation are asymmetrical, and when they are molded by the prevailing ways of decision-handling so that the particular type of unanimity is clearly distinct from every other type. The following matrix represents the typology:

Ways of interest Articulation	Ways of Decision-Handling: *Consensual*	*Political*	*Ministerial*
Group-specific / *Individual-diffuse*	(1) Ancestral	(3) Bargained	(5) Functional
Group-diffuse / *Individual-specific*	(2) False	(4) Projected	(6) Injunctive

Ancestral Unanimity

If the group's interests are specific, but individual interests are diffuse, and if, at the same time, decisions are handled consensually, there is likely to be a very strong commitment to make unanimous decisions, partly because there is long-standing agreement on what, under certain circumstances, should be done, and partly because the maintenance of group solidarity requires that it should be done unanimously. Individual interests, being diffuse, are submerged in group interests, and there is, therefore, little opportunity for individual interests to be sufficiently crystallized to affect the decisional situation and to occasion division. Alternatives facing the group are decided by traditionally ordered priorities, with little likelihood that group agreement will be disturbed by the intrusion of specific individual interests. Whatever private interests an individual may have are fulfilled in the achievement of the group's interests. Unanimity may be said to be ancestral.

This type of ancestral unanimity seems to be implicit in Keefe's hypothesis concerning unanimous decisions in American state legislatures:

> The area of agreement on legislative questions is so large in some two-party states that significant divisions along discernible lines (e.g., party, rural-urban, sectional, conservative-liberal, etc.) must necessarily be something less than frequent. It may not be so much a matter of "leadership" as simply a case of like-minded legislators moving from bill to bill in the broad fields of state public policy where consensus rather than conflict obtains.[25]

The hypothesis implies that even in modern, functionally highly differentiated political systems there remain vestiges of traditional, customary understandings of what things should or should not be done by the polity. These group preferences are so firmly established and so widely shared that they preclude the emergence of specific individual interests that might be at odds with group interests.

False Unanimity

An altogether different configuration characterizes the decisional situation in which the interests of the group are diffuse, but those of the individual members are specific, yet where decision-handling is essentially consensual. The group's inability to order its interests preferentially, but the existence of specific individual interests, creates a situation that is potentially full of tension and conflict. Yet, the habit of handling decisions consensually and the need to maintain group solidarity, though group interest articulation is diffuse, makes for superficial agreement that prohibits the airing of individual interests inimical to group solidarity. As a result, individual interests, though specific, are suppressed or concealed in the name of the group. Mediators or conciliators cannot function because they have no way of identifying the sources and parties of conflicts. As group interest articulation is diffuse, decisions, even though unanimous, are not genuine expressions of group consensus. Unanimity may be said to be false.

An illustration of false unanimity is the detailed description of the "politics of unanimity" by Vidich and Bensman in their study of the village and school boards of a small, rural community. The school board, for instance,

> reaches its decisions through a process of discussion which results in an inchoately arrived-at unanimous decision in which no vote, or only a perfunctory one, is taken. . . . It becomes central to the psychology of the members of the board to attempt to minimize or avoid crises, and this leads to further demands for unanimity and concealment.[26]

25. Keefe, *op. cit.*, p. 311.
26. Arthur J. Vidich and Joseph Bensman, *Small Town in Mass Society* (1960), p. 176.

As a hypothesis, the notion of concealment or "false unanimity" is probably more viable in small legislative bodies such as city councils or committees than in large institutionalized groups like state legislatures or the Congress, where a façade of unity is practically impossible in normal conflictual situations, and where partisanship rather than friendly agreement is the public expectation.

Bargained Unanimity

Where the task of decision-making is to integrate diffuse individual interests in terms of specific group interests in a decision-handling structure that is "political," unanimity, if it occurs, probably stems from successful trading and bargaining among the individual members. The bargaining process is facilitated, on the one hand, by the diffuseness of the individual interests: No intransigent positions are likely to be taken, and the spirit of compromise prevails. Moreover, the specificity of group interests sets limits to the bargaining process—not everything goes, for, if everything goes, bargaining will not lead to compromise. In this situation, then, conflicts are resolved through compromise in terms of specific group interests. Unanimity may be said to be bargained.

Bargained unanimity is implicit in Truman's explanation of unanimous decisions in larger legislative bodies. He suggests that

> even where virtual unanimity prevails in the legislature, the process of reconciling conflicting interests must have taken place—though perhaps at an earlier stage wholly or partly outside the legislature and the formal institutions of government. When this happens, the legislature merely registers the decision.[27]

There is the assumption, then, first, that conflict has in fact occurred, but second, that the conflict has been so successfully resolved that it culminates in unanimity.

Projected Unanimity

If, on the other hand, group interests are diffuse, yet individual interests are specific, the political bargaining process encounters difficulties. The absence of an articulated group interest makes the political game appear to be fragmented

27. Truman, *op.cit.,* p. 392. Unfortunately, Truman then gives what seems to me a rather dubious example. The last sentence quoted here continues: ". . . as the Congress did in its declaration of war after Pearl Harbor." I am not clear what conflict Truman had in mind that was resolved prior to the declaration of war. If he means the battle between internationalists or interventionists and isolationists, it is inaccurate to say that it had been solved prior to Pearl Harbor. It would be more appropriate to say that it was "tabled." Moreover, as I suggested in footnote 8, the unanimity accompanying the declaration of war is not likely to be one that can be considered due to a process of free choice.

and kaleidoscopic. Conflict is not suppressed as it is in the case of false unanimity, and the game is played as in the case of bargained unanimity. But as political decision-handling is not altogether formal and contains informal patterns, there is likely to be a tendency to go along with a somewhat fictitious group consensus. The consensus is fictitious because the group interest is not really articulated. How can unanimity be explained in this situation? I shall suggest a hypothesis.

Because group interests are poorly articulated and diffuse, the decisional situation will appear ambiguous to the decision-makers. Yet, as there is a pressure for decision–individual specific interests are promoted–some perceptual structuring of the ambiguous situation is needed. Therefore, the individual decision-maker will tend to project his own preferred interests on the group as a whole. Not knowing where others stand, such projection provides the individual with a perceptual anchorage point. He expects others to decide in the way in which he himself decides. This psychological ordering of the ambiguous situation involves a great deal of perceptual distortion.[28] But it may have the effect of creating a cognitive environment in which psychological pressure towards a unanimous decision becomes very great. If it is believed that everybody agrees with everybody else, the image of unanimity can serve as a kind of protective screen from responsibility for failure to resolve an issue in those terms in which it was originally defined by the individual with specific interests himself. Unanimity may be said to be projected.

Projected unanimity seems to be implicit in an interesting finding by Crane concerning party cohesion in the Wisconsin legislature. One might surmise that the absence of division in a legislative party is simply a function of legislators' indifference concerning a piece of legislation. Party cohesion, for instance, should occur only in policy matters where the group's interest is specific enough for legislators to feel strongly about the stakes at issue. Yet, Crane reports, "party cohesion was most easily maintained on those issues about which legislators were least concerned and apparently regarded as least important." [29] In other words, cohesion within the parties occurred on unimportant rather than, as one might expect, on important issues. Though we are dealing here with a subgroup rather than the full group, it would seem that in the situation described by Crane we encounter a case of projected unanimity for the subgroups in question. Individually specific interests seem to be surrendered in favor of a psychologically satisfying, if unreal, unanimity.

28. For other examples of the projection hypothesis in politics and some proof, especially in electoral voting, see A. Thomsen, "Psychological Projection and Election," *Journal of Psychology*, II (1941), 115–117; Paul F. Lazarsfeld, Bernard Berelson, and Hazel Gaudet, *The People's Choice* (1948), p. 168; and Heinz Eulau, "Class Identification and Projection in Voting Behavior," *Western Political Quarterly*, VIII (1955), 441–452.

29. Wilder Crane, Jr. "A Caveat on Roll-Call Studies of Party Voting," *Midwest Journal of Political Science*, IV (1960), 246–247.

Functional Unanimity

The impact of ministerial decision-handling on a situation in which individual interests are diffuse, but group interests are specific, is likely to produce a kind of unanimity that is compelling because alternatives are drastically reduced. Decision-makers, whether themselves in a ministerial position, as judges are, or whether acting on the advice of persons in ministerial positions, as legislators do on recommendations from administrative experts, appeal to and accept "authority" precisely because individual interests, being diffuse, do not intrude strongly on the decision process. At the same time, the specificity of group interests provides an evaluative reference point for what action must be taken. This does not mean that disagreements over group interests do not exist. But they are clarified and resolved in terms of rather impersonal criteria, such as routine, precedent or specialized knowledge. Unanimity may be said to be functional.

To illustrate functional unanimity, let us shift to judicial decision-making. For instance, speaking of the "powerful factors normally operating to achieve unanimity in the decisions of the Supreme Court," Pritchett attributes unanimous decisions, among other reasons, to "the generally settled character of the American legal system, fairly strict adherence to the principle of stare decisis, and the broad similarities in training and background which tend to characterize Supreme Court justices. . . ." Pritchett also points out that "the influence of a strong and skillful Chief Justice is of great importance in leading to the discovery of solutions satisfactory to all members of the Court." [30] In other words, an issue is resolved by appeal to the authority of precedent.

Analogous to the authority of precedent in judicial decision-making is probably the authority of routine in legislative action. In city councils, for instance, routine handling of issues serves as an impersonal criterion for deciding what should or should not be done. Or a legislative group may accept the recommendations of an administrative specialist—an engineer who advises on the location of a bridge, or a city manager. Acceptance of an expert's judgment is presumably based on his professional disinterestedness that stems from his specialized know-how rather than from his personal relations with his clients.

30. C. Herman Pritchett, *The Roosevelt Court* (1948), p. 24. Pritchett names other factors as well, such as "the discussion which goes on around the judicial conference table, out of which consensus can often be achieved." This suggests that judicial unanimity can also be explained as "bargained unanimity." And "false unanimity" through concealment seems to be relevant in explaining the Court's behavior under Chief Justice Marshall. See John R. Schmidhauser, *The Supreme Court* (1960), p. 114: "The price of maintaining the fiction of judicial certainty, decisiveness, and unity was the camouflaging of real doubt, and occasionally, the acceptance by individual justices of positions which they personally knew to be erroneous. Justice Story was, without doubt, the most careful legal scholar on the Supreme Court during this period. Yet he was persuaded, on several occasions, to accept erroneous decisions silently for the sake of the Court's reputation and unity." In other words, one should not confuse a given type of unanimity with a particular institution.

Injunctive Unanimity

This is, of course, the behavioral situation which underlies the constitutional unanimity rule. The constitution itself becomes a ministerial-like reference point. Individual interests are so specific and group interests so diffuse that unanimity is the only way of protecting individual interests from each other or preventing the emergence of a collective decision to which individual members cannot subscribe. As suggested earlier, unanimity in this situation may either create deadlock or serve to resolve it. The formal rule of unanimity enjoins the individual members from imposing their specific interests upon each other. Unanimity may be said to be injunctive.

But unanimity of this kind can be present without being constitutionally required. The consensus of the Quaker meeting seems to be of this order. Although formal voting is eschewed, an issue is discussed until a solution emerges to which all individuals can agree or, at least, from which any one individual will not dissent.[31] In the case of the Quaker meeting, the appeal to "conscience" serves as the impersonal criterion for giving or withholding consent. This procedure is functionally equivalent to the constitutional unanimity rule. It is because the process involved is costly and time consuming that democracy is willing to deviate from the unanimity rule and accept that degree of coercion which majority voting, in the Quaker view, implies.

The typology of unanimity here outlined is probably not exhaustive, for it is necessarily an artifact of the dimensions that were used in constructing it. However, it suggests that unanimity is a multi-faceted behavioral phenomenon that cannot be treated as a monomorphic structure. Moreover, the typology seems to be sufficiently comprehensive to accommodate various empirical descriptions of or hypotheses about unanimous voting. We are now in a position to examine the kind of rationality that may be involved in the various types of unanimous decision-making.

VI

As mentioned earlier, one need not start off from the behavioral assumptions of the individualistic theory of rationality in order to use the conditions of constitutional unanimity as criteria in appraising the rationality of unanimous decisions in real-life situations that are not controlled by the formal rule. Let me restate both the assumptions and the conditions for "spontaneous unanimity" (unanimity not constitutionally required) as they have emerged from the discussion, so that they can be referred to in the following appraisal.

Behavioral assumption: There is no necessary conflict between individual and group interests (though there may be), and both individual and group interests can be attained through collective action. Because each participant

31. See Francis Pollard, *Democracy and the Quaker Method* (1949).

decision-maker expects to attain his individual interests and the interests of the group through collective action, he will accept the costs of unanimity as being less than the costs of deadlock. Unanimity has the effect of making each participant in the decision equal in status and power to every other participant, and it assures him membership in the decisive group.

First condition: A unanimous decision is rational if it is made in a situation that has the potential for free choice among alternate decisional patterns (such as majority voting or dictatorship). This condition states essentially a requirement made of the environment of choice.

Second condition: A unanimous decision is rational if it is consciously chosen from among alternate decisional patterns. This condition states essentially a requirement made of the individual actor.

To what extent, then, do the types of unanimity developed in the previous section conform to the behavioral assumptions and meet the conditions of rationality here specified?

Ancestral Unanimity: Prerationality

Ancestral unanimity does not seem to invalidate the behavioral assumptions, but it does not satisfy the first condition. The decision-handling structure is such that alternate decisional patterns are not contemplated. The behavioral style of ancestral unanimity seems to be prerational, in the sense that long-standing agreement on unanimity as a way of making collective decisions precludes the availability of alternatives. The consensus is genuine enough, but as there is no potential for free choice among alternate patterns of decision-making, it is prerational rather than rational.

False Unanimity: Counterrationality

In the case of false unanimity, the behavioral assumptions seem to be falsified. There is no gurarantee in this situation that individual interests can be achieved through collective action, for they are suppressed in the name of group solidarity. On the other hand, unanimity is chosen as a preferred decisional pattern over alternate patterns, and consciously so. The rationality involved, if it can so be called, is a kind of counterrationality of fear which deters individuals from pursuing certain of their interests and which leads them to act counter to these interests in order to achieve a group interest that is poorly articulated. The consensus of false unanimity is counterrational rather than prerational, as is the consensus of ancestral unanimity.

Bargained Unanimity: Satisfying Rationality

The process that culminates in bargained unanimity seems to meet all the behavioral assumptions as well as the conditions of rationality. However, as the ways of decision-handling call for trading, bargaining, and compromise among diffuse individual interests in terms of group-specific interests, the latter are themselves subject to negotiation. The rationality involved is more likely to be of the kind which Simon calls "satisficing." Therefore, unanimity is by no means the "best" decisional pattern under the circumstances, but it is "good enough" for the attainment of the individual interests at stake. Majority voting might well be a better alternative, but it seems to be consciously ruled out if the participants in the decision-making situation can arrive at a satisfying solution through unanimity. This kind of bargained unanimity, then, is satisficingly rational.

Projected Unanimity: Irrationality

Projected unanimity fails to meet both conditions of rationality. It gives the participants the impression of being able to attain individual and group interests through collective action without really doing so. The decisional process of projected unanimity seems to stymie the ways of decision-handling that one should expect. Because group interests are diffusely articulated, the individual decision-maker is left without a stable point of reference for trading, bargaining, and compromising–a situation in which alternate decision patterns cannot be consciously chosen. The decisional impasse is resolved through unconscious projection of individual upon group interests–a process that violates the behavioral assumptions and is unlikely to attain individual or group interests. Insofar as a decision is unanimously reached in this way, it is irrational in the sense of being accidental or essentially random. Any other decisional pattern is equally plausible.

Functional Unanimity: Procedural Rationality

In situations where the group's interests are specifically articulated and decision-handling is largely ministerial, reliance on authority or precedent would seem to make for a kind of rationality that is procedural in appraising the relevance of alternate decisional patterns, given the group's specific and individual's diffuse interests. Though the process of cumulatively procedural-rational decision-making might ultimately tend to reduce alternatives in contravention of the first condition, there is little probability that decisional alternatives in the final stages of decision-making will ever be exhausted. Unanimity itself is almost self-evident proof of the procedural rationality involved in the process, for it is likely to occur only after alternate decisional patterns have been consciously eliminated as a result of convincing argument that the choice to be made cannot be anything but unanimous.

Injunctive Unanimity: Maximizing Rationality

Injunctive unanimity presents the situation in which the individual participant with his specifically articulated interests uses his dissent whenever collective action seems to threaten his interests. The rationality involved is essentially maximizing from the individual's point of view. However, injunctive unanimity would seem to falsify our behavioral assumptions. If carried to its ultimate logical conclusion, the attempt to maximize one's individual interests at the expense of the group's interests through unanimity would be self-defeating by creating deadlock, a situation which the rationally maximizing actor does not prefer. Insofar as he prefers some action to deadlock, he will continue to debate an issue until unanimity is reached. Insistence on unanimity in this sense meets both conditions of rationality, for alternate decisional patterns are consciously rejected.

What general observations can be made about the logic of rationality in different unanimous decision-making situations? First of all, only one type—injunctive unanimity—meets the requirements of rationality derived from the classical individualistic conception of the maximizing individual. Because the requirements of maximizing rationality are severe, we should expect that only very few of the spontaneous unanimous decisions reached in the real world of politics would be of the injunctive type. Indeed, the sparse use of the formal unanimity rule in modern circumstances suggests that injunctive unanimity does not recommend itself to rational men except in the most extreme cases where they feel their "vital interests" to be at stake.

Second, only one type of unanimity—projected unanimity—is clearly irrational. It is irrational because unanimity emerges as the outcome of unconscious psychological mechanisms in a situation where one should expect division. Little is known about this type of irrationally projected unanimity, but it should be of considerable empirical research interest. For there is reason to believe that this type of unanimity is not uncommon in large political systems where neither consensual nor ministerial ways of decision-handling provide feasible behavioral alternatives.

Third, a distinction must be made between the irrational behavior involved in projected unanimity and the counterrational behavior of false unanimity. The difference is largely due to the two different ways of decision-handling, but whereas in projected unanimity the process of decision-making remains altogether obscure, in false unanimity it is all too evident. Here decisions are made in self-conscious, if not widely shared, awareness of the consequences that would ensue if the decision-makers were to promote their specifically articulated interests. Yet, they act purposefully counter to their individual interests in the name of a unity that is largely fictitious. Counterrationality might be thought of as a kind of mixture of prerationality and irrationality, perhaps as a kind of pseudorationality. It approximates both kinds, but is precluded from being completely prerational or irrational by virtue of its consciousness of alternatives of decisional patterns.

Fourth, the notion that decisions can be made unanimously in the sense of prerationality, as the concept is used here, should not strike one as particularly novel. That a group's consensually validated ways of doing things have an influence on current behavioral patterns has been widely observed in simple societies, and it has been hypostatized into principle by conservative ideologues who distrust the maxims of utilitarian rationality. That this type of prerational, ancestral unanimity is also found in modern decision-making situations should surprise only those who write off as irrelevant the pertinacity of informal, personal ways of decision-handling in complex collectivities.

Fifth, the typology certainly supports the notion that there is a point where the achievement of group interests is halted and circumscribed by the free play of individual interest-seeking through trading, bargaining, and compromise. This point is not likely to be the optimal point for either the attainment of group interests or the attainment of individual interests. But it is likely to satisfy the requirements of rational men. The point is reached not through maximizing but through "satisficing" rational conduct. The extent to which the "satisficing"-rational type of bargained unanimity is characteristic of unanimous decision-making in real-life politics is unknown. In all probability it is rather rare, for "satisficing" rationality does not require unanimity as a decisional pattern that is preferable to others. Satisfaction of interests can be more readily achieved through plurality or majority decisions.

Finally, the typology identifies procedural rationality as a companion of the kind of unanimity that has been called functional. A great deal of unanimity found in modern legislative bodies, as in judicial and administrative institutions, is procedurally rational. It is a kind of rationality that is "built in," so to speak, the kind of situations where the attainment of interests is sought by reliance on available resources. This has long been recognized in judicial and administrative settings, but the presence of procedural-rational unanimity in more immediately political situations, as those of legislative bodies, would seem to defy the conventional categories of institutional analysis. However, recent research on legislative processes and legislative behavior shows that specialization and reliance on expertise are not alien to primarily political decision-making.[32] The notion of procedural-rational unanimity is likely to be fruitful in explaining much of the unanimous decisional outcomes in democratic institutions such as legislatures and other deliberative bodies where, in general, majority voting is the norm.

VII

We may return now to the starting point of this inquiry: Why unanimity in democratic decision-making? Is such unanimity rational? The typology of unanimity suggests that unanimous decisions may be stimulated by the confluence of diverse types of interest articulation and decision-handling. From the

32. See John C. Wahlke, Heinz Eulau, William Buchanan, and LeRoy C. Ferguson, *The Legislative System: Explorations in Legislative Behavior* (1962), pp. 193–215.

perspective of interest articulation, the typology intimates that there may be some pressure towards unanimity whenever either group interests are specifically articulated, yet individual interests are diffusely articulated, or vice versa. The incidence of these occurrences is an empirical research question. At the same time, different ways of decision-handling give unanimity, when it occurs under one or another condition of interest articulation, a characteristic style or format. The task of research is to locate and classify unanimous decisions in terms of the critical ways in which decisions are generally handled in choice-making situations.

What of the rational character of unanimity? Quite clearly, great caution is called for in assessing the kind of rational conduct involved in the various types of unanimity that have been identified. One result of the argument is beyond doubt: The assumption that unanimity in democratic decision-making is necessarily irrational does not seem to be warranted. Only one type—projected unanimity—could be called irrational. Other types of unanimity seem to meet various criteria of rationality, while other types are prerational or what I have called counterrational. Even if one were to combine the latter with the irrational type, it would seem that unanimity is not inevitably a deviation from some norm that requires majority voting (or some other decision rule) as the only legitimate form of democratic decision-making. Moreover, what was called bargained unanimity is eminently rational in the "satisficing" sense. Unanimity appears to be a legitimate form of democratic decision-making, though the kind of rationality involved always requires specification. One might well argue that it is perhaps more difficult to get men in responsible decision-making posts to disagree than to agree, just as in the world of business it seems more difficult to provide for competition which must often be "enforced" in the face of a "natural" inclination towards monopoly. But the central point to be made is that unanimity is not necessarily dysfunctional and symptomatic of a breakdown of the democratic process.

Chapter 2

Manifest and Latent Functions in Legislative Politics

Congressional reform is an area where political scientists should fear to tread. For, whatever other virtues political scientists may possess, they do not have at their disposal a knowledge of good or evil, of right or wrong. In fact, even on matters where we can make a claim to knowledge, it is the better part of wisdom to speak with restraint and not to claim too much. But though our knowledge is often fragmentary and even unreliable, we cannot abandon either the critical or the creative functions that our role as politically as well as scientifically responsible observers of and participants in public life calls for—provided we adhere to our own professional standards of appropriate conduct.

One of these standards is that we make as explicit as possible the assumptions, both normative and behavioral, that underlie whatever recommendations we make about public policies. This standard is by no means always adhered to. Yet, behind any proposal for reform of congressional structures, functions, and processes are assumptions about the role of the Congress in the total American governmental system. Unfortunately, only rarely are these assumptions fully articulated. In fact, articulation may sometimes be deliberately avoided, lest it mobilize opposition to a particular proposal, not because of its actual contents so much as because the assumptions behind it seem obnoxious and unacceptable. Avoidance of stating assumptions can therefore on occasion become a strategy of reform. But this cannot be our strategy. As scientists, we have no alternative but to clarify and articulate our assumptions. For our role is primarily to enlighten rather than to persuade.

Originally published as "The Committees in a Revitalized Congress" in Alfred de Grazia, Ed., *Congress: The First Branch of Government* (Washington, D.C.: American Enterprise Institute for Public Policy Research, 1966) pp. 213–56. Reprinted by permission.

As one reviews the many recommendations made by members of Congress, interested citizens and organizations, and political scientists concerning reforms of congressional operations, one is struck, first, by the nit-picking character of criticisms of this and that aspect of congressional life—criticisms that are rarely informed by a comprehensive view of the Congress in the American system of checks and balances. Secondly, one is struck by the casual, *ad hoc* character of most of the proposals and by the fact that they do not add up to a coherent program for reform. The purpose of a normative model—such as the model of a vigorous, independent Congress presented in this symposium—is to give direction to particular proposals and to see to it that they constitute a logical, consistent whole.

From the vantage point of our own model, the main feature of the great variety of proposals so far put forward for committee reforms is their limited perspective. At their best, they are oriented to the *contemporary* configuration of power within the Congress or between the Congress and the White House. That the configuration may change in a short time, because of changing personal or party fortunes, is intentionally disregarded. For instance, quite recently we have seen liberal congressmen rise in defense of seniority, a principle of organization that not too long ago was high on the agenda of liberal denunciation. Hence, when viewed in this way, "reform" comes to have a very particular meaning. It comes to mean the creation of temporary devices designed to serve the temporary advantage of partisan groupings, ideological factions, interest-group combinations, or the President. The long-range role of the Congress in the system of balanced powers is ignored, or else the Congress is assigned a secondary role in the scheme of governmental things.

At their worst, proposals for reform are advanced to redress special grievances which are generalized, though we do not know how widely they are held—that a chairman does not schedule bills as they should be scheduled, or that junior comittee members are not given a chance to shine at public hearings, or that administrative officials must spend too much time on the Hill. Reform proposals to alleviate these defects, which may indeed occur, are usually so innocuous that they fail to draw blood. That grievances stemming from the human condition can be redressed by structural changes remains largely an act of faith. True, there is always the *possibility* of correcting or at least harnessing human frailties through changes in institutional arrangements. The men who framed the Constitution and thought of the living constitution as one of checks and balances were eminently sensitive, perhaps too sensitive, to the problem of controlling human passions and errors through institutional safeguards. But one need not be a conservative to recognize that not even the subtlest structural controls can entirely eliminate human folly.

Therefore, it is a modest assumption of this paper that, no matter what proposals for committee reform are made or adopted, there will always be difficulties stemming from the human factor. Whatever system of chairman selection be adopted by a legislative body, for instance, there will always be good and bad presiding officers, and many who are in between. Whatever financial inducements are necessary to attract a presumably competent staff, there will always be good, in-between, and bad staff members. This does not mean that behavior patterns should not be optimized through appropriate structural arrangements. It only means that perfection is not the issue.

It is for just these reasons that framing proposals for reform merely in terms of a normative model is not enough. If the proposals are to be viable, they must also take into account the emergent properties of collective bodies like committees which result from individual and interpersonal behavioral patterns. The congressional structure is not a bloodless mechanism, but a living organism—a system of complex interpersonal and intergroup relations that must be thoroughly understood if proposals derived from the normative model are not to remain altogether utopian. The fact is that we *know* relatively little about the behavioral system that is Congress, at least if by "knowledge" we mean empirically tested propositions as opposed to casual (albeit possibly profound) insights or hunches. This is especially true of the behavioral patterns of congressional committees. We know less about them than about other aspects of congressional behavior and functioning, say the role of the parties or the constituencies. If the few excellent studies of committee structures and functions conducted in the last few years by political scientists tell us anything, it is that the congressional behavioral system as mirrored in the life of the committees and subcommittees is even more complex and manifold than we had hitherto suspected.

Because almost no committee or subcommittee behaves like any other, generalizations about committee behavior are hazardous. Any set of proposals for changes must therefore take this fact as its point of departure. Each committee has its own needs and requirements for effective functioning, its own traditions and norms of behavior, its characteristic tasks and goals, its unique subject matter and relevant skills. If they are to serve any useful purpose, reform proposals must take all these factors into account; and further, reformers must seek to assess how proposed changes would affect committee behavior.

The purpose of the proposals about committees presented in this paper is neither to serve partisan, ideological, or any other advantages, nor to redress familiar grievances. They are derived from a model of Congress that is geared, on the one hand, to the behavioral realities of the present as we know them and, on the other hand, to the developmental context of the future as we hope to shape it. My proposals do not touch, therefore, on every conceivable aspect of committee structures and functions. Rather, they are located in the context of broad, basic problems. They are based on the assumption that the future can be shaped according to man's preferences, that there is nothing inevitable about the future (as there is about the present) if men are prepared to seize their opportunities. Whatever may motivate the other authors represented in this symposium, be they liberal or conservative, my own preference for a strong, independent, representative, responsible, and responsive Congress in the American system does not stem from the conservative's hankering after the past. Rather, it flows from the liberal conviction that, over the long haul, the elected representatives of the people assembled in Congress are at least as qualified to give direction to the American democracy as the President and the federal bureaucracy.

THE PROBLEM OF FUNCTIONS: MANIFEST AND LATENT

Proposals for reorganizing congressional committees with a view to strengthening the Congress vis-à-vis the President and the bureaucracy must proceed from a clear view of congressional functions and of committee functions. It is a rather widespread, if simplistic, view that because committees are "creatures" of Congress in the formal sense, they have no functions that can be distinguished from those of the Congress as a whole. This view ignores a number of considerations. In the first place, the functions of Congress cannot be identified independently of the functions of its committees because, for all practical purposes, the work of Congress is done in the committees. Notwithstanding the formal derivation of committees, therefore, identifying the functions of Congress requires prior identification of committee functions.

Second, while it is easy enough to identify those functions which are defined in the Constitution, they do not exhaust the list of functions actually performed by committees in practice. Some of these additional functions are "manifest," like the investigatory function which was inherited, so to speak, from the English Parliament and the early state legislatures. Others, however, may be described as "latent"; these latent functions are difficult to identify and have come to be scrutinized by political scientists only in recent years.

These distinctions are important because changes in congressional structure may have consequences for committee functioning which, from the perspective of one model or another, may be harmful. In turn, changes in committee functions may have important consequences for the position of Congress in the total governmental system. This "structural-functional" view of the congressional process suggests that concrete proposals for committee reform, no matter how picayune they may appear to be, must be appraised in terms of their possible consequences for the total constellation of congressional operations. While this is not the place to do so, it is my strong impression that quite a few proposals recently made would have to be considered detrimental from the standpoint of the model of a strong Congress presented in this symposium.

If possible harmful consequences are to be avoided, perhaps one of the most immediate tasks of the Joint Committee on the Organization of the Congress ought to be to bring into the open, through an appropriate statement, exactly those latent functions that tend to strengthen the Congress as a countervailing power to the President and the bureaucracy. To insist that just the traditional, formal functions of Congress–lawmaking proper, participation in nominations and treaty-making, or investigation–should be strengthened, will not contribute very much to solving the critical problem of congressional-presidential relations. It is my belief that some of the latent functions performed by the committees may be more relevant than the better-known manifest functions. My intent here is to be only suggestive. We shall discuss merely two of the more important latent functions performed by committees—the congressional "veto" and the conflict-resolving function.

Under the Constitution, the veto is a presidential prerogative, introduced precisely because the framers distrusted legislative majorities. The President still has the right to veto and, on proper occasion, he exercises his right. But over the years Congress has gradually come to perform a veto function that was not provided for in the Constitution. Whenever a committee or subcommittee bottles up executive-initiated legislation, votes it down, or refuses to report it out of committee, it is exercising an effective, if latent, veto function. From the perspective of our model, this function is highly desirable, even though it may at times be abused.

The second latent function I wish to discuss is the conflict-crystallizing and conflict-resolving function that is inherent in the complex congressional committee and subcommittee structure. This function is not always appreciated sufficiently. All too many reformers—whether those who would subordinate the Congress to the President, or those whose ideal is a Congress which resembles an efficient business organization—ignore the fact that the Congress is, above all, a broadly representative body, and as such, because it is representative of so many potentially and actually conflicting interests, preeminently a political body. If the conflicts of society that find their way into Congress are not to be resolved by authoritarian means but through mutual accommodation of interests and compromise, the facilitation of the conflict-resolving function ought to be high on the list of structural requirements. Moreover, it would seem that this function can be better performed by the committees and subcommittees than by the Congress as a whole.

Let us consider only two aspects of the relationship between function and structure in this connection. First, there is the factor of size. It is generally agreed that small committees are more accessible to interests-in-conflict than large groups. From the point of view of those who take a negative stance towards interest-group politics this fact may appear to be harmful. From the point of view of our model, however, committee accessibility is a strong feature of congressional structuring. For this reason, proposals to combine committees with related jurisdictions may seriously interfere with the functions of conflict resolution. In other words, what is often called the "proliferation" of committees is in fact highly functional from our perspective. And precisely because it is functional, I believe that it will always occur, even if for some reasons the committee superstructure is "simplified."

Second, there is now good evidence to suggest that committees and subcommittees each evolve norms of their own which may be either highly conducive or non-conducive to conflict resolution. In a careful study of the House Appropriations Committee, Professor Richard F. Fenno, Jr., has shown that this committee is faced with basic problems of integration, defined as "the degree to which there is a working together or a meshing together or mutual support among its roles and subgroups"—which are directly relevant to the performance of its manifest functions. In other words, successful integration in this committee has important consequences for its work; for instance, on the acceptability of its recommendations, the reduction of party influence on appropriations decisions, the stability of appropriations procedures, and others.[1]

What these merely suggestive comments add up to is this: there is a high probability that almost any structural change in one sector of congressional life—say, the leadership structure or House-Senate relations—will affect many other sectors; since, if functions are eliminated from one sector, they will probably be performed by another. Before structural change is undertaken, therefore, it is important to identify as many functions as possible so as to assure that the total complex of functions necessary for a vigorous Congress is not undermined by inappropriate structural changes. These considerations will in part guide us in the following sections of this paper. But before I go on, one proposal: Congress should allocate funds for a continuing survey of its structures and functions, to be conducted by a team of disinterested analysts, for the purpose of permitting Congress to reorganize and strengthen itself from session to session rather than from decade to decade or more. What use Congress would make of this continuing survey would be symptomatic of its commitment to remaining a viable institution in our age of executive dominance. But even if the survey should turn out to be more of a *pro forma* operation than a real one, it could serve to alert the Congress to the consistency or inconsistency—from the perspective of a strong legislature—of those piecemeal, incremental changes in structure and functions that are bound to occur over the years.

THE PROBLEM OF JURISDICTION: CONFLICT AND COORDINATION

Efforts to improve the internal organization of Congress necessarily center in what is felt to be a need for the orderly arrangement of the respective jurisdictions of the standing committees. But what criteria should guide this arrangement? Perhaps too much routine, and too little imaginative thinking has been devoted to answering this question. How else can one explain the general agreement that the organization of the committees along the more or less broad policy lines laid down in the Legislative Reorganization Act of 1946 has

1. Richard F. Fenno, Jr., "The House Appropriations Committee," *American Political Science Review,* June 1962, pp. 310–24. But, for a negative case of integration, see Charles O. Jones, "The Role of the Congressional Subcommittee," *Midwest Journal of Political Science,* November 1962, pp. 327–44.

worked reasonably well, even though jurisdictional conflicts continue? At least at the present time, there is no widespread demand for reorganization of the standing committee structure as such. Such proposals as are made are largely cast within the "spirit" of the 1946 Act.

The chief argument in favor of the present arrangement is that though almost every committee must deal with several administrative departments or agencies, there is sufficient parallelism between the various congressional and bureaucratic sectors to guarantee efficiency in relations and operations at both ends of Pennsylvania Avenue. The argument is plausible but deceptive. In reality, it is an argument derived from the executive model of the legislature's role in the federal government. If it were really taken seriously, the argument would weaken rather than strengthen the Congress vis-à-vis the bureaucracy.

For the assumption underlying the argument, and implicit in the executive model that strengthening Congress is mainly a matter of achieving greater efficiency through the clarification of committee jurisdictions and the avoidance of jurisdictional conflicts, is the ideal of the public administrator. Needless to say, perhaps, insofar as the quest for efficiency relates to the myriad of routine tasks which the Congress must perform, one can only endorse appropriate efforts (always keeping in mind the possibility that valuable latent functions may be harmed). But what reason is there to believe that efficiency in congressional operations will strengthen the position of Congress as a *policy-making* institution in the total governmental system? Indeed, one might argue that rather than making the Congress more independent of presidential domination, proposals to increase its efficiency will actually make it even more susceptible to executive and administrative pressures and demands. Surely, more efficient reaction to these pressures and demands is not in the best interests of Congress as a strong and independent legislative body.

But the efficiency argument is faulty on another ground as well. It ignores the facts of Washington political life. As a close academic observer of the scene, Professor Richard Neustadt, has pointed out, the actual relationship between Congress and the bureaucracy is just the reverse of what it is often assumed to be: "Both organizationally and in terms of personnel the new bureaucracy is a projection of congressional committee jurisdictions—or, more precisely, since 1946, of standing subcommittee jurisdictions." This, perhaps, overstates the true case, as Neustadt himself acknowledges: "Of course, committee jurisdictions have been influenced, in turn, by organizational developments downtown." [2] In other words, respective congressional and agency structuring appears to be a reciprocal process, and hence tends to make for structural parallelism. Unfortunately, we do not really know whether this parallelism is an advantage or a disadvantage for committee operations vis-à-vis the bureaucracy—say, in regard to their oversight function, for instance.

2. Richard E. Neustadt, "Politicians and Bureaucrats," in David B. Truman (Ed.), *The Congress and America's Future* (Englewood Cliffs, N.J.: Prentice-Hall, 1965), pp. 103–04.

In any case, as Neustadt also suggests, the very rigidity introduced by efforts to attain jurisdictional neatness actually has the adverse effect of depriving committees of their influence on administrative operations: "As a forum for administrative bargaining, our legislative process has its uses in securing and defending fixed positions, not in reaching or applying operational accommodations suited to the job in hand." [3]

If Neustadt is correct, and I believe that he partly is, then, surely, not too much effort should be expended in attempts to clarify and sharply delineate jurisdictions. Such attempts will only impede just those conflict-resolving bargaining processes which an elected legislative body, perhaps better than any other organ of government, is especially capable of performing. Moreover, most modern legislation is usually so complex that it cannot easily and unambiguously be assigned to one or another committee or subcommittee. In other words, setting up neat and sharply separated jurisdictional structures is dysfunctional from the viewpoint of contemporary legislation. It tends to create difficulties where none need to exist. Insistence on defining sharp jurisdictional boundaries between committees, in terms of some purely hypothetical subject matter contributes to legislative confusion because, as Professors William J. Keefe and Morris S. Ogul rightly point out, "policy interrelationships may be missed, emerging policies may begin or come to work at cross-purposes, and committees may wrangle with each other over the custody of measures and activities." [4]

Of course, committee and subcommittee jurisdiction cannot be helter-skelter. As I shall argue later on, committee expertise is an essential requirement for vigorous congressional functioning. But it is only a necessary and not a sufficient condition. The committee structure must remain sufficiently flexible to maximize political bargaining, for which committees are the governmental instruments par excellence. But how can the bargaining process be facilitated so that it has the dual effect of strengthening the hand of Congress in its brushes with the White House and the agencies and of keeping the committee structure as flexible as possible?

It seems to me that proposals for clearly defining committee jurisdictions miss the crucial point that jurisdictional conflicts may be harnessed to maximize congressional bargaining operations. Their proponents tend to look on jurisdictional conflicts as malfunctions that interfere with efficient legislative behavior because they seem to defy organization charts. Hence, they usually call for "coordination" procedures of various sorts—parallel committees in the two houses, interlocking memberships, joint committees, simultaneous bill referrals, intervention by the central leadership, cooperation through staff assistants, exchange of information, and so on. Although such demands do not necessarily imply an assumption that the existing committee structure repre-

3. *Ibid.*, p.108.

4. William J. Keefe and Morris S. Ogul, *The American Legislative Process, Congress and the States* (Englewood Cliffs, N.J.: Prentice-Hall, 1964), p. 156.

sents the best of all possible worlds, it appears to be taken for granted that jurisdictional purity, if not possible in fact, is desirable in principle, and that jurisdictional conflicts between committees and subcommittees are to be avoided at all cost.

From the perspective of the model pursued here, however, jurisdictional conflicts can be seen as the first signals that a given piece of legislation may involve a great variety of complex and technical issues whose solution calls for bargaining and also for expertise. The problem involved in resolving these conflicts is not simply one of coordination. Coordination is an administrative, not a political way of doing things. From a political standpoint, and assuming that jurisdictional conflict signalizes a need for political adjustments, structures are not ends in themselves but means. And if the executive agencies pattern themselves after congressional structures, it follows that Congress should experiment with new structures better suited to its own needs than quasi-administrative stopgaps. Instead of becoming embroiled in inter-committee entanglements in the wake of coordinative efforts—entanglements which are usually interpreted as further proof that Congress is an outmoded institution—Congress should be given the opportunity to create new structures as need for them arises. But this requires, above all, that the ongoing committee structure—and there always must be such a structure, if for no other reason than that the bulk of congressional business is routine rather than innovative—should not be frozen to a point where it can no longer respond flexibly to the complexity of public issues.

If, as has been suggested, such new structures are to meet the requirements both for bargaining and for expertise, then clearly conventional notions of coordination, leadership, or authority—geared to hierarchical organizations rather than to collegial bodies like legislatures—are out of place. My proposal is, therefore, that Congress experiment with a new type of committee—a kind of intercommittee committee—composed of members of those committees or subcommittees which claim jurisdiction over a given piece of legislation. This type of committee would meet our two requirements. On the one hand, its members would bring to the new committee the expertise of their standing committees; on the other hand, the bargaining process could go on without being impeded by jurisdictional jealousies. The members of our new committee will not be regarded as delegates from their standing committees and would not be required to report back to the committees from which they are recruited. In other words, the new committee would differ in significant ways from the so-called "select" or "special" committees that are also part of the congressional committee structure. These committees, established for a variety of reasons, do not ordinarily influence congressional decision-making; and as they do not have formal power "to report a bill," they are not on an equal footing with the standing committees.[5] By way of contrast, the type of inter-

5. See V. Stanley Vardys, "Select Committees of the House of Representatives," *Midwest Journal of Political Science*, August 1962, pp. 247–65.

committee committee proposed here would have the power to bring bills to the floor, following whatever procedures are followed by the regular standing committees. It might even happen that this new type of committee becomes a new standing committee—an outcome that would attest to its creativity.

THE PROBLEM OF POWER: AUTONOMY AND INTEGRATION

A good deal has been said about the so-called usurpation of legislative "power" by the committees of Congress. Interestingly, complaints along this line often come from those who, following the executive model, see in this alleged usurpation an obstacle to strong congressional party government, which, they assume, would support the President's legislative program. But sometimes these complaints also come from those who vaguely feel that the power of the committees in some way undermines the vigor of Congress as a whole vis-à-vis the presidency, because it deprives the Congress (and the House much more than the Senate) of the opportunity to deliberate in an atmosphere that forces the eyes of the nation upon the Hill. Taking the two sets of complaints together, the committee system comes to be blamed for both congressional obstinacy in the face of presidential needs and for congressional weakness.

Textbooks on Congress are generally agreed in their explanations of the power of committees. Committee power is said to be a product of the voluminous business before Congress, the need for specialization and expertise, the close bond between the committees and administrative agencies, the ease of access the committees afford to supportive interest groups, the existence of greater opportunity for bargaining and compromise in small groups, and so on. Whether this power is "good" or "bad" remains a matter of dispute precisely because these explanations are rarely derived from an explicit model of the congressional system.

Let me illustrate the consequences of this instability in criteria. Take, for instance, a hypothetical advocate of the executive model who does not quite know what he is advocating. If he is a member of the majority party, if his party controls both the Congress and the White House, and if he is a strong partisan supporter of the President's program, then he would be likely to deplore committee power, should a committee happen to be composed of a coalition hostile to the presidential program or be chaired by a man who is only reluctantly in favor of it. On the other hand, should a committee happen to be well disposed to the President's program, our hypothetical congressman would be inclined to welcome the committee's power, since it would speed up the process of legislation. Indeed, he might even argue that, given the fact that members cannot inform themselves about all bills as well as they perhaps should, congressmen ought to trust the committee's recommendation and support its bills—in other words, cast a blind vote. It is just such blind voting that worries those who see in committee power a threat to a vigorous, independent Congress.

It is evident that no appraisal of committee power, and certainly no recommendation as to how much power the committees should have, can be built on such opportunistic considerations. No reasonable committee system can be built on the ever-shifting configurations of congressional-presidential and intra-congressional power relations.

But though the actual explanations for committee power may be sound enough, must there necessarily be a conflict over power between the committees and the houses of which they are a part? As far as our model is concerned, we take it for granted that, in the foreseeable future, we cannot expect radical changes in the circumstances that make the committees what they are. However, our model does not assume that power is a zero-sum game, an assumption that seems to underlie the complaints about committee power. The assumption is false because power can be generated out of power, and moreover, it can be distributed–much as wealth can be created out of wealth and distributed. In other words, if one wishes to "restore" the power of the houses of Congress as wholes, one need not necessarily take away from the committees whatever power they may have. Let me illustrate this point and suggest at least one way in which this might be done.

Of the explanations that are offered for committee power, none seems more relevant to the problem than that which attributes committee power to the opportunity they provide for negotiation, bargaining, logrolling, and compromise. This potential, in turn, stems from the fact that, contrary to a common belief, the committees are patently not microcosms of the Congress as a whole —despite the fact that the majority and minority parties are almost proportionately represented on the committees. Congress is not now and is unlikely to be a body in which disciplined majority and minority parties are pitted against each other. Rather, it is a quilt of criss-crossing ideological, regional, and interest-centered coalitions. These coalitions tend to shift from issue to issue. And, moreover, they are not necessarily represented in the committees.

The result of these conditions is that what comes out of a committee need not necessarily coincide with the preferences on an issue that may crystallize in certain coalitions on the floor. To argue, therefore, that the committees have usurped the functions of the houses, because the latter would only be duplicating the work done in committees, if they were to take their lawmaking tasks more seriously, is a spurious argument. If, as the critics complain, the committees have "usurped" the powers that rightly belong to the houses as wholes, the fault does not lie with the committee systems. Rather, it lies with those who view the legislative process as an exercise in "efficiency." There is, admittedly, no easy answer to the problem. But to justify "blind" voting on the floors in the name of efficiency is clearly counter to our model of a vigorous legislative body.

More to the point, therefore, is the committees' ability to perform the latent function of conflict resolution. There is overwhelming logical as well as empirical ground for believing that small groups are more suitable arenas than large collectivities for the negotiations and compromises that must be made in the course of decision making.[6] Not only is a committee more accessible to the interests that have a stake in legislation, but the intimacy of personal relations in the committee setting facilitates the bargaining process. This being so, relations between the committees and the houses as wholes could be enormously improved if each committee were required, in the case of controversial legislation, to issue a report, accepted by proponents of both sides of an issue (and not necessarily party sides), which would inform the houses of those compromises that have been made and the reasons for these compromises. Even if the average congressman does not and often cannot understand the technical aspects of a bill, he can be expected to understand and be highly interested in the political implications of legislative decisions. Since he is, above all, politically responsible, the least one should guarantee him is a clear statement of the political aspects of what he is going to vote for or against. His vote is a political, not a tehnical act. The fact is, of course, that he already relies on political advice and not on technical advice before casting his vote. However, my proposal would enable him to appraise a committee's work from the perspective that is most salient to him.

My proposal would also have the effect of restoring the legislative floor to a position of prominence, if not power, especially in the House. Once again, the political principles involved in controversial legislation could be openly and meaningfully debated, instead of being as now smuggled into the statute books. No doubt, passions would be stirred. But such stirring would once more direct the attention of the nation from the White House to the halls of Congress. And the power of the houses would be increased without detriment to the power that the committees must have to go on with their job.

THE PROBLEM OF NUMBER AND SIZE: MAGIC FORMULAS

How many committees each house of the Congress should have, and how large the size of these committees should be, are questions much discussed, but discussed as if they were matters of magic formula rather than of practical requirements. Too many committees is bad, it has been argued for a variety of reasons (which we need not bother with here); on the other hand, too few committees is bad, it has also been argued on a variety of grounds. Somehow, out of the wisdom which such prejudgments generate, an "ideal" number is contrived; and this number becomes a more or less hard and fast rule for relevant thought on the subject, if thought it can be called. Under the Legislative Reorganization Act of 1946, the number of standing committees was set

6. See Mancur Olson, Jr., *The Logic of Collective Action* (Cambridge, Mass.: Harvard University Press, 1965), pp. 53–65.

at 15 in the Senate and 19 in the House of Representatives. Apparently, some magic formula had been satisfied. But the emergence of strong subcommittees in the years since, some of them almost autonomous of the parent committee and powerful in their own right, would seem to belie the effectiveness of trying to organize through magic formula. Organizers are often happy if things look "good" on paper. It satisfies the bosses and silences the critics, they think. But few are fooled, except the organizers themselves. The harm consists in the fact that a *strategem* of organization becomes a *formula* for organization.

It may be desirable to have more committees or fewer committees. It may be desirable to combine committees or partition them. It may be desirable to abolish old committees or create new ones. It may be desirable to elevate a subcommittee into a standing committee. But what is desirable or not depends on an appraisal of usefulness, and usefulness, in turn, due to the nature of the beast that Congress is, can refer only to political and not to administrative criteria. In other words, deciding on the number of committees is necessarily a matter of political bargaining, because politicians are likely to disagree on what is and what is not a useful committee. To turn the job over to business management consultants, as has been proposed, is an admission of congressional impotence. But this impotence is self-imposed and avoidable. I propose, therefore, that there be a biennial review of committee structures, functions, jurisdictions, workloads, and so on, by the Joint Committee on the Organization of the Congress as a permanent body, for the purpose of keeping the committee structure as flexible as possible and adjusting it, as nearly as possible, to the political contingencies of the Congress. This review should be based on the continuing survey of Congress suggested in the first section of this paper.

Magical thinking about the number of committees is even more common in connection with discussions about the size of committees. Though it is not fashionable any more to speak about the size of human groups in terms of "span of control"—long a magic formula of those addicted to models of administrative efficiency—there remains the belief that it is possible and desirable to fix some ideal size of legislative committees and subcommittees. We are told that a committee should not be too large, but that it should also not be too small. This talk barely disguises the assumption that it is possible to fix an optimum committee size, an assumption which the authors of the Legislative Reorganization Act of 1946, for instance, seem partly to have acted upon. Under the Act, all Senate standing committees, with the exception of appropriations, were given 13 members. A more variable quota was used for the House, but there, too, assumptions about optimum size were made. In part, of course, committee size in the Senate was subjected to the principle that, with certain exceptions, no senator should serve on more than two standing committees.

Yet, the important fact is that under the legislative Reorganization Act *exceptions were* made, apparently on the contrary, though sound, assumption, that some committees need more staffing than others. For instance, Senate Appropriations was given 21 members, House Appropriations 50, House Armed Services 35, House Un-American Activities 9. These exceptions, it would seem, made more sense than the standard formula. The rigid formula has not been observed strictly in practice, but even so hampers full flexibility of numbers and party divisions.

On balance, I favor adaptability over stability in this connection, trusting that committee stability can be achieved in other ways. I would suggest the general practice of having each committee recommend how large it should be: no one is better qualified to assess a committee's work load than the committee itself. There is no reason to believe that a committee cannot be enlarged or reduced during the course of a session, as it becomes clear just what its work load will be.

What is needed, clearly, is a continuing appraisal of a committee's workload for the forthcoming sessions. If it can be anticipated that the load of a committee will increase (which, under current conditions, can be gauged from the President's program), then its membership ought to be increased and also the number of its subcommittees, just as a committee's membership should be decreased if its workload is expected to be reduced. This, of course, touches on the problems of seniority and expertise (discussed below), and adjustments in other aspects of congressional life would be necessary. But the proposal would serve the purpose of adapting committee size to the actual work requirements of the Congress; and it would have the further advantage of not impeding the politics of committee composition along party, ideological, or any other lines of cleavage. Once a committee's recommendation is made, the Speaker and Majority Leader in the House can continue their present practice of suggesting the final sizes and political compositions of committees to the whole body for final approval. A similar process is recommended for the Senate.

THE PROBLEM OF COMPOSITION: ASSIGNMENT AND SENIORITY

In the Congress organized according to our model, the assignment of members to the committees would be made to vary explicitly—rather than implicitly, as is now the case—with the particular needs of a given committee or subcommittee. Not the least important source of the tensions now accompanying the assignment process is the discrepancy between members' expectations and what actually occurs. As Professor Nicholas Masters has shown in an illuminating study of the assignment process, the number of both formal and informal criteria used is great, but they are often rather casually or even arbitrarily used.[7] In other words, in reorganizing the committee appointment process

7. Nicholas A. Masters, "Committee Assignments in the House of Representatives," *American Political Science Review,* June 1961, pp. 345–57.

any mechanical formula would be sure to fail. Rather, an effort should be made to exploit the inevitable flexibility of the process in such a way that arbitrariness will be reduced and functionality optimized. In short, the process should satisfy both the aspirations of congressmen and the needs of the committees. In some cases this may be impossible, but as our model of Congress does not presume an ideal world, our analysis need not concern itself with inevitable imperfections.

In fact, however, there is reason to believe that our model of Congress does approximate to real world conditions. The criterion probably uppermost in a congressman's mind is the question whether his assignments will maximize his chances of re-election. One must incline to the view that it is in the interest of our model of a strong Congress and of the effective committee to help members in their electoral battles, since too rapid a turnover of congressmen creates discontinuities which tend to interfere with effective committee operations. But much of this aspect of the assignment process can be left to selection, for congressmen are likely to prefer committees whose work either harmonizes with their own personal abilities and experiences or with those constituency interests which they represent. It would be folly, therefore, to legislate into assignment practices a criterion which many believe should be mandatory —namely, that each committee's composition be proportional not only to party strengths in the houses as wholes but also to the variety of sectional, ethnic, or other interests in the two houses. As already pointed out, the conception of the committees as microcosmic replicas of the houses is not desirable as a criterion in assignments, since it would make the legislative process—negotiation, bargaining, and compromise—even more difficult than it is now.

This does not, however, preclude the criterion of balance from being used in connection with assignments to certain committees, especially those which, like the appropriations or ways and means committees, must carry the burden of congressional resonsiveness to public demands or needs. The tendency to name to these committees members with seniority—that is, members from relatively safe districts—is understandable but basically undesirable. For, rather than being responsive, these members can afford to be irresponsive—being safe and senior, they can elude the wrath of the electorate. (This is not to say that these members are in fact "irresponsible" from the standpoint of some ethical norm.) But if the wishes of the electorates are to have an effect on congressional actions and decisions, not only should the members of these key committees come from districts where sanctions can be effectively imposed by the public, but the burden of their responsibility should be equitably distributed among the variety of interests that constitute the congressional quilt. In these cases, then, the balance criterion may well be in place. There are, of course, disadvantages, both of a structural and functional kind. Structurally, the tenure of committee members might be shorter and reduce the corps of experienced members available for committee work. As to functions, because shorter-term members are more likely to be subject to local pressures, there might be a tendency toward greater "public spending." Nevertheless, the proposal would aid in making such committees more responsive to public wants and prevent congressional insulation from extra-congressional political life.

Congressmen's personal preferences and committee needs would also seem to coincide in regard to the problem of providing adequate committee expertise. The congressional division of labor and ensuing specialization, one might argue, should not be directly predicated on the need for expertise. A committee should be so composed that it can bring to bear on a piece of legislation the broad views of the generalist rather than of the expert. But this argument is counter to the requirements of our model of Congress. In the latter part of this century the Congress can ill afford the amateurism that characterized the classical nineteenth century legislative assemblies, if it wishes to stand up to the professionalism of the bureaucracy. Congressional committees in the model of a strong Congress require more expert guidance than they have at present—not from professional staffs, but from their own members.

It is, of course, a moot question whether specialization makes for expertise or expertise makes for specialization. No relevant research about the interlocking of congressional expertise and specialization has ever been conducted. However, it is not implausible to assume that as a legislator comes to specialize, he tends to become an expert in his area of specialization. But this in turn presupposes that he has sufficient opportunity to become familiar with the often highly technical aspects of modern legislation. This he cannot do if his committee tenure is of short duration. From this vantage point at least, there is much to be said for retaining seniority as a criterion in guiding committee assignments. But it should also be emphasized that seniority can be regarded as only one criterion among several. Indeed, in some cases the members responsible for assignments ought perhaps deliberately to ignore it—as for instance when a senior member clearly fails to show interest in the work of a committee, or when he is blatantly incapable of comprehending the business before a committee no matter how much claim he may have by virtue of seniority for appointment to a prestigious committee.

Expertise is facilitated, of course, in those committees whose jurisdictional focus is fairly clearly defined, as in the agricultural or judiciary committees. In the case of the former, most members will come from agricultural constituencies having direct interests in the committee's subject matter.[8] In the case of the latter, most members are likely to come from the legal profession.[9] In our model Congress these circumstances of uniformity of background would be frankly recognized and taken into account in committee assignments. On the

8. See Charles O. Jones, "Representation in Congress: The Case of the House Agricultural Committee," *American Political Science Review,* June 1961, pp. 358–67.

9. See Heinz Eulau and John D. Sprague, *Lawyers in Politics: A Study in Professional Convergence* (Indianapolis: The Bobbs-Merrill Company, 1964).

other hand, a committee like the House Committee on Education and Labor is severely handicapped by the inevitable heterogeneity of its tasks; and expertise is most difficult to come by, precisely because political considerations necessarily enter the assignment process.[10] In the case of such committees, our model of a strong Congress suggests the need for countervailing measures to reduce partisanship and ideological inflexibility.

THE PROBLEM OF SPECIALIZATION: WHAT PRICE COHERENCE?

Just as committees are set up to enable Congress to cope with its voluminous business and bring to bear on that business as much expertise as possible, so subcommittees are set up to divide the labor further and maximize detailed attention. In general, there is agreement that the degree of specialization and expertise mobilized through the subcommittee structure serves well the interests of both individual congressmen and the Congress as a whole. The subcommittees provide meaningful employment especially for able and aspiring junior members, permitting them to concentrate their talents on tangible tasks, and giving them a better opportunity than they would otherwise have to prove themselves.

For the Congress and its standing committees, the subcommittee structure serves a myriad of functions, of which specialization and expertise are only a part. Perhaps most important is the communication function. The subcommittee structure links the Congress with the organized interest groups which find in the subcommittees reasonably clearly marked points of access to the legislative process. It facilitates contact, consultation, and coordination with, as well as control of, relevant subdivisions in the federal bureaucracy. Lastly, it facilitates discussion in a face-to-face setting, bargaining, and compromise.

Yet, a number of apprehensions have accompanied what is often alluded to as the "proliferation of subcommittees." Some of these apprehensions are quite well articulated, others are only vaguely felt. But not all of them are equally valid from the perspective of our model of a vigorous, independent Congress. Many are the apprehensions only of those who would make the Congress subordinate to the presidency. In such cases apprehension may express itself in a tendency to translate what should be a functional problem into a structural problem of power and authority. So that instead of asking, "do the subcommittees perform their functions well or not?" the question becomes, "do the subcommittees have too much autonomy vis-à-vis their parent committees or the houses as wholes, and is not congressional power too fragmented?"

The second set of questions provides its own answers because it is invari-

10. See Richard F. Fenno, Jr., "The House of Representatives and Federal Aid to Education," in Robert L. Peabody and Nelson W. Polsby (Eds.), *New Perspectives on the House of Representatives* (Chicago: Rand McNally and Company, 1963), pp. 195–235.

ably predicated on self-answering assumptions. For instance, one assumption seems to be that Congress should somehow develop a "coherent legislative program." One supposes that by this is meant the President's legislative program, since neither the possibility nor the feasibility of a "coherent congressional program" is ever seriously proposed. But even if one were to believe that it is not the President's program that is intended but a genuinely Congress-centered program, the whole assumption of a coherent program is predicated, in turn, on the notion that coherence is attainable only through top-level coordination, supervision, and control. Even if one were to agree that a coherent *congressional* program is desirable, the facts of congressional life suggest that top-level control is most unlikely in the foreseeable future. On the contrary, if a coherent program were to emerge, it would have to result from successful bargaining and compromise between the various congressional decision centers.

But is a coherent program desirable? To answer this question, one must appreciate the unique position which the Congress occupies in the American federal system. In this system, one of the most critical functions of Congress is to represent the diverse interests and tendencies of a pluralistic society. Hence, the very notion of a "coherent program" becomes of doubtful utility, since such a program could probably only be imposed from above. And if it were to be imposed in this manner, it would be clearly in conflict with the representational requirements of a strongly centrifugal system. Whatever programs Congress comes up with, these programs must reflect the great variety of interests and preferences and demands that, like the tributaries of a river system, contribute to the main stream. The main stream has an identity of its own (and given the fact of executive ascendancy over legislation, one really need not worry too much about it). But great care must be taken to ensure that the tributaries do not dry up and deprive the main stream of its vital nurture and sustenance. It is the peculiar function of the subcommittee structure to keep the tributaries open, to see to it that fresh ideas and interests are continuously fed into the main stream. The task of Congress is not to evolve a coherent program, if by such a program is meant a plan promulgated at the top, but to facilitate the emergence of many programs in the crucible of legislation and public policy.

Once it is accepted that a coherent program is not the issue, then the question of subcommittee autonomy becomes largely irrelevant. Quite apart from the fact that the relations between subcommittees, committees, and houses vary a great deal, so that no common pattern can be easily identified, the whole view that sees Congress as a hierarchy of decision centers seems to be mistaken. A hierarchy of sorts there certainly is, but its structure defies the prescriptions of the conventional hierarchical models of organization. The advocates of establishing clear lines of responsibility between the various decision levels in the congressional web of authority-relations often talk as if the lower centers in the hierarchy were children who must be supervised, controlled, and disciplined. Just what it means to "control" a committee or subcommittee is never spelled out. And why, in a collegial body, should a subcommittee be more controlled than the leadership cadre of the houses? The Congress is not an army post with generals, master sergeants, and privates.

Subcommittees, like any other human group, are subject to human errors and exposed to human dangers. Being small groups, they are characterized by emergent properties that are two-edged: they provide access to interests, but are therefore easily pressured; they develop informal understandings, but their points of view may be therefore parochial; they facilitate easy relations among their members, but are therefore easily manipulated by an aggressive chairman. However, and this is a point all too often overlooked in the complaints about Congress, the subcommittees are composed of congressmen, all elected to their jobs, and all not much better or worse than the American people as a whole. The issue ought not to be the authority or autonomy of these groups vis-à-vis other decision centers in the Congress, but what they make of their power. If a subcommittee, or committee, bottles up legislation for which there is strong support elsewhere in Congress, it certainly misuses its power; if it succeeds in persuading other decision points to accept its labors, its authority is well justified.

The coherence of legislative programs in a collegial body—and we would surely want to keep the Congress collegial rather than make it over into a bureaucratic structure—depends, under modern conditions, on the subcommittees' and committees' reciprocal deference to the authority of expertise.[11] The lesson to be learned, it would seem, is that the subcommittee structure should be so strengthened that each subcommittee can speak with authority in its own domain of expertise, and that the function of bringing about coherence in programs, insofar as this is desirable, can be performed through informal channels of deference and through reciprocity of expertise, rather than through central direction from the top of the congressional hierarchy.

THE PROBLEM OF CONTROL: WHO SHALL RULE?

No aspect of committee operations occasions more criticism than what is usually referred to as the "committee oligarchy," which, invariably, is seen to be composed of "dictatorial chairmen." This criticism is mainly made by advocates of the executive model because they see the committee oligarchy, so-called, as the main obstacle to strong House leadership, anchored in a disciplined two-party system. And they propose centralized authority as the only effective remedy for what are felt to be the evil ways of the committee oligarchy. What should be said here about both diagnosis and cure can be said very simply and briefly. First, the diagnosis is inadequate; it is usually based

11. For an opposite view, see Clem Miller, *Member of the House* (New York: Charles Scribner's, 1962), p. 51.

on the insufficient evidence of a few cases of improper chairman behavior, for the behavior of congressional chairmen has never been systematically investigated. Second, the prescribed cure does not follow from the diagnosis but rather from the underlying premises. Internal committee democracy would seem to be at least as feasible a remedy as centralized House leadership.

The existence of the committee oligarchy is often inferred more from the formal privileges of chairmen than from their actual behavior. That the chairmen possess a good deal of formal authority cannot be denied; but whether or not they make use of it in an authoritarian manner is another matter. Until chairman behavior is inspected more thoroughly than it usually is, a good case can also be made out for the opposite argument. My own admittedly casual, at-a-distance observations are that chairmen differ a great deal in their ways of running their committees, and that they are by no means inevitably the oligarchs which they are made out to be. Moreover, committee and subcommittee chairmen are not invariably or necessarily the real leaders of committees; there are many important and influential committee members who are not chairmen. All of this is not to deny the presence of some chairmen who may be called oligarchs; it is to assert that the existence of a general committee oligarchy cannot be confirmed.[12]

But if we accept, for argument's sake, that under present arrangements the chairman is *potentially* an oligarch, and if we assume that oligarchical control is undesirable, we may ask what changes in the procedures are necessary to bring about a change in the substance of committee operations. Invariably, the first item that comes to mind is the practice of selecting chairmen according to seniority. The succession of the member of the majority party who has served longest on a committee is seen as the first cause of the chairman's power, for it makes it virtually impossible to depose and replace him. But does it follow that the chairman chosen on this basis is necessarily an oligarch? Clearly not. For one thing, it is much too simple to assume that the chairman will always ride roughshod over his committee. If he is a leader, then like any leader who wishes to retain his position, the chairman must ultimately have the backing of his committee and especially of his subcommittee chairmen. He may have at his disposal certain sanctions, but, given the congressional culture of mutual accommodation, he is more likely to attain his goals through persuasion and negotiation. In short, while it may be difficult to replace the chairman because of the seniority tradition, one must not underestimate the "countervailing power" that committee members have at their disposal.

What, then, of the seniority procedure itself? Is it the best way to select committee chairmen who will be leaders? Our answer must be generally negative. Seniority does not guarantee ability and competence; moreover, the procedure favors one-party areas and sectional interests, and it tends to make for

12. This appraisal agrees, I think, with the observations of Richard F. Fenno, Jr., "The Internal Distribution of Influence: The House," in Truman, *op. cit.*, pp. 55–56.

political irresponsibility, to mention only a few items in a large catalogue of familiar complaints. Nevertheless, the practice is as lustily supported as it is attacked. Seniority, its defenders say, makes for committee stability and continuity, and it avoids the competition for office and resultant strife that would enormously harm the atmosphere of good will and conviviality that is so essential to political relations in a collegial legislature; precisely because seniority is an impersonal criterion, it assures friendly relations and harmony within Congress.

The trouble with this argument (or should we say folklore?) is that it cannot be really disproved, for to disprove it one would have to have numerous cases of chairman selection where seniority was not the tradition. What evidence there is for the presumably harmony-creating consequences of seniority comes largely from the testimony of individual congressmen or from journalistic observers of Congress.[13] In state legislatures the question of seniority also has some influence on the selection of committee chairmen and on committee appointments, but in general plays a much less important role than in Congress, and practices very considerably from state to state. Moreover, as far as I know, no study has ever been made of the effects of varying practices with respect to legislative harmony or disharmony.[14] My inclination is to be rather skeptical of the beneficial effects of the seniority procedure. I see no reason to believe that some form of electoral procedure, for instance—and many varieties of such a procedure have been proposed—would create such turmoil as to prevent the committees from doing their work.

After all, congressmen encounter many conflict situations in other arenas of congressional life and manage to live with each other reasonably well. As masters of bargaining and compromise, as elected politicians who must face the possibility of defeat at the polls in primaries or general elections, congressmen often find themselves in situations which make severe demands on their personal sensitivities. And, in fact, the bitter struggles that have often been waged for positions of party leadership in Congress[15] or over the composition and power of the House Rules Committee,[16] do not suggest that any detrimental consequences would inevitably follow from the competitive struggles for chairmanships if the seniority practice were abandoned.

Nor do I find much more convincing the argument that seniority guarantees the kind of experience and expertise so necessary to committee functioning.

13. The one article devoted to the subject reports these impressions but does not really cope with the problem. See George Goodwin, Jr., "The Seniority System in Congress," *American Political Science Review*, June 1959, pp. 412–36.

14. For a comparative study of chairman behavior in four states—California, New Jersey, Ohio, and Tennessee—see John C. Wahlke, Heinz Eulau, William Buchanan, and LeRoy C. Ferguson, *The Legislative System* (New York: John Wiley & Sons, 1962), pp. 170–92.

15. See, for instance, Nelson W. Polsby, "Two Strategies of Influence: Choosing a Majority Leader, 1962," in Peabody and Polsby, *op. cit.*, pp. 129–64.

16. See Robert L. Peabody, "The Enlarged Rules Committee," in Peabody and Polsby, *op. cit.*, pp. 129–64.

The argument is not necessarily false, for senior men may in fact have acquired much experience and relevant knowledge as a result of long service. What is wrong with the argument is that it rules out by presumption the possibility that junior men, even though less experienced, can be good committee chairmen. Moreover, the whole concept of the seniority practice seems to violate the spirit of American culture with its stress on equality of opportunity. By establishing norms that are opposed to the surrounding cultural norms, Congress isolates itself from one of the mainsprings of vitality in the American culture.

It is exactly this anomaly which is responsible for producing the kind of tensions between congressional behavior and expectations that often lie at the bottom of criticisms of Congress. Like other vital organizations in the American culture, and notably the bureaucracy where merit is an important criterion for advancement, Congress should similarly reward those members who have earned it through their achievements. Bringing into the limelight of publicity its best talent in the shortest possible time would therefore strengthen the Congress vis-à-vis the bureaucracy where talent and merit perhaps contribute more heavily to advancement. And it is with those at the top of the bureaucracy with whom committee chairmen must deal. If the bureaucrats often seem to have the advantage over their congressional counterparts, Congress need only blame itself.

However, most proposals that have been so far put forward as alternatives to the seniority system do not measure up to the requirement that the most talented members be brought to the top of the committees. Electoral processes, whether within a committee, the majority party, or the houses as wholes, do not assure its fulfillment, for elections are just as likely to result in promoting the most popular as in rewarding the most talented and gifted. Arbitrary rotation of the chairmanship among all majority party members is likely to produce even worse results than those criticized by the opponents of seniority. Appointment of those who are considered by the majority leader as being most capable is undesirable from the point of view of our model, for it would make for centralized authority sensitive to presidential pressures.

My own proposal is a radical one: abolish the chairmanships as now constituted with their familiar rights and privileges! Instead, let the housekeeping functions and the administrative work of the committees and subcommittees be handled by a "presiding officer" assisted by a competent head of staff. If this were done, we would expect that the legislative, investigative, and oversight work of the committee, and especially the work on major legislation, would fall into the hands of those who take on the responsibility of seeing to it that the work is done. In other words, the proposal would allow the committee to evolve a "natural" leadership team. This may sound utopian, but it is not. In the first place, as I have pointed out already, most committees already have such "natural" leaders who give the committee its orientation and direction. Second, precisely because the committees are in fact "little legislatures" (though not micro-replicas) whose decisions are influential in determining final legislative outcomes, abolition of the permanent chairman would increase the collegiality of Congress and give each member of Congress an opportunity to count for more than he does now. It might even serve to attract more capable people to seek a seat in the Congress.

But how to select the "presiding officer"? I would suggest this: nobody is as qualified to know about and assess the skills and competences of committee members as committee members themselves. From this it follows, clearly, that the "presiding officer" should be selected by his peers—his colleagues on the committee. And I am prepared to retract some of the negative appraisal of seniority that I expressed earlier. That is, I would say that while the present seniority system does not possess the virtues it is so often alleged to possess, it may possess *some* virtue. And one of these virtues, certainly, is the possibility that long tenure does enable certain members to acquire skills and abilities less likely to be possessed by more recent members. For this reason, I would have the presiding officer elected from among the three ranking members of the majority party, on the assumption that at least one among the top ranking members is better qualified than the rest of all the members.

Finally, I am inclined to believe that in any case the more senior members of a committee (and not just the presiding officer or leading minority member alone) have a greater need for staff assistance than the more junior members. Having been around longer, their workload, arising out of the cumulative net of connections with fellow members of Congress, with interest groups, constituents, and with departmental agencies, is likely to be heavier. I would propose, therefore, that in the assignment of staff the senior committee members, of both the majority and the minority party, be given appropriate staff help, such as is necessary and feasible.

THE PROBLEM OF ASSISTANCE: THE NEED FOR NONPARTISANSHIP

The objection will be raised that this proposal for the abolition of chairmanships and reliance on staff for conducting the routine business of the committees will create a congressional bureaucracy with too much independence and undue influence over committee decisions and the shaping of public policies. I do not wish to minimize the weight of this objection. But I feel that if the goal of a vigorous and independent Congress is to be realized, Congress must take a chance and not be too much concerned about the possible ill effects of staff bureaucratization before they have occurred.

In fact, I do not believe that whatever ill effects may occur will be so widespread and disastrous that they cannot be remedied. Just as, at present, the internal life of different committees, the role of committee chairmen, and the power and prestige of the committees in the houses vary considerably, so we can expect that under the presiding officer and staff assistance plan the relations between staff and committee will also vary a great deal. Whether the responsible policy officials or the hired administrative officials are dominant in an organization always depends upon the kind of persons who occupy given positions and the kind of interpersonal relations that develop between them. The multiplicity of possible patterns is great. To mention just one example from another arena of government where policy officials and administrative officers confront each other, take the relationships between city councils and city managers in the hundreds of American cities which have this arrangement (and which seems appropriate here because it involves small groups). Whatever the formal features of the relationship, we know that city councils and city managers meet each other in manifold ways—ranging from submission of one to the other to close cooperation, from manager withdrawal in policy matters to active initiation, and so on. I would expect that the congressional committee staff patterns under my schema would resemble such informal patterns.

From an organizational viewpoint, the possibility of genuinely complementary relationships between committees and their staffs opens up new possibilities for invigorating congressional life. Where a committee fails to produce "natural leadership" from among its members, a competent and aggressive staff can do a great deal to offset committee sluggishness. Where a committee is saddled with apparently unending routine tasks, a reliable and intelligent staff can perform many of these tasks. The staff schema will thus free the committee members for the kind of creative and innovative thinking that should be done by the committees.

The trouble with most proposals for additional staff assistance for committees is that they are predicated on the assumption that the committee structure will remain pretty much what it is. Hence, while there is usually a demand for a larger and more competent staff, and while there is even a quest for methods of integrating staff operations more fully into legislative policymaking, the benefits to be derived from merely augmenting staff assistance remain doubtful. As so sensitive and experienced an observer of Congress as Professor Bertram M. Gross has noted, increased staff assistance does not automatically strengthen the Congress vis-à-vis the executive agencies, and it does not automatically lighten the workload of congressmen.[17] In my own proposal, on the other hand, the increased staff assistance would be used in a directed manner for specific purposes. For under this proposal, congressmen would themselves do things now assigned to the staff, and the staff would do things now done by congressmen. This, it might be objected, would make the individual committee member even more anonymous than he now is and even less of a symbolic force. Perhaps. But I do not believe that the proposal would undermine the

17. Bertram M. Gross, *The Legislative Struggle* (New York: McGraw-Hill, 1953), pp. 421–22.

prestige of the Congress as a whole. In fact, it might strengthen it, because committee members would be doing more significant things than they do now.

In the first place, much routine committee work now absorbing a good deal of the members' or chairmen's time—scheduling, investigation, hearings, markup, and so on—would be done by the staff, as would much of the liaison work with and the oversight of the executive agencies. The collecting, sorting, and analyzing of data and the preparation of studies and committee reports would also be staff matters in this division of labor. On the other hand, the really creative aspects of committee work, now often delegated to the staff, would revert to where they properly belong, to the committee members. Somehow the notion has developed that staffs are more competent, more expert, and even perhaps more intelligent than the average congressman. Then it is said that the task of identifying problems and suggesting policy alternatives should be preeminently a staff rather than a political function. This, it seems to me, is false. If the staffs are enlarged, as most proposals suggest they should be, and more fully integrated into the work of the committees (so that committee and staff become a team in the best sense of the word), it should be possible for the committee members to develop that broader perspective on problems, issues, and policies which a vigorous and innovative legislative body requires.

The proposal would also tend to remove some of the nit-picking criticisms that are often made of how at present staffs are used (or misused) by the committees. In a collegial committee without a permanent chairman, no staff member could become the "property" of any one member. Committee staff could no longer be used to do the chairman's case work. Moreover, because staffs would be less concerned with the policy aspects of legislation, the whole debate over whether staff members should be picked on the basis of partisan, bipartisan, or nonpartisan criteria would subside. Our model, of course, suggests the need for a politically neutral and nonpartisan staff, equally available to majority and minority party members. This objective would be attainable because the selection of staff personnel would no longer be the prerogative of a chairman or presiding officer, but would be handled by a congressional personnel office. Since a nonpartisan staff would be unaffected by shifts in the committee's majority control, it would contribute stability and continuity to routine committee work. Finally, the cooperation between the staff directors of various committees would be less encumbered by partisan considerations and would become more task- than strategy-oriented.

The debate over whether staffs should or should not be partisan, and over whether the minority party should have staff personnel of its own, has usually proceeded on the assumption that lines of cleavage in committees mostly follow party lines. They may in fact often do so, but the few solid studies made of congressional committees suggest that splits along other than party lines are also frequent. And if such non-party splits occur, with majorities and minorities emerging along ideological, regional, urban-rural, or sundry interest lines, how can these majorities and minorities have the staffs they need if the staff members are recruited along party lines? As with so many proposals for the various aspects of congressional reorganization, the demand for separate majority and minority party staffs is based on the wishful belief that Congress ought always to divide more closely along party lines, in order to facilitate what has been called "more responsible party government." But this is undesirable from our perspective, since it spells executive ascendancy over the Congress.

THE PROBLEM OF INTELLIGENCE: SCARCITY OR ABUNDANCE?

Proposals for giving congressional committees more staff assistance are not infrequently justified in terms of the committees' lack of adequate data necessary for intelligent decision and their inevitable (but presumably undesirable) reliance for information on the administrative agencies. As is so often the case, if an alleged shortcoming is repeated enough times, first by those who claim to feel it directly, then by those to whom they complain (in this case by congressmen to each other and to the press), and then by those whose job it is to study the problem (i.e., by political scientists), the shortcoming tends to assume a reality which comes to be defined more in subjective than in objective terms. The general problem of the amount and kind of information needed by congressmen in order to do their work is being discussed elsewhere in this symposium. As far as committees are concerned, my own impression is that the problem has been exaggerated or, to put it better, that the accent has been usually placed on the wrong aspect of the problem. The problem, it seems to me, is not one of scarcity, but of an abundance of information, most of which remains unassimilated and undigested.

As one peruses the hundreds and thousands of committee hearings and committee reports on every conceivable topic of public interest, one is appalled by the huge bulk of information that comes to congressional attention. In any case, whether abundance or scarcity prevails, I am not aware of any scientific study ever having been attempted to test either allegation. Of course, all this is not to say that committees should not have at their disposal all the background material and immediate data necessary for arriving at a considered judgment. But to say this is largely platitudinous. For all the information that comes in, from whatever source—the administrative agencies, interest groups, disinterested scholars, or the Congress' own Legislative Reference Service—is of no avail if it is not collated and digested.

I find it rather interesting that congressmen simultaneously complain about lack of information and about their inability to keep up with the information they do receive. It would seem to follow, then, that congressmen do not receive the right kind of information. But what is the right kind of information? Here, I think, one must be rather hard-nosed. Whether one likes it or not, whether congressmen like it or not, the fact is that "objective" information, so-called, has only marginal utility in committee work. For congressmen, being human, act like humans: they take positions first and seek to back them up with data and rationalizations later on.[18] This being so, what congressmen in committee need is information that supports their positions and seems to confirm the rationality of their actions.

Having made this perhaps startling statement, I would like to retract somewhat and elucidate the point. It must be viewed in the context of my general emphasis on the fact that individual congressmen are different from each other, and that the various committees are also different from each other. Therefore, while I think it is correct to say that most people most of the time seek information to reinforce their own predetermined positions, there are, of course, exceptions. And certainly there are well-known exceptions where congressmen have genuinely sought very specific information about highly complex economic and technical matters, about matters of vital interest to their constituencies, and about departmental operations, on which they had open minds, or were at least ambivalent. It is for these congressmen, in particular, that the Congress should provide the necessary means, discussed elsewhere in this symposium, to satisfy their thirst for factual knowledge, in order to facilitate their efforts at diagnosis and prognosis of problems.

Some of the criticisms that have been leveled against committee hearings as information-gathering devices seem to miss the main point. For instance, the fact that hearings sometimes assume the character of a court of law with its adversary system of seeking the truth is often criticized. Actually, hearing the pros and contras on particular issues is probably more useful to a committee member than lengthy reports from administrative agencies, interest groups, or scholars which pretend to objectivity. Available evidence indicates that committee hearings reach their high points of usefulness if and when committee members themselves participate in the hearings in a variety of active roles, notably those of protagonist and antagonist.[19]

Insofar as hearings are the main avenue by which committee members inform themselves, their various functions should be clearly differentiated. My concern here is not with those functions of hearings, whether legislative or investigative, which Professor David B. Truman has identified as "propagandistic" and "safety-valve" functions.[20] Rather, my concern is with the communication function of hearings. Two types of hearings can be distinguished—those designed to produce technical information and those designed to pro-

18. For congressmen's confessions on this point, see Charles L. Clapp, *The Congressman—His Work as He Sees It* (Garden City, N.Y.: Doubleday & Company, 1964), p. 303.

19. See the study of the Senate Committee on Banking and Currency by Ralph K. Huitt, "The Congressional Committee: A Case Study," *American Political Science Review*, June 1954, pp 340–65.

20. David B. Truman, *The Governmental Process* (New York: A. A. Knopf, 1951), p. 372.

duce political information. It has been argued that if the purpose is purely technical, experts from the agencies or interest groups should be invited to testify, and no others. But experts and technicians are often notoriously unable to communicate their knowledge, and to place restrictions on the kind of witnesses who should testify strikes me as altogether useless. Moreover, more often than not, we have the spectacle of experts—all equally well-trained and well-informed—testifying on opposite sides of a question. The committee member exposed to this spectacle is more likely to discount expert testimony altogether than to be impressed by it. Similarly, the sheer repetition of much expert testimony stifles rather than excites the member's interest. There is good reason to believe that committee members prefer succinct résumés of arguments pro and con on a bill by those who can speak with the authority of a department or organization behind them.

Proposals to make legislative committee meetings and hearings resemble fact-finding procedures, such as those which have been developed in investigative or oversight situations, are ill-conceived. They ignore the fact that Congress is above all a political body—that its vitality and maintenance as an independent branch of the government depend on its successful performance of its political functions. Congress needs help in keeping informed; but the information must be adapted to the most relevant needs of congressmen and committees—in other words, political needs. Hearings, other impressions notwithstanding, are the most effective devices for committees to inform themselves in a *political* context. This is not to say that committee hearings should not be improved. Certainly, many of the criticisms that have been made—the badgering of witnesses beyond what a fair adversary system would permit, the tendency to limit the scope of hearings, insufficient planning, hearing the same witnesses over and over again, preventing junior members from playing an active role, and others—should be remedied. But to reduce hearings to a kind of directors' meeting that benignly and passively listens to experts, bureaucrats, technicians, engineers, and so on, is counter to our model of the Congress as a strong, independent legislative and representational body.

CONCLUSION

It has been my purpose in this paper to review, from the perspective of a model that envisages a strong and independent Congress in a governmental system of checks and balances, a number of problems faced by congressional committees; to analyze, from the same perspective, just what is problematic about these problems; to evaluate and criticize, again in terms of the model, some of the assumptions and proposals for committee reforms made by advocates of other models; and to present, on the basis of our model, certain propositions and recommendations about committee behavior under varying conditions. It has not been my intention to exhaust all possibilities, but rather to be suggestive. The important point to be made, in conclusion, is that, hopefully, the propositions and recommendations that were made here are in accord with the basic assumptions of a model for a strong and independent Congress. Even if they are so outrageous as to remain unrealized, it is my expectation that they can and will serve as criteria against which to assess changes that may occur in the congressional committee system, regardless of whether they are purposefully instituted or spontaneously created in the course of events.

Chapter 3

Changing Views of Representation

My theme is the invention of institutions, the role that ideas play in their survival, and the obsolescence of political theories. My target is the problem of representation, because, it seems to me, the development of structurally discrete and functionally specific agencies of government was predicated, historically, on the invention or discovery of the technique of representation; and because government, whatever its constitutional form, remains based on representative institutions.

At the outset, let me simply say that our common conceptions of representation are obsolete! Please note that I am not saying that representation is obsolete, but only that our common conceptions of it are. This, at least, is the conclusion I draw from all the studies of representation which in recent years have finally subjected our ordinary notions of representation to the crucial test of empirical validation. Regardless of whether the empirical attack has come from the study of representatives, as in my own work and the work of many others,[1] or from the study of the represented, as in the work of that extraordinary team of researchers assembled at Michigan's Survery Research Center,[2] we can finally say with some confidence what representation is not. But,

Originally published in Ithiel de Sola Pool, Ed., *Contemporary Political Science* (New York: McGraw-Hill Company, 1967), pp. 53–85. Reprinted by permission.

1. See John C. Wahlke *et al., The Legislative System: Explorations in Legislative Behavior,* John Wiley & Sons, Inc., New York, 1962; Frank J. Sorauf, *Party and Representation,* Prentice-Hall, Inc., Englewood Cliffs, N.J., 1963. For a review of recent studies, see Heinz Eulau and Katherine Hinckley, "Legislative Institutions and Processes," in James A. Robinson (Ed.), *Political Science Annual,* The Bobbs-Merrill Company, Inc., Indianapolis, 1966, Vol. I.

2. See Warren E. Miller and Donald E. Stokes, "Constituency Influence in Congress," *American Political Science Review,* Vol. 57, pp. 45–56, March, 1963; Donald E. Stokes and Warren E. Miller, "Party Government and the Saliency of Congress," *Public Opinion*

in spite of many centuries of theoretical effort, we cannot say what representation is.

This state of affairs in the theory of representation confronts us as a scientific challenge. Thirty years ago, when I was a student, there was much talk about the "crisis" of representation. From today's perspective, I think that those who spoke of crisis mistook their particular conceptions of what representation should be with representation as a institutional requisite of any political system larger than an ideal-type polis. Because representative institutions did not work as preferred models of representation said they should work, the institutions were blamed rather than the models. It is an indication of the profound transformation in our approach to political phenomena that we have overcome the normative fallacy. As propositions derived from normative doctrines of representation have been exposed to empirical scrutiny, their obsolescence has become evident.

If there is a crisis, then, it is a crisis in the theory of representation and not in the institution of representation. I find it enormously interesting that the recent literature on the politics of the developing nations only very rarely uses the concept of representation as an explicitly analytical tool. This does not mean that representation is not a problem in the new nations; on the contrary, it is a central problem of nation building. But, apparently, our colleagues in the field of comparative politics do not deal with it in the familiar terms because they do not find our inherited formulations of representation particularly germane to the real-world problems with which the new nation builders must deal.[3]

The obsolescence of theories of representation, evident in the crucible of modern empirical research and evident in the crucible of modern nation building, makes my assignment quite tantalizing. For, I had to ask myself in preparing this chapter, can a look at history really help us as practicing political scientists? Can it fruitfully aid us in better explicating the problems with which a modern and as yet unborn theory of representation should concern itself? I am still not sure whether such an exercise can and will have the payoffs that the investment of time and effort would lead one to hope for. For I fear that of all the muses, Clio, the Muse of History, is the most treacherous. I could not proceed without coming to grips with History.

Quarterly, Vol. 26, pp. 531–46, Winter, 1962; and Warren E. Miller, "Majority Rule and the Representative System of Government," in E. Allardt and Y. Littunen, *Cleavages, Ideologies and Party Systems*, Transactions of the Westermarck Society, Helsinki, 1964, pp. 343–376.

3. I am gratified to note that the problem of representation is dealt with in its own terms by Lucian W. Pye in his recent *Aspects of Political Development*, Little, Brown and Company, Boston, 1966, pp. 21, 24–26. But I also note that "representation" does not appear as an entry in the book's index, just as it does not appear in the indexes of any number of books on the new nations that I have perused. What I find fascinating is that the problems which Pye identifies resemble the problems with which medieval theorists had to cope.

I

Because any attempt to link modern developments in the study of politics with older forms of theorizing about things political necessarily involves historical reconstruction, it is likely to encounter the danger of misconstruction. In general, sciencing, the activity in which the scientist is engaged, proceeds without being unduly hampered by the history of Science, with a capital S. It is therefore less prone to be victimized by Clio than is the study of the arts and letters. But only scientists altogether barbarian in outlook would be oblivious to or deliberately ignore the historical rootedness of their enterprise. And, precisely because any scientific enterprise has historical roots which, in many ways, define its outlook and commitments, no scientist can ultimately avoid doing battle with History.

The alienation of the study of political theory from the rest of political science, which began at the turn of the present century, is a well-known story.[4] And it has become fashionable to deplore it. But the story is more complicated than it appears to be. Indeed, I believe that the separation of the history of political theory from the empirical concerns of political science has not been completely dysfunctional. For as long as the study of political theory involved the regurgitation and exegesis of the classical texts, it could only be an obstacle to scientific development. Galileo's enemy was Aristotle. In freeing himself from the dead hand of Aristotle, Galileo liberated modern physical science.[5] In rejecting many of our inherited political ideas, empirical political science opened up new vistas for scientific inquiry. It could come to deal with problems that historicist and legal-positivist political science had failed to recognize—and these problems were almost everything that was interesting in contemporary politics: modern mass movements, charismatic leadership, popular apathy, problems of nation building and development, the growth of bureaucracy, political bargaining, the articulation of social interests, political pathology, and so on.

But, perhaps, the pendulum has swung too far, and the time has come to assess the reciprocal contribution which traditional political theory can make to empirical political science and which empirical political science can make to political theory. This is not to say that Clio, the Muse, is a faithful leader on the road ahead. Although we sometimes speak of "historical method" as if it were a straigthforward and unambiguous guide to understanding, nothing could be further from what in fact is the case. Indeed, it was the mistaken identification of chronological description with history that, for so long, put the study of political theory in the bind it was

4. See David Easton, *The Political System,* Alfred A. Knopf, Inc., New York, 1952 pp. 37–63, 233–265.

5. See Kurt Lewin, "The Conflict between Aristotelian and Galileian Modes of Thought in Contemporary Psychology," in *A Dynamic Theory of Personality,* McGraw-Hill Book Company, New York, 1935, pp. 1–42.

in. The simple assumption that meticulous attention to historical detail and faithful reconstruction of "exactly what happened and what was said" are sufficient to make history serviceable can no longer be entertained.[6] The analysis of what Aristotle or Hobbes "really meant," or the minute, sequential tracing of particular concepts through time, so widely practiced by the historians of political thought, hardly meets the requirements of empirical political science. Whatever broadly humanistic purposes this method may serve, it fails to tell the scientist just what he most wants to know, namely, what concepts are viable, what theoretical formulations are valid, or what propositions have withstood the test of falsification.

But I also find it impossible to accept the alternative of using history to explain "how things have come to be what they are." [7] The evolutionary bias implicit in this formulation of the historical method is not the sole reason why I find it unpalatable. Although this approach implies a frank recognition that the historian's look at history is inevitably colored by his contemporary circumstances,[8] it introduces a level of uncertainty into historical writing which empirical science, though itself now accustomed to think in probabilities rather than in certainties, cannot possibly accept with any degree of confidence.

Quite recently, an enterprising political scientist has attempted to make the classics of political theory relevant to our contemporary concerns by juxtaposing some ancients and some moderns, not for the purpose of implying causal relationships or of tracing influences, but for the purpose of noting "significant similarities and differences." [9] I find this effort intellectually stimulating for the teacher and student, but I very much doubt its utility for the modern researcher. The problems of the researcher, as he approaches the history of political theories, are somewhat different. If, as researchers, we go to history at all, we must ask of the history of political theory what we are asking of empirical political science. And this is something other than noting similarities or differences between theoretical formulations.

What we are asking of empirical science is that it help us solve problems in the real world. The dilemma we face in empirical research often is, of course, that the real-life problems we wish to solve are not the problems which are theoretically interesting. Therefore, the first task of the scientist invariably is

6. For the original formulation of this view of historical method, see Leopold von Ranke, *Saemmtliche Werke,* 3d ed., Leipzig, 1877, Vol. 33, p. vii.

7. See Frederick J. Teggart, *Theory and Processes of History,* University of California Press, Berkeley, Calif., 1960.

8. J. T. Merz, in *A History of European Thought in the Nineteenth Century,* Edinburgh, 1896, Vol I, p. 7, quotes Goethe: "History must from time to time be rewritten, not because many new facts have been discovered, but because new aspects come into view, because the participant in the progress of an age is led to standpoints from which the past can be regarded and judged in a novel manner."

9. William T. Bluhm, *Theories of the Political System,* Prentice-Hall, Inc., Englewood Cliffs, N.J., 1965, p. 14.

to translate real-life problems—what John Dewey once called "problematic situations"—into scientific problems.[10] Formulations of problematic situations and formulations of scientific problems are not identical. It is well to remember that however much we get immersed in purely scientific problems, some real-life problem or problematic situation lurks in the background of our scientific endeavors. The older political science, inordinately preoccupied with practical problems of governmental reform, tended to minimize the distinction between the practical and the scientific. The newer political science, it seems to me, all too often loses touch with reality in its preoccupation with scientifically interesting problems. But just as a practical political science is inevitably predicated on some scientific assumptions, no matter how inarticulate, so a theoretical political science is inevitably rooted in real-life problematic situations.

All of this is relevant to our strategy of looking at the history of political theories. When I say, therefore, that we should ask of that history what we are asking of empirical political science, I mean that we should study the political theories of the past in a double perspective: first, in the perspective of the real-life problems to which the theorists addressed themselves; and second, in the perspective of how these real-life problems were "solved," that is, translated into theoretical terms. Otherwise, it seems to me, the history of political thought becomes what it has so often been—either textual exegesis, or ideological handmaiden, or merely intellectual game.

Needless to say, perhaps, I do not subscribe to the attitude of those who promise themselves from the study of political theories in history some novel and unexpected revelations. I think they are thoroughly mistaken, for we go to the history of political thought not only to learn, but also to unlearn. If I read the history of science correctly, and admitting that one may read the history in different ways, it seems to me that, along with learning from his predecessors, the creative scientist is particularly successful in unlearning. Copernicus had to unlearn Ptolemaic astronomy; Galileo had to unlearn Aristotelian physics; and a scientist like Darwin was fortunate in that his immediate predecessors had already unlearned the dogma of creation. In general, not the proposition that is true, but the proposition that is false is the beginning of scientific discovery. Only if we know what is false are we motivated to continue the search for what may be true.

Now, this kind of self-consciousness is likely to occur only if the scientist is faced with anomalies in his work for which there are no easy solutions. The formidable output of political scientists assessing their discipline is probably symptomatic of the crisis in basic orientation that, as Thomas S. Kuhn has so well demonstrated in a recent work, sooner or later revolutionizes science. By way of contrast, what Kuhn calls "normal science," or "the activity in which

10. John Dewey, *Logic: The Theory of Inquiry,* Holt, Rinehart and Winston, Inc., New York, 1938; quoted in F.S.C. Northrop, *The Logic of the Sciences and the Humanities,* The Macmillan Company, New York, 1947, pp. 12–13.

most scientists inevitably spend almost all their time," is based "on the assumption that the scientific community knows what the world is like." [11]

In spite of much historical scholarship on the theory and history of representation,[12] and in spite of all the contemporary research on the representational process, we do not know what representation "is like," at least not under the conditions of political life that characterize our own time. Hence our efforts, of which this book is typical, to recover from the shock of recognition that our "normal science" is in transition.

But I think we are troubled by something else as well. Put as a question, we are increasingly asking: "Just what contribution has our knowledge, whatever the state of this knowledge, made to the art of government?" This question may come as a shock to those among us who are practicing "normal science." In asking the question, I am not assuming that the practical application of scientific knowledge is the sole or ultimate justification of scientific activity. I would argue that even if empirical political science had no practical payoffs at all, it would still be worthwhile to pursue it. It would probably have survival difficulties, but survive it would, for no other reason than that men have been, are, and will continue to be curious about the world they live in. Nevertheless, asking about practical payoffs is appropriate, for empirical inquiry is, in fact, evaluated in these terms.

We often shrink away from payoffs as a standard for appraising our work as political scientists because it invariably leads to invidious comparisons between the physical and the social sciences. But these comparisons become invidious only if we ignore what I think is a profound difference between the study of man and his works and the study of nature.[13] The difference does not lie, as is sometimes said, in the logics or methods of the natural and the social sciences; these, I believe, are generic to all the sciences. Rather, the difference lies in the "raw materials" with which the natural and social sciences deal.[14]

What is this difference in raw materials? The raw materials of the natural sciences are given by nature as they are in nature; they are, indeed, "raw" as the word implies. By way of contrast, the materials with which the social sciences deal are, in most respects, already fashioned by human intervention even before the social scientist comes to deal with them. They are not raw, but

11. Thomas S. Kuhn, *The Structure of Scientific Revolutions,* The University of Chicago Press, Chicago, 1962, p. 5.

12. For the American context, see Alfred de Grazia, *Public and Republic: Political Representation in America,* Alfred A. Knopf, Inc., New York, 1951.

13. How often it is said that the social sciences do not "deserve" the kind and amount of research support which the physical and biological sciences receive because they are less "useful"! To just what useful applications can the social sciences point by comparison with the natural sciences? Even if their usefulness is not altogether denied, they cannot claim to have had the same revolutionary consequences for the shape of human affairs that can be attributed to the natural sciences.

14. In other words, I reject the argument that, because it is perhaps possible to reduce social to biological phenomena, the materials of the social sciences are not unlike those of the natural sciences.

they are invariably artifacts of human endeavor. Even the simplest phenomena with which the social sciences deal—say the mother's care of her child, or primitive economic exchange—are creations of man and not creations of nature.

The differences between the natural and the social sciences, then, lie in the character of the objects with which they deal—"natural facts" in the case of the former, "artifacts" in the case of the latter. My only point in making the distinction is that man has established a great deal of control over his social environment without the benefit of an empirical social science, whereas his control over the physical environment has often had to await the prior discoveries of physical science. Of course, man has also made inventions for the control of nature without the benefit of science, and science has sometimes had to catch up by way of post-facto theories or experiments. But the difference in the degree to which this occurs in the two types of science is still considerable. For almost all the things that we study in the social sciences have been largely inventions unencumbered by prior scientific investigations, often going back to times immemorial. Correspondingly, we should not try to measure the payoffs of empirical social science on the same scale as that used in measuring the payoffs of physical science.

In dealing with representation as an invention or a discovery that preceded theoretical or scientific analysis,[15] as an artificial rather than as a natural phenomenon, we are not only forced to journey into history, but we are also put in a better position to explain its relationship, at a particular moment in time, to some of the other functional problems which any political system is likely to face in the course of its development—notably the problem of interest articulation, the problem of integration, the problem of authorization, and the problem of legitimization. Not all historical or contemporary discussions of representation were or are concerned with all four of these problems. In fact, preoccupation with one or another has not infrequently obfuscated understanding of the representational aspects involved. Because representation is then treated as ancillary or auxiliary to other problems—in democratic representation, say, those of equality in voting or political responsibility—the tendency has been to substitute "real" definitions as obiter dicta of low or no explanatory power for genuine analysis.[16] Actually, the juxta- or counterpositioning of definitions in lieu of relating representational to other functional

15. Representation, wrote James Mill in *An Essay on Government,* 1820, is "the grand discovery of modern times" and "the solution of all the difficulties, both speculative and practical . . ." (Cambridge University Press, New York, 1937, p. vi). Karl Loewenstein, in *Political Power and the Governmental Process,* The University of Chicago Press, Chicago, 1957, p. 40, states: "In retrospect it appears that the invention or discovery of the representative technique was as decisive for the political evolution of the West and, through it, of the world as the mechanical inventions—steam, electricity, the combustion engine, atomic power—have been for man's technological evolution."

16. Note the rather hopeless enterprise by John A. Fairlie, "The Nature of Political Representation," *American Political Science Review,* Vol. 34, pp. 236–248, 456–466, April and June, 1940.

problems may be scientifically harmful, because it gives an impression of theoretical closure where there is none.[17]

Finally, if representation refers to the structure of the relationship between representative and represented, and to the functions which this structure performs for the political system, it precludes self-fulfilling usages that are empirically nondemonstrable and therefore nonfalsifiable. I have in mind the metaphysics of Prof. Eric Voegelin who, in making representation "the central problem of a theory of politics," sees in it "the form by which a political society gains existence for action in history," and who seeks to explore "the symbols by which political societies interpret themselves as representatives of a transcendent truth." [18]

I shall, in the remainder of this chapter, deal with three historical "cases" which are instructive from the perspective developed so far. I shall first review the failure of the Greek philosophers to understand representation, a failure that points up the importance of theory, even if it is post-facto theory, for the survival of political systems. I shall then jump the centuries and discuss the efforts of medieval theorists, notably the conciliarists, to come to grips with representation and some of its functional implications. My third case will be Edmund Burke's now classical treatment of representation which has had a more profound impact on our own thinking than that of any other theorist. I shall not deal with the populist treatment of representation, and especially the problem of responsibility that looms so large in democratic theory, because I think it is only a special case of the more generic problem with which Burke was concerned. In conclusion, I shall make a few remarks about the consequences of contemporary empirical research for a modern theory of representation. In fact, I shall conclude that our contemporary real-life problems are such that none of the traditional formulations of representation are relevant to the solution of the representational problems which the modern polity faces.

II

If we approach an institutional artifact, like representation, as a problem of invention or discovery, the case of the Greeks–their failure to comprehend what they were practicing–is especially instructive. We are then in a better position to advance empirical theory and relevant research than when we treat representation as a matter of definitions. That the Greeks, and later the Romans, did in fact conduct a good deal of public business through represen-

17. See, for instance, Harold F. Gosnell's attempt at synthesis in *Democracy: The Threshold of Freedom,* The Ronald Press Company, New York, 1948, pp. 124–142.

18. Eric Voegelin, *The New Science of Politics,* The University of Chicago Press, Chicago, 1952, p. 1. Voegelin elsewhere refers, evidently for demonstration, to the early Asiatic empires which "understood themselves as representatives of a transcendent order, of the order of the cosmos. . . ." In this conception, "the ruler himself represents the society, because on earth he represents the transcendent power which maintains the cosmic order." *Ibid.,* p. 54.

tative institutions has been reasonably well established by contemporary historical scholarship.[19] This is not to say that the Greek system of representation was highly developed or that it was properly appreciated as a technique of governance. Moreover, it would be a grievous mistake to read into what representative institutions there were meaning that the Greeks could not possibly have entertained. On the contrary, as a technical invention, representation seemed to have been designed for the purpose of limiting rather than extending the participation of citizens in government. Yet even this use of representation as an instrument of power escaped theoretical understanding. Aristotle, for instance, discusses the situation in Mantinea where the people,

> . . . although they do not all share in the appointment of offices, except through representatives elected in turn out of the whole people, as at Mantinea;—yet, if they have the power of deliberating, the many are contented.

He interprets this case as follows: "Even this form of government may be regarded as a democracy, and was such at Mantinea." [20] In interpreting this interpretation, one must keep in mind that by "democracy" Aristotle did not mean "representative democracy," but what we think of as "direct democracy." Although the *boule* or council finally became the only institution of the Greek polis that mattered, it was not and probably could not be perceived as a representative institution in the sense that it was a council of individuals who represented the community as a whole.[21] The representative institution could not be visualized as an instrument of power because the aristocratism of Greek democracy was effectively camouflaged by the ideology that every citizen directly and personally participated in the government of the polis. Both Plato and Aristotle were deceived by the prevailing myth, and their approach to knowledge prevented them from penetrating to reality.

So strong was this myth that even after the federalistic experiments of the various Hellenic confederacies—which, as J. A. O. Larsen has conclusively shown, provided for representative assemblies based on population, though they were insufficiently empowered to make collective decisions—the principle of representation was not understood. Even Polybius, Larsen notes,

> . . . gives us no theory of representative government. The reason seems to be that Greek formal political theory was so dominated by the city state that even a laudation of a federal government took the form of the claim that it was almost a polis.[22]

19. See J.A.O. Larsen, *Representative Government in Greek and Roman History,* University of California Press, Berkeley, Calif., 1955.

20. Aristotle, *Politics,* Modern Library, Inc., New York, 1943, Book VI, Chap. 4, p. 264.

21. See V. Ehrenberg, *Der Staat der Griechen I. Teil: Der Hellenische Staat,* Teubner, Leipzig, 1957, pp. 44–48.

22. Larsen, *op. cit.*, p. 104.

The price which the Greeks paid for this theoretical failure to understand their own governmental inventions has often been commented upon. As Professor Friedrich has pointed out,

> . . . necessity for personal participation became fatal whenever such a city reached larger proportions. The attempts at solving this problem through a federal organization foundered upon the inability of the ancients to work out a representative scheme.[23]

The failure of practice, then, was partly predicated on a failure of theory. The Greek case is of interest, therefore, precisely because it emphasizes the role of political theory in practical governance.[24] Whether the Greek city-state or the Greek confederacies could have survived the Macedonian and Roman onslaughts if they had been successful in solving the problem of representation is a matter of speculation of no relevance here. Of interest is the question of just why the rudimentary representative institutions that they did have could not be properly conceived for what they were.

Political theory failed the Greeks in their most fateful hours because it was based on an epistemology that obscured political reality. This is not the place to belabor all the points often made about Aristotle's approach to knowledge. But they do help us understand, I think, why even Aristotle could not see representation as an important discovery of the Greek city builders. In the first place, what stood in the way of a theory of representation was the practice of essentialist definitions which were presumed to identify both the essence and the meaning of a phenomenon.[25] In the Aristotelian universe of definitions concerning the forms of the polis and the processes of politics, there was no place for the kind of behavior that the existence of representative modes of governance entailed. Second, "knowledge" for Aristotle meant the compilation of the definitions of essences, a sort of encyclopedia of names, together with their defining formulas, which becomes an "authority." But knowledge does not grow by way of authoritative definitions, but by way of challenging hypotheses, such as that the earth is not flat. Finally, though Aristotle was less inclined than Plato to hold that knowledge is a matter of intellectual intuition, we should not overestimate, as is sometimes done, the empirical temper of his thinking about politics. It is true that Aristotle collected over 150 constitutions: but this was done, it seems, not for the purpose of empirical inference, but rather for more or less illustrative purposes *after* the foundations of his polit-

23. Carl J. Friedrich, *Constitutional Government and Democracy*, Ginn and Company, Boston, 1946, p. 267.

24. For an opposite view, denigrating the role of ideas in institutional survival, see Edward M. Sait, *Political Institutions: A Preface,* Appleton-Century-Crofts, Inc., New York, 1938, p. 475. However, Sait's chapter on representation is still one of the best succinct historical accounts I have seen.

25. Karl R. Popper, *The Open Society and Its Enemies,* Routledge & Kegan Paul, Ltd., London, 1945, Vol. II, pp. 12–13.

ical theory had already been formulated.[26] Observation, then, does not function to verify or falsify propositions, but rather to stimulate the mind in its task to comprehend universal essences.

Let me reemphasize that it is not my intention to beat a dead dog from the vantage point of modern scientific epistemology. My emphasis is on what happens when in our quest for knowledge we depart too far from the real-life problems that are at the base of inquiry. Benjamin Farrington, in an illuminating book on Greek science, concerns himself with just this aspect of knowledge making. He writes:

> In the earlier period of Greek thought, when the sciences were not distinguished from the techniques, science was plainly a way of *doing* something. With Plato it became a way of knowing, which, in the absence of any practical test, meant only talking consistently. . . . The kind of science they [i.e., Plato and Aristotle] aimed at creating was a science for citizens who would not directly engage in the operational control of the physical environment. Their modes of explanation necessarily excluded ideas derived from the techniques.[27]

The tragedy of Greek political theory was that it served as an ideology of defense of the master-slave system that, by Plato's time, had become dominant. In this apologia, there was no room for interest in techniques, including techniques of government, even though they were practiced. Representation as a technique could not be accommodated in a teleological thought system that in assuming men to be born as either masters or slaves, sought to help nature realize its intentions. Farrington sums up this "real paralysis of science":

> During four hundred years there had been, as we have seen, many extensions of knowledge, much reorganization of the body of knowledge, fresh acquisitions of skill in exposition. But there was no great forward drive, no general application of science to life. Science had ceased to be, or had failed to become, a real force in the life of society. Instead there had arisen a conception of science as a cycle of liberal studies for a privileged minority. Science had become a relaxation, an adornment, a subject of contemplation. It had ceased to be a means of transforming the conditions of life.[28]

If the writers of antiquity did not lay even the barest foundations of a theory of political representation, those of the Middle Ages got it off to a wrong start. Representation was discovered, or rather rediscovered, as an instrument of power wielded by medieval monarchs to facilitate the conservation of peace, the administration of lucrative justice, and the replenishment of royal treas-

26. See *Ibid.*, Vol. II, p. 275, note 32.
27. Benjamin Farrington, *Greek Science*, Penguin Books, Inc., Baltimore, 1963, p. 141.
28. *Ibid.*, p. 302.

uries.[29] Although, later, representation was also seen as a technique to limit the power of the ruler, the universalistic, sacerdotal, and traditional outlook on society—that strange mélange of Aristotelian and Christian ideas which had been fused by St. Thomas into a grand design of order—could not conceive of representation in other than hierarchical terms. As a result, and as long as the medieval order was relatively undisturbed by the later controversies over rulership, representational theory was a theory of impersonation that legitimized the power of the ruler. The king or prince represented in his person the realm as a whole, just as the Pope impersonated the whole of Christendom.

As a theory of personification, representational theory could not cope with the important functional problem of integration that was as basic to the medieval order as it later became to the modern order and as it is today in the developing nations. Given the controversies of the later Middle Ages—between emperor and Pope, between king and states, between bishops and cathedral chaplains, between the old monastic orders and the self-governing new ones, and finally between the papacy in Avignon and the conciliar movement—one wonders how the problem of integration in state or church would have been solved if representational theory had not been transformed in such a way that it could at least take cognizance of the changes in relationships between the effective political forces of the time. Clearly, a theory which only asked, "*Who* represents the *whole?*" however the whole was defined, could not possibly break out of tautological polemics. For the claim to authority by one would-be representative was as good as the claim by another. Indeed, most of the arguments, even many of those made at a relatively late date by some conciliar theorists, led nowhere because they were legitimizing rather than analytical propositions. History being what it is, we cannot say what might have happened in the real world if theoretical development had failed to transcend the medieval paradigm of a hierarchical social structure in which the parts were both unequal and subordinate to each other. For this paradigm, if it ever corresponded to reality, was increasingly in conflict with it. All we can say is that the problem of integration was solved, and that a new conception of representation, along with other theoretical developments, played a role in its solution.

A theory of representation that would take account of the relationship between representative and represented had to be based on a view of politics that was sensitive to the interplay of diverse interests—whether of persons, groups, or territories. Such a view could not emerge as long as political thought was in the Aristotelian bondage of definitional essentialism, with its emphasis on a primary classification of politics and its fascination with universal categories. Nominalism, in rejecting "real" definitions and starting with the individual

29. See Charles A. Beard and John D. Lewis, "Representative Government in Evolution," *American Political Science Review*, Vol. 26, pp. 223–240, April, 1932, reprinted in John C. Wahlke and Heinz Eulau (Eds.), *Legislative Behavior*, The Free Press of Glencoe, New York, 1959, pp. 22–30.

phenomenon rather than with the whole as its unit of analysis, was an epistemological revolution. It not only produced a new paradigm for the comprehension of all social formations, but was also of critical importance for the emergence of a rudimentary theory of representation as delegation. It thus enabled theorists to catch up with the custom of the "imperative mandate" that was practiced in early representative government.[30] Moreover, once the superiority, by definition, of the whole over the parts, or of the general over the specific, was questioned, the theoretical door was opened for seeing politics as an arena of conflicting interests. And finally, the legitimacy of all claimants to be represented in collective decision making was recognized. Though such writers as Marsilius of Padua, William of Ockham, or Nicholas of Cusa took different stands in the struggles between emperor and Pope and in the controversies within the Church, the focus of theoretical attention shifted to the represented as significant parties to the representational relationship.

This is not to say that nominalism alone was responsible for the breakthrough in thinking about representation. Any adequate appreciation of the new view of representation as delegation rather than impersonation cannot ignore the confluence of all those factors that laid the foundations for constitutional government in the late Middle Ages, notably the rejuvenation of Roman law and the pervasiveness of the German Law of Corporations. Moreover, the budding medieval constitutional thought was strongly supported by the Christian conception of equality. So Roman legal notions of agency and consent were combined with the Christian idea of all being equal before God. In secular terms, all were conceded the equal right of being heard and represented in law making. And Aristotle's concept of the right of citizens to participate in all decisions affecting the polis, which previously had purely rhetorical meaning, reduced the tension between the built-in radicalism of the Christian concept of equality and the conservative view of social structure. Note how Marsilius presents the solution:

> Let us say, then, in accordance with the truth and the counsel of Aristotle in the *Politics,* Book III, Chapter 6, that the legislator, or the primary and proper cause of the law, is the people or the whole body of citizens, or the weightier part thereof, through its election or will expressed by words in the general assembly of the citizens, commanding or determining that something be done or omitted with regard to human civil acts, under a temporal pain or punishment. The aforesaid whole body of citizens or the weightier part thereof is the legislator regardless of whether it makes the law directly by itself or entrusts the making of it to some person or persons, who are not and cannot be the legislator in the absolute sense,

30. See, for instance, Alice M. Holden, "The Imperative Mandate in the Spanish Cortes of the Middle Ages," *American Political Science Review,* Vol. 24, pp. 886–912, November, 1930, reprinted in Wahlke and Eulau, *op. cit.*, pp. 30–34.

but only in a relative sense and for a particular time and in accordance with the authority of the primary legislator.[31]

Once limitations on rulership—something the Greeks had failed to work out—had been accepted as legitimate, representation could be conceived as the effective technique to limit political power, provided that the representative institution took cognizance of diverse claims. But all the theoretical creativity involved in this new synthesis of partly inherited, partly novel notions of politics would have been impossible, it seems to me, without the decisive metamorphosis in the *ways* of thinking about the world which the new approach of the nominalists made possible.

But, again, we must guard against reading modern democratic notions into the evolving view of the representational process. Men like Marsilius of Padua or William of Ockham were not advocates of what later came to be called "individualism." That the representative stood for the many was clearly recognized, but the many themselves still constituted largely indivisible wholes—be it an individed church, or the people as a whole, or the estates as wholes. As Professor Sabine pointed out, "certainly, William had no thought of representing Christians individually, as so many discrete units, or territorially, as the inhabitants of such and such districts." [32] Rather, the demand of these writers was for a more perfectly ordered social organism, in the sense that the church would approximate this ideal if all the members and groups of Christianity were represented in a more adequate way.

The *legislator humanus* in Marsilius's thought, for instance, differed from the traditional view only in that his legitimacy derived from popular consent rather than from divine inspiration. His "role," to use a modern term, was more that of a judge than that of a delegate as we understand it today. Nicholas of Cusa's complaint largely centered in the point that the Pope represents the Church only "in a very confused fashion," whereas the universal council is more representative because "it is always better in judgment than the single pontiff who is a more uncertain representative." [33] In fact, then, the conception of representation used here is still in part one of impersonation. As one recent interpreter of Nicholas put it, "the council is not superior to the pope because it is made up of representatives chosen by others to take their places, but because a larger number are present who 'figure' or 'personify' the lesser hierarchical groupings in the church." [34] If anything, then, this conception is closer to the Burkean notion of "virtual representation" than to the view of

31. Alan Gewirth, trans., *Marsilius of Padua: The Defender of Peace*, Vol. II, *The Defensor pacis*, Columbia University Press, New York, 1956, Chaps. 12, 3, p. 45.

32. George H. Sabine, *A History of Political Theory*, Holt, Rinehart and Winston, Inc., New York, 1937, p. 310.

33. Quoted in Paul E. Sigmund, *Nicholas of Cusa and Medieval Political Thought*, Harvard University Press, Cambridge, Mass., 1963, p. 166.

34. *Ibid.*, pp. 166–167.

representation as delegation. On the other hand, Nicholas also entertained ideas of delegation. His *legati,* members of Church councils, including the college of cardinals, do not simply personify the Christian community, but are presumably answerable to electors, or in the case of the cardinals, responsible to the *praesides*—the heads of the various hierarchical ranks in the provinces whose places they were taking in Rome.

The intellectual turmoil apparent in Nicholas of Cusa's treatment of representation suggests that the conciliar theorists did not completely surmount the traditional holistic paradigm of the political order. Though the authority of representatives was increasingly constructed as deriving from a mandate, taking for granted the sovereignty of the people and the contractual basis of rulership, both representative institutions and the collectivities represented were still seen as wholes. The council or assembly of representatives was treated as an analog of the *ecclesia universalis* or of the *universitas populi.* The method of theory construction was one of extrapolation from the macrocosm of a universal, hierarchical order to the microcosm of the particular assembly of representatives. In other words, the council or assembly was also a *universitas,* for it was only a substitute for the larger unit of which it was a part.[35] But this construction hardly disguises the changes in political relationships that were at the base of the theoretical efforts to free theory from the holistic paradigm. Nevertheless, as Gierke has pointed out, referring to the difficulties involved in these constructions, "the persistent cult of the antique was a hindrance to the progress of the representative idea, while the absolutist doctrine of Bodin was positively hostile." [36]

The medieval case is instructive because it suggests that a theory of the relationship between representative and represented cannot be fruitfully pursued independent of the prevailing status relations in a society. I am reluctant to link representation with considerations of status in this connection. But a theory of representation clearly cannot ignore what both representative and represented, be they superiors or subordinates, can in effect do to each other as a result of occupying different status positions. For instance, reverting to the medieval case, representation as delegation is bound to fail if the represented occupy status positions that in effect prevent them from issuing instructions. Yet, as status relationships were in fact changing, medieval representational theory confronted the dilemma of taking account of these changes without, however, disturbing the social order as such. It was therefore supremely unconcerned with the problem of how the relationship between representative and represented could be instrumented. The solution, as I suggested, was

35. For similar doctrinal difficulties with federalistic theories, see Heinz Eulau, "Theories of Federalism under the Holy Roman Empire," *American Political Science Review,* Vol. 35, pp. 643–664, August, 1941, reprinted in Heinz Eulau, *Journeys in Politics,* The Bobbs-Merrill Company, Inc., Indianapolis, 1963, pp. 3–27.

36. Otto von Gierke, *The Development of Political Theory,* W.W. Norton & Company, Inc., New York, 1939, p. 244.

found in isomorphic constructions: smaller organisms were seen as replicas of the larger organism. But the question of effective linkage between representative and represented remained unanswered.

The isomorphic view of the representative assembly became a theoretical straitjacket that, later on, plagued representational theory. For once church, or sovereign people, or estates gave way to area as the unit of representation, and even after representatives were seen as delegates from geographic constituencies, the latter were assumed to be represented as wholes. But this conception, in turn, could only yield a paradox: if that which is represented constitutes a whole, particularistic interests within the whole cannot be articulated, and as Professor MacIver has rightly observed, "the only policy he [i.e., the representative] can logically stand for is the presumptive interest of the whole he represents." [37]

What becomes of interest, then, is how later theorists coped with this paradox. Clearly, no representative can speak for the whole except in a formalistic sense. As I shall point out, Edmund Burke tried to solve it by asserting that, in order to represent the whole, the representative must speak and act according to his own judgment. From this perspective, then, Burke's formulation was truly "progressive." Virtual representation, as he understood it, was the only alternative to a holistic view of representation, on the one hand, and to an individualistic view, on the other hand.

III

Before discussing Edmund Burke's theory of representation, we must once more take a leap through the centuries in order to appreciate the change in paradigms from the holistic conception of representation in the Middle Ages to the individualistic conception that took root in the seventeenth century. Yet, I shall not dwell on Hobbes' logical perversion of the individualistic paradigm or on Rousseau's sentimental radicalism that led him to reject the technique of representation as a violation of the individualistic principle.[38] I shall almost immediately turn to Burke, for a number of reasons. That our contemporary thinking about representation derives from Burke's suggestive polemic rather than from Hobbes or Rousseau is perhaps most relevant. But almost equally interesting is the location of Burke's statement in the development of representational theory. What Burke told the electors of Bristol in his famous speech of 1774 could not have been said without the profound change in paradigms that had taken place in the centuries between the conciliar movement and his own time. In other words, behind Burke's view of representation lay an alto-

37. Robert M. MacIver, *The Web of Government,* The Macmillan Company, New York, 1947, p. 210.

38. For an excellent discussion of Rousseau, see Allan Bloom, "Jean-Jacques Rousseau," in Leo Strauss and Joseph Cropsey (eds.), *History of Political Philosophy,* Rand McNally & Company, Chicago, 1963, pp. 514–535.

gether new view of social relationships. The individual, either as representative or as represented, had become the primary unit of theoretical analysis.

But Burke, unlike Hobbes and Rousseau, and perhaps also unlike Montesquieu, had to come to practical grips with the consequences of individualism for the representational process. If the individual is the unit of any representational relationship, the problem clearly is how it comes about that the community, also, is represented. Hobbes had solved the problem by liquidating the individual through contracting him out of the political process. Rousseau had simply denied that any problem existed, very much as the Greeks had done, though he knew better. Montesquieu was perhaps the first theorist who presented a pragmatic conception of representation by geographic districts, on the ground that a locally elected representative is better acquainted with the needs of his own locality and with his own neighbors than any other would-be representative.[39] But even though Montesquieu recognized the individual as the unit of the representational relationship, he viewed representation as resting on a collective mandate, in the sense that representatives act on behalf of the community which is itself vested with legislative power. Representation, then, is simply a convenience. The problem—just how individual representation gives rise to collective representation—is treated by absorption: the people as individuals may be capable of choosing representatives, but they are not themselves capable of taking an active part in government, despite their being vested with legislative power. In arguing against a delegate view of representation, Montesquieu simply postulated that representation somehow takes place, without paying attention to the question of how representative and represented are linked.[40]

All of these "solutions" were not solutions, though they gave the impression of being so. If we turn to Burke, I think the reason his formulation, in contrast to those of Hobbes, Rousseau, or Montesquieu, is still so suggestive today is the fact that he did *not* present a pseudosolution to the puzzle of how individual representation can become collective representation. Burke's failure is our legacy. To appreciate it, we must place Burke into the English historical context.

After emerging from the holistic preoccupations of the medieval period, representational theory was above all a theory of legal relationships, a theory of authority. Whether the legal accent was put, as by Hobbes, on the sovereignty of the ruler, or as by the Levellers on the sovereignty of the people, with parliament having only purely delegated authority, there was little theoretical concern with the instrumentation of the actual relationships between representative and represented.[41] The change in paradigm was evident enough. The

39. Baron de Montesquieu, *The Spirit of the Laws,* Trans. Thomas Nugent, Hafner, Publishing Company, Inc., New York, 1962, Book IX, Chap. 6, pp. 154–155.

40. See Gierke, *op. cit.*, p. 247.

41. For a detailed treatment of their thought on representation, see H.N. Brailsford, *The Levellers and the English Revolution,* Stanford University Press, Stanford, Calif., pp. 10–11, 275–287, 354–357.

Levellers, as Sabine has stated, "conceived parliament as standing for the actual human beings that composed the nation, and not as representing corporations, vested interests, and rights of property or status." [42] True, as Gierke mentioned, certain "weighty maxims" gradually came to prevail in England, "to the effect that every member of parliament should represent the whole nation and not merely his district, that he is not bound to obey instructions or to render account to his constituents." [43] But these weighty maxims did not cut much ice. Down to Burke's day, it seems, parliamentary representation was conceived as delegation—a type of relationship between representative and represented not different from the ordinary legal relation of agency.

What, we wonder, touched off Burke's polemic and his attack on the mandate theory? One might argue, as Burke himself argued in his speech, that it was his fellow M.P. from Bristol who, Burke tells us, "expresses himself (if I understand him rightly) in favor of the coercive authority of such instructions." But why should this occasion Burke's outspoken attack on the notion of mandate—an attack which, as a clever politician, he might surely have expected to backfire? Why did he dwell on the problem of his relationship with the voters of Bristol at all? He could have remained silent.

Burke's attack was not a simple reply to a familiar and common doctrine reiterated by a colleague. He was not so naïve politically as it might seem if we were to take his argument at face value. On the contrary, as I shall suggest, his argument was designed to conceal rather than reveal his true intentions as one of Bristol's representatives. Some years ago, employing the technique of textual exegesis, I thought that

> . . . Burke postulated two possible foci of representation: local, necessarily hostile interests, on the one hand; and a national interest, on the other hand. He rejected the former as an improper and advocated the latter as the proper focus of the representative's role. But in doing so, he also linked these foci of representation with particular representational styles. If the legislature is concerned with only one interest, that of the whole, and not with compromise among diverse interests, it follows that the representative cannot and must not be bound by instructions, from whatever source, but must be guided by what Burke called "his unbiased opinions, his mature judgment, his enlightened conscience." Moreover, Burke buttressed his argument by emphasizing the deliberative function of the legislature—presumably in contrast to its representational function.[44]

I can no longer leave it at that. For if we leave the argument at this point, Burke's view of virtual representation could hardly be challenged, or to put it differently, his hypothesis could hardly be falsified. We must ask, therefore,

42. Sabine, *op. cit.*, p. 487.

43. Gierke, *op. cit.*, p. 246.

44. Heinz Eulau *et al.*, "The Role of the Representative: Some Empirical Observations on the Theory of Edmund Burke," *American Political Science Review*, Vol. 53, p. 744, September, 1959.

just what Burke had in mind when he confronted the diverse interests of different constituencies with the one interest of the nation as a whole. His claim that this national interest would somehow emerge out of the deliberations of an assembly of men endowed with reason and judgment, provided they are unencumbered by instructions, does not sound true. For Burke's whole orientation to politics was a kind of pragmatic aristocratism. This aristocratism, by the third quarter of the eighteenth century, had found institutional expression in an incipient party system. Yet, nowhere in his speech to the voters of Bristol is there any acknowledgment of his commitment to a particular party.

Burke's speech oozes an air of political innocence. But how innocent was Burke? We are indebted to a delightful essay by Ernest Barker on "Burke and His Bristol Constituency" to disabuse us of any illusions we might cherish about Burke's political innocence. Who was the politician who, in 1774, stood for election in Bristol? After having been private secretary to the member for Petersfield, known as "single-speech Hamilton," Burke had entered similar confidential employment in 1765 with the Marquis of Rockingham, a week after this leader of one of the Whig factions had become Prime Minister. And soon, Barker narrates,

> . . . his nature working powerfully on Rockingham's affection, he became his right hand, his goad to action, his trumpeter, his manager, his plague, his inspiration. A seat in Parliament was immediately found for him, by the influence of Lord Verney, at the foot of the Chilterns, in the borough of Wendover.[45]

Through his connection with Rockingham, Burke became a party man. The party leaders included Rockingham, the Duke of Portland, the Duke of Richmond, and when he was not engaged in fox hunting, Lord John Cavendish. These men were cajoled by Burke, Barker tells us,

> . . . that they would not stay immured in their castles, on the plea of health or foxes or private affairs; that they would come to London before the session began in order to concert a policy; that they would brave the Court and the crowd for the sake of their policy; in a word, that they would work for their party, live for their party, and, if necessary, die for their party, in the grand old manner of the seventeenth century. A passion of activity is natural to a zealous party organizer, and Burke, if we may use a modern name, was the Rockingham party organizer. He suggested policies, drafted petitions, arranged for meetings, looked after elections, arranged everything and goaded everybody.[46]

The man who was put up for election in Bristol was a party man. In fact, he was put up *because* he was a party man. In putting him up, his supporters broke a "polite arrangement" made toward the end of the reign of George II,

45. Ernest Barker, "Burke and His Bristol Constituency, 1774–1780," in *Essays on Government,* Oxford University Press, Fair Lawn, N.J., 1945, p. 170.

46. *Ibid.,* pp. 172–173.

"under which Whigs and Tories were to share its [i.e., Bristol's] two seats for the next three Parliaments." But the local Whigs had become ever more restless as the sitting Tory member had voted consistently for an anti-American policy that annoyed the merchants and traders of Bristol. In settling on Burke as a second Whig candidate, his Bristol friends thought they knew what they were getting. As the virtual leader of the Rockingham faction, he was eminently sound on the American question; he "was the man with whom North corresponded on the business of the House, as a Prime Minister corresponds today with the Leader of the Opposition." Burke, in turn, was aware of the advantages that would accrue to his parliamentary position if "he could sit for one of the great popular constituencies, which would lend authority to his protests and weight to his policies." [47]

But the alliance between Burke and Bristol was an uneasy one from the start. Even during the election an anonymous writer had urged, "it is plain that ye have greatly mistaken one another, and the best thing that can now be done is to make explanations and apologies on all sides and part." [48] Another pamphleteer had asked:

> Do you know that he is the agent and instrument of the Rockingham party? Do you know he has written a book recommending the principles of that party? That they amount to this . . . that they will invest themselves with the people's rights, who shall be free in their power but not otherwise, for that *they* shall have virtue and ability enough for you all? [49]

But what does Burke's being a party man and being known as a party man tell us about his theory of representation? It tells us, I think, that taking words out of historical context, as we have done for so long, can be highly misleading. In coming down on the side of independent judgment as the proper style and in preaching the supremacy of the whole over the parts as the proper focus of representation, Burke in fact translated the interests of his party into a universal principle of politics. And in doing so, Burke would become the victim of his own dissemblances. Burke could say what he did say in his Bristol speech only because in 1774 he and his constitutents happened to be of similar mind on economic questions. On the Irish issue and American matters, Burke's policies and the interests of the Bristol merchants chanced to coincide. But their agreement was only apparent. Burke was a free trader by conviction; his demand that parliament legislate for the whole nation in the national interest meant for him, in this context, a demand for free trade. But the merchants of Bristol favored free trade only as long as it served their particular interests; if they thought restricted trade served their interests better, they would favor rigid protection. Similarly, Burke's advocacy of toleration on the Catholic

47. All quotes *ibid.*, p. 179

48. Quoted in *ibid.*, pp. 183–184.

49. Quoted in *ibid.*, pp. 184–185.

issue could only succeed if parliament would identify toleration with the national interest. Bristol's Protestants saw it otherwise. Burke was never defeated in Bristol, as is commonly believed. On Saturday, September 9, 1780, Barker recounts, "he appeared at the Guildhall, on the opening of the second day of the poll, and declined the election." [50] He withdrew from the polls and retired from a contest which, he knew, could only end in defeat.

Burke's difficulties were not limited to the discrepancy between his policy views and those of his constituents. In the decade prior to the Bristol speech of 1774, the view that representatives should be instructed delegates had found wide acceptance. Burke's own view was that the representative is a free and responsible agent, to be left free in his decisions but accountable for them after they were made. No doubt, this conception had grown deep roots in his political thought. For eight years prior to 1774, he had been free, in the sense in which he thought the representative should be free, because the rotten borough of Wendover had hardly made demands on him. And he had associated himself with aristocrats who, by virtue of their status, considered themselves as free in the same sense. But, above all, freedom from local connections and instructions was for Burke a necessary and very practical condition to work for a parliamentary party, be its leader, and accept the commitments of a party man. Burke never envisaged the possibility that his own judgment and his party's policies could ever come into conflict.

Professor Barker, in his essay, on which I am drawing so much in this chapter, admires Burke's candor, for he might have circumvented the issue by avoidance. But he did not. He did not, and could not avoid it, it seems to me, because he knew that he would be challenged as a party man in any case, as indeed he was. Granted that he believed what he said, we cannot ignore what he did not say but might have said. And what he did not say was that he was bound to the principles of his party as strongly as he did not want to be bound to instructions from his constituents. True, as Barker points out, "the question raised between Burke and his constituents was more than personal and psychological; it was, in its essence, as we have seen, a grave constitutional question, which went to the impersonal roots of politics." [51] But, as Barker had also to admit, "to espouse without reserve the cause of Burke against Bristol would be, in effect, to deny the cause of democracy." [52] The real issue, it seems to me, was not the constitutional question. The real issue was the political question of who should rule England—and on this issue Burke had committed himself as much as any man of his time. At issue, too, was the future of his party—"a body of men united, for promoting by their joint endeavours the national interest, upon some particular principle in which they are all agreed" [53]—and the role of his party in the future of England.

50. *Ibid.*, p. 204.
51. *Ibid.*, p. 197.
52. *Ibid.*, p. 199.
53. Edmund Burke, *Works,* S. & C. Rivington, London, 1803–1827, Vol. III, p. 335.

Needless to say, perhaps, Burke's notion of political party is far removed from our own notion of the party as an agent of interest aggregation in a pluralistic or polyarchic society. Yet it is an astounding fact, now confirmed by many empirical studies of representational roles, at least in the American context, that Burke's conception of the representative as a trustee is widely held. But, as in the case of Burke himself, what we must look for is not what the trustee orientation tells us about the representative who holds it, but what it does not tell us. What it does not tell us is anything significant about the exchanges that occur between the representative and those—party leaders, colleagues, lobbyists, even some constituents—from whom he receives his cues, and about the processes of politics that, in the end, lead to the self-serving assertion of independent judgment. The dichotomy in terms of which Burke has made us think—and this includes radical democratic thought as well—does not correspond to the political realities of our time. Burke's trustee was, in the end, a party man—in the sense of party as he understood it. But what is today's trustee? I do not think that we can say. And so, Burke too, has failed in solving the problem of representation—how individual relationships are transformed into representation of the whole.

IV

With Edmund Burke, theoretical thinking about representation reached an impasse. The pendulum of preference swung heavily in the direction of the mandate or delegate interpretation of the representational relationship. The theories of proportional and functional representation that became prominent in the later nineteenth and early twentieth centuries were either party-centered or interest-centered interpretations of the basic relationship between representative and represented. Their immediate purpose was to maximize meaningful popular participation in the governing process and to maximize governmental responsiveness. As normative doctrines they were largely obiter dicta, and no efforts were made to answer the question of whether schemes of representation based on these theories actually attained the promised objectives. On the other hand, a small but influential group of writers continued to advocate notions of virtual representation and actually succeeded in writing these notions into some modern constitutions.

My purpose in reviewing the failure of the ancients to develop a theory of representation, the struggle of the medieval writers to formulate a theory, and Burke's attempt to diagnose the basic issue, has not been to describe, but to point up the problematic situations involved in these theoretical postures and to suggest how theoretical formulations are anchored in problematic situations. My purpose has been to see just what it is that we, as empirical political scientists, can learn from the theoretical failures, struggles, or dilemmas of the past. It is my point of view that we can learn something from the history of political theories if we ask of it what we ask of empirical science. The first demand which we must make on ourselves as empirical researchers is that we have as accurate, as unembellished, a picture of the problematic conditions that give rise to our theorizing in the first place. This, it seems to me, is all too often forgotten as we practice "normal science." Normal science necessarily sees the world in terms of its own conventional, agreed-on ways. But we can be sensitive to the presuppositions that determine what we see in the real world. In part, the difficulties of the past were the result of the fact that presuppositions of an epistemological kind—essentialism in the Greek case, holism in the medieval case, and rationalism in Burke's case—powerfully circumscribed the diagnoses that were made of the problematic situations that were at the base of theorizing about representation.

We have witnessed, in the last ten years or so, an outpouring of empirical studies which, in one way or another, concerned themselves with a great variety of political relationships connected with problems of representation. Most of this research has been conducted in the American context, but some of it has also been undertaken abroad, especially in Western Europe. Most of this research has been conceived, wittingly or not, within the broad theoretical framework that Edmund Burke bequeathed to us. We have been practicing normal science. In doing so, we have largely taken for granted just what the problems are that interest us when studying representation, and we have largely overlooked the possibility that a change in basic paradigms may have taken place in the intervening years. And we have failed to make this change as explicit as might be desirable.

As a result, it seems to me, we are in a curiously ambiguous research situation. On the one hand, we have subjected to empirical testing a broad range of propositions translated from normative formulations, and we have found that these formulations do not square with our findings. This, you will recall, is what I had in mind in the opening of this chapter when I said that we know what representation is not. On the other hand, because we have not really addressed ourselves to problematic situations in our current reality, we have been unable to come up with relevant knowledge as to what representation means in our own time. In this respect, I believe, we are closer to the Greeks, for whom knowledge had become an idle pastime, than to the medievalists or to Burke, who were deeply involved in a search for solutions to troubling situations. In the medieval case, this was the quest for political integration and legitimization; in the case of Burke, it was the quest for solving the problems of party, responsiveness, responsibility, and the national interest.

Burke—I once more turn to him, because he defined our scientific problems for us in regard to representation—really formulated a dilemma, and this dilemma is still with us. If the critical real-life problem of representation—even under the very much changed conditions of our time—is the responsibility of the governors to the governed, then indeed virtual representation, as Burke understood it, is probably the appropriate style in an era when "mandate uncertainty"[54] and the complexity of governmental policy making create a deep and wide gap between representative and represented. In this situation, the representative can act responsibly only if he has sufficient freedom and discretion to act as he sees fit in the face of the intricate, rapidly changing issues which he must decide on. Prior consultation of the represented is out of the question.

But if we see as the critical problem the responsiveness of the representative to the represented, then a mandate or delegate conception would seem to be appropriate. Responsiveness implies that the representative be at least alert and sensitive to the preferences and wishes of the represented. Burke was eminently conscious of the conflict that necessarily arises out of these alternative formulations of the problem of representation.

In general, we have continued to formulate the problem in Burkean terms, in spite of all the evidence to the contrary. The circumstances of modern government are such that neither responsibility nor responsiveness can be assured through the technique of representation. Despite all the oratory of the politicians, they cannot possibly be responsive, in the traditional sense, to individual constituents whose numbers are in the hundreds of thousands or millions, whose interests are enormously diverse, and whose understanding of the complexities of public policy is minimal. At the same time, and for very much the same reasons, it is increasingly impossible to hold the representative responsible for his decisions. As we observe the electoral process, still considered the main technique to enforce responsibility, it is evident that the electorate is chiefly guided by rather vague and often confused moods about the drift of public policy in general rather than by a clear perception as to whether the individual representative has acted responsibly or not within his discretionary capabilities.

It seems to me, therefore, that much of our research on representation, geared as it is to the problem as formulated by Burke, does not really come close to the problematic situation of modern government. And although responsiveness annd responsibility remain the norms in terms of which we would like to see government conducted, the difficulties involved in practicing these norms challenge us to discover just what it is that makes representative government tick. I cannot possibly present here a modern theory of representation, and doing so was not my assignment. However, I would at least like to suggest, in conclusion, the threshold for such a theory.

Whatever the scheme of representation, the core problem involved in representation is the relationship that exists between representative and represented. Burke and the research based on the Burkean formulation dealt primarily with the role of the representative. But the relationship between representative

54. I am indebted for this term to Kenneth Janda, "Democratic Theory and Legislative Behavior: A Study of Legislator-Constituency Relationships," unpublished Ph.D. thesis, Indiana University, Bloomington, Ind., 1961 pp. 169–179.

and represented is problematic because not only the roles but also the statuses of the counterplayers are likely to be ambiguous, so that the exchanges occurring between them are likely to be misperceived, creating all kinds of difficulties for the polity's other functional problems. Where there is little or no ambiguity in the relationship, it is not really very interesting from a theoretical point of view. For instance, if the representative is a dictator and the represented are subjects, and if this model really corresponded to an actual situation, our theoretical curiosity would hardly be mobilized. Similarly, if the "imperative mandate" guided the relationship between representative and represented, our research interest would not be aroused. The fact is, of course, that in reality—even in dictatorships or radical democracies—the representational relationship rarely corresponds to such models. On the contrary, it is likely to be ambiguous and, therefore, becomes theoretically interesting because of the tensions for the political system that arise out of the ambiguity. Dictators, for instance, are invariably concerned with their legitimacy; or assemblies based on mandate are concerned with their authority.

A viable theory of representation cannot ignore, therefore, the status of each party to the representational relationship. Status refers to the position of superordination, subordination, or equality of the actors; role refers to the expectations of how the incumbent of each status should behave in the relationship. Contemporary research is primarily concerned with representation as a system of role relationships and avoids the admittedly ticklish problem of representation as a status system. This, perhaps, is one of the reasons why the research literature on the new nations, where status is even more problematic than in the West, avoids dealing with representation. I mention this matter here only because we tend to take the status relationship between representative and represented in the modern democratic polity for granted, and because we take it for granted we fail to see it as a critical problem of representation. It seems to me that a future empirical theory of democratic representation should not foreclose the problematics of status in the representational relationship by simply identifying, *ex definitione,* the representative with governor, ruler, or elite, and the represented with governed, ruled, or mass. Who governs whom in the representational relationship is an empirical question that cannot and should not be answered by definition.

At the bottom of all theories of democratic representation is the behavioral assumption that responsibility and responsiveness are best assured by some similarity, achieved mechanically through appropriate governmental structures or empathically through relevant psychological processes, between the characteristics, attributes, attitudes, or goals of the representative and the represented. I think that this behavioral assumption is totally false. On the contrary, I believe we must proceed from the behavioral assumption of a built-in difference between representative and represented—built-in in the sense that representation always involves a difference in status between representative and represented. And if this is so, a viable theory of democratic representation must be based on this assumption of an inevitable status difference rather than on the democratically pleasing, but false assumption of some basic similarity between representative and represented.

Let me put this a bit more concretely. It is an error, I think, to assume that the "chosen"–whether elected or selected–are or can ever be "like" their choosers. The very fact of their having been elected or selected–having been "elevated" through some mechanism of choice from one position into another –makes the "chosen" fundamentally different from their choosers. Having been chosen, the representative has at least one attribute that differentiates him from the represented, no matter how similar, socially or psychologically, he may be in all other respects. Status differentiation, then, is a crucial property of any representational relationship. Whether he was born in the proverbial log cabin or in the mansion of the high and mighty, the fact of having been "chosen" sets the representative off as someone "special."

It is on the basis of this status relationship, then, that a viable empirical theory of democratic representation must build its axioms, theorems, and research hypotheses. These axioms, theorems, and hypotheses will have to deal with the tensions arising out of the status differentiation between representative and represented that representation entails and the role expectations that a democratic polity entertains with respect to its representative's conduct. I shall leave it at that. But one thing seems clear to me: Whatever solutions are found concerning the proper modes of conduct in the representational relationship, they are unlikely to be as simple as our conventional conceptions of the representative as either a delegate, bound by mandate to follow his constituency's instructions, or a trustee, committed to pursue the interests of his constituency, however he defines it, according to his own conscience or best judgment. Once status is introduced as a variable into the representational equation, the formula is bound to be more complex than we hitherto suspected.

We have come a long way in the last fifteen years since Oliver Garceau, in his seminal recommendations for research on the political process, enjoined us

> . . . to observe the flow of communication from constituency to legislator and the pattern of response to these multiple pressures, together with a broad gauge field study of the constituency itself, its economy, social stratification, group organization, media of communication and party organization, in order to record simultaneously the circumstances originating this flow of information. In this way the multiple roles of the representative may be illuminated and judgments made in regard to our contradictory and normatively colored hypotheses of representation.[55]

We have done all and more than what Garceau asked us to do. We have come to know what representation is not. This is the challenge to theory of

55. Oliver Garceau, "Research in the Political Process," *American Political Science Review*, vol. 45, pp. 78–79, March, 1951, reprinted in Heinz Eulau *et al.* (Eds.), *Political Behavior*, The Free Press of Glencoe, New York, 1956, p. 48.

these years of travail. Our conceptions of representation are obsolete. We have representative institutions, but like the Greeks we do not know what they are about. Continuing with normal science will not get us out of our theoretical quandary. I am not suggesting a moratorium on empirical research. But I do feel that we must break the spell of Burke, just as Aristotle's spell had to be broken by late medieval theory. This, I believe, is the lesson to be learned from the history of representational theory.

Part II

Accent on Method

Chapter 4

H. D. Lasswell's Developmental Analysis

The existence of a scientific discipline hinges on the simultaneous presence of two minimum requirements: first, it must have a body of theory or, at least, a conceptual schema within which empirical data can be so selected and organized that they will derive their meaning and significance from relevance to a theoretical structure; and, secondly, it must develop methods of inquiry which are consistent with the canons of scientific investigation.

Until recently, political science has been devoid of a consistent conceptual schema conducive to empirical inquiry. Only in the last few years has there been a gradual emergence of consensus among political scientists to the effect that the central problem of their discipline is not "the state" or "political power," but rather those processes of action through which, in David Easton's terms, values are authoritatively allocated in what may be conceived of as "political system." [1] Politics, then, means decision-making in situations involving, to use a Lasswellian expression, "the shaping and sharing of values," and policy formation appears as the focus of political investigation.

Concern with methodology has not been a hallmark of political science. One seeks in vain in the vast literature of politics for the kind and degree of methodological awareness easily found in the work of economists, sociologists, or psychologists. Again, there has been some change in recent years. Younger scholars, under the influence of the neighboring social sciences, have increasingly paid serious attention to methodological matters.[2] But their efforts have

Originally published in *Western Political Quarterly,* Vol. II (June, 1958), pp. 229–42. Reprinted by permission.

1. David Easton, *The Political System* (New York: Knopf, 1953).

2. See, for instance, Oliver Garceau, "Research in the Political Process," *American Political Science Review,* XLV (1951), 69–85; Samuel J. Eldersveld, "Theory and Method in Voting Behavior Research," *Journal of Politics,* XIII (1951), 70–87; Avery Leiserson,

remained random and noncumulative. The only persistent and consistent discussion of methodology can be found in the work of Harold D. Lasswell,[3] and there it is scattered through numerous books and articles of three decades.

THE NATURE OF DECISION: FACTS, VALUES, AND EXPECTATIONS

In specifying decision-making behavior as its proper focus of attention, political science deals with a most complex series of human actions. Lasswell is acutely aware of this complexity. Rational decision-making, he suggests in clarifying the concept, "depends on clear conception of goals, accurate calculation of probabilities, and adept application of knowledge of ways and means." [4] In other words, a decision is an act, or a series of acts, involving the simultaneous manipulation of facts, values, and above all, expectations. The decision-maker cannot do without expectations about the future—expectations relating, for instance, to the probability of a long or short war, rising or falling national income, the stability or instability of foreign governments. Being explicit about one's expectations necessitates their assessment in terms of values, goals, or objectives, on the one hand, and in terms of whatever factual knowledge may be available, on the other hand. While every decision "turns in part upon a picture of significant changes in the emerging future," it is the task of the decision-maker "to think creatively about how to alter, deter, or accelerate probable trends in order to shape the future closer to his desire." [5]

Each of these components of decision-making behavior is predicated on three different types of thought. Lasswell refers to these types as goal-thinking, trend-thinking, and scientific-thinking. Goal-thinking relates to the analysis and selection of values or objectives towards which decisions are directed. Trend-thinking involves the analysis of past tendencies and future probabilities. And scientific-thinking refers to the analysis of limiting conditions through the application of appropriate skills. In other words, each of the three aspects of decision-making behavior has "built in," so to speak, three quite different, and possibly even conflicting, modes of thought or universes of discourse.

It seems to me that at the base of the difficulties characteristic of political science as a scientific discipline lies the problem of clarifying the three forms

---

"Problems of Methodology in Political Research," *Political Science Quarterly,* LXVIII (1953), 558–84. All of these articles are reprinted in Heinz Eulau, Samuel J. Eldersveld and Morris Janowitz, *Political Behavior: A Reader in Theory and Research* (Glencoe: Free Press, 1956).

3. See David Easton, "Harold Lasswell: Policy Scientist for a Democratic Society," *Journal of Politics,* XII (1950), 450–77; George A. Lipsky, "The Theory of International Relations of Harold D. Lasswell," *Journal of Politics,* XVII (1955), 43–58.

4. Harold D. Lasswell, "Legal Education and Public Policy," in *The Analysis of Political Behavior* (New York: Oxford University Press, 1948), p. 30.

5. *Ibid.*, p. 32.

of symbolic behavior outlined by Lasswell, to keep them distinct in the analysis of decision-making activity, and yet to see their interrelations in the process of actual decision-making. The methodological problem is nothing less than to connect statements of value or preference, statements of fact, and statements of expectation. All three types of statement are essential in decision-making and in thinking about decision-making behavior.

It is not possible here to examine the problem of just how these patterns of thought are interrelated or can be interrelated, and whether Lasswell succeeds in doing so. As a matter of fact, it seems to me that Lasswell sidesteps the issue—perhaps because it cannot be resolved. The following is typical of the kind of statement he makes in this respect:

> For maximum rationality it is necessary to use each tool, with no excessive reliance upon one. Each tool is part of the total process by which the mind can seek and perhaps find correct orientation in the entire manifold of events. . . . The thinker can rely first upon one line of attack upon his problem, then another. By moving back and forth from one "lead in" to the next, he can increase the likelihood of arriving at policies that facilitate democracy.[6]

Lasswell's concern with the problems of expectation has, however, successfully culminated in the conception of "developmental analysis" and of "developmental constructs." And it is with this phase alone of Lasswell's formulations that I want to deal. For here, it seems to me, Lasswell's work is especially suggestive. That this should be the case is not surprising. Preoccupation with decision-making necessarily leads to developmental notions. For decision-making is predominantly future-oriented. It is, Lasswell points out, "forward-looking, formulating alternative courses of action extending into the future, and selecting among the alternatives by expectations of how things will turn out." [7] The accent is clearly on "expectations of how things will turn out." In fact, one may say that the other ingredients of decision-making, to be successful, are predicated on correct expectations of how things will turn out.

It follows, too, that a theory of the political process or, at least, a conceptual schema that has decision-making behavior as its empirical referent is predicated on the availability of constructs which are descriptive of the emerging future. Such constructs presumably make possible "the planned observation of the emerging future [which] is one of the tasks of science." [8] The name Lasswell gives such planned observation is "developmental analysis." A "developmental construct," the tool of developmental analysis, is a statement of expectations concerning the future expressed in certain core concepts. In

6. Harold D. Lasswell, *Power and Personality* (New York: Norton, 1948), pp. 203–4, 208.

7. Harold D. Lasswell and Abraham Kaplan, *Power and Society* (New Haven: Yale University Press, 1950), p. xvi.

8. Lasswell, "General Framework: Persons, Personality, Group, Culture," in *The Analysis of Political Behavior*, p. 219.

the study of international relations, for instance, Lasswell advances "inter-determination," "bipolarization," "militarization," or "totalitarianization," as developmental constructs.[9] Thinking in developmental terms is to be explicit about one's anticipations of the shape of things to come.

One may ask how developmental analysis differs from other procedures designed to deal with the problem of uncertainty as far as the future is concerned. Formal methods of decision-making rely on the rules of probability in making rational choices. A probability prediction means that one possibility in a given range of possibilities is more likely to occur than another—on the assumption that extraneous factors are randomly distributed so that an outcome is unlikely to occur by chance alone and is therefore to be attributed to non-chance events. Lasswell is not altogether happy with probability models as far as policy-making is concerned—for the reason that it is not easy for the decision-maker to enumerate in advance the range of possibilities that will be open to him.[10]

Lasswell therefore proposes developmental analysis as "another method of estimating the future. It does not throw away the available stock of trend information or of scientific knowledge." But, he continues,

> it does not attempt to limit the mind of the decision-maker (or advisor) to precisely ordered trend or scientific information. On the contrary, the accent is upon scrutinizing the whole context in which the precise data and relationships have been obtained and established. The result may be to direct attention to the unrepresentative character of some of the information at hand.[11]

Elsewhere Lasswell has described developmental analysis as an effort to achieve "productive insight into the structure of the whole manifold of events which includes the future as well as the past." [12] In order to approximate this objective developmental analysis requires configurative methods. It utilizes

> several interrelated and mutually facilitating patterns of thought, which we may abbreviate as the clarification of goal *values,* the assessment of *trends,* the review of scientific knowledge of conditioning *factors,* the *projection* of developmental constructs of the future, and the invention and estimating of policy *alternatives* designed to increase the probability of the realization of the goal values.[13]

9. Harold D. Lasswell, *The World Revolution of Our Time* (Stanford: Stanford University Press, 1951), pp. 29–39.

10. Harold D. Lasswell, "Current Studies of the Decision Process: Automation versus Creativity," *Western Political Quarterly,* VIII (1955), 392.

11. *Ibid.*, p. 392.

12. Lasswell, "The Garrison State and Specialists on Violence," in *The Analysis of Political Behavior,* p. 147.

13. Harold D. Lasswell, "Democratic Character," in *The Political Writings of Harold D. Lasswell* (Glencoe: Free Press, 1951), p. 473.

SOCIETY AS A CONTINUUM OF SOCIAL CHANGE

Developmental analysis proceeds from the assumption that societies are constantly changing. It follows, as a postulate, that "any given society, at any given period of time, can be conceived as an interval on some continuum of social change." [14] A developmental construct specifies the terminal phases of the continuum—"the 'from what' and 'toward what' of developmental sequences." [15] It represents a provisional pattern of the from what-toward what relationship, with one set of terms referring to selected features of the past, another to the future. Or, as Lasswell puts it elsewhere, "a developmental construct characterizes a possible sequence of events running from a selected cross-section of the past to a cross-section of the future." [16]

A developmental construct, these definitions suggest, is tentative and hypothetical. In view of its futuristic component it can be nothing else. For this reason Lasswell also refers to developmental constructs as "speculative models of the principal social changes of our epoch. . . . They specify the institutional pattern from which we are moving and the pattern toward which we are going." [17]

Although developmental analysis selects different points at which to observe, in cross-section, the characteristics of a given epoch, it is not concerned with "stages" of development, but with "patterns of succession of events." [18] In its full stress on time developmental analysis differs from those approaches which seek to subject the future to inner logical restriction by thinking in terms of stages. Developmental analysis makes use of the conception of stages, but it does not allow itself to be subordinated to this method. Rather than emphasizing stages as significant aspects of social change, developmental analysis "throws the time axis—the 'from what, toward what'—into relief." [19]

Developmental analysis must not be confused with trend analysis. Extrapolation is a necessary part of developmental analysis, but building expectations about the future on extrapolation alone is, in Lasswell's terms, an essentially "itemistic procedure." [20] Extrapolation, he suggests, is only "a prelude to the use of creative imagination." [21] For a trend "is not a cause of social change; it is a register of the relative strength of the variables that produce it." [22] Never-

14. Harold D. Lasswell, Daniel Lerner and Ithiel de Sola Pool, *The Comparative Study of Symbols* (Stanford: Stanford University Press, 1952), p. 27.

15. *Power and Society,* p. xv.

16. *Comparative Study of Symbols,* p. 7; *World Revolution,* p. 4.

17. Harold D. Lasswell, "The Policy Orientation," in Daniel Lerner and Harold D. Lasswell (eds.), *The Policy Sciences* (Stanford: Stanford University Press, 1951), p. 11.

18. *Power and Society,* p. xv.

19. *World Revolution,* p. 5.

20. "Garrison State," p. 147.

21. "Legal Education," pp. 32–33.

22. *Ibid.,* p. 32.

theless, because trend curves summarize many features of the past, they must be carefully considered in the formulation of developmental constructs. But a developmental construct, in contrast to a trend curve, "is frankly imaginative though disciplined by careful consideration of the past." [23] In other words, trends derive their significance from being imbedded in developmental constructions.

Developmental constructs, like most models in the social sciences, "are actuarial rather than purely theoretical." [24] Most of the constructs of social science are based on estimates of the parameters from the statistics derived from observation. It is inspection of the data that suggests the main variables and their relative weights in prediction. The process yields an empirical model which can then be tested against new data.

Finally, it requires emphasis that developmental constructs are not scientific propositions. This may be seen if they are compared with equilibrium models. Equilibrium analysis is concerned with the systematic interaction of variables which constitute a system in that they tend toward the maintenance of a particular pattern of relationships. Equilibrium analysis seeks to isolate such systems and investigate the conditions of their maintenance. Developmental analysis has an equilibrium component—"laws of change in addition to characterizations of the process of change." But, Lasswell warns, "confusion between these components may interfere with sound appraisal of both." [25] Contrasting examples are the Darwinian and Marxian conceptualizations of development. Darwin's developmental analysis of the evolutionary process can be clearly distinguished from statements of those conditions and mechanisms which are supposedly operative in the process of evolution. But Marxian "laws" of social change, so-called, are seldom explicitly distinguished from the description of a specific historical process—"data confirming the account of that process is often mistakenly construed as evidence for the supposed laws according to which the changes occur, and conversely." [26] Moreover, the Marxist construct of the emerging classless society involves a claim of inevitability which cannot be accepted, for "events in the future are not knowable with absolute certainty in advance: they are partly probable and partly chance." [27] Conceptions like the Marxist construct of the classless society, or the liberal notion of continued progress, are not developmental constructs, Lasswell points out, "since it was usually assumed by the forecaster that he was making a deduction about the future from a valid scientific law." [28]

23. "Garrison State," p. 147.
24. *Comparative Study of Symbols,* p. 64.
25. *Power and Society,* p. xv, note 9.
26. *Ibid.*, p. xv.
27. "Policy Orientation," p. 11.
28. *Comparative Study of Symbols,* pp. 7–8.

DEVELOPMENTAL CONSTRUCTS AND KNOWLEDGE

Developmental constructs are not to be considered predictions, even when confirmed by future events. Yet, developmental constructs are anticipatory in nature. But if they refer to the future, then, why are they not predictions? A prediction, Lasswell suggests, not only "refers to a category of events rather than a unique occurrence," but also "puts the stress upon an estimate of probability (or randomness)," and it "is made contingent upon the occurrence of conditions which, on the basis of past observations, have controlled the phenomenon being considered." [29]

If this is the meaning of prediction, it is evident why developmental constructs are not predictive statements. For, Lasswell maintains, "we cannot depend upon the future to conform to the ordinary postulates of probability theory, such as that a series of uniform events is in prospect (as in the tossing of the same penny to show 'heads' or 'tails')." It is necessary, therefore, "to appraise the degree to which the more familiar probability postulates will apply." [30] For instance, it might have been reasoned in 1900 that the non-European world was likely to increase its power in the next fifty years, and that this development would be accompanied by a tendency of European nations to unite in the face of the non-European threat. This prediction would have miscarried. For it would have been based on the erroneous inference that Europeans are sufficiently identified with each other and sufficiently alert to change to feel jointly threatened rather than individually advantaged by the growth of non-European states. In other words, had the prediction been based on an inference from conditions, it could be said that "a scientific proposition is being deductively applied." But in 1900, as Lasswell points out, "it would not have been clear what conditions were to be assumed to hold before the proposition might have been supposed to apply." [31]

The task of prediction, then, is more complicated than simply extrapolating a trend or applying relevant scientific laws and hypotheses. It is precisely the task of developmental constructions to help surmount the difficulties involved in anticipating the future. But are developmental constructs wholly arbitrary? The answer is "no." For it can be tested "whether the stated conditions actually hold–whether the trends in the past and present have been, in fact, toward" the state of affairs anticipated by the given construct.[32]

As speculative models, then, developmental constructs are of value in suggesting significant hypotheses that can be tested. In so far as these hypotheses derive their significance from their origin in a developmental framework, their utility in research is guaranteed, for "in research, as elsewhere, activity direct-

29. *Ibid.*, p. 6.
30. *World Revolution*, p. 5.
31. *Comparative Study of Symbols*, p. 7.
32. *Ibid.*, p. 66.

ed by an explicit and important purpose is bound to be more relevant, economical, and lucid than activity which is routinized."[33] Or, as Lasswell writes elsewhere, a developmental construct "can at any given moment be taken as the point of departure for gathering and appraising data about trends and conditions on a global scale."[34] This discussion clarifies the meaning of developmental constructs further. Rather than being a direct statement concerning the future, it appears that a developmental construct primarily serves as "a means of improving judgments of the future."[35] As a tool of analysis it may be particularly valuable in situations in which extrapolations of trends and extrapolations of conditions collide. For it may help "to estimate which factors are likely to resolve the conflict."[36]

But as developmental constructs are not statements of fact, and because they are statements of expectations, their hypothetical quality raises certain questions of knowledge. If the term "knowledge" is reserved to statements of fact, that is, statements concerning what is actually observed, Lasswell suggests that it "does not properly apply to statements about future events." But one may ask whether there are criteria of knowledge relevant to choosing among different developmental constructs, particularly if interpretations of trends seem to be conflicting. Lasswell takes the position that "under certain restrictions it is reasonable to extend our knowledge of the past into the future."[37] By "restrictions" Lasswell means the available knowledge of conditioning relationships that have held true in the past. For instance, available knowledge may suggest that population growth is affected by pessimistic expectations about world politics. On the further assumption, therefore, that in a prolonged crisis of insecurity the factor of pessimism will have to be taken into account, it seems reasonable to modify the population curve in accordance with such knowledge.

In other words, as projections of trends into the future developmental constructs do not have the status of knowledge. But they may be appraised in a scientific frame of reference. For any future trend will register and interact with the equilibrium of those factors that condition each other. A developmental construct such as Lasswell's famous concept of the "garrison state," he asserts, is "neither a dogmatic forecast, nor, methodologically, a simplistic extrapolation of past trends into the future. . . ."[38]

Of course, developmental constructs are less generalized than the concepts used in equilibrium analysis. For instance, if we speak of the world as moving from a multipolar towards a bipolar state system, the constructs employed here lack the generality of a concept like "political system." But, Lasswell

33. *Ibid.*, p. 75.
34. *Power and Personality,* p. 207.
35. *World Revolution,* p. 4.
36. *Comparative Study of Symbols,* p. 7.
37. *World Revolution,* pp. 3–4.
38. *Comparative Study of Symbols,* p. 66.

points out, "the lesser generality of the developmental standpoint gives it a correspondingly more direct purport for action." [39]

DEVELOPMENTAL ANALYSIS AND POLICY SCIENCE

We may ask how developmental constructs are elaborated and how their relevance is assessed. Lasswell's reply is crisp and, on the face of it, scandalizingly simple: "Select according to goal values." As grounds for his position Lasswell mentions "the characteristics of rational thought." For, he points out, "rational thinking takes the consequences of its own exercise into account." Moreover, he continues, "among the factors moulding the future are interpretations of the future." And since expectations of the future have an impact on action, notably policy decisions, "we proceed rationally when we operate with a clear conception of our possible effect upon the shape of things to come." [40] Since it is the particular function of policy to achieve goal values, a first step in the creation of developmental constructs is the clarification of the values presumably to be realized by decision-making.

This is not the place to discuss the particular values in terms of which Lasswell creates his developmental constructs. While he specifies "human dignity" as a central value, he maintains that "the relative significance of values for persons and groups is to be discovered by inquiry and not settled by definition." [41]

In pleading for the inclusion of values in the construction and selection of developmental constructs, Lasswell deviates from the positivistic bias of much of social science. "In some ways," he writes, "the thinking in the United States about human relations has been unnecessarily one-sided in the amount of emphasis put upon derivation [justification] and upon science. This has meant a relative de-emphasis upon the *clarifying* of goals, the projection of future developments, including especially the *invention* of future lines of policy." [42]

Lasswell has increasingly come to speak, therefore, of "policy science" as a convenient term which distinguishes positivistic social or political science from an approach where "knowledge is mustered for clear-cut objectives, and is fully related to the most likely contingencies to appear in the unfolding processes of history." [43] One of the distinctive functions of policy science is "to facilitate the modification of trends by making explicit what the trends in fact have been and whither they lead with respect to social goals." [44] In this task developmental analysis and projective thinking have a central role:

39. *Power and Society*, p. xv.
40. *World Revolution*, p. 5.
41. *Ibid.*, p. 6.
42. *Power and Personality*, p. 204.
43. *Ibid.*, p. 204.
44. *Comparative Study of Symbols*, p. 74.

> This mode of thinking is indispensable for responsible action, which invariably consists in selecting programs in the light of expectations about future contingencies. No one plans a military campaign, a party program or business enterprise without modifying his conceptions of policy in the light of estimates of what will happen under various circumstances.[45]

In other words, because developmental analysis implies a picture of the future—"a picture of the alternatives by which goals are likely to be affected by what we, or anyone else, will probably do"—it also "includes the evaluation of new *invented* ways of moving toward the goal, and embraces the products of creative imagination about the ways and means of policy." [46]

Developmental constructs, evidently, are the products of a mutual cross-fertilization of goal-thinking, trend-thinking, scientific-thinking, projective-thinking, and probability-thinking. The five types are clearly discernible in what is probably Lasswell's most complete and also recent description of what he means by a developmental construct:

> A "developmental construct" is a speculative model in which the present is characterized as a transition between a selected pattern of events located in the past and a pattern imputed to the future. No claim of scientific validity is made for the model, although the present state of knowledge is taken into account in setting up the hypothesis. The developmental construct is not a simple extrapolation of recent trends, but a critical weighing of future outcomes considered as an interacting whole. By highlighting some major possibilities we may be led to revise our previous estimates of the situation, and to guide research and policy activities with a view to taking advantage of emerging opportunities for analysis, insight, and perhaps control.[47]

In short, a given developmental construct, such as that of bipolarization, is nothing less than an "ideal-type" concept of a social process symbolized in its nomenclature. It represents an ideal-type exaggeration of the relationship between empirical and hypothetical (or past and future) situations.

But why did Lasswell seek to fashion developmental constructs as tools of analysis? Indeed, what purpose does it serve to seek to comprehend complex patterns of human behavior in terms of such relatively simple constructs as bipolarization or garrison state? Do these constructs not oversimplify complicated processes of action? Needless to say, perhaps, these constructs do oversimplify the problems implicit in their construction. But all scientific constructs oversimplify. And in simplifying problems they presumably aid in the understanding of reality.

45. *Power and Personality*, p. 204.

46. *Ibid.*, p. 203.

47. Harold D. Lasswell, "The World Revolutionary Situation," in Carl J. Friedrich (Ed.), *Totalitarianism* (Cambridge: Harvard University Press, 1954), p. 360.

DEVELOPMENTAL ANALYSIS AND THE SELF

One of the most recurring themes in Lasswell's writings is the idea that political analysis is "nothing less than correct orientation in the continuum which embraces the past, present, and future." [48] By such orientation Lasswell means self-orientation in the context of time. Such orientation, he writes, "can be expedited by the self-conscious consideration of details," and both developmental and equilibrium patterns of thinking may be helpful.[49] Otherwise "details will be incorrectly located." [50] Developmental constructs, then, are deliberately created "for the purpose of orienting ourselves in the succession of significant events, past and future." [51]

But developmental constructs serve not only the task of correct self-orientation. They also serve that of self-stimulation. The developmental standpoint, Lasswell writes, is designed to bring "the process of inquiry into closer accord with the needs of policy, when this standpoint is deliberately taken as a technique of self-stimulation in the envisioning of alternative futures." [52] As a technique of self-stimulation, developmental analysis will serve the policy-maker as well as the social scientist. Once he has clarified his goals, Lasswell suggests, the policy-maker "must orient himself correctly in contemporary trends and future probabilities. Concerned with specific features of the future as they are ever emerging from the past, he needs to be especially sensitive to time, and to forecast with reasonable accuracy passage from one configuration of events to the next." [53] Similarly, discussing the utility of the garrison state construct for the social scientist, Lasswell emphasizes that "it is to stimulate the individual specialist to clarify for himself his expectations about the future, as a guide to the timing of scientific work. Side by side with this 'construct' of a garrison state there may be other constructs; the rational person will assign exponents of probability to every alternative picture." [54]

Lasswell's concern with correct self-orientation of the policy-maker or the social scientist has its source in his long-term interest in the psychology of politics and the application of psychiatric techniques in the study of political behavior.[55] The central task of psycho-analysis or psychiatry is to help the disturbed patient to orient himself correctly vis-à-vis his social environment.

48. Harold D. Lasswell, *World Politics and Personal Insecurity* (1934), reprinted in *A Study of Power* (Glencoe: Free Press, 1950), p. 4.

49. *Ibid.*, p. 16.

50. *Ibid.*, p. 4.

51. Lasswell, "Skill Politics and the Skill Revolution," in *The Analysis of Political Behavior*, p. 136.

52. *Power and Society*, p. xvi, note 10.

53. "Legal Education," p. 32.

54. "The Garrison State," pp. 146–47.

55. See Lasswell, "Psychopathology and Politics" (1930), in *The Political Writings of Harold D. Lasswell*, pp. 1–282.

In aiding his patient, the therapist is essentially future-oriented. It is not accidental, therefore, that as Lasswell's interests turned from the pathology of political behavior to its creative possibilities, he was to make use of the notion of correct self-orientation. In a recent paper he explicitly states that the ways and thoughts of the therapist and those of the policy-maker are very much similar:

> The therapist is always oriented toward the future since he must guide his intervention in the life of the patient according to an estimate of contingent outcome. . . . It is well known to every policy maker who influences or estimates the future that systematic knowledge is always insufficient for his purposes. Hence he becomes accustomed to employ whatever information is at hand that will provide a basis of inference about the future. . . . Some of the available information is unsystematic, yet helps in imagining and assessing a "developmental construct" of the sequence of future events. . . . With a clearer image of order the pertinence of scientific knowledge can be better appraised. The therapist goes further. He may invent courses of action designed to increase the likelihood that desired outcomes will in fact occur.[56]

A second task of analysis is to create insight and understanding in the total context. Both patient and therapist are modifiable by exposure to information about the patient's conduct in past situations. "The great and creative insistence by Freud on the efficacy of insight," Lasswell continues,

> carries with it a challenging and dynamic implication for the future of man in society. It puts into a special category the data obtained by scientific procedure and the generalizations on hand at any given cross-section in time, when they relate to human interactions. . . But knowledge of interaction may produce insight and in this way modify future events in ways that result in changing the scientifically established relationships themselves. It is not that scientific laws are unverified; it is simply that they are always to be taken as historical summaries of event relations, and the assessment of the likelihood that they will obtain in the future is a special problem.[57]

The special problem to which Lasswell refers is, of course, the central problem of the analysis of decision-making and, for that matter, of all social action. It is more generally known as the problem of the "self-fulfilling" or "self-denying" prophecy. It is this problem which developmental analysis seeks to surmount by incorporating in the developmental constructs of the future those very predictions of the future which, by becoming known, may affect the future. In other words, developmental analysis makes a virtue of the fact—

56. Harold D. Lasswell, "Impact of Psychoanalytic Thinking on the Social Sciences," in Leonard D. White (Ed.), *The State of the Social Sciences* (Chicago: University of Chicago Press, 1956), p. 114.

57. *Ibid.*, pp. 114–15.

which gives social science in general a great deal of trouble—that a prediction, by becoming itself a factor in the definition of the situation, guarantees or prevents the emergence of anticipated results. But because once a prediction becomes known the individual can change his behavior in such a way as to confirm or deny the validity of a social law, Lasswell emphasizes that "an element of free choice is thereby introduced which reduces our reliance upon prediction." [58]

Lasswell touches here upon a theme that has occupied him for over twenty years. As he pointed out in *World Politics and Personal Insecurity,* published in 1934:

> Now it is impossible to abolish uncertainty by the refinement of retrospective observations, by the accumulation of historical detail, by the application of precision methods to elapsed events; the crucial test of adequate analysis is nothing less than the future verification of the insight into the nature of the master configuration against which details are construed. Each specific interpretation is subject to redefinition as the structural potentialities of the future become actualized in the past and present of participant observers. The analyst moves between the contemplation of detail and of configuration, knowing that the soundness of the result is an act of creative orientation rather than of automatic projection. The search for precision in the routines of the past must be constantly chastened and given relevance and direction by reference to the task of self-orientation which is the goal of analysis.[59]

Developmental constructs, then, are acts of the creative imagination. As imaginative estimates of the future they enable policy-makers or social scientists to orient themselves in the pursuit of their activities. For, as Lasswell puts it in another recent publication, "even in an automatizing world some top-level choices must be made. In that sense at least discretion is here to stay." [60]

CONCLUSION

It was not my purpose to criticize Lasswell's notion of developmental analysis, but rather to piece together in reasonably orderly fashion his widely dispersed references on the subject. Ultimately, of course, the test of a method's usefulness in scientific inquiry is its application in empirical research.

On the positive side, it seems to me, Lasswell has successfully come to grips with two problems: first, he has dealt with the implications for political science of the fact that political behavior is value-oriented or goal-seeking, by pointing out that values or goals are not independently existing ontological entities, but are shaped in and by the very processes of behavior of which they are a part; and, secondly, Lasswell has brought into sharp focus the fact that

58. *World Revolution,* p. 4.
59. *World Politics,* p. 17.
60. "Current Studies of the Decision Process," p. 399.

political behavior is oriented toward the future and anticipatory, as well as related to the past and retrospective.

On the negative side, it seems to me, Lasswell's undisciplined ways of presentation have tended to make his total work seem disjointed. His dependence on readily available examples or analogies rather than on meticulous research have made his work suggestive but hardly evidential.

This is quite clear in his discussion of the relationship between developmental and equilibrium models of analysis. His treatment of the problem is not satisfactory. The relationship between the two methods of analysis is probably the central methodological problem on which he touches, and Lasswell gives the impression of having solved it without actually having done so. He seems aware of the fact that equilibrium models in social science, in rejecting or avoiding the possibility of entropy, do not cope with the problem of change. Developmental analysis, on the other hand, though specifying initial and terminal states, does not say anything about the character of these states in the pattern of change. One should expect, therefore, an attempt at the integration of developmental and equilibrium models. Lasswell's discussion in this respect is suggestive, but there appears to be a failure of theoretical nerve at the most crucial point of his methodological work. Instead, Lasswell is satisfied with stating that both models may be strategically employed when needed. The question remains, it seems to me, whether it is possible to say, without taking account of developmental sequences as elaborated by developmental analysis, that any given system is in equilibrium or not. Talcott Parsons, in discussing the relationship between equilibrium theory and processes of change in the social system, sticks his neck out in asserting that equilibrium analysis is necessarily prior to an analysis of change: "The essential point is that for there to be a theory of change of pattern . . . there must be an initial and a terminal pattern to be used as points of reference." [61] These initial and terminal points are assumed to be in equilibrium, of course. If Lasswell were to carry developmental analysis to its logical conclusion, he would have to assert the opposite—that it is impossible to know whether the points are in fact in equilibrium, or entering or departing from an equilibrium condition, without a prior analysis of the developmental sequences which would reveal past changes of the system or suggest possible future changes. But this Lasswell does not do, and in not doing it he seems to miss a methodological opportunity.

61. Talcott Parsons, *The Social System* (Glencoe: Free Press, 1951), p. 483. Reprinted from *The Western Political Quarterly*, Vol. XI, No. 2, June, 1958.

Chapter 5

The Maddening Methods of Harold D. Lasswell: Some Philosophical Underpinnings

HDL's methods are maddening of course only to those who do not want to understand them in the first place. This is as true today as it was thirty years ago when I first encountered the opening chapter of *World Politics and Personal Insecurity,* entitled "The Configurative Analysis of the World Value Pyramids." I was a student then of something called "international relations," a rather dissonant potpourri of diplomatic history, international law, and current events. His book was quite a shocker—an encounter, as I said. I sought to get some guidance from my teachers, but they shrugged him off as an eccentric and inconsequential. (Needless to say, perhaps, this was at U.C., Berkeley, not U.C., Chicago.)

To this day I am not sure whether it was what Lasswell said or how he said it that offended the sensibilities of political scientists. In conversations about him I sensed a good deal of respect for an intellectual effort that was not understood, but there was always some comment that he was slightly mad, and that what he wrote should not be taken too seriously. There was, of course, the overt resistance to the psychoanalytic vocabulary and to his neologisms, but I felt that this was not the real source of scholarly discomfort. More relevant, I think, was the dim realization that Lasswell was a more consistent and threatening advocate than others of the "behavioral revolution" in political science that smoldered at the University of Chicago in the late twenties and thirties.

Originally published in *The Journal of Politics,* Vol. 30 (February, 1968), pp. 3–24. Reprinted by permission.

He seemed the most uncompromising in a movement which conventional political science could not easily co-opt precisely because its incorporation would mean the end of the ancestral order. But as long as the behavioral revolution was only a one-campus revolt, the prevailing attitude was one of condescension toward Lasswell and the happy few who appreciated him.

All this changed in the late forties and early fifties. The seeds planted at Chicago had spread across the prairies of academe and grown into plants. Chicagoans turned out to be the most innovative of American political scientists. Herbert Simon had published his attack on conventional public administration in 1947;[1] V. O. Key had breathed new life into American studies in 1949;[2] Gabriel Almond had tackled the ticklish relationship between public opinion and foreign policy in 1950;[3] David Truman had established contact with neglected pioneer Arthur Bentley's group notions in 1951;[4] and Lasswell himself, with the help of Abraham Kaplan, had codified much of his thinking in 1950.[5] The ferment of the early fifties brought with it a change in attitude among political scientists toward Lasswell. Criticism became more relevant and appropriate. No longer was it possible to shrug his work off as peripheral to or inconsequential for the main stream of political science.

There are few ideas in contemporary political science that cannot be found in Lasswell's early work. Too much emphasis, I think, is often put on his psychoanalytically influenced interest in political personality. It is, of course, an important part of his total work, but it is only one component. Many other current enthusiams can be found in his early writings. He anticipated the current interest in system theory, in functional analysis, in the study of roles, in the diagnosis of symbolic behavior, in the science of public policy, and in many methodological topics, such as content analysis, participant observation, objectifying interviews, or experimental designs. Careful reading of his work shows that these things are all there, even if, at times, the nomenclature is different. I am not saying this because I want to make Lasswell a fountainhead of contemporary virtues. A propagandist for his points of view he was and is, but a savior he was and is not. Yet, many political scientists could have saved themselves a lot of travail if they had paid more attention to his messages. As it was and still is, they had and have to discover for themselves and then rediscover Lasswell. This, perhaps, is all to the good. It made for the eclecticism of the behavioral movement and, through this eclecticism, for its pervasiveness. Moreover, not being chained to an entourage of disciples, though often aided by able collaborators, Lasswell was able to continue as the spear-

1. Herbert A. Simon, *Administrative Behavior* (New York: Macmillan, 1947).

2. V. O. Key, Jr., *Southern Politics in State and Nation* (New York: Knopf, 1949).

3. Gabriel A. Almond, *The American People and Foreign Policy* (Princeton: Princeton University Press, 1950).

4. David B. Truman, *The Governmental Process* (New York: Knopf, 1951).

5. Harold D. Lasswell and Abraham Kaplan, *Power and Society* (New Haven: Yale University Press, 1950).

head of the movement. Where he would go next was always something that fascinated even those who knew him best.

Although contemporary political science bears the mark of the Lasswellian influence, Lasswell remains an enigma to many of his professional colleagues. Despite all the words he has written, there seems to be something inscrutable about his ideas that proves elusive. It is my feeling that there has been a failure to understand and appreciate the philosophical underpinnings of his theoretical, methodological, and substantive writings. For this reason, going back to Lasswell's early work may prove to be especially fruitful. For, unlike most of us, he was profoundly concerned with philosophical matters that were the current coin of the realm in his formative years.

The major premises of his approach to politics are well known. His adaptation for the study of political behavior of Freudian propositions about the powerful working of unconscious and often irrational motivations is common knowledge. The sources of his interest in values and public policy, on the other hand, are less clearly understood. One must go back to the *Psychopathology's* chapter on "The Politics of Prevention" to appreciate Lasswell's strong and lasting commitment to political science as a therapeutic enterprise.[6] But these are only the more obvious premises that fertilized his work. Others are more difficult to identify, for Lasswell's simultaneously curt style and discursive form of presentation do not easily lend themselves to textual exegesis. Moreover, because Lasswell made this philosophical underpinnings his *working* assumptions, he evidently did not feel compelled to explicate them except only occasionally, and then in the barest manner. Much of the failure of political scientists to understand what Lasswell is all about has been due to their failure to concern themselves with the philosophical assumptions of his work beyond its most obvious aspects. And I think that even today few appreciate the philosophical complexity of his thought.

II

There are some overt clues that are suggestive. In what is still the most significant methodological essay he ever published, "General Framework: Person, Personality, Group, Culture," Lasswell explicitly states that his terminology "owes something to the Cambridge Logical School, and especially to A. N. Whitehead. The debt is evident in the use of such expressions as 'event' and 'event manifold.' "[7] What interests me is Lasswell's use of the notion of "manifold of events" and the methodological implications of this use for some of the problems of political science as a behavioral science.

6. Professor Easton is wrong, I think, in dating Lasswell's commitment to democratic values as of the beginning of the second World War. See David Easton, "Harold Lasswell; Policy Scientist for a Democratic Society," *Journal of Politics*, Vol. 12 (1950), pp. 450–77.

7. Harold D. Lasswell, "General Framework: Person, Personality, Group, Culture," in *The Analysis of Political Behavior* (New York: Oxford University Press, 1948), p. 195. This essay first appeared in *Psychiatry*, Vol. 2 (1939), pp. 533–61.

As far as I know, Lasswell never discussed Whitehead's cosmology in detail. Useful as he apparently found the British philosopher-scientist's concepts, he did not subscribe to his intricate metaphysics. One can only do violence to Whitehead's thought by seeking to summarize it in a few lines. I shall do so at the risk of enormous simplification, but I hope that this summary will pinpoint Lasswell's indebtedness to Whitehead.

For Whitehead the world is due to a "creative advance of nature"—a process that pervades the whole of nature and produces "events" that never existed before. The world is always incomplete, but it moves toward novelty and further completeness through the workings of something that Whitehead called the "Principle of Concretion." As nature is a purposive process moving toward achievement, indeterminate actualities are transmuted into determinate ones. Actualities and potentialities are the two poles of nature that the process of emergence seeks to link and unify.

It is easy to see why this philosophy of emergence should be attractive to Lasswell. Throughout his work he was preoccupied with actualities and potentialities. But, unlike Whitehead, the potentialities were for Lasswell not teleological properties inherent in nature. Rather, they resided in man as an action-oriented purposive animal.

In using the concept of "event manifold," Lasswell confronted a central and critical problem of political analysis that still confronts us today. "Implications," he wrote in the last chapter of *Psychopathology and Politics,* captioned "The State as a Manifold of Events,"

> have continually been drawn in the foregoing pages about the bearing of the intensive study of *individual* personalities upon the *meaning* of the political process as a *whole.*[8]

I am taking the liberty of italicizing three key words in the sentence because they bring out the problem. How can one make meaningful, empirically reliable statements about wholes—that is, human collectivities—on the basis of knowledge about individual behavior? For, Lasswell continues,

> since the psychopathological approach to the individual is the most elaborate procedure yet devised for the study of human personality, it would appear to raise in the most acute form the thorny problem of the relation between research on the individual and research upon society.[9]

Why did Lasswell see a problem where most other political scientists saw none? The simplest answer is that political scientists saw no problem because they had no problem. They largely ignored individual behavior and concerned

8. Harold D. Lasswell, *Psychopathology and Politics* (Chicago: University of Chicago Press, 1930), p. 240.

9. *Ibid.*

themselves only with large-scale institutions and processes. But once the strange fruit of individual behavior had been tasted, the joy was soured by the "thorny problem." Lasswell set out to cut the Gordian knot of the familiar dualism between individual and society:

It may be asserted at the outset that our thinking is vitiated unless we dispose of the fictitious cleavage which is sometimes supposed to separate the study of the "individual" from the study of "society." There is no cleavage; there is but a gradual gradation of reference points. Some events have their locus in but a single individual, and are unsuitable for comparative investigation. Some events are widely distributed among individuals, like breathing, but have no special importance for interpersonal relations.* Our starting-point as social scientists is the statement of a distinctive event which is widely spread among human beings who occupy a particular time-space manifold.[10]

But denying the dualism of individual and society by mere assertion is not enough. Lasswell's denial involved a search for philosophical underpinnings. To follow his search, one must appreciate the fact that philosophy, and notably the philosophy of science, is a search for answers to certain recurring questions. Often these questions are put in the form of dualism. Perhaps best known is the dualism of "soul" and "body" inherited from primitive thought and Greek philosophy, a dualism that still persists, if in diluted form, in the distinction between psychological processes and the processes of the nervous system. In biology the dualism between the "organic" and "inorganic," or in physics the old dualism between "force" and "matter," are other instances from the history of scientific thought. The dualism of individual and society is of the same generic class.

Often a dualism is of such long standing that it becomes part of the cultural heritage, hardened and resistant to resolution precisely because its reality is taken for granted. A dualism, then, assumes the existence of two kinds of entities or processes which are seen as interacting, but the interaction is yet to be explained. Once a dualism "exists," it serves as a powerful stimulus to thought, but it represents a "Problem" because the interaction of the two poles of the dualism proves elusive. Moreover, the problem involved may be a pseudo-problem if the dualism is merely a figment of the intellectual imagination. In that case, the problem has only subjective significance and is not a soluble scientific problem. If, on the other hand, the dualism has been empirically discovered, as for instance the dualism between consciousness and unconsciousness, the problem is genuinely scientific because, though two kinds of reality may be involved, their relationship is presumably connected in some causal manner that can be investigated and explained.

*I don't think Lasswell would give this example of a widely distributed individual event today. With air pollution a major physical problem of collective survival, the interpersonal importance of breathing is evident.

10. *Ibid.*

But a dualism may be the result of both intellectual imagination and empirical inquiry. In this case it is extremely difficult to disentangle its speculative and empirical components. As it is in the nature of a dualism to make for increasing polarization and hardening of the lines between its end terms, the dualism is likely to give rise to antagonistic "schools of thought" that stress the primacy of one pole over the other. Not surprisingly, the history of political and social theory has often been written as a history of conflict between the individual and society.

Decomposing the speculative and empirical components of a dualism has been the achievement of logical positivism in that it distinguished between *statements* that are subject to falsification and those that are not. The specific problem of resolving the question of whether the dualism of individual and society is an empirically viable phenomenon or a pseudo-phenomenon was facilitated by the scientific theory of "emergent evolution" or the philosophical idea of "emergence" that became prominent in the 1920's and had its most distinguished philosophical exponent in A. N. Whitehead. Though Lasswell never explicitly and directly discussed emergence as a philosophical assumption, his frequent use of the terms "event manifold" and "emergent" indicates his acceptance, if not of the doctrine of emergent evolution, at least of the philosophical notion of emergence. For instance:

> If the significant political changes of the past were signalized by revolutionary patterns which rose and spread until they were blocked or superseded by new revolutionary innovations, the future may well follow the same course of development. Hence our "present" would be transition between the latest and the impending world revolutionary emergent.[11]

Lasswell's consistent emphasis on the need for developmental analysis of political processes, from his earliest major writings to his latest, supports this contention.[12] Moreover, the topography of his "General Framework" is predicated on a necessary corollary of the assumption of emergence—the conception of discrete levels of organization and analysis.

Because in attacking the problem of the individual-society dualism Lasswell also called for a new form of thinking about social phenomena, it may be useful to review, if only superficially, earlier attempts to cope with the dualism problem in cognition. Materialism—from Thomas Hobbes to the behavioristic psychology of John Watson—eliminated the dualism of mind and matter by reducing everything to a single basic reality, material substance. For Hobbes thinking was but the motion of some unidentified substance in the head; for Watson thinking was simply "subvocal speech." On the other hand, idealists

11. Harold D. Lasswell, *World Politics and Personal Insecurity* (New York: McGraw-Hill, 1935), p. 4.

12. See Heinz Eulau, "H. D. Lasswell's Developmental Analysis," *Western Political Quarterly,* Vol. 11 (1958), pp. 229–42.

from Bishop Berkeley on sought to abolish the dualism of the physical and the psychical by reducing everything to some fundamental spiritual reality. As a result of these formulations, instead of being resolved, the dualism was aggravated by the arguments and counter-arguments of the materialist and idealist warriors. Escape from the materialist-idealist *cul-de-sac* could be had only if it was possible to occupy a new observational standpoint. Such a new standpoint was also sought by the theory of "emergent evolution."

This aspect of the new philosophy of emergent evolution must have been attractive to Lasswell in his attempt to overcome the dualism of logical and free-associational modes of thinking. The "new position" he came to occupy, and for which he became famous in his own right, was of course his insight that Freudian psychology could serve not only as an instrument of mental therapy, but also as a powerful instrument of thought. In chapter III of the *Psychopathology,* "A New Technique of Thinking," Lasswell attacked the prevailing emphasis on logic as the sole mode of thinking about politics:

> A totally different technique of thinking is needed to get on with the task of ridding the mind of the distorting results of unseen compulsions. . . . Logical thinking is but one of the special methods of using the mind, and cannot itself achieve an adequate inspection of reality because it is unable to achieve self-knowledge without the aid of other forms of thinking.[13]
>
> . . . The mind is a fit instrument of reality testing when both blades are sharpened—those of logic and free-fantasy.[14]

III

"Emergent evolution" was a philosophical doctrine that was bred by crossing Darwin and Hegel. It implied, therefore, two conceptions—one of *existential* emergence and one of *functional* emergence. These conceptions are by no means opposed to each other. Existential emergence means that in the course of development certain qualities, objects, or events come into existence which did not previously exist, and that knowledge about such novel types of existents—that is, emergents—cannot be derived from knowledge of what previously existed. Functional emergence means that the functioning of different types of existents is irreducible so that no single theory can explain the characteristic functions of all types. These functional discontinuities are due to the existence of "levels of organization," regardless of whether these levels are novel or were always present. If novelty is stressed, the notion of functional emergence, like that of existential emergence, holds that the emergents cannot be explained by propositions that could explain previously existing phenomena; if levels of organization are emphasized, the doctrine holds that explanations

13. *Psychopathology*, pp. 31–32.
14. *Ibid.*, p. 37.

of lower-level phenomena cannot be applied to the functioning of higher-level phenomena. But regardless of where the accent is put, the notion of emergence assumes an ultimate pluralism in the propositions that are needed to describe and explain the functioning of different types of phenomena. Both existential and functional emergence assert the non-deducibility of the phenomena with which they are concerned. In the case of existential emergence, this non-deducibility can be called "unpredictability." In the case of functional emergence, it can be called "irreducibility."

I don't know whether Lasswell, had he been explicit, would have preferred the notion of existential emergence or the idea of functional emergence. It does not matter in any case because for Lasswell ideas are never rigid formulas whose internal logic is to be respected, but rather suggestive starting points for innovative thinking. In other words, it is not clear whether he viewed emergence as descriptive of an actual process of progressive development in the cosmos whereby the present variety of physical, biological, and social phenomena emerged from a primitive stage characterized by undifferentiated and isolated elements, while the future contains unpredictable novelties; or whether he accepted emergence as a conception of an irreducible hierarchical organization of phenomena or processes and of the existence of properties at "higher" levels of organization that cannot be deduced or predicted from properties characteristic of "lower" levels.[15] My inclination is to believe that he toyed with both conceptions, but did not adopt either in its pristine purity.

The notion of emergence has aided in overcoming many old dualisms. Just as such "nothing but" ways of thinking–pluralism versus monism, determinism versus free will, or materialism versus idealism–could be abandoned by philosophy, so Lasswell could dispose of the logic versus free-fantasy dualism and suggest a compromise. In this new mode of thought it was unnecessary to make a choice between extreme views. What appears to be antithetical is reconciled on a new plane. It represents a position which Lasswell has repeated time and again in his various writings when he enjoins us to occupy as many observational standpoints as possible in the analysis of individual, social and cultural phenomena.

But what of the "thorny problem" of research on individual and society that bothered Lasswell? We can see now that it was linked in his mind to the problem of utilizing appropriate ways of thinking about the phenomena involved. In the *Psychopathology* he had probed deeply into the micro-behavior of individuals, but there remained the problem of how such knowledge could be made relevant to an explanation of the behavior of social entities. Lasswell did not assume, as is sometimes assumed by less sophisticated students of

15. For a discussion of the distinction between emergence as part of an evolutionary cosmogony and as a thesis about hierarchical organization, see Ernest Nagel, *The Structure of Science* (New York: Harcourt, Brace & World, 1961), pp. 366–80. Nagel argues that the evolutionary version of the emergence doctrine is not entailed by the conception of emergence as irreducible hierarchical organization.

individual behavior, that societal phenomena can be solely explained by means of a theory concerning their micro-structures. Insight into societal behavior at the level of the individual may be a necessary condition for explanation of social phenomena, but it is not a sufficient condition. Lasswell came to identify classes of events in society and culture which could not be explained by theoretical propositions about the behavior of individuals in terms of personality. His concern, clearly, was a theory of classes of events that were unexplained. Similar concerns were at the roots of the doctrine of emergence.

IV

Emergence, we have seen, refers to the process by which *new* effects (or processes or events) arise from the operation of antecedent causes (or processes or events). As a result of emergence new *wholes* (or configurations) appear which include or show *novel* properties that are qualitatively different from the sum of the properties of their constituent parts. This is not to say that aggregation of individual properties is not a legitimate operation to describe new wholes. For instance, if we speak of the median age of a group, the property "age" is stated in the form of a summation. But when we speak of a group's cohesion or integration, we do not refer to some arithmetic value, but to something new—an emergent property that cannot be reduced to some characteristic of its individual members. The new phenomenon is a "whole" that cannot be dissected or taken apart like an automobile and then reassembled. We can see better now, I think, what Lasswell meant when he characterized the state as a manifold of events. What he meant was that state behavior cannot be analyzed by disassembling it into parts. In this connection, we must not make too much of Lasswell's use of the term "state" which, at the time, was still the prevailing theoretical concept in political science for what we would call today "political system." A political system can be any political whole whose boundaries are identifiable—the historical "state" as much as a "legislature" or a "party" or a "party system." The important point to keep in mind is that in leading to a conception of the whole, the idea of emergence called attention to the manifold of events that constitutes the whole.

Lasswell articulated the relationship between thinking in terms of emergence and wholes, as follows:

> . . . Sound political analysis is nothing less than correct orientation in the continuum which embraces the past, present, and future. Unless the salient features of the all-inclusive whole are discerned, details will be incorrectly located. . . .[16]

> . . . The gradual creation of a sense of wholeness, and of assurance in the discovery of interdetail connections within the all-encompassing totality, also requires new methods of formal exposition.[17]

16. *World Politics*, p. 4.
17. *Ibid.*, p. 16.

Lasswell's words and concepts, as I suggested earlier, sounded strange to his contemporaries in political science (but not to behavioral scientists in other disciplines who recognized his stature earlier, I think, than political scientists did). It is by now abundantly clear that Lasswell was not playing with neologisms for effect, as some of his critics alleged. As his future research and the research of those whom he influenced has amply demonstrated, these were not empty or meaningless words. Yet, Lasswell felt compelled to defend himself when he wrote that "our function is not to introduce a new cult but to give a sounder general analysis than has been possible heretofore." [18] His approach to politics was not a cult because he knew, as his critics did not know, that in utilizing the ideas of emergence and wholeness he was anticipating the course of social scientific inquiry in the next few decades, with its emphasis on *gestalt* thinking, interdisciplinary frames of reference, development, functional categories and procedures and, last but not least, the distinction between levels of analysis.

To understand the levels of analysis "problem," we must keep in mind a distinction between resultant effects and emergent effects. Resultant effects—as in the parallelogram of forces model of mechanics—are analyzable in terms of the independent forces or vectors whose confluence can be expressed algebraically or geometrically. In the case of emergent effects, on the other hand, the component "events" interact to produce a new whole in such a way that they are no longer independent of each other. Emergent wholes like "personality," "society," or "culture" are units that are something more than the sum of the items, elements, or traits that constitute them individually. An emergent whole differs, for instance, from the collection and arrangement of pieces of furniture in a room where individual pieces may be introduced or removed without disturbing the basic arrangement. A configuration is an emergent whole, made up of parts, of course; but statements about its "shape" or "pattern" can neither be deduced from knowledge of the properties of its individual parts nor be reduced to the properties of the constituent parts.

If it is correct, then, that in the course of interaction of individual parts new properties appear or emerge that characterize the whole, the behavior of parts and whole must be analyzed on different levels—a macroscopic and a microscopic level. And as behavior on the macro level is new and emergent, it requires new descriptive concepts and possibly new empirical propositions that are independent of the concepts and propositions relevant to the micro level. Confusion of levels has disastrous consequences for scientific explanation and interpretation. If macro level explanations are simply extrapolated from observations of behavior on the micro level, as for instance in the older "national character" studies, the behavior of the whole is likely to be misunderstood and misinterpreted. On the other hand, if the behavior of the whole, say a society, is used to explain the behavior of its component individuals, violence is done

18. *Ibid.*, p. 17.

to the explanation of the constituent parts. For instance, if it is proper to characterize German society as "authoritarian," in the political-structural sense on the macro-level of analysis, it does not follow that the behavior of all Germans or even most Germans is "authoritarian" in some psychological sense on the micro-level of analysis.

The notion that human behavior in its totality can and must be analyzed from the perspective of different analytical levels does not imply empirical discontinuity from one level to the next. On the contrary, as the new macro-level configuration emerges out of the behavior of the constituent parts that is also observable on the old or micro level, empirical continuity is implicitly assumed. Macro level phenomena, then, are not mere epiphenomena or in any sense less "real" than micro-level phenomena. The behavior involved, whatever the level of analysis, is the same. A group, for instance, is a unit of interacting individuals whose behavior is the same, regardless of whether the analyst occupies a micro-level or macro-level standpoint of observation. But if the behavior of the individuals is observed from the group or macro-level perspective, it is possible to identify qualities which are new because they do not exist if any one constituent individual is observed as a single unit. For instance, no analytic operation whatever on the micro-level of the individual enables the analyst to describe a group's "cohesion" or "solidarity." (In other words, an individual's *feeling* of solidarity is a property of the individual, not of the group; "group solidarity" is an analytically distinct property of the whole group). It is for just this reason that the conception of levels of analysis and the notion of emergence are complementary. Emergence entails the appearance of new levels of organization; the recognition of new levels entails a developmental perspective and the need to distinguish between levels of analysis.

Although he did not directly deal with considerations of this kind, they are clearly implicit in Lasswell's "General Framework." The key concepts that constitute the framework—person, personality, group, culture—refer to different levels of behavioral organization and to different levels of analysis. The "thorny problem" that he had identified in "The State as Manifold of Events" —the relation between research on the individual and on society—was the problem of how one can move empirically from one level to another. The answers he gave are of different degrees of strength and scope. Minimally, there is the issue of frequency: many new patterns that emerge out of individual behavior at the group level of analysis can be analyzed as statistical regularities. Lasswell's early commitment to quantitative analysis did not stem from some compulsion to "count" for the sake of counting. Rather:

> What is known as the "quantitative method" provides a valuable discipline for the student of culture because it directs his attention toward the discovery of events which are often enough repeated to raise a strong presumption that a particular sequence does actually exist. These events must be so defined that similar events

can be identified by other workers. This necessitates an operational definition of the concept, which is to say, terms must be used to specify the position of the observer in relation to the configuration which it is proposed to describe.[19]

Lasswell was, above all, sensitive to the deficiency of macro-level explanations. He complained about "the impatience among students of culture with the slow-footed quantitative approach" which

is partly due to the diffuse, implicit nature of the experiences upon which is based the judgment about a subjective event outside one's self, and the resulting bias of the student of culture against exaggerating the significance of items in the pattern.[20]

This theme is continued in "General Framework" and linked to the theme of configurative analysis:

Although we have defined culture trait and personality trait, we have not defined culture or personality. These terms refer to wholes, and as wholes they include *not only* the traits of which they are composed, but the interrelationships of these traits (italics added).[21]

Lasswell's emphasis on quantification led, as is well known, to his pioneering studies of political elites and symbols whose objective it was to uncover the emergence and shape of the world configuration of values.[22] But his acceptance of the notion of emergent levels as real phenomena that are empirically continuous also implied the further analysis of the causal conditions under which the new phenomena occur and of the immanent conditions that maintain them independent of the component events. Hence his attention turned to the analysis of wholes as developmental as well as equilibriated phenomena. And just as he had encountered opposition to the "slow-footed" method of quantification, so he noted opposition to "systemic" analysis: "To some extent, there has been resistance against this mode of conceiving the task of students of personality and culture." [23] Not that this resistance was due to a lack of knowledge of the calculus of variations on the part of social scientists. Psychologists, for instance,

have operated with variables, but they have not undertaken to select a list in terms of which they could describe the fluctuations of the whole personality in relation to its environment. The essential point about the "systemic" pattern of analysis is not

19. *Psychopathology,* p. 251.

20. *Ibid.*

21. *Analysis of Political Behavior,* p. 202.

22. See Harold D. Lasswell, Nathan Leites and Associates, *Language of Politics* (New York: Stewart, 1949); and Harold D. Lasswell, *The World Revolution of Our Time* (Stanford: Stanford University Press, 1951).

23. *Analysis of Political Behavior,* p. 208.

that it uses variables, but that it chooses a list whose interrelations are studied with regard to fluctuations in the environment.[24]

In part, then, the problem was to develop specific categories and modes of observation for systematic analyses of such configurative wholes as personality or culture. Yet, Lasswell pointed out, "science seemed to be growing by the discovery and exploration of new standpoints, and by the discovery of inter-part relations independent of explicit modes of describing 'wholeness.' "[25] Organic metaphors and analogies were suspect on political grounds. Here Lasswell once more acknowledges the suggestiveness of the doctrine of emergence: "It is not one of the least distinctive achievements of Whitehead that he lifted the conception of the organic from the battle-scarred phraseology of preceding centuries." [26]

V

My task is not to review Lasswell's particular substantive formulations. The significant point is that, in "General Framework," he clearly distinguished between levels of organization and raised the issue of the relationship between levels. The methodological issue is, essentially, that of reduction and non-reduction, or of continuity and discontinuity of levels. I don't think that the issue has been in any way resolved. The reductionist standpoint envisages a unified science of human behavior in which all the sciences are integrated in terms of a micro-level theory of behavior. This theory, it is argued, is the only guarantee of scientific knowledge of any phenomenon, on whatever level it is observed, for it alone gives insight into the "inner workings," so to speak, of phenomena. But if levels are seen as discontinuous, analysis on each level presumes the generation of empirical propositions appropriate to that level and not applicable to another. Hence the continued autonomy of the three basic behavioral sciences, each primarily concerned with the study of human behavior from a particular level-relevant perspective–psychology with behavior at the level of the individual person, sociology with behavior at the level of the group (society), and anthropology with behavior at the level of culture. However, as behavior on different levels gives rise to independent empirical phenomena, the study of the interstices between levels makes for the development of intermediate disciplines, such as social psychology, political sociology, or culture-and-personality, that are in search of principles which can connect macro and micro characteristics of behavior as parts of total analysis.

If I understand it correctly, the "General Framework" was Lasswell's attempt to come to grips with the problem of inter-level relations. Just what motivated him to deal with the problem was, I suspect, his desire to avoid the

24. *Ibid.*, p. 210.
25. *Ibid.*, p. 211.
26. *Ibid.*

reductionist trap into which his preoccupation with individual psychological mechanisms might have led him, as indeed is the case with many psychologists interested in societal phenomena. He was too much of a social and political scientist not to sense that behavior at the level of group or culture followed laws that were quite independent of propositions about microscopic behavior items. Yet, though he resisted reduction, or perhaps because he resisted it, Lasswell recognized problems of interlevel or translevel relationships that must necessarily arise if reduction is not feasible. The amazing thing is, I think, that his essay is as suggestive today as it was almost thirty years ago, for we have made little progress in the solution of the problem. Although the essay was reprinted in a volume devoted to political behavior, its original appearance in *Psychiatry* as well as its unfamiliar vocabulary seem to have deterred political scientists from following up on his suggestions; and this despite the fact that political science occupies an eminently interstitial position between the three basic behavioral sciences. I am confident that in the future, as political scientists must come to terms with the interstitial position of their discipline and hence with the problem of emergent properties in the macro structures and processes that interest them, they will have to turn to the "General Framework" for guidance and enlightenment.

Careful reading of the essay will also show, I think, that Lasswell was concerned with another problem—namely, whether and how, after the emergence of higher-level phenomena, the behavior of the lower-level units might be changed so that the behavior of these units follows empirical laws not discoverable when there is no "intervention" of the emergent phenomenon. Lasswell must have had this problem in mind when he referred to an observer who

> uses the expression "trait of a specified culture" to refer to an act which is expected to appear and which does occur with at least a specified minimum frequency in a given field of observation. Our observer may use the word "conduct" to refer to an act which conforms to a culture trait and the word "behavior" to refer to an act which does not conform. We may note that an act which is behavior in one community may be conduct in another community, but it is also possible that an act may conform to no pattern anywhere.[27]

In another example a person's "career line" rather than culture is the emergent. The observer

> is also interested in placing the act in proper relationship to another dimension of this manifold of events. The act is one of the acts which compose the career line of the actor. Some of the acts are representative of the person under specified conditions.[28]

27. *Ibid.*, p. 200.
28. *Ibid.*

In other words, because the behavior of individuals takes place in what Lasswell called "the personality-culture manifold," the behavior should be expected to follow empirical laws which are not operative if it took place independent of such higher-level phenomena as personality or culture. In simpler language, we would say that the cultural content of behavior permeates otherwise non-patterned acts of behavior. Culture is, of course, the most pervasive emergent in human relations. But on the social level, too, the impact of an emergent phenomenon on its constituent parts can be observed. Recent studies of "structural effects" or "compositional effects" seek to measure the impact of emerging group properties on the behavior of the individuals who constitute the group.[29]

In Lasswell's terminology, the possibility of analyzing behavior on several and diverse levels brings into play what he has sometimes called the "contextual principle," sometimes the "principle of interdetermination." Precisely because certain phenomena, say "value systems" or the "language of politics," can have considerable internal independence so as to constitute distinct levels of organization in society or culture, they may be analyzed on their own level. But they may also be analyzed in terms of development from presumably prior or lower levels to present levels. The traditional procedure of nineteenth-century social science had been to search for single-factor explanations. In rejecting single-factor approaches, Lasswell did not simply substitute a multi-factor design. Let us listen carefully:

> This standpoint [i.e., of interdetermination, as against overdetermination] is sometimes formulated as a principle of "multiple causation." *But more is involved than multiple causes;* there are multiple effects as well, and more important, there are patterns of interaction in which it is impossible to distinguish between cause and effect (italics added).[30]

Or he may speak of a "principle of situational reference":

> Empirical significance requires that the propositions of social science, rather than affirming unqualifiedly universal invariances, state relations between variables assuming different magnitude *in different social contexts* (italics added).[31]

Contextual analysis and developmental analysis may go hand in hand. Individuals, Lasswell stated early in "Configurative Analysis,"

> may be investigated by special methods to disclose the genetic sequence of personality development and to place the individual career line in relation to the career

29. See Peter M. Blau, "Structural Effects," *American Sociological Review*, Vol. 25 (1960), pp. 178–93; James A. Davis, "Problem and Method: Compositional Effects and the Survival of Small Social Systems," in *Great Books and Small Groups* (New York: Free Press, 1961), pp. 1–25.

30. *Power and Society*, p. xvii.

31. *Ibid.*, p. xxi.

line of others living in the same epoch. *It is a question solely of expediency and not of principle* whether the total configuration is approached extensively or intensively by the individual observer, since either starting point draws the investigator toward the opposite (italics added).[32]

Here, once more, we encounter the impact of thinking in modern terms of emergence with an emphasis on avoiding the mistakes and simplifications of nineteenth-century evolutionary thought. Rather, whatever phenomena are to be observed on whatever level of analysis—political institutions, social structures, cultural patterns, norms of conduct, symbolic systems, and so on—they are to be observed in relation to the total context in a given stage of human development. Just as developmental analysis is predicated on the existence of stages in terms of which the developmental process can be ascertained, so contextual analysis is predicted on the existence of levels in terms of which behavior is given meaning. For meaning changes from level to level.

It is for all of these reasons that the behavioral scientist must at all times be cognizant of the level of analysis that defines for him the frame of reference or observational standpoint from which he generalizes about the phenomena at his focus of attention. What on one level, say that of culture, may appear as a generic value, also may, on the social level, appear as a norm of interpersonal conduct; and it may appear, at the level of personality, as a rationalization of hidden motives. The behavior that is observed is the same; what is different is the emergent level—be it culture, society, or personality—that defines the appropriate mode of analysis and guides interpretation. Confusion of levels is to be avoided. A system of values as a cultural phenomenon cannot be analyzed as a set of mechanisms of defense that may be appropriate on the level of personality. Similarly, a group's "interest" is something different from the private agendas that are rooted at the level of personality. Mobilizing all levels of analysis in behalf of understanding or explaining the manifold of events that constitutes any one particular phenomenon, like Lasswell's "state," is a strategy of research, not a confusion of levels of analysis.

VI

The conception of emergence has certain implications for the problem of scientific prediction in human affairs. If emergent properties at a higher level of organization cannot be deduced with logical rigor from statements about the constituent parts of a whole, prediction is not always possible. But this does not foreclose the making of anticipatory statements that are sometimes more than fortunate guesses. In other words, emergents as altogether novel phenomena are unpredictable only in a strictly logical sense. But this does not necessarily mean that an emergent phenomenon, *on its own level of analysis,* cannot

32. *World Politics,* p. 24.

be predicted from determinate conditions for the occurrence of all events, whatever the level. Put differently, emergence is not incompatible with assumptions about causation. It does not involve some acceptance of either indeterminism or teleological principle. An emergent property is not some ontological, immanent aspect of a phenomenon. Rather, one can assume that the probability of its being observed is relative to the state of theoretical knowledge at a given time. An emergent property may lose its emergent status as level-relevant theoretical propositions become available, so that the phenomenon can be explained or predicted on its own level. For instance, a group's cohesion may vary with varying threats to the group's survival. In other words, an emergent phenomenon is always contingent on the total configuration in which the emergent event occurs. The difficulty is that the configuration may be unique and for this reason make prediction hazardous. Note Lasswell's early statement of the predicament:

Now the whole world of "causation" is implicated in any event, and the whole number of significant mechanisms which may be discerned in the "mind at the moment" is infinite. So our hypothetical volume might conclude by accepting the assumption that some events can be brought about by more than chance frequency, subject to the reservation that experimental confirmation is never reliable as to the future. *The critical configurations may never "reappear."* We commonly say that the probability of an event's future repetition is greater if it has been oft repeated in the past. *But there is no means of demonstrating that the future contains analogous configurations to the elapsed.* The probability of the future repetition of an event is "no probability." If events appear to be predictable, this is so because our knowledge of contingencies is limited, and our sequences of similar configurations may still be treated as special instances of "no sequence." The stable is a special case of the unstable, to put the ultimate paradox (italics added).[33]

The problem of prediction, then, is not just a matter of logical deduction but of multi-level empirical investigation into the manifold of events that constitutes the context of emergence. Lasswell stated this problem in "Configurative Analysis" as follows:

Now it is impossible to abolish uncertainty by the refinement of retrospective observations, by the accumulation of historical detail, by the application of precision methods to elapsed events; the crucial test of adequate analysis is nothing less than the future verification of the insight into the nature of the master configuration against which details are constructed. Each specific interpretation is subject to redefinition as the structural potentialities of the future become actualized in the past and present of participant observers. The analyst moves between the contemplation of detail and of configuration, knowing that the soundness of the result is an act of creative orientation rather than of automatic projection. The search for precision in the routines of the past must be constantly chastened and given rele-

33. *Psychopathology,* p. 260.

vance and direction by reference to the task of self-orientation which is the goal of analysis.[34]

In this quotation Lasswell's indebtedness to A. N. Whitehead is most evident. The problem of relating actualities to potentialities is a problem of the creative orientation of the observer. The evidence is overwhelming that Lasswell was fascinated by this problem, and that it was this problem, perhaps more than any other, that led him to his deep interest in what, in later writings, he called the "problem-solving approach." In a magisterial statement addressed to his colleagues in *The Future of Political Science,* he stated his position succinctly:

Any problem-solving approach to human affairs poses five intellectual tasks, which we designate by five terms familiar to political scientists—goal, trend, conditions, projection, and alternative. The first question, relating to goal, raises the traditional problem of clarifying the legitimate aims of a body politic. After goals are provisionally clarified, the historical question arises. In the broadest context, the principal issue is whether the trend of events in America or throughout the world community has been toward or away from the realization of preferred events. The next question goes beyond the simple inventories of change and asks which factors condition one another and determine history. When trend and factor knowledge is at hand, it is possible to project the course of future developments on the preliminary assumption that we do not ourselves influence the future. Finally, what policy alternatives promise to bring all preferred goals to optimal fulfillment?[35]

In its cool simplicity this statement conceals the intellectual labor that has gone into it over a professional career of forty years. There are still those who accuse Lasswell of braggadocio and empty phrase-making. What they miss is Lasswell's profound and life-long concern with the most subtle philosophical underpinnings of a science of politics and social science in general. While he may have had an image of the complex problems involved early in his career and envisaged in a broad perspective possible solutions, his incessant quest led him to touch all bases rather than only one or two. In Lasswell's master orientation—I cannot think of a better expression to describe his intellectual style and stance—there is little room for exclusiveness. But there is ample room for a great variety of approaches to knowledge. Because, perhaps more than any other contemporary behavioral scientist, he disdained intellectual simplicity in a world of great practical complexity, he was not satisfied with occupying just one or two observational standpoints—a task which, for most of us, is a life-time effort. He could not afford to be a "pure" theoretician, and he could not afford being satisfied with doing empirical work alone; he could not afford being a student only of the past or the present, but always had to

34. *World Politics,* p. 17.

35. Harold D. Lasswell, *The Future of Political Science* (New York: Atherton, 1963) pp. 1–2.

occupy himself with the future; he could not limit himself merely to the analysis of values, but had to recommend their application in the crucible of public policy-making; he could not sacrifice causal for functional analysis, just as he could not surrender an interest in details to an interest in wholes. The intellectual edifice he erected resembles a Gothic cathedral with its turrets and spires and arches and niches which, on close inspection, may evince flaws of one kind or another. But, like a Gothic cathedral, the edifice is built on firm foundations, and it is wondrous to behold in its total complexity and splendor.

Chapter 6

Comparative Political Analysis

Not as a matter of scientific logic but as a quirk of history—that bottomless pit for anything that cannot be explained otherwise—discourse on "comparative method" in political science was, quite properly, appropriated by the students of "comparative government" who in doing so, inadvertently, expropriated the rest of the discipline. This is not to say that, at least until recently, "comparative government" reached great heights of methodological sophistication by its monopoly of comparative analysis. In fact, comparative analysis, truly to deserve its name, might have fared better, and done so earlier, if all students of government—the domestic brand as well as the foreign—had been concerned with a method which comes closer to the laboratory experiment than any other we have in controlling a few variables. For if "control" is the *sine qua non* of all scientific procedure, it would certainly seem easier to obtain in a single culture, even one as heterogeneous as that of the United States, than across cultures. There are enough units in the American political system to keep a whole generation of scholars busier than bees in perfecting comparative analysis. Instead, "case analysis" has been the dominant mode of inquiry in American government and politics (and, I daresay, in the foreign field too).

But this is not to be an exercise in exorcism. There has been enough of it. If methodological discourse remains nothing but a promising prospectus unrelated to the problems of empirical research strategy and tactics, it is likely to be a rather sterile, scholastic exercise. Therefore, I shall use some of the experiences of the State Legislative Research Project (SLRP)—a strictly domestic operation—as a point of departure for some methodological observations on comparative analysis.[1]

Reprinted from *Midwest Journal of Political Science,* Vol. 6 (November, 1962), pp. 397–407 by permission of the Wayne State University Press.

1. SLRP was a comparative study of the legislative systems of California, New Jersey,

When SLRP began, in 1955, there was much discontent with comparative work which seemed to consist primarily of descriptive statements about formal institutions, made seriatim or in juxtaposition, with little generalized comparison of processes or functions.[2] In the arena where comparative method seemed most appropriate—the cross-national study of political institutions or even whole political systems—so many variables were involved that the specification, not to say explanation, of particular factors making for differences was operationally difficult, if not impossible. Research in American state politics seemed to be a particularly opportune way of advancing comparative analysis because the number of uncontrolled variables would be substantially reduced: a considerable degree of institutional similarity and behavioral uniformity could be assumed to exist from state to state. Descriptive emphasis on a variety of discrete and almost unique categories of analysis was to give way to conceptualization of political variables in terms of a smaller number of more inclusive categories—the objective being, hopefully, to arrive at statements of some generality beyond the immediate situation. Increased sophistication in the use of comparative analysis seemed to be a methodological requisite for the development of reasonably reliable generalizations about political institutions and political behavior.

From its very beginnings, then, SLRP was self-consciously concerned with the critical problem of comparability. It is unnecessary, in this connection, to report why it was decided to study legislatures, and why the four states of California, New Jersey, Ohio, and Tennessee were chosen as research sites. These decisions had, of course, consequences for some of the tactical aspects and substantive findings of the project, but they are not particularly relevant to the generic problems of comparative method. The choice of other institutions or research sites would have involved pretty much the same methodological dilemmas as far as comparative analysis is concerned.[3]

SLRP was not only a comparative but also a collaborative enterprise. Comparative analysis and collaborative research must not be confused. It is undoubtedly possible to conduct comparative research without the collaboration of others, but SLRP's experience was that comparative analysis, especially if it involves comparison of several units, is greatly facilitated by the collaboration of several researchers, not the least important reason being efficiency and economy in data collection. Collaboration, of course, creates its own difficulties. There is no need for dealing with these difficulties here, but as the

Ohio and Tennessee, conducted between 1955 and 1960 under the auspices of the Committee on Political Behavior of the Social Science Research Council. For a full report of the project, see John C. Wahlke, Heinz Eulau, William Buchanan and LeRoy C. Ferguson, *The Legislative System: Explorations in Legislative Behavior* (New York: Wiley, 1962).

2. It should be recalled that the Committee on Comparative Politics of the Social Science Research Council, responsible for much of the innovative thinking on comparative analysis in recent years, only got underway in 1954, and that SLRP did not have the benefit of its deliberations.

3. These matters are fully discussed in *The Legislative System*, Chapters 2 and 18.

SLRP experiment in "leaderless" collaboration has shown, the advantages far outweigh the difficulties if the latter are intelligently handled and solved.[4] Certainly, given limited resources, SLRP would have been impossible as a comparative study if it had not also been a collaborative operation. It is, therefore, only for the sake of analytical simplicity that, in this paper, I shall abstract from the total SLRP experience some of those features which are most directly pertinent to discussion of the problems of comparative method.

If the methodological objective of reasonably controlled comparison was to be achieved, certain strategic decisions had to be made in the very earliest stage of the research process. These decisions involved theoretical, technical and analytical considerations—the latter requiring a good deal of prognostication. In presenting them here in more or less orderly fashion I do not want to give the impression that they were actually always made in the order prescribed by all the good books on how to conduct social-scientific research. Of course, these strategic decisions were modified or expanded from time to time as experiences in later stages of the project required. But, in general, the early strategic decisions had a determinative influence on SLRP planning, field work, and analysis.

THEORETICAL DECISIONS

To achieve its comparative objectives, the research had to be conducted in a theoretical framework flexible enough not to do violence to variations in the empirical data to be collected, yet also sufficiently abstract to accommodate these variations in a schema of analytical categories which would permit comparison in terms of similarities and differences. Such a theoretical framework is a logical prerequisite of comparative analysis because it alone can provide that *tertium comparationis* without which comparison is impossible. Of course, theory has other functions in research as well, but in comparative analysis it is especially critical because it provides a standard which itself is not empirical. In particular, the conceptual schema had to be such that formal structural differences would not obscure functional similarities.

These considerations led to a number of theoretical questions and decisions. First, what are the functions of a legislature? Clearly, answering this question in the textbook manner—"to make the laws" and so on—would not have been very useful for comparative purposes, for apart from being tautological, this definition would not have told us just what to look for that might be profitably compared. Instead, we postulated that, whatever other functions there might be, legislatures function to crystallize, clarify, and resolve political conflicts. This theoretical specification, in turn, oriented us towards collecting certain

4. For a succinct statement of the collaborative features of SLRP, see John C. Wahlke, Heinz Eulau, William Buchanan, and LeRoy C. Ferguson, "The Annals of Research: A Case of Collaboration in Comparative Study of Legislative Behavior," *The American Behavioral Scientist,* 4 (May, 1961), 3–9.

data rather than others, and in due time guided us in the elaboration of suitable analytical categories for coding the data.

Second, we asked: who are the actors who participate in this functional process? To say that "the legislature" does was theoretically not sufficient. In addition to the legislature as an institution, other "collectivities" are involved in the legislative process conceived as conflict crystallization and resolution: pressure groups, parties, constituencies, and administrative agencies. "Legislature" or "party" are names for concrete structures, but they are not very useful analytic concepts with which to proceed in theorizing. We therefore postulated "legislative system" as the theoretical macrounit of analysis in which the legislature, along with parties, pressure groups, and so on, can be conceived as subsystems. The concepts of system and subsystem raise, of course, the question of how different subsystems are coupled or linked to constitute a system. Had we left the formulation at this point, we would have been required to study not only the legislature, but also the other subsystem components of the legislative system. This was beyond the resources of the project.

Third, we asked whether it made sense to say that an institution "acts." We agreed—readily enough because of our behavioral bias—that only human beings act, and that speaking of the legislature or a pressure group as "actor" is shorthand language perhaps permissible for theoretical but not useful for empirical research purposes. It was necessary, therefore, to distinguish between empirical and theoretical units of analysis not only on the macro- but also on the micro-level. Our empirical unit, then, was the individual legislator (and it could have been, had we expanded the research, the individual lobbyist or constituent, and so on). But what should be our basic theoretical unit of analysis? We needed a unit which (a) would be sufficiently precise to make it operational, and (b) would help in solving the ticklish problem of linking the subsystems of the legislative system in terms of the behavior of the individual actors whom we had chosen as our empirical units, i.e., the legislators incumbent in four legislatures.

Fourth, we chose therefore as our theoretical and basic units of analysis the roles which legislators take in the pursuit of their legislative tasks. This is not the place to elaborate or defend the theoretical usefulness of the role concept, or to discuss how we operationalized it for the purposes of empirical research.[5] Suffice it to say that role commended itself as the basic theoretical unit because it calls attention to the interrelatedness and interdependence of human actors. Legislators take the roles they do, we postulated, in response to the expectations of all the actors in the legislative system, including themselves as well as those significant others with whom they come into contact by virtue of their participation in different legislative subsystems. Their roles, then, orient legislators to what, in shorthand, we call parties, constituencies, pressure groups, and so on, as subsystems (or foci of legislative input and output, as we

5. For a full discussion of the role concept as employed in SLRP and the project's entire conceptual schema, see *The Legislative System,* Chapter 1.

came to think of them). We hoped that by identifying legislators' roles we could at least come up with some reasonably valid and genuinely comparable inferences about the functioning of the legislative system in four political environments.

This is a highly abbreviated statement of SLRP's analytical schema. To summarize even more, our basic model postulated a legislative system of which the concrete structure called "legislature" is a subsystem. This subsystem was conceived as a "role system" which means that, in empirical reality, we expected the roles taken by legislators to vary systematically from one concrete legislature to the next, depending on the whole network of roles in any one system. Finally, we postulated that each system as a whole would vary structurally and functionally in terms of the types and degrees of conflict characteristic of the politics in each state.

These theoretical decisions and anticipations were of critical importance in SLRP's empirical work. Without raising the empirical findings in the four states to this high level of abstraction, it would have been impossible to make meaningful comparative analysis and interpret the findings comparatively. By subsuming a great amount of empirical material under relatively few analytical categories, we could identify theoretically significant similarities and differences in the structure and process of eight legislative chambers.[6] The desirability of conducting comparative research within a unified theoretical framework has long been emphasized in methodological discussions of comparative politics, but, as far as I know, no empirical research following this prescription on SLRP's scale has ever been conducted.[7] In this respect, then, the SLRP represents a breakthrough at the frontiers of comparative analysis.

TECHNICAL DECISIONS

Choice of the individual legislator as the empirical unit and of his roles as the theoretic units of analysis entailed a number of technical decisions of immediate relevance in a discussion of comparative method. Although without a theoretical schema it would have been impossible to specify just what *variables* are crucial to what problems or how the variables are to be related to each other, SLRP could have proceeded without agreement on just what *particular data* were to be collected as evidence and how to collect them. Therefore, the

6. The results are report in *The Legislative System,* Part V.

7. For instance, in the very excellent volume edited by Gabriel A. Almond and James S. Coleman, *The Politics of the Developing Areas* (Princeton: Princeton University Press, 1960), the particular country analyses seem to be quite independent of the theoretical schema presented in the introductory chapter as well as of each other. Clearly, a distinction must be made between conducting empirical research in different sites within a unified theoretical framework which is uniformly operationalized in all phases of the research process, and *post-facto* interpretation of separately conducted research, no matter how much that research may have been "influenced" by prior theoretical understandings among individual researchers. The latter is an operation quite legitimate in its own right, of course.

choice of "role" as the central conceptual tool of analysis was critical: if genuine comparison of the four legislatures as role systems was to come off, construction of the roles required, at the very minimum, the collection of exactly the same empirical data in the four states. This requirement, in turn, entailed the application of uniform techniques of data collection and, once the data were in, of uniform techniques in data processing.

In the early stages of the project, when these strategic technical considerations came up, the members of the SLRP "team" were by no means committed to collaboration in all the phases of the research. For instance, the team could have been broken up after the theoretical work had been finished, or after it had been agreed to collect the same data by uniform techniques. In retrospect, it seems, it was the gradual continuation of collaboration which oriented the project more and more towards comparison, rather than the requirements of comparative analysis which called for increased collaboration. While comparative analysis—whatever it might have meant to individual SLRP members at the time, and I am sure it meant different things—was seen as a desirable goal, the more direct advantages of collaboration probably kept the team together. These advantages included mutual discussion of technical matters to which particular members of the team brought their particular skills. Only gradually did the notion of four "single-state studies" or even four individual "cross-state functional studies" yield to the conception of a joint comprehensive comparative analysis. Indeed, an early outside criticism of the study design expressed doubt about the possibility of achieving this objective in stating that "it may be necessary in this kind of research to sacrifice something of formal comparability in order to attain the desired degree of substantive understanding and insight."

The choice of the individual legislator as the empirical unit of the research and the need to come up with the same empirical data suggested the interview as the main data-gathering technique and the administration of the same interview schedule to the populations which SLRP was to study. Again, this is not the place to review how the schedule was constructed, pretested, and administered.[8] However, it seems important to point out that comparative considerations made for certain technical decisions which are probably less salient in a single-population study. For instance, the questions had to be so worded that they would be specifically meaningful to, i.e., answerable by, the respondents in terms of their own experiences in a given state and that state's political culture. Yet they also had to be so worded that they would be sufficiently general to be equally applicable in all four states to make comparison possible. As SLRP discovered by hindsight, not all questions "worked" equally well in all four states—and this despite their having been pretested in other states as well. As a result, some data had to be sacrificed in the final comparative analysis which might have been quite useful in a single-state analysis. On the

8. For detail, see *The Legislative System*, Chapter 2 and 18, and Appendix Six.

other hand, the "failure" of some questions to "work" allowed identification of those "deviant cases" or "deviant situations" whose very departure from otherwise regular patterns can serve the purpose of testing a hypothesis. In this respect, then, comparative method proves to be very useful: it dispels some of the mystique of the unique which, in the comparative perspective, turns out to be unique not because of an "intrinsic" or "essential" characteristic, but because it deviates from what one might theoretically expect and from what, in fact, one finds empirically in most situations.

If the administration of a uniform interview schedule assured identical data which were necessary if comparative analysis was to be attained, the processing of the data—i.e., the translation of the statements made by the legislators into categories of variables which would permit analytic manipulation—could not be left to whimsy. The data, many of them stemming from open-ended questions allowing for a wide variety of response patterns, had to be coded along theoretical lines designed to make for valid comparisons. Here the earlier theoretical decisions paid off well. As the data reported the verbal responses of individuals which were to be handled quantitatively, yet statements of a comparative character were to be made about theoretic units larger than "role" alone, problems of aggregation of individual data in comparative analysis had to be dealt with in the coding stage. In other words, coding had to follow theoretical lines which would, in the analysis, facilitate making statements not only about individual legislators and their roles, but about larger units of action, such as party delegations, leadership groups or legislative chambers. In fact, in some of the SLRP analyses comparisons are made not only between four legislatures, but at times also between eight chambers, sixteen party delegations, and other categorical subgroups.

Although SLRP is reasonably confident that errors in the collection and processing of the data were reduced to a point where statistical measuring of the errors would not invalidate the data, there remain technical problems which, in comparative analysis more than in a case study, require solutions. For instance, the tactics of interviewing employed in the four states varied a good deal. The time, place, and order of the interviews are variables in the research situation which we did not control (largely because we did not foresee their possible relevance in affecting comparative analysis). However, possible error springing from this source was sufficiently overcome by the use of the uniform interview schedule so that SLRP had at its disposal data enough alike to warrant their being considered both reliable and valid from a comparative point of view.[9]

ANALYTICAL DECISIONS

Just as the choice of the individual actor as the empirical unit of inquiry commits the investigator to a search for individual data, the collection of indi-

9. These problems are discussed in *The Legislative System,* Chapter 18.

vidual data has consequences of a determinable sort for the kind of analysis that is made. In general, most of the statements made in *The Legislative System* are about legislators' roles and other behavioral items—perceptions, attitudes, expectations, and so on. These statements are comparative in saying something about similarities and differences in individual legislators' attributes from one state to the next.

However, as political scientists we are interested not only in similarities or differences in individual behavior, but also in the consequences of political behavior for the functioning of larger groups and institutions. I believe that comparative analysis of political institutions and processes will not get off the ground until it uses systematic data. These, as in the case of SLRP, may be individual data, but they may also be aggregated data.[10] Of course, aggregated data may conceal a good deal of variance in political phenomena which the use of individual data reveals. Statements about collectivities or institutions, especially if they are of a comparative sort, are necessarily molar in character. Political analysis and interpretation cannot avoid this type of statement, but necessity should not be made into a virtue. The necessity stems from the fact that institutional analysis on the empirical level of the individual is very expensive. For this reason comparative institutional analysis usually relies on well-placed informants, if such informants are available and accessible, and on public documents. These sources require molar language which conceals a great deal of variance, and the statements made in this language are not easily controlled. As a result, comparative analysis as practiced in political science has often compared what cannot or should not be compared. This is not said as criticism, but only in order to make explicitly articulate a dilemma involved in macro-analysis of political institutions or systems.

On the other hand, individual data have the advantage that they can not only be treated individually, but can also be aggregated, so that units other than the individual can be examined. Such aggregation, involving the use of proportions, ratios, averages, correlations and so on, presents its own difficulties. These need not be discussed here. But aggregation was used to good advantage in some SLRP analyses in cases where the individual data were analytically difficult to handle in any other way. Individual analysis would have been preferred, but in some cases the data did not lend themselves to this treatment. This was sometimes partly due to insufficient theoretical preparation at the time when the interview schedule was designed. For instance, the data on "party roles" were such that they could not be handled in the analysis as individual data. But they could be aggregated, and the aggregated analyses of party delegations proved very suggestive and convincing for comparative purposes. Moreover, this procedure shows how great the variance may be which aggregate statistics or broad institutional language are likely to conceal.

Another dilemma in the use of individual data for comparative institutional

10. This has been imaginatively shown by Seymour M. Lipset, *Political Man* (Garden City, N. Y.: Doubleday, 1960), Chapter II.

analysis stems from their numerical paucity. Though in SLRP we did not face the conventional sampling problems because in each state almost the population universe was interviewed,[11] the fact that most state legislative chambers are very small made it difficult to do more than bivariate analyses (for instance, the New Jersey Senate has only 21 members). Multivariate analysis —permitting control of several variables—requires relatively large numbers to fill the cells of a complex analytical table. I would argue, of course, that despite this limitation bivariate analysis of individual data can tell us more in comparative institutional study than the even less refined molar type of analysis. But the dilemma must be recognized. To conduct meaningful analysis, it was at times necessary to combine data across the states, washing out differences between the states and giving undue emphasis to the data from the numerically larger legislative chambers—that is, to give up comparison of institutional units in order to make comparisons between certain categories of individual legislators. This "out-of-context" analysis is legitimate (most sample surveys of the electorate do just that), and it is useful because it can serve as a way of generating hypotheses which might then be tested within particular institutional contexts. But this is not to deny that the treatment of individual data in their "natural" institutional setting is, from the political scientist's point of view, by far preferable to the non-institutional, quasi-sampling approach.[12] The latter is strictly a matter of making the best out of numerically limited data.

On the other hand, individual data, even if numerically small, can fruitfully serve the purpose of comparative analysis if the data are *institutionally* controllable. In the case of SLRP, we had the opportunity to use the two chambers *within* each state as the *institutionally* critical units in the final analysis of the legislature as a subsystem of interrelated roles. In other words, hypotheses concerning how legislators' roles should be characteristically related to each other in the four state systems, and how the relationships should differ from one system to the other, could be tested in two institutional settings—the upper and the lower houses. Comparison of this sort within a political subsystem can be thought of, and really serves as a kind of, internal replication of a very persuasive character. Of course, some difference in the hypothesized pattern from one house to the other within a state was to be expected, due to the existence of institutional variables over which we had no control—for

11. All New Jersey legislators were interviewed; 94 per cent, respectively, in California and Ohio; and 91 per cent in Tennessee. By "conventional" sampling problems I mean, of course, problems of selecting a sample from a larger universe whose parameters are known. In SLRP, we faced our own sampling problems—some stemming from non-responses to particular questions, some from uncertainty concerning the universe referred to by data collected in only four states at a particular point in time, and so on. These matters are discussed in *The Legislative System,* Chapter 18.

12. I am speaking of "quasi-sampling" because though, in SLRP's case, 474 legislators from four states undoubtedly were a sample, it is difficult to say of just what universe this sample is representative.

instance, the larger size of the lower houses in all four states, or the usually longer legislative experience of the members in the upper houses. Despite minor variations, the same over-all pattern of role relationships emerged in each state's two chambers; and these within-state patterns of both houses varied considerably from one state to the other, as theoretically expected. This analysis is, I think, as good a test of the validity of SLRP's use of the comparative method as can be devised.[13]

13. I might add that this fortunate result was one of those critical consequences of a research decision the books on methodology sometimes talk about. At one point in planning the research SLRP entertained the idea of interviewing in only one chamber in each state. The decision to collect data in both chambers, whatever other reasons for doing so there were, was certainly not due to anticipation of this type of analysis, which was only designed long after the data were in.

Chapter 7

The Behavioral Treatment of Politics

My assignment, if I understand it correctly, is to assess the promises of behavioral research in different substantive areas of political science. It is not my task, then, to be programmatic—to prescribe what behavioral research in political science should or might do—or to be codificatory—to review or systematize past and current research. Rather, my assignment involves specification of criteria of relevance in terms of which appraisal of the question posed by the title of this chapter can be made. This, immediately, creates a predicament.

Practitioners of behavioral approaches in political science are by no means agreed on the standards by which to judge the strong points and the weak points of their enterprise. What in one perspective appears to be an element of strength may, in another perspective, appear to be an element of weakness. For instance, many agendas for future research notwithstanding,[1] the fact that behavioral research in politics has not been committed to a single strategy may represent a point of weakness.[2] Were it possible to follow a definite strategy, criteria of relevance and significance, not now available, would facilitate appraisal. Yet, this very absence of a master strategy and clear directions also represents a point of strength. It protects the behavioral enterprise from pre-

Originally published as "Segments of Political Science Most Susceptible to Behavioristic Treatment" in James C. Charlesworth, Ed., *The Limits of Behavioralism in Political Science* (Philadelphia: American Academy of Political and Social Science, 1962), pp. 26–48. Reprinted by permission.

1. For an early agenda of the behavioral persuasion, see Charles E. Merriam, *New Aspects of Politics* (Chicago: University of Chicago Press, 1924); for more recent statements, see some of the articles in Heinz Eulau, Samuel J. Eldersveld, and Morris Janowitz, *Political Behavior: A Reader in Theory and Research* (Glencoe: The Free Press, 1956).

2. The argument for a strategy of inquiry has recently been made by James A. Robinson, "The Major Problems of Political Science," in L. K. Caldwell (Ed.), *New Viewpoints on Politics and Public Affairs* (Bloomington: Indiana University Press, 1962).

mature closure, from being cut off from alternatives which may be dictated by future contingencies. This being so, it is admittedly difficult to say just what "segments of political science" are or are not—more or less, or not at all—"susceptible to behavioristic treatment."

Having stated a predicament and made a reservation, I shall nevertheless throw caution to the winds and assert rather categorically that potentially at least, *all* segments of political science can be treated behaviorally—depending, of course, on a clarification of the terms used in this chapter's title. But, whatever such clarification may entail, it seems to me that human creativity, and especially scientific creativity, knows of no predetermined limitations. Of course, limitations there are. But they are conditional: limitations of time, opportunity, and resources; limitations arising out of bias, fear, and shortsightedness; limitations inherent in the scientific enterprise itself—false starts, wrong moves, errors of omission and commission; and limitations in the armory of available research tools and methods. But, if inquiry remains open, these limitations are surmountable. We may not as yet know how to overcome them, but this, precisely, is the challenge which the behavioral sciences in the study of politics present. Man has smashed the atom and defied the gravity of the earth—whether for better or for worse we may disagree on. And, perhaps, as Albert Einstein once said, politics is so much more difficult than physics. But only the assumption that politics is not immune to scientific inquiry into human relations and behavioral patterns can justify the entire venture called "political science."

To state an assumption, however, is one thing, to appraise future possibilities, another. The future is always contingent, and contingencies are difficult to foresee. Needed for appraisal, then, are not criteria of relevance but also conceptions of future conditions. These conceptions may differ. Political science, despite its roots in the great tradition of classical political theory, is a very young discipline as an empirical study. As a behavioral science, it is even younger. The time perspective of youth is short range. The future always looks brighter than it is likely to be. Not long ago, a distinguished political scientist, Peter H. Odegard, took "a new look at Leviathan":[3]

There is a new look in the study of politics; an increasing awareness of the baffling complexity of what since Aristotle has been called the queen of the sciences—the science of politics. No longer a hostage to history, and freed at last from its bondage to the lawyers as well as from the arid schematism of the political taxonomists, political science is in the process of becoming one of the central unifying forces for understanding why we behave like human beings. As the dominant mood of the interwar period was one of specialization and isolation among the major disciplines, so the mood of this postwar generation is one of specialization and integration.

3. Peter H. Odegard, "A New Look at Leviathan," in Lynn White, Jr. (Ed.), *Frontiers of Knowledge in the Study of Man* (New York: Harper and Brothers, 1956), p. 94.

Such is the short view. As I commented on Professor Odegard's statement elsewhere, it seems to me an unduly hopeful view:[4]

Certainly, those laboring in the vineyards of political behavior research can take heart from such acclaim. Certainly, too, it is true that much progress has been made in political science in recent years. But a sober, second look also suggests that Professor Odegard's picture is still more in the nature of a snapshot of a possible future than of a richly painted current canvas. In fact, there is no surer way to kill the newer trends than to "co-opt" the label "political behavior" without reservations. As one considers the requisites of behavioral research, one must recognize a continuing need for intellectual humility. For few are those who can say that they have fully mastered these requisites.

In retrospect, this rejoinder sounds almost prophetic. Only a few years after Professor Odegard's hopeful appraisal, another distinguished political scientist, Professor Robert A. Dahl, announced the demise of what he called the "behavioral mood":[5]

Where will the behavioral mood, considered as a movement of protest, go from here? I think it will gradually disappear. By this I mean only that it will slowly decay as a distinctive mood and outlook. For it will become, and in fact already is becoming, incorporated into the main body of the discipline. The behavioral mood will not disappear, then, because it has failed. It will disappear rather because it has succeeded. As a separate, somewhat sectarian, slightly factional outlook it will be the first victim of its own triumph.

This may be the long view, but I do not think it is the correct view of the immediate future. Professor Dahl overestimates what he calls the "triumph" of the behavioral persuasion and underestimates the resilience of "the main body of the discipline"—whatever that is. His prognostication is sufficiently ambiguous to permit varying interpretations. But, if he means, as I have reason to assume, that the historical, legal, or doctrinal approaches to the study of politics will succumb under the onslaught of the behavioral movement, his view must be very long indeed. On the contrary, I believe that these approaches will persist. And it is for just this reason that I believe the behavioral approaches in politics will continue as separate and distinct—unless, of course, there is an unpredictable failure of nerve.

In stating conditions, then, I shall try to avoid the short view and the long. If one takes a closer look at particular developments in the behavioral study of politics, what is most evident is the very unevenness of the rate of growth, output, and quality of behavioral research in different subfields of the disci-

4. Heinz Eulau, "Political Science," in Bert F. Hoselitz (Ed.), *A Reader's Guide to the Social Sciences* (Glencoe: The Free Press, 1959), p. 126.

5. Robert A. Dahl, "The Behavioral Approach in Political Science: Epitaph for a Monument to a Successful Protest," *American Political Science Review,* Vol. 55 (December 1961), p. 770.

pline. In public administration, for instance, following Herbert A. Simon's trenchant criticism of the field, one might have expected a flowering of behavioral research.[6] But none occurred.[7] On the other hand, in the field of judicial decision-making, where one might least have expected such development even a few years ago, a growing number of venturesome scholars are producing a sophisticated list of behavioral studies.[8] These are extremes. I can only guess why this is so. But it suggests that between past and future there is an intervening, conditional present. What present conditions of behavioral research in political science, then, are likely to fashion future conditions in different segments of the discipline?

Before tackling this question, it is necessary to come to definitional grips with the terms used in my assignment. I must confess to some hesitation in accepting the assignment in terms which were not of my own choosing. But some conceptual clarification may contribute to enlightenment about assumptions which may be implicit in the assignment.

MEANINGS OF TERMS

First of all, what is meant by "behavioristic"? The term is unfortunate in this connection because it was used in the 1920's to denote a particular school of psychology known as "behaviorism." Modern behavioral inquiry has little in common with the physiological stimulus-response psychology of behaviorism which, in some departments, sought to exorcise from social science what were considered "merely mental" phenomena—drives, motivations, attitudes, defenses, and so on. On the contrary, modern behavioral science is eminently concerned not only with the acts of man but also with his cognitive, affective, and evaluative processes. "Behavior" in political behavior, then, refers not simply to directly or indirectly observable political action but also to those perceptual, motivational, and attitudinal components of behavior which make for man's political identifications, demands and expectations, and his systems of political beliefs, values, and goals. "Behavioral" is, therefore, preferable to "behavioristic," and I shall use it in this dynamic sense.[9]

Moreover, it is a particular characteristic of modern behavioral science,

6. Herbert A. Simon, *Administrative Behavior* (New York: The Macmillan Company, 1947).

7. Of course, there has been vigorous development in organizational theory, decision-making theory, and empirical research on bureaucracy—but by sociologists and social psycholigists, not by political scientists specializing in public administration. For instance, only a handful of political scientists are listed in the comprehensive bibliography in James G. March and Herbert A. Simon, *Organizations* (New York: John Wiley and Sons, 1958), pp. 213–248.

8. See Glendon A. Schubert, *Quantitative Analysis of Judicial Behavior* (Glencoe: The Free Press, 1959) and Glendon A. Schubert (Ed.), *Judicial Decision-Making* (New York: The Free Press of Glencoe, 1963).

9. The most useful inventory of behavioral definitions is still Harold D. Lasswell and Abraham Kaplan, *Power and Society: A Framework for Political Inquiry* (New Haven: Yale University Press, 1950).

including political behavior research, that it is concerned with man's behavior not simply in psychological terms at the level of the individual personality but also at the levels of the social system and culture.[10] Its orientation is multi-causal or multidimensional and, therefore, necessarily interdisciplinary. In being interdisciplinary, political behavior research makes use not only of the theories and findings of the behavioral sciences but also of those of their methods and techniques which may be appropriate. It is necessary, therefore, to distinguish between the study of political behavior and the behavioral study of politics. The distinction is not simply a play on words. It is possible to do research on political behavior without making use of the concepts and methods of the behavioral sciences. The only requirement for the study of political behavior is that the individual actor be the empirical unit of analysis whose behavior is described–though probably not explained. Much of the work in the fields of voting and legislative behavior during the 1920's and early 1930's was of this kind.[11] In the behavioral study of politics, on the other hand, the individual remains the empirical unit of inquiry, but the theoretical units of analysis may be role, group, institution, organization, culture, or system, and so on, whatever conceptual tools may be most adequate for the purpose of a particular investigation. Though I cannot pursue this distinction further here, it is critical in appraising the promises of behavioral research in political science.[12]

Second, how are we to interpret the term "treatment"? I have partly answered it already. Treatment, presumably, refers to the application of the methods and techniques of the behavioral sciences to political data. But what is to be treated? The title of the chapter suggests that segments of political science are to be investigated by these methods. This, again, is a somewhat circuitous formulation. On embarking on a piece of research, one does not first ask whether it falls within this or that segment of political science and whether the segment is or is not susceptible to behavioral analysis. Rather, one asks: "What is the problem?" And, in trying to define the problem to make it amenable to research on the level of the individual as the empirical datum, one tries to mobilize all the resources that might be helpful in doing so: personal experience, common sense, existing information, normative doctrine, available theory, preliminary observation, inventories of techniques, and so on–regardless of whether this involves invasion of one or another academic territory. At this stage of behavioral research, nothing is rejected out of hand–either because it may be doctrinally obnoxious or counter to common sense, or because

10. See Talcott Parsons and Edward A. Shils (Ed.), *Toward a General Theory of Action* (Cambridge, Mass.: Harvard University Press, 1951). For an application of the Parsons-Shils schema in political science, see Gabriel A. Almond, "Comparative Political Systems," *Journal of Politics,* Vol. 18 (August 1956), pp. 391–409.

11. See, for instance, Stuart A. Rice, *Farmers and Workers in American Politics* (New York: Columbia University Press, 1924).

12. For fuller and more explicit discussion of this matter, see my essay, *The Behavioral Persuasion in Politics* (New York: Random House, 1963).

it might be difficult to handle conceptually or impossible to pursue operationally, and certainly not because it may "belong" in someone else's bailiwick. In other words, "treatment" must mean attacking a problem in the most intuitive, speculative, and imaginative ways possible—proceeding from studied openness to cultivated closure. The choice of behavioral methods of analysis and the specification of empirical data requirements are the last steps, not the first, in the design of political behavior research.

Third, as follows from what I have just said, "segments" is best translated into "problematic areas" or simply "problems." The notion of segment implies that it is possible and necessary to define the boundaries of an area of inquiry. Indeed, the fine art of boundary-setting is both exhilarating and troublesome. It is exhilarating because skillful classification and codification make for intellectual order in and control over the huge array of theoretical propositions, approaches, and empirical findings which constitute an arena of scholarship. If done creatively and imaginatively, boundary-setting is very useful in locating a problem and orienting the scholar towards it. But, boundary-setting is also troublesome, because boundaries may rigidify an intellectual enterprise and impede both the finding and the solving of problems.[13]

In contemporary political science, the problems of empirical research defy the necessarily arbitrary limits of scholarly occupations and preoccupations. How to ask questions and how to define a problem has always been at the core of inquiry, regardless of whether the answer was sought in supernatural magic, speculative philosophy, or empirical science. It is only a matter of habit, convenience, or ignorance that we initially tend to pose our questions in terms of those boundaries in which we feel most at home. Each subfield, with its own traditional subject matters, propositions, and methods, becomes a principality of specialists, fearful and jealous of encroachments.

There is, of course, much functional advantage to be derived from this division of labor. Even within a single major discipline, the range of problems, theories, and methods is so great that expertise is ever more difficult to come by. How much more the contemporary student of government and politics must master to earn his sheepskin than his predecessor of only twenty-five years ago! I do not believe that specialization means, as some contend, that we know more and more about less and less. This easy metaphor ignores the fact that, along with specialization on particular problems, we also expand the frontiers of investigation. But, as the frontiers expand in depth, contact is also made with subfields and neighboring disciplines, and boundaries are difficult to respect. Those working at the frontiers are, therefore, less inclined to draw exact boundaries than those who travel in the hinterland. They come to see things as their neighbors do. Indeed, they may come to have more in common with the neighbors than the old core. This is, of course, a matter of more or

13. See Robert K. Merton, "Notes on Problem-Finding in Sociology," in Robert K. Merton, Leonard Broom, and Leonard S. Cottrell, Jr., *Sociology Today: Problems and Prospects* (New York: Basic Books, 1959), pp. ix–xxxiv.

less, varying from researcher to researcher. Specialization makes for cross-fertilization.

All of this suggests, perhaps, why behavioral researchers in political science seem to be rather disrespectful of intra- and inter-disciplinary boundaries yet refuse to allow themselves to be pigeonholed as a subfield, some pressure in this direction notwithstanding.[14] The traditional boundaries between the subfields of political science are not particularly viable avenues in terms of which to explore the promises of behavioral research, though they may represent contingencies. The latter may be illustrated: a subfield which can state its *problems* specifically is more likely to expose itself to behavioral research than a subfield that remains unproblematic in its formulations. This, perhaps, accounts for the difference I noted earlier between behavioral development in public administration and in public law. Public administration likes to state programs; public law likes to state problems. If my speculation is at all plausible, the difference may well lie in the different intellectual styles taken by these two fields. Nevertheless, it seems to make more sense to ask what problems are susceptible to behavioral research than to ask in what subfields it is more likely to advance.

Finally, a few comments on the meaning of "most susceptible" in the title. Implicit in this formulation seems to be the assumption that there must also be "segments least susceptible" to behavioral investigation. It is more fruitful to ask, therefore, which problems are more likely to be solved under certain conditions than others. This at least avoids the polarization implicit in the title. But even this reformulation leaves me somewhat uncomfortable. For it still seems to assume that susceptibility is a function of the problem alone and not a function of the kind of analysis that may be made, as if a problem had certain intrinsic or essential qualities which do not lend themselves to behavioral investigation. But this assumption, it seems to me, precludes by fiat what is to be concluded upon investigation.

The medical analogy seems relevant. Success in a patient's treatment is both a function of the patient's relative state of health and the physician's relative therapeutic skills which, in turn, depend on the state of medical knowledge. Admittedly, some patients and their problems react to treatment better than others, and some may not react at all. But it must also be admitted that recuperation may have something to do with the kind of treatment that is administered. For most medical problems, there are alternate solutions. There are alternate theories and methods of medical research. In any case, medical science does not proceed on the assumption that some problem is per se more susceptible to solution than another. It assumes that, given time, resources, and inventive skills, all problems of disease are soluble–more or less satisfactorily at any one time, to be sure, but soluble nevertheless. Finally, as my medical friends tell me, almost every problem solved is, more often than not,

14. See Heinz Eulau, *Recent Developments in the Behavioral Study of Politics* (Stanford: Stanford University Department of Political Science, 1961), pp. 4–7. (Out of print.)

the take-off point for discovering new problems. In other words, problems are not given but found, if not created. How one finds or even creates problems in research is likely to have a great deal to do with how one solves them. A political problem stated in terms of theoretical propositions amenable to translation into empirical indicators is necessarily susceptible to behavioral research. Whether the traditional problems of politics—the great issues of politics, so-called—can be stated in behavioral terms is for the future to decide. The possibility of doing so, though it depends on many conditions and contingencies, cannot be ruled out by prejudgment.

LIMITATIONS ON DEVELOPMENT

Even if a complete inventory were possible, no attempt can be made here to attend to all of the conditions and contingencies which, in one way or another, are likely to circumscribe developments in the behavioral study of politics. I shall, therefore, deal with only three conditions which, it seems to me, are particularly relevant because they are most likely to change: the state of theory, the state of research technology, and the state of professional skills.

Of these, the state of theory is the most critical because our ability to formulate problems in behaviorally feasible yet politically significant terms depends on it. Here the traditional boundaries between the subfields of political science have been especially impedimental in extending the range of behavioral analysis. The segmentalization of political theory very early in the development of political science as an autonomous academic discipline has had unfortunate consequences in a dual sense: on the one hand, for decades political theory failed to fertilize the other subfields of the discipline with more empirical-institutional or policy concerns; on the other hand, political theory, as history of political doctrines, became a rather scholastic enterprise unrelated to experiences in the real world of politics. As an even more immediate result, especially germane in this connection, those trained in political theory were altogether incapacitated for having what I can only describe as a feel for the methodological needs and empirical dilemmas of political science. There were, of course, exceptions, such as Charles E. Merriam, who "came out of" political theory, and a few others. But, as a group, political theorists, if not concerned with the history of political thought, busied themselves with values in the speculative tradition of philosophy.

When, at long last, books like David B. Truman's *The Governmental Process,* David Easton's *The Political System,* or Robert A. Dahl and Charles E. Lindblom's *Politics, Economics and Welfare* appeared, their impact was impressive, not because they were just good books or even excellent, but because they were directly oriented in a behavioral perspective.[15] Yet, relevant behav-

15. David B. Truman, *The Governmental Process* (New York: Alfred A. Knopf, 1951); David Easton, *The Political System* (New York: Alfred A. Knopf, 1953); Robert A. Dahl and Charles E. Lindblom, *Politics, Economics, and Welfare* (New York: Harper and Brothers, 1953).

ioral research was still largely laggard, and they could be debated as if they were statements of knowledge rather than suggestive theoretical leads useful in the process of creating knowledge. Yet, it seems to me, the virtue of these theoretical efforts was not to be found primarily in either the logic or validity of their arguments–which could be and were challenged, as is to be expected –but in the fact that they were cast in a theoretical frame of reference which could, and did, stimulate empirical research along behavioral lines. The next step–theoretical work which could build on or at least rely on empirical research of a behavioral sort–has been altogether slow in coming, though books like Dahl's *A Preface to Democratic Theory* or Seymour M. Lipset's *Political Man* are suggestive of new theoretical departures from behavioral research as a base.[16] But, even today, those specializing in political theory do not expend enough effort on theoretical work that could advance the frontiers of behavioral knowledge of politics.

It seems appropriate here to point to a very interesting and understandable paradox in theory construction. There seems to be an inverse relationship between theorizing as an independently creative activity and the empirical accessibility of the phenomena theorized about. I find that the most exciting theoretical work of potential behavioral research relevance now being done falls into the range of problems traditionally of interest to the student of international relations–precisely the area where access to behavioral data is perhaps most difficult to come by.[17] On the other hand, theorizing has been sluggish in problem areas where empirical research is relatively easy–for instance, the study of elections and voting behavior. Here we are now facing an enormously rich mine of empirical research for which there does not exist even a comprehensive conceptual schema within which to organize and order the data.[18] What theory there is is largely of a middle-range, post-factum variety.[19] These two extremes underline the need for research in which behaviorally relevant political theory and theory-relevant behavioral analysis go hand in hand.[20] There is a range of problems where self-conscious theoretical formulation and empirical behavioral research can fruitfully meet to extend

16. Robert A. Dahl, *A Preface to Democratic Theory* (Chicago: University of Chicago Press, 1956); Seymour M. Lipset, *Political Man* (New York: Doubleday and Company, 1960).

17. For an excellent collection of this genre, see James N. Rosenau (Ed.), *International Politics and Foreign Policy: A Reader in Research and Theory* (New York: The Free Press of Glencoe, 1961) and Klaus Knorr and Sidney Verba (Ed.), *The International System: Theoretical Essays* (Princeton: Princeton University Press, 1961).

18. But, for an attempt to organize the data in a "funnel of causality," see Angus Campbell, Philip E. Converse, Warren E, Miller, and Donald E. Stokes, *The American Voter* (New York: John Wiley and Sons, 1960), pp. 18–37.

19. See, for instance, Bernard Berelson, Paul F. Lazarsfeld, and William N. McPhee, *Voting* (Chicago: University of Chicago Press, 1954), pp. 305–323; or Morris Janowitz and Dwaine Marvick, *Competitive Pressure and Democratic Consent* (Ann Arbor: Bureau of Government, University of Michigan, 1956).

20. See Robert K. Merton, *Social Theory and Social Structure* (rev. ed.; Glencoe: The Free Press, 1957), pp. 85–117.

the margins of political knowledge. I might mention Dahl's recent study of urban-community decision-making, *Who Governs?*,[21] and the work of John C. Wahlke and colleagues on legislative behavior reported in *The Legislative System*.[22]

The important point to be made here is not that there is legitimate room for theoretical disagreement but that efforts are being made to resolve such disagreements by demonstrating the validity of theoretical propositions, or at least their utility, by subjecting them to empirical tests in the crucible of research rather than by debating them in the fashion of dialectics where it is usually convenient to set up one's intellectual adversary in his weakest posture and then strike him down with one's strongest arguments.[23] Whatever entertainment value it may have, I have always found this bit of "theoretical" polemics rather incongruous with the aspirations of a discipline which presumably does not subscribe to the comfortable assumption that theory is the same thing as knowledge. In any case, increasing remarriage of political theory and empirical research is one of the most important conditions likely to facilitate the development of behavioral analysis in politics.

The earlier observation on the inverse relationship between theoretical development and access to data should not be interpreted to mean that I believe accessibility to be somehow an absolute limitation on extending the range of behavioral research. On the contrary. It seems to me that accessibility is itself a variable subject to the progressive development of instruments and techniques of inquiry. A second condition likely to influence the future of behavioral inquiry in different problem areas is, therefore, the state of technical know-how and methodological sophistication at a given time. Indeed, what has been called the revolution in the behavioral sciences is, to no small extent, a technological revolution—though I would not say that its impact on political science is only a technological breakthrough.[24] The range of problems susceptible to behavioral treatment is, therefore, always also a function of advances in research methodology and technology.

It is true, of course, that behavioral researches have been initially successful

21. Robert A. Dahl, *Who Governs? Democracy and Power in an American City* (New Haven: Yale University Press, 1961). The lively debate in this range of problems is likely to extend the range of empirical concerns covered. See, for instance, Raymond E. Wolfinger, "Reputation and Reality in the Study of 'Community Power,'" *American Sociological Review*, Vol. 25 (October 1960), pp. 636–644, and Lawrence J. R. Herson, "In the Footsteps of Community Power," *American Political Science Review*, Vol. 55 (December 1961), pp. 817–830.

22 John C. Wahlke, Heinz Eulau, William Buchanan, and LeRoy C. Ferguson, *The Legislative System: Explorations in Legislative Behavior* (New York: John Wiley and Sons, 1962).

23. See, for instance, Bernard Crick, *The American Science of Politics* (Berkeley: University of California Press, 1959).

24. See David B. Truman, "The Impact on Political Science of the Revolution in the Behavioral Sciences," in Brookings Lectures, 1955, *Research Frontiers in Politics and Government* (Washington, D.C.: The Brookings Institution, 1955), pp. 202–231.

in problem areas where data could be most easily harvested, processed, packaged, and, if not sold, at least freely distributed. For a time, political behavior was more identified with voting behavior than anything else. Stores of data were readily available in the aggregated election statistics of many jurisdictions, large and small, and cutting across international frontiers.[25] But it was the development of the random sample survey in the last twenty years and the use of panels, first introduced in the memorable Erie County study of 1940,[26] which made possible the analysis of problems in the area of mass political behavior not even dreamed about when I went to college. The success of the systematic interview in the study of voting and public opinion is gradually encouraging researchers to use these techniques in the study of institutionalized populations like legislatures or bureaucracies.[27] The use of the interview in institutionalized groups, in turn, makes possible much more carefully controlled comparative analysis, at least of relatively small political systems like local administrative bodies or city councils.[28] In any case, much can still be done in perfecting the interview as an instrument of behavioral-institutional research.

The bias long held against systematic interview research was characteristic of a state of mind in the discipline which even today is still widely shared. Similar biases exist against other techniques which are simply denied out of existence because they are new and strange. Yet, once these techniques are applied to political problems, the range of phenomena accessible to behavioral research increases enormously. For instance, the use of roll calls in the study of legislative policy, introduced into the discipline by A. Lawrence Lowell as long ago as 1901, did not seem to yield remarkable new findings as long as the technology involved in their use remained relatively rudimentary.[29] Stuart A.

25. This identification of "political behavior" and "voting behavior" was probably due, in part, to the use of "political behavior" in the Swede Herbert Tingsten's *Political Behavior: Studies in Election Statistics* (London, 1937).

26. See Paul F. Lazarsfeld, Bernard Berelson, and Hazel Gaudet, *The People's Choice* (New York: Columbia University Press, 1948).

27. When the data were collected for V. O. Key's *Southern Politics in State and Nation* (New York: Alfred A. Knopf, 1949), there was still much hesitation about the systematic interview. While the interviewers had been sensitized to the kind of information that was sought, they had to assume considerable responsibility for the kind of interview they were conducting and the kind of data they tried to elicit. Yet, Key's project represented a noteworthy breakthrough in interviewing in political science. As Key's associate, Alexander Heard, later reported, the project accepted "the conviction that much significant information could be obtained only from politicians themselves or from their close associates." See "Interviewing Southern Politicians," *American Political Science Review,* Vol. 44 (December 1950), p. 886.

28. See Robert L. Peabody, *Organizational Authority* (New York: Atherton Press, 1964), who systematically interviewed and compared responses concerning authority and responsibility in three formally differently structured small agencies—a school system, a police department, and a welfare agency.

29. A. Lawrence Lowell, "The Influence of Party upon Legislation in England and America," *Annual Report of the American Historical Association,* Vol. 1 (1901), pp. 321–542.

Rice extended their use in the 1920's with his indexes of "cohesion" and "likeness,"[30] and subsequently Julius Turner applied chi-square analysis.[31] But only very recently have roll calls again yielded fresh results. These results had to await technological developments which escaped our vision not so long ago. The application of Guttman scaling[32] and factor analysis[33] once more increased the range of problems which can be fruitfully investigated.

It is not my purpose to review technological developments systematically, but to suggest, by way of some illustrations, that the susceptibility of problems in political science, as in other disciplines, is always conditioned by the state and development of research technology. What this technology will be in the future is difficult to say, because developments are rapid and radical. For instance, the use of electronic computers is likely to have important consequences for the kind of behavioral analyses of politics that may be possible in the near future. But the application of new techniques depends, of course, on the availability of skilled personnel to handle them. For, as Harold D. Lasswell has put it succinctly, "discretion is here to stay."[34] The extent to which behavioral research is possible depends, therefore—a third condition—on the training given at this time to students interested in research. This training, I daresay, if compared with the training given in neighboring disciplines, is at present generally deficient in view of the technological opportunities which are on the horizon of behavioral political science.

I do not want to labor it, but I find a peculiar line of reasoning in a rather unreasonable resistance to the kind of research training which, I think, a political science deserving of its name requires. If we have to learn calculus and probability theory, content analysis, factor analysis and what not, questionnaire construction and computer work, so the reasoning goes, we might as well drop politics and take up physics. Few would admit to being too stupid to study mathematics or statistics as a requisite for theoretical and empirical work in political science.[35] Instead, shelter is sought and found in the image

30. Stuart A. Rice, "The Behavior of Legislative Groups," *Political Science Quarterly*, Vol. 40 (1925), pp. 60–72.

31. Julius Turner, *Party and Constituency: Pressures on Congress* (Baltimore: The Johns Hopkins University Press, 1951).

32. See Duncan MacRae, Jr., *Dimensions of Congressional Voting* (Berkeley: University of California Press, 1958).

33. For this and other techniques of legislative study, see the section on "Research Orientations and Techniques" in John C. Wahlke and Heinz Eulau (Eds.), *Legislative Behavior: A Reader in Theory and Research* (Glencoe: The Free Press, 1959), pp. 355–413.

34. Harold D. Lasswell, "Current Studies of the Decision Process: Automation versus Creativity," *Western Political Quarterly*, Vol. 8 (1955), p. 399. For a report on computer handling of voting data, see Ithiel de Sola Pool and Robert Abelson, "The Simulmatics Project," *Public Opinion Quarterly*, Vol. 25 (Summer 1961), pp. 167–183.

35. How a political scientist might go about studying the relevant mathematical literature in a year's time is suggested by Richard R. Fagen, "Some Contributions of Mathematical Reasoning to the Study of Politics," *American Political Science Review*, Vol. 55 (December 1961), pp. 888–900.

of a political science which protects the student from having to involve himself in what appears to be such dismal and difficult preparation. Instead, the student will dutifully learn two foreign languages which he may never use! And, because he has not acquired the newer research skills, our student, once he becomes a teacher, will protest that the problems of political science are not amenable to behavioral investigation. The circle is full: *quod erat demonstrandum!* What this line of reasoning really says is this: "I don't want to do what I don't want to do"—a case of scientific infantilism. As long as this attitude prevails, many potential problems of political science will, in fact, escape behavioral treatment.

Not that I would require every political scientist to acquire all the skills now available! In the first place, as I said earlier, historical, legal, and normative approaches are here to stay. And, second, not all skills are needed in every piece of behavioral research, though one might expect at least a speaking acquaintance, if for no other reason than communication, if needed, with skilled technicians. Yet, the curious thing is that, sooner or later, at least those with an open mind in the matter who are oriented toward research confront or pose problems which seem to force them into technological ventures. When this point is reached by a particular group facing particular problems I cannot say. That it is reached is quite clear. Those of my generation who came to behavioral analysis are largely self taught. The important point I wish to make is that what stimulated this retooling was not simply some more or less vaguely felt dissatisfaction with the state of political science as a whole but that we confronted some particular research problem which could not be handled satisfactorily by legal or historical treatment. This point, it seems to me, has been missed by those who in very general terms have written about the behavioral approach or behavioral mood. Though there may have been general protest, it is dissatisfaction with theory, research, or method in a particular problem area which stimulates interest in the new technology. It stands to reason that, if theory, research, and method were not useful in solving a new problem one encounters, there would be little incentive to involve oneself in the expensive and time-consuming business of retooling and fresh study. Yet, there are those who are generally dissatisfied with their discipline but who do very little about it except argue their conviction at professional meetings or write a manifesto. They rarely take a year out to study statistics or spend endless hours learning how to do a reliable content analysis.

The discovery and susceptibility of problems to behavioral treatment depend, then, on the quality and quantity of trained personnel that may be available in the future. How lack of proper training—even of training that is eminently qualitative—retards disciplinary growth is perhaps best illustrated by the inability of younger political scientists to follow the pioneering leads of Harold D. Lasswell's *Psychopathology and Politics*.[36] One need not accept

36. First published in 1930. But see the most recent edition "With Afterthoughts by the Author" (New York: The Viking Press, Compass Books, 1960).

Lasswell's particular formulations, but all political scientists, whether they know it or not, make assumptions about "human nature" in their varying approaches to political problems. I think this is particularly true of those who take pride in their concern with political values and political ethics. It would seem, therefore, that the intensive study of personality in politics would rank high on the agenda of political science as a whole. Yet, perhaps less has been done here than in any other problem area of political science, though a few exceptions are noteworthy.[37] Little has been done, not because the study of political personality is not susceptible to one or another kind of intensive behavioral inquiry, but because the skills needed to do an adequate job are difficult to come by. But possibly even more important is resistance to personality analysis as a mode of inquiry. Again, as in the case of objections to quantitative treatment, I have heard it said that, if personality were what politics is "all about," we might as well be psychologists! This is, of course, a very feeble argument, for no one, and Lasswell least of all, has ever asserted that politics is "all about" personality. In this range of political inquiry, I suspect, resistance to training stems less from cultivated ignorance than from irrational fear.

NEW DILEMMAS

The susceptibility of particular problem areas of political science to behavioral treatment, I have argued, varies and will continue to vary with the state and development of relevant theories, appropriate techniques, and available skills. But if, as I have also asserted, the behavioral approaches are complementary and supplementary to the more traditional methods of the discipline, there arise a number of methodological questions about the relationship between the older and the newer approaches which present certain dilemmas on whose solution the behavioral persuasion is in turn contingent. Needless to say, perhaps, I can only indicate very superficially here what some of these dilemmas are, but even a few comments might be suggestive for an elaboration of the theme assigned to me.

In the first place, taking it for granted that political science is not only interested in the behavior of individuals but, above all, in the actions and policies of groups, institutions, and "states," the problem arises as to how meaningful statements about large systems can be made on the basis of inquiry into the behavior of individual political actors. This is the problem of the relationship between macro- and microanalysis. For, clearly, only if the rela-

37. Especially the work in progress by Robert E. Lane. See his "The Fear of Equality," *American Political Science Review,* Vol. 53 (March 1959),pp. 36–51, and "Fathers and Sons: Foundations of Political Belief," *American Sociological Review* Vol. 24 (1959), pp. 502–511. Dynamic depth analyses based on documentary materials are Alexander L. and Juliette L. George, *Woodrow Wilson and Colonel House* (New York: John Day, 1956) and Alex Gottfried, *Boss Cermak of Chicago* (Seattle: University of Washington Press, 1961).

tionship between macro- and microanalysis is satisfactorily settled can it be legitimate to say that, as I have said, all problems of interest to political science are potentially susceptible to behavioral treatment. In trying to solve this methodological problem, it is easy to fall into various errors. For instance, there is the fallacy of extrapolation from micro- to macrophenomena. Small systems are treated as analogues of large systems, and the findings on the microlevel are extended to the macrolevel.[38] There is, secondly, the fallacy of personification: large-scale phenomena are "reduced" to the individual level, as in the more grotesque descriptions of "national character." [39]

This is not the place to suggest solutions. One solution, I believe, will involve the recognition that the distinction between macro- and microunits as the empirical objects of inquiry is relative to the observer's standpoint, and that units like individual, primary group, organization, community, or even state are not polar but continuous variables of political analysis. If this is so, it should be possible to order these units on a macro-micro continuum, and the task of research will be to link these units in terms of vertical and horizontal patterns of relationship as parts of a continuous chain.[40]

The issue is not, as it is sometimes posed in normative political theory, one of individual versus group or group versus state. Rather, from whatever point on the continuum one proceeds, the task of research is to build, by patiently linking one unit with another, the total chain of interrelations which link individual to individual, individual to primary group, primary group to primary group, primary group to secondary group, secondary group to secondary group, secondary group to organization, organization to organization, and so on, until the total vertical system of interpersonal and intergroup relations has been given a continuous order. In this order, what is to be considered macro or micro will always depend on the observational standpoint occupied by the investigator. Behavioral analysis of units larger than the individual depends, it seems obvious, on some construction of the total system in which the individual is a necessary link. Let me emphasize that I am not thinking here of theoretical linkage alone but of empirical linkage also. Clearly, the susceptibility of a broad range of "large" problems, like war or peace, or freedom and responsibility, and so on, to behavioral analysis is contingent on the solution of this methodological dilemma.

Second, and not unrelated to the macro-micro problem, is the problem of using both discrete and aggregate data in behavioral analysis. The difficulty arises out of the fact that what may be true of aggregates need not be true of the individuals who compose them. The reason for this is simple enough:

38. For an example of the fallacy, see Ralph K. White and Ronald O. Lippitt, *Autocracy and Democracy* (New York: Harper and Brothers, 1960).

39. But, for an imaginative use of the concept, see David M. Potter, *People of Plenty* (Chicago: University of Chicago Press, 1954).

40. See Oliver Garceau, "Research in the Political Process," *American Political Science Review,* Vol. 45 (March 1951), pp. 69–85.

moving from statements about the behavior of aggregates, such as electoral districts, to the behavior of any one individual within the aggregate involves an inference which may be wrong. The dubious procedure involved was pointed out over ten years ago in a widely read article by the sociologist W. S. Robinson.[41] Indeed, in the case of voting behavior, for instance, the sample survey has made this procedure unnecessary. As Warren E. Miller has shown, generalizations from aggregate data about the "presidential coat-tail" are untenable if tested against information about the behavior and attitudes of individuals.[42] Similarly, Wilder Crane, Jr., found, though on legislative roll calls members of both parties vote alike, that party may yet be a salient variable influencing individual behavior and that the occurrence of party conflict in legislative divisions need not mean that the party is, in fact, the crucial factor in bringing about a party-line division.[43]

The use of aggregated data, therefore, is likely to conceal a good deal of the variance in the behavior of individual political actors which the use of discrete data reveals. This does not mean that statements based on aggregate data can be abandoned. Aggregate data are often the only kind of behavioral data available for the purpose of making statements about groups or larger collectivities. But this necessity should not be made into a virtue. For the problem remains that, if behavioral statements are to be made about large systems, aggregate data are evidently not sufficient. On the other hand, even if individual data are available and are aggregated to permit statements about super-individual units to be made, such aggregation may still do violence to findings about individual behavior. It has the advantage of showing how great the variance may be which aggregate or broad institutional language conceals. But, what we empirically mean when we speak of a group's loyalty, a party's cohesion, or an organization's morale remains unanswered. Do we speak about a "group property" which is independent of the behavior of the individuals composing a group, party, or organization, or are we really speaking only about the aggregated characteristics of individuals? It seems that the extent to which certain problems of politics are susceptible to behavioral treatment depends on an answer to these questions.[44]

Finally, as a third example among many other dilemmas that could be cited, I want to mention only briefly the methodological problems involved in closing the gap between case analysis and systematic analysis. I am not concerned here with the use of cases as pedagogic devices but as instruments of research. In this connection, a number of questions arise. Though a great many cases

41. W. S. Robinson, "Ecological Correlations and the Behavior of Individuals," *American Sociological Review*, Vol. 15 (June 1950), pp. 351–357.

42. Warren E. Miller, "Presidential Coattails: A. Study in Political Myth and Methodology," *Public Opinion Quarterly*, Vol. 19 (Winter 1955–1956), pp. 353–368.

43. Wilder Crane, Jr., "A Caveat on Roll-Call Studies of Party Voting," *Midwest Journal of Political Science*, Vol. 4 (August 1960), pp. 237–249.

44. See Hanan C. Selvin, *The Effects of Leadership* (Glencoe: The Free Press, 1960).

have been accumulated with respect to various problematic areas of politics—from the administrative process to legislative decision-making to party and pressure-group politics—the grounds on which these cases were selected are somewhat obscure. In general, the substantative interests of the researcher and his convenience, such as accessibility of documents and persons, seem to be the guiding criteria—hardly scientific criteria. Moreover, most of the cases now available deal with the exciting, spectacular, and perhaps critical situations rather than with more modal situations. As a result, the degree to which the cases are typical or not, and of what they might be typical, is always open to doubt. I have also always wondered about the reliability of case studies: would a second researcher, working with the same materials and having access to the same respondents, come up with findings—leaving aside the matter of interpretation—reasonably similar to those of the first researcher, so that findings cannot be attributed to chance? Finally, few cases are cast in a theoretical framework that controls the cases, making inferences from a variety of cases extremely hazardous.

Although cases are said to be rich sources of hypotheses about politics for future systematic research, few follow-up studies of that character have ever been made. One of the few exceptions is James A. Robinson's *Congress and Foreign Policy-Making* which also deals rather ingenuously with the difficulties involved in trying to cope systematically with several dozen other cases, presumably covering similar policy processes, yet prepared by as many researchers.[45] Perhaps the most successful and certainly the most sophisticated use of cases has recently been made by Edward C. Banfield in *Political Influence,* a behavioral-institutional study of the politics of decision-making in a metropolitan area.[46] Not only were the cases shaped by an identical theoretical framework, but inferences and generalizations were made on both middle-range pragmatic and high-level systematic bases. Both Robinson's and Banfield's works are important steps in broadening the range of problems susceptible to systematic behavioral analysis through the use of relatively few but intensively studied cases.

CONCLUSION

I have argued in this paper that, potentially at least, all problematic areas of political science are amenable to political behavior research, provided certain conditions are met and dilemmas resolved. The future success of behavioral research depends, first, on the construction of empirical theory which is behaviorally relevant; second, on the continuing progress in research technology; third, on the recruitment into behavioral research of properly trained and

45. James A. Robinson, *Congress and Foreign Policy-Making* (Homewood, Illinois: The Dorsey Press, 1962).

46. Edward C. Banfield, *Political Influence* (New York: The Free Press of Glencoe, 1961).

skilled personnel; fourth, on the closing of the gap between macro- and micro-analysis; fifth, on the reciprocal uses of discrete and aggregated behavioral data; and sixth, on the reconciliation of case and systematic analysis. The discussion was intended to be suggestive rather than exhaustive, to illuminate the road which the behavioral persuasion in politics is traveling rather than to guide along it.

Part III

Accent on Analysis: Linkages

Chapter 8

Dimensions of Political Involvement

If, as George Herbert Mead suggested long ago, communication consists in "a taking of the role of the other," the mass media are of vast importance in the social process because "they report situations through which one can enter into the attitude and experience of other persons." But, continues Mead, "you have to presuppose some sort of co-operation within which the individuals are themselves actively involved as the only possible basis for this participation in communication." [1]

In most studies of political behavior, involvement is usually conceived as prior to political activity in a causal sense, rather than, as Mead hinted, an activity phenomenon in itself. Not until recently have participation and communication been seen as simultaneous dimensions of political involvement. Communication and participation are not independent phenomena, but variables in a broad cluster of motivational, perceptual, and atittudinal dimensions variously subsumed under such concepts as political "interest," "involvement," or, as we shall call it, "relatedness."

Merriam and Gosnell, in their pioneer study of political activity, *Non-Voting,* were not unaware of the limited character of their inquiry.[2] But a more dynamic approach had to await the absorption of psychological and sociological concepts into political behavior research. In the Erie County study of 1940, respondents' self-rating of "interest" was considered the best index of

Originally published, with Peter Schneider, in *Public Opinion Quarterly,* Vol. 20 (Spring, 1956) pp. 128–42. Reprinted by permission.

1. Mead, George H., *Mind, Self & Society,* Chicago: The University of Chicago Press, 1934, pp. 73, 257.

2. Cf. Charles E. Merriam and Harold F. Gosnell, *Non-Voting: Causes and Methods of Control,* Chicago: University of Chicago Press, 1924.

psychological involvement in the presidential election.[3] A 1944 national survey, conducted by the National Opinion Research Center, was exploited by Korchin who interpreted the quality of voter participation in the election in terms of the concept of "ego-involvement." [4] In a pilot study, based on a small, non-representative sample, Rosenberg isolated three general determinants of political apathy: the threatening consequences of political activity, its futility, and the absence of spurs to interest and participation.[5] Meanwhile, Riesman and Glazer, developing criteria of political apathy, specified "affect" and "competence" as factors particularly relevant to the diagnosis of political commitment.[6] Finally, in the nation-wide survey conducted in 1952 by the Survey Research Center, University of Michigan, "sense of political efficacy" and "sense of citizen duty" (or "responsibility") were introduced as indices of political motivation.[7]

The following analysis examines the inter-relations of selected dimensions of political involvement, in particular, "efficacy" and "responsibility." In order to assess the simultaneous impact of these two criteria relevant scales were combined into an "index of political relatedness." The discriminating power of this index will be compared with other indices of involvement: (1) competence; (2) affect; (3) identification; (4) exposure; and (5) participation.

SOME THEORETICAL CONSIDERATIONS

The diversity and heterogeneity of indices of political involvement suggest the definitional ambiguity and index instability so characteristic of research in the social sciences.

Riesman and Glazer, as has been noted, define political involvement in terms of two inter-related variables which they characterize as "competence" and "affect." The problem arises whether these criteria are useful in a study of a nation-wide sample. Riesman and Glazer themselves would probably be inclined to deny their applicability. For, as they point out, the distinction they make between "genuine" and "spurious" affect or competence "leads us away from any quantitative or quasi-quantitative use of either affect or competence as isolable criteria." [8] Nevertheless, we feel that affect and competence, if

3. Lazarsfeld Paul F., Bernard Berelson, and Hazel Gaudet, *The People's Choice,* New York, Columbia University Press, 1944.

4. Korchin, Sheldon J., *Psychological Variables in the Behavior of Voters,* unpublished Ph.D. thesis, Harvard University, 1946, p. 55.

5. Rosenberg, Morris, "Some Determinants of Political Apathy," *Public Opinion Quarterly,* Vol. 18, Winter, 1954–5, p. 350.

6. Riesman, David and Nathan Glazer, "Criteria for Political Apathy," in A. W. Gouldner, Ed., *Studies in Leadership,* New York: Harper and Brothers, 1950, pp. 505–559.

7. Campbell, Angus, Gerald Gurin and Warren E. Miller, *The Voter Decides,* Evanston: Row, Peterson and Company, 1954.

8. Riesman and Glazer, *op. cit.,* p. 540.

conceptualized more broadly, are susceptible to quantitative treatment as significant dimensions of involvement.

Our own principal indicators of political involvement are the concepts of "efficacy" and "citizen responsibility" developed in the 1952 Survey Research Center study of a national sample. Sense of political efficacy is defined as "the feeling that individual political action does have or can have an impact upon the political process, i.e., that it is worthwhile to perform one's civic duties. It is the feeling that social change is possible, and that the individual citizen can play a part in bringing about this change." [9] Rosenberg has suggested that in expressing his sense of futility, the individual can on the one hand "focus on certain characteristics of himself: e.g., he is insignificant, powerless, or incompetent. On the other hand, he can focus on the characteristics of the objects to be influenced; e.g. political representatives pay no attention to him, political machines run things just as they please, and so on." [10] It is in this dual sense that we shall use the concept of efficacy.

However, sense of one's efficacy alone is not a sufficient condition of involvement in the political process. A person may feel inefficacious, insecure or anxious in political matters, and he may yet have a strong conviction that it is his duty to participate in politics. Hence he may be a regular voter. We believe that "sense of responsibility" is a deeply ingrained American cultural attribute, regardless of class or educational level, though related to both. Moralizing about good citizenship may not be enough to relate the individual to politics, but we feel that if the moral appeal is successful through time, i.e., properly internalized, it becomes an independently operating commitment to the political process.

Participation in politics, then, is largely determined by (1) the degree to which an individual has internalized political expectations and (2) the degree to which he appraises his role as being politically significant and effective. Both of these facets constitute the concept of "relatedness" as used here.

METHOD AND SAMPLE

In the following paragraphs we shall briefly describe the two scales on which our "index of political relatedness" is based, how they were derived, and how they were combined.

The "efficacy scale" is a Guttman-type scale based on the following items asked of the sample population: [11]

1. I don't think public officials care much what people like me think.
2. Voting is the only way that people like me can have any say how the government runs things.

9. Campbell, Gurin and Miller, *op. cit.*, p. 187.

10. Rosenberg, *op. cit.*, pp. 354–5.

11. For technical aspects of both scales, including co-efficients of reproducibility and statements of per cent error for items, see Campbell, Gurin and Miller, *op. cit.*, pp. 187–99.

3. People like me don't have any say about what the government does.
4. Sometimes politics and government seem so complicated that a person like me can't really understand what's going on.

"Disagree" responses to these four items were coded as "efficacious."

The "responsibility scale" is likewise a Guttman-type scale based on these items:

1. It isn't so important to vote when you know your party doesn't have a chance to win.
2. A good many local elections aren't important enough to bother with.
3. So many other people vote in the national elections that it doesn't matter much to me whether I vote or not.
4. If a person doesn't care how an election comes out he shouldn't vote in it.

Respondents disagreeing with these statements were coded as being "responsible," i.e., they must feel that political participation is a citizen's duty.

The response patterns of both scales were converted into scale types, and the latter were cross-tabulated to yield the "index of relatedness." The resultant scale types and index categories are indicated in Table 8.1.

Table 8.1. Distribution of Respondents on Political Relatedness

Index Category	*Efficacy Scale Type*	*Responsibility Scale Type*	*N*	*%*
High	High	High	205	18
Medium High	High	Medium		
	Medium	High	447	39
Medium Low	Medium	Medium		
	High	Low		
	Low	High	352	30
Low	Medium	Low		
	Low	Medium		
	Low	Low	142	13
Total			1146	100%

An original sample of 1,614 respondents, selected by the method of area probability sampling and interviewed by the Survey Research Center both prior to and after the presidential election of 1952, was reduced for this analysis, for two reasons: (1) a disproportionate number of Southern respondents fell into the low relatedness category. As Table 8.2 shows, inclusion of the Southern sub-sample would have seriously distorted the meaning of the analysis for the country as a whole. (2) Another 33 respondents could not be

Table 8.2. Distribution of Respondents on Political Relatedness, by Region

Index Category	*Northeast* $N=379$	*Midwest* $N=569$	*Far West* $N=198$	*South* $N=435$
High	20%	19%	12%	9%
High Medium	37	37	47	25
Low Medium	31	30	31	34
Low	12	14	10	32
Total	100%	100%	100%	100%

classified on either the efficacy or responsibility scale. The final sample used in this analysis was thus reduced to 1,146 respondents.

As the variables in this study may be influenced by "third" factors, making for spurious results if not controlled, Table 8.3 presents the distribution of respondents according to their relatedness category among a number of selected demographic groupings. As the table indicates, people who score high on political relatedness are more often found among the well-to-do, those of high-

Table 8.3. Distribution of Respondents on Index of Political Relatedness By Selected Demographic Characteristics

Relatedness	*High*	*High Medium*	*Low Medium*	*Low*	*Total*	*N*
Income						
$5,000 +	31%	40%	24%	5%	100%	339
$2,000–4,999	13	39	34	14	100	639
$2,000 –	8	39	32	21	100	147
Occupation						
Professional/manager	28	42	26	4	100	272
Other white collar	28	38	26	8	100	130
Skilled/semi-skilled	15	37	35	13	100	385
Unskilled	9	34	35	22	100	116
Farm operators	9	39	36	16	100	128
Community						
Metropolitan areas	23	40	27	10	100	390
Cities/towns	20	36	32	12	100	375
Open country	10	41	33	16	100	359
Education						
College	32	44	22	2	100	176
High School	19	42	30	9	100	559
Grammar School	10	32	36	22	100	409

er occupational status, urbanites, and the better educated, while low scorers are more often found at the opposite end of these demographic groupings. Of these factors, education—which, of course, also correlates with higher income and higher occupational status—seems particularly relevant in a study of political involvement. Unless specifically mentioned in the text, educational controls do not interfere with the patterns observed.

ANALYSIS

1. *Competence.* By competence, as a dimension of political involvement, we do not mean "knowledge" of politics in the bookish sense or the "know-how" of the professional politician. Rather, we mean an awareness of, and sensitivity to, those aspects of the political process that are crucial, if political behavior is to bring about social change.[12]

Table 8.4. Political Relatedness and Perception of Differences Between the Parties on Two Specific Issues

Perception of differences between Democrats and Republicans on economic controls and intervention in foreign affairs.	RELATEDNESS *High* *N = 205*	*High Medium* *N = 447*	*Low Medium* *N = 352*	*Low* *N = 142*
Democrats go further	42%	30%	26%	20%
Parties about the same	53	56	55	55
D.K., not ascertained, mistaken	5	14	19	25
Total	100%	100%	100%	100%

For instance, an individual's sensitivity to differences between the Democratic and Republican parties with regard to such issues as government control of the economy and intervention in foreign affairs may be considered as an index of competence. We should expect that those more highly related to the political process are also more perceptive of differences between the parties concerning issues. As Table 8.4 indicates, this is in fact the case. There is a significant difference between those more highly-related and those more low-related in their perception of the Democratic Party's stand on the issues. Also the proportion of those who do not know or whose perception was mistaken (i.e., who believed the Republicans would go further), increases progressively as level of relatedness decreases.

A more refined measure of competence may be derived from combining

12. This definition is considerably broader than that of Riesman and Glazer, *op. cit.*, pp. 542–3.

people's degree of sensitivity to differences between the parties with the amount or extent of attention to public issues, such as Governmental Social Welfare Activity, Taft-Hartley Labor Law Revision, U. S. Foreign Involvement and U. S. China Policy. A person attentive to all four, or at least three, of these issues may be considered highly "involved," regardless of his partisan stand. Combination of the sensitivity measure with issue involvement yields an "index of issue orientation." Table 8.5 presents the relationship between political relatedness and issue orientation. The more highly related people are to politics, the more highly concerned are they with issues. In other words, the highly related person perceives differences between the parties and chooses between them with regard to specific issues.

Table 8.5. Political Relatedness and Issue Orientation

	RELATEDNESS			
Degree of Issue Orientation	*High N = 198*	*High Medium N = 425*	*Low Medium N = 332*	*Low N = 132*
High orientation	77%	61%	51%	40%
Medium orientation	15	22	25	23
Low orientation	8	17	24	37
Total	100%	100%	100%	100%

2. *Affect.* The concept of "affect" as used here is defined more broadly than by Riesman and Glazer who distinguish between "genuine" and "spurious" or "idling" affect. We do not believe that affect derived from personal tensions is necessarily different in its social consequences from affect derived from sources inherent in political activity—at least not as long as other factors, like those of an ideological or structural sort, support the continuance of democratic politics.

One way of ascertaining whether an individual is affectively related to the political process is to ask him a direct question, giving him the opportunity to express the intensity of his feeling regarding the outcome of an election. As Table 8.6 indicates, relatedness, as defined in this study, and "caring," in an affective sense, about the outcome of an election, are clearly inter-related. The higher respondents are in relatedness, the more do they care about the outcome of the election. And the less related they are, the less do they care about the result.

A more convincing measure of affect is the degree of partisanship an individual may exhibit on a number of issues. An "index of issue partisanship" was derived by combining respondents' partisan answers on four issues with a scale measuring their perception of differences between the parties. It was

Table 8.6. Political Relatedness and Concern About Election Result

Concern About Outcome of Election	RELATEDNESS *High* *N = 205*	*High Medium* *N = 447*	*Low Medium* *N = 352*	*Low* *N = 142*
Care very much	49%	30%	22%	18%
Care somewhat	36	43	39	31
Don't care very much	12	17	25	29
Don't care at all	2	7	10	20
Don't know, not ascertained, It depends	1	3	4	2
Total	100%	100%	100%	100%

hypothesized that those not highly related to the political process are also less likely to take extreme partisan positions, more likely to be in conflict over issues and hence non-partisan with respect to issues. As Table 8.7 shows, our data support the hypothesis, with strong partisans more concentrated in the highly-related group, and with non-partisans most evident in the low-related group.

Table 8.7. Political Relatedness and Issue Partisanship

Degree of Issue Partisanship	RELATEDNESS *High* *N = 198*	*High Medium* *N = 425*	*Low Medium* *N = 332*	*Low* *N = 132*
Strongly partisan	30%	20%	17%	10%
Weakly partisan	56	51	51	49
Non-partisan	14	29	32	41
Total	100%	100%	100%	100%

A third measure of affect, similar to the previous one, is candidate partisanship. In the course of the interview respondents had an opportunity to make *spontaneous* references to the candidates, both positive and negative. For the purpose of this analysis "strong" Eisenhower and Stevenson supporters were combined into a "strongly partisan" category, and "moderate" supporters of either candidate were combined into a "moderately partisan" grouping. Those highly related should be expected to be strongly partisan in their candidate orientation. As Table 8.8 indicates, the data support this hypothesis.

However, there is the possibility that these findings are spurious. As the candidate partisanship measure is derived from spontaneous responses, partisan answers may in part be a function of verbal facility. And as verbal facility is likely to vary with education, it seemed advisable to control for possible variations in education. However, even with education as control, the general pattern observed in Table 8.8 holds. Education does play an independent part in determining the degree of partisanship, but on all educational levels relatedness continues to operate as an independent variable in relationship to partisanship.

Table 8.8. Political Relatedness and Candidate Partisanship

	RELATEDNESS			
Degree of Candidate Partisanship	*High* $N = 205$	*High Medium* $N = 447$	*Low Medium* $N = 352$	*Low* $N = 142$
Strongly partisan	35%	32%	26%	18%
Moderatey partisan	34	29	28	26
Indifferent	31	39	46	56
Total	100%	100%	100%	100%

3. *Identification.* "A primary determinant of political participation," the Chicago Seminar in Political Behavior emphasized in 1951, "is the individual's identification and association with the group and social structure." [13] It has been suggested that it was the "isolation of the individual" that "impelled the American to herd with his fellows in the party fold." [14] If this hypothesis were correct, one should expect that those least related to the political process would nevertheless be very strong party identifiers. It might be well to recall that "relatedness" means that the individual feels "responsibility," and the sense that the performance of his citizen role has an effect on the political process.

But identification with a party, rather than being a desperate effort of the isolated individual to make himself at home in the political world, is predicated on ability to enter into continuing social relationships. One should expect, therefore, as Table 8.9 shows, that those more highly related to politics in general also tend to be more strongly identified with a political party. Weak identification is more connected with low relatedness.

13. "Research in Political Behavior," *American Political Science Review,* Vol. 46, December, 1952, p. 1017.

14. Quoted from M. Ostrogorski, *Democracy and the Party System in the United States, 1926,* by Sebastian De Grazia, *The Political Community,* Chicago: University of Chicago Press, 1948, pp. 151–2.

Table 8.9. Political Relatedness and Party Identification

	RELATEDNESS			
Strength of Party Identification	*High* $N = 205$	*High Medium* $N = 445$	*Low Medium* $N = 350$	*Low* $N = 142$
Strong identifiers	43%	35%	32%	30%
Weak identifiers	27	38	43	42
Independents	30	27	25	22
A-political	0	*	*	6
Total	100%	100%	100%	100%

Table 8.9 also shows, however, that relatedness seems to be positively connected with "independence" or non-identification. There is some reason to believe that this result is due to respondents' educational status as a "third factor." Our data seem to bear out the general observation that we are probably dealing with two different types of "independents"–those who are independent because their higher educational status makes them less dependent on the parties as "anchorage points," and those who are independent because they are less related to politics and hence find it difficult to identify with a party.

4. *Exposure.* Political participation, the 1951 Chicago Seminar suggested in a terse sentence, "ranges from overt activity to mere interest (such as exposure to mass media)." [15] The sentence is illuminating. For in most studies of political behavior "interest" is usually conceived of as an index of involvement causally prior to political activity, rather than as an activity phenomenon in itself. Hence these studies are often stained in distinguishing between "interest" as a measure of "involvement," and interest in the sense of "spectator interest." We frankly think here of interest in the latter meaning. Interpreted in this way, interest is not a measure of affect, but rather a preliminary index of people's predisposition to expose themselves to campaign activities.

In line with the propositions of this study, one should expect that those more highly related to the political process are also more interested in following campaign activities. As Table 8.10 indicates, this is in fact the case.

Similarly, people's exposure to public affairs may be measured by the knowledge they possess on an issue which has been widely discussed in the mass media. Respondents were asked if they had ever heard anything about the Taft-Hartley Law. Although this law had received substantial publicity in the years preceding the 1952 election, only 57 per cent of the low-related respondents indicated having heard anything about it, as against 88 per cent of the highly-related (see Table 8.11).

15. "Research in Political Behavior," *op. cit.*, p. 1016.

Table 8.10. Political Relatedness and Interest in the Campaign

	RELATEDNESS			
Degree of Interest in the Campaign	*High* N = 205	*High Medium* N = 447	*Low Medium* N = 352	*Low* N = 142
Very much interested	64%	46%	28%	14%
Somewhat interested	27	36	44	28
Not much interested	9	17	28	55
Don't know, not ascertained	*	1	*	3
Total	100%	100%	100%	100%

Respondents were asked a series of questions concerning various mass media—newspapers, magazines, radio and television. An "index of exposure" was derived from these questions. A low score on this index would indicate that the respondent had used anywhere from one to four sources, but none of them actively. A medium score represents the use of one or two sources, at least one of them actively; and a high score indicates the use of three or four sources, at least one of them actively.

Table 8.12 shows a positive relationship between political relatedness and degree of exposure to the mass media, supporting the hypothesis that the highly related person is also one who exposes himself to the major media of political communication. Actually, although we have used relatedness as the independent variable, a good case can be made for the converse, i.e., that relatedness is dependent on exposure. On the one hand, those who are highly related will be sensitive to the need of exposing themselves to important sources of political information. On the other hand, those who are highly exposed tend to become highly related to the political process. Both variables are inter-related, and probably in both directions simultaneously. Finally, it may be well to mention that with educational status controlled, the relationship between re-

Table 8.11. Political Relatedness and Knowledge of the Taft-Hartley Law

	RELATEDNESS			
Knowledge of Taft-Hartley Law	*High* N = 205	*High Medium* N = 447	*Low Medium* N = 352	*Low* N = 142
Yes, had heard	88%	80%	74%	57%
No, had not heard	11	19	25	37
Don't know, not ascertained	1	1	1	6
Total	100%	100%	100%	100%

Table 8.12. Political Relatedness and Exposure to the Mass Media

	RELATEDNESS			
Degree of Exposure	*High* N = 205	*High Medium* N = 447	*Low Medium* N = 352	*Low* N = 142
High	65%	52%	36%	26%
Medium	21	25	27	21
Low	14	23	37	53
Total	100%	100%	100%	100%

latedness and exposure is still operative in spite of the fact that education is also related to the tendency to expose oneself to the media of communication.

5. *Participation.* The ultimate test of a person's relatedness to public affairs is the degree of his participation. Degree of participation may be measured by two behavioral indicators–the "vote-no vote" dichotomy in a single election, and voting regularity through time, i.e., the persistence of the voting "habit" in more than one election. Of these, voting behavior in a single election is, of course, the simpler and probably less reliable measure. For voting in a single election may be motivated by factors peculiar to that election, such as issues or candidates of singular emotional meaning to the individual. This consideration should be kept in mind in connection with Table 8.13. As one should expect, there is a direct relationship between degree of relatedness and vote turn-out in the 1952 election. The same pattern holds when relatedness is controlled by respondents' educational level.

Table 8.13. Political Relatedness and Vote Turn-out in 1952

	RELATEDNESS			
Vote Turn-out in 1952	*High* N = 205	*High Medium* N = 447	*Low Medium* N = 352	*Low* N = 142
Voted	93%	88%	80%	67%
Did not vote	7	12	20	33
Total	100%	100%	100%	100%

In order to determine whether relatedness had an effect on voting participation independent of the particular character of the 1952 election which brought out a record vote, probably because of the great attractiveness of both candidates, we controlled relatedness by the candidate partisanship measure. If voting was due to candidate partisanship, to the extent of eliminating the significance of relatedness as a motivating factor in participation, the pattern observed in Table 8.13 would break down. But, as Table 8.14 demonstrates, even with relatedness controlled by candidate partisanship, the highly related still tend to vote more than any other category.

Table 8.14. Political Relatedness and Vote Turn-out in 1952, Controlled by Candidate Partisanship

	RELATEDNESS			
Vote Turn-out in 1952	*High*	*High Medium*	*Low Medium*	*Low*
Strong Partisanship	*N = 71*	*N = 143*	*N = 92*	*N = 25*
Voted	96%	94%	89%	80%
Did not vote	4	6	11	20
Total	100%	100%	100%	100%
Moderate partisanship	*N = 70*	*N = 131*	*N = 99*	*N = 37*
Voted	92%	89%	81%	76%
Did not vote	8	11	19	24
Total	100%	100%	100%	100%
No partisanship	*N = 64*	*N = 173*	*N = 161*	*N = 80*
Voted	91%	82%	74%	59%
Did not vote	9	18	26	41
Total	100%	100%	100%	100%

Voting "regularity," i.e., voting through time, is a more difficult phenomenon to measure. A question asked in the Michigan survey whether respondents had voted in all, most, some elections or none did not yield satisfactory results once responses were controlled by education. This is probably due to a number of reasons: (a) people erred in recalling their whole record of past voting behavior; (b) people in the lower educational levels confused the response categories; and (c) people intentionally deceived the interviewer.

For these reasons we found respondents' answers concerning their voting behavior in only one past presidential election, 1948, combined with their 1952 behavior, more reliable as an index of voting regularity. Respondents were sorted into three groups; (1) those who had voted in both the 1948 and 1952 elections; (2) those who had voted in only one; and (3) those who admitted having not voted in either. As Table 8.15 shows, eight times as many of the low-related respondents failed to vote in both elections as of the highly-related respondents. The same pattern holds when the 1948–1952 voting behavior combination is controlled by education (except in the case of the college-educated in the highly-related category, some of whom apparently failed to vote in 1948, probably because they did not consider the choice between Truman and Dewey an attractive one).

Table 8.15. Political Relatedness and 1948–1952 Vote Pattern

	RELATEDNESS			
1948–1952 Vote Pattern	*High N = 201*	*High Medium N = 434*	*Low Medium N = 346*	*Low N = 137*
Voted in both elections	82%	73%	65%	50%
Voted in one election	15	18	20	25
Did not vote at all	3	9	15	25
Total	100%	100%	100%	100%

Other facets of participation may be measured by examining people's behavior in the election situation prior to the voting act. Do they talk to other people to convince them? Do they make financial contributions? Do they attend political rallies? Do they engage in other work for a party? Do they belong to a political club? As Table 8.16 indicates, there is a direct connection between degree of political relatedness and various types of participation. Invariably, the more highly related are also more active in the campaign. Moreover, there is an abrupt drop in type of activity from mere "talking" to personally more demanding forms of participation in all relatedness levels.

An "index of political participation" permits classification of respondents into these activity types: (1) high: those who voted in 1952 and engaged in some campaign activity; (2) medium: those who merely voted; and (3) low:

Table 8.16. Political Relatedness and Types of Political Participation

	RELATEDNESS			
Types of Participation	*High N = 205*	*High Medium N = 444*	*Low Medium N = 351*	*Low N = 142*
Talk to other people	42%	32%	24%	14%
Give money	12	4	3	0
Attend political rallies	15	8	6	2
Do other party work	7	4	2	1
Belong to political clubs	6	3	2	2

those who did not even vote. As Table 8.17 shows, those most highly related to the political process are also most active in electoral politics. The same general pattern prevails when relatedness is controlled by education, though the latter also has an independent effect on level of participation.

Table 8.17. Political Relatedness and Participation in the 1952 Campaign

	RELATEDNESS			
Index of Participation	*High* N = 205	*High Medium* N = 447	*Low Medium* N = 352	*Low* N = 142
High	46%	34%	25%	16%
Medium	46	53	55	52
Low	8	13	20	32
Total	100%	100%	100%	100%

SUMMARY

It has been an assumption of this study that an individual's "relatedness" to the political process is largely a function of (1) the degree to which he has internalized his role as a citizen, and (2) the degree to which he evaluates this role as being an efficacious one, in the sense that performance of the role will make a difference in political affairs. On the basis of 1,146 interviews concerning the 1952 election, an "index of political relatedness" was derived from two scales measuring "sense of citizen responsibility" and "sense of political efficacy." This index was tested against other dimensions of political involvement, such as competence, affect, party identification, exposure to political information, and participation in the 1952 electoral contest.

It was found that those more highly related to the political process are more sensitive to differences between the parties (Table 8.4), more issue-oriented (Table 8.5), more concerned about the outcome of the election (Table 8.6), more partisan on issues (Table 8.7), more partisan in their choice of candidates (Table 8.8), more likely to have strong party identifications (Table 8.9), more interested in the campaign (Table 8.10), know more (Table 8.11), are more exposed to the mass media (Table 8.12), more likely to vote (Tables 8.13 and 8.15) and otherwise participate in the campaign (Tables 8.16 and 8.17), than the less related.

Chapter 9

Identification with Class and Political Role Behavior

Research in political behavior is based on the assumption that the political process is characterized by the ceaseless inter-action of two major types of determinants: those "situational" factors which shape political activity irrespective of the personalities, motivations or perceptions of the participants; and those "psychological" factors which relate political activity to the motives, attitudes, or expectations of the political actors. It is the task of political behavior research to investigate the inter-penetration of specific situational and behavioral data in terms of empirically-oriented theory.[1]

It is the most general purpose of this study to report certain findings concerning the relationship between people's position in the social structure, or class, and various behavioral manifestations accompanying their role as democratic citizens in the presidential election of 1952. However, the findings are of interest not only because they may add to our knowledge of political behavior, but also because they necessitate reconceptualization of the data in terms of theoretical considerations not originally anticipated. In other words, this is in many respects a case study on the connection between empirical research and political theory.[2]

Social class has long been recognized as a significant factor in political

Originally published in *Public Opinion Quarterly,* Vol. 20 (Fall, 1956), pp. 515–29. Reprinted by permission.

1. See Avery Leiserson, "Problems of Methodology in Political Research," *Political Science Quarterly,* 1953, Vol. 68, pp. 558–84; and David Easton, *The Political System.* New York: Alfred A. Knopf, 1953, pp. 149–218.

2. See Robert K. Merton, "The Bearing of Sociological Theory on Empirical Research," and "The Bearing of Empirical Research on Sociological Theory," in *Social Theory and Social Structure.* Glencoe, Ill.: The Free Press, 1949, pp. 83–111.

behavior.[3] Research concerning the relationship between class and political behavior is, however, made difficult by two obstacles implicit in the concept of class. The first is "index instability" which not only hampers quantification of political hypotheses, but also restricts theoretical generalizations to specified social situations; the second is lack of agreement as to whether "objective" or "subjective" indices are more relevant in linking class to social behavior.[4]

The first of these obstacles will not concern us here. As to the second, it can be successfully argued that meaningful explanation of the relationship between people's objective position in the social structure and their political behavior requires the introduction of an "intervening variable" in the form of their self-identification with a particular social class. For high correlations between objective class position and manifestations of political behavior may be a necessary, but need not be a sufficient condition for class-relevant political behavior. In other words, it may be held that the way in which class is *experienced* by participants in the political process makes a significant difference in their political behavior. Yet, it is not our intention to enter into this controversy. It is simply suggested that if identification with class does make a difference, it is a difference in degree rather than in kind. As Theodore M. Newcomb has pointed out, to have both objective and subjective information about a person is better than either alone.[5]

IDENTIFICATION WITH CLASS

Richard Centers defines classes as "psycho-social groupings, something that is essentially subjective in character, dependent upon class consciousness (i.e., a feeling of group membership), and class lines of cleavage [which] may or may not conform to what seem to social scientists to be logical lines of cleavage in the objective or stratification sense." [6] Class, Centers continues, "can well be regarded as a *psychological* phenomenon in the fullest sense of the term. That is, a man's class is a part of his ego, *a feeling on his part of belongingness to something;* an *identification* with something larger than himself." [7] Centers evidently equates class identification with class consciousness, and he uses people's self-identification as a criterion of their class consciousness.

As an index of identification with class Centers uses responses to this ques-

3. But see Heinz Eulau, "Perception of Class and Party in Voting Behavior: 1952," *American Political Science Review,* 1955, Vol. 49, pp. 364–384.

4. See Paul K. Hatt, "Stratification in the Mass Society," *American Sociological Review,* 1950, Vol. 15, pp. 216–22.

5. Newcomb, Theodore M. *Social Psychology*. New York: The Dryden Press, 1950, p. 559.

6. Centers, Richard, *The Psychology of Social Classes.* Princeton, N. J.: Princeton University Press, 1949, p. 27.

7. *Ibid.*, p. 27.

tion: "If you were asked to use one of these four names for your social class, which would you say you belonged in: the middle class, lower class, working class or upper class?" [8] For instance, in a survey conducted in July, 1945, by the quota control method, and presumably representative of the adult white male population of the United States, Centers found that three per cent identified themselves as upper class, 43 per cent as middle class, 51 per cent as working class and one per cent as lower class, while two per cent said they didn't know to which class they belonged or didn't "believe in" classes. These answers, according to Centers, "will convincingly dispel any doubt that Americans are class conscious, and quite as quickly quell any glib assertions like *Fortune's* 'America is Middle Class.'" [9] And he asserts that "one can find textbook and dictionary definitions enough, to be sure, but these do not serve us here, for, in essence, *a class is no more nor less than what people collectively think it is.*" [10]

To support this hypothesis, Centers cites significant differences between occupational strata in regard to class identification, and he shows that class identifiers place different emphases on relevant class membership criteria. But this does not really prove that "class consciousness" is revealed by self-identification with class. Awareness of socio-economic differences may help one in identifying one's class, and people do not necessarily think or act alike because they belong to the same stratum. It is precisely for these reasons that subjective assessment of their social position may be important. But this cannot be construed to the effect that *only* subjective evaluations matter.

Centers himself does not seem to be sure of his evidence. He feels that "more evidence, something in the way of a crucial test, is demanded to support such an hypothesis." He finds a test, "although in a rather crude sense, in a comparison of the class criteria in use by people of common occupational position but of different class allegiance." [11] "If people in the same broad occupational stratum, but of different class affiliations do have interests in common with the classes with which they identify themselves they should differ in attitudes or politico-economic orientations, i.e. in conservatism-radicalism, from the 'members' of their own occupational stratum and differ in the direction characteristic of the classes with which they identify themselves." [12]

Centers' data bear him out. When attitudes on socio-economic issues and voting preferences of identifiers and non-identifiers within a given objective stratum are compared, Centers finds that "the differences are substantial, statistically reliable, and in the predicted direction." [13] After having partialed

8. *Ibid.*, p. 76.

9. *Ibid.*, p. 76. Centers was referring to a *Fortune* survey, conducted in 1940, which showed 79 per cent of respondents identifying themselves with the middle class.

10. *Ibid.*, p. 78.

11. *Ibid.*, p. 103.

12. *Ibid.*, p. 126.

13. *Ibid.*, p. 129.

out objective stratification indices, however, Centers concludes that subjective class identification is far more a function of socio-economic classification than anything else. "The several variables that are correlated with class identification to some extent or other are seen to derive most of their concomitancy of variation with those functions mainly from the strength of their association with stratification itself." [14]

Centers' theoretical formulations, sample and other methodological procedures have been severely criticized. Lipset and Bendix, for instance, have pointed out the circular nature of Centers' class concept, the likelihood of streotypy involved in self-identification, and the abandonment of concern with social theory.[15] Walter Goldschmidt has emphasized that Centers' correlations are positive where one would expect them to be, but that they are low. In other words, people behave in the expected manner more often than not, but the population does not behave consistently with Centers' class analysis.[16]

Our own concern is less with these aspects of Centers' work than with the uses to which the concept of class identification has been put. Centers relates class identification exclusively to other *attitudinal* dimensions of political behavior—such as conservative-radical orientations, voting preferences, and other psychological differences—, but not to any behavioral manifestations of political *conduct,* such as political participation, political interest, exposure to the mass media, political effectiveness, and so on. In other words, whether class identification has an effect on conduct, in the sense that the self-identifier actually takes the *role* of the identified-with class, remains unanswered. Examining this problem is the particular purpose of this study.

NEED OF RECONCEPTUALIZATION

The present analysis is based on data from a national area probability sample survey collected both prior to and after the 1952 presidential election by the Survey Research Center, University of Michigan.[17] Of a total sample of 1,614 twice interviewed, 482 respondents had to be dropped from the study because they either failed to identify themselves as middle class or working class, or could not be located on an objective Index of Status Characteristics.[18] Table

14. *Ibid.,* p. 202.

15. Lipset, Seymour M, and Reinhard Bendix, "Social Status and Social Structure," *British Journal of Sociology,* 1951, Vol. 2, pp. 150–68; 220–54.

16. Goldschmidt, Walter, "Social Class in America—A Critical Review," *American Anthropologist,* 1950, Vol. 52, pp. 483–98.

17. See Angus Campbell, Gerald Gurin, and Warren Miller, *The Voter Decides.* Evanston: Row, Peterson and Company, 1954.

18. In order to develop an Index of Status Characteristics, forty-five different combinations of occupational, income and educational status were placed in a cross-tabulation matrix which permitted each respondent to occupy different positions in the three status hierarchies, and which yielded nine summary scores for every combination of status positions possible in the matrix. The resultant status categories were combined and dichoto-

Table 9.1. Distribution of 1,132 Respondents in Terms of Objective Classification and Self-Identification

	OBJECTIVE CLASSES		
Self-Identification	*Working Class* $N = 766$	*Middle Class* $N = 366$	*Total* $N = 1{,}132$
Working Class	76%	36%	63%
Middle Class	24	64	37
Total	100%	100%	100%

9.1 shows the distribution of the final sample in terms of both objective classification and self-identification. This cross-tabulation was made in order to isolate the operation of class identification as a variable independent of the respondents' objective class position. With objective class controlled, it was then possible to divide respondents into four class groupings:

1. Those objectively classified as Working Class and self-identified as Working Class—Working Class Consistents or WW.
2. Those objectively classified as Working Class but self-identified as Middle Class—Middle Class Affiliates or WM.
3. Those objectively classified as Middle Class but self-identified as Working Class—Working Class Affiliates or MW.
4. Those objectively classified as Middle Class and self-identified as Middle Class—Middle Class Consistents or MM.

It was initially hypothesized, in line with Centers' procedure, that the affiliate groupings (WM and MW) should differ significantly from the consistent groupings (WW and MM, respectively) with regard to various manifestations of political behavior. Such differences would be indicative of the operation of class identification as an independent variable.[19] Tabulations revealed that

---

mized into "working class" and "middle class" on the basis of the frequency distribution of all respondents located in the matrix. The terms "middle class" and "working class" were assigned to the dichotomized aggregates for convenience only, largely because on the self-identification instrument 94 per cent of objectively classified respondents accepted these terms as descriptive of their class affiliation.

19. Chi square (χ^2) was used as the statistical test to determine significant differences. The 5 per cent level of probability was accepted as the standard of significance. Degree of association between class identification and dependent political behavior variables was measured by T, which is the square root of T^2 where $T^2 = \dfrac{\chi^2}{n \sqrt{(t-1)(s-1)}}$. T would equal 1 if the association were perfect. See Lilian Cohen, *Statistical Methods for Social Scientists.* New York: Prentice-Hall, 1954, pp. 134–5.

this was in fact the case. But closer scrutiny of the relevant tables indicated that the differences between each pair of contrasted class groupings were quite dissimilar for the attitudinal dimensions of political behavior, on the one hand, and manifestations of political conduct, on the other. Identification with class seemed less effective in helping self-identifiers take the political roles of the identified-with groups than in helping them develop relevant attitudes and preferences. It became necessary, therefore, to clarify the concept of identification.

Two steps were taken. First, rather than define identification as a feeling of belonginguess with its static implications, identification was conceptualized as a process, partial or limited, which involved locomotion away from and towards a region of valenced activity. It was assumed, then, that class identification might make for conflict, with the result that dependent attitudes or behaviors could be inconsistent.[20] This notion of identification as movement permitted measuring along the class identification continuum. The distance between the two consistent groupings reported on an Index of Class Identification Strength could serve as a standard for measuring the extent of identification by the affiliates in regard to dependent political behavior.[21]

Second, as inspection of the data suggested that identification conceived as locomotion away from and towards a region of valenced activity indicated more movement in regard to attitudinal than conduct patterns of political behavior, it seemed desirable to sharpen the distinction between identification in terms of attitudes, such as other identifications, demands or expectations, and identification in terms of political roles.

The literature on identification offered little guidance. Parsons and Shils, possibly because they are sociologists rather than social psychologists, seem to sense the multi-modal complexity of the concept of identification. Though they relegate their pregnant observation to a footnote, they distinguish "(1) the internalization of the values but not the role of the model from (2) internalization of his specific role." [22] But they do not follow up this distinction. Stuart M. Stoke, in a critical appraisal of the concept, points out that "an emotional identification cannot produce a behavioral manifestation if *capacity* for the behavior is lacking. It also seems reasonable that different degrees of capacity are bound to produce different degrees of behavioral identification,

20. For more detail, see Heinz Eulau, "Identification with Class and Political Perspective," *Journal of Politics,* 1956, Vol. 18, pp. 232–253.

21. This index is derived by subtracting one extreme position (i.e., proportion of voters within each class grouping) along each dependent variable continuum from the other extreme position. Resulting scores may be compared, and the *distance* between consistent and affiliate groupings may serve as a measure of locomotion. As it should be expected that the distance between the two consistent groupings is always greater than that between each contrasted pair, the more the distance score of the latter approximates that of the former, the less partial or limited is identification with respect to a particular aspect of an affiliate group's political behavior.

22. Parsons, Talcott, and Edward A. Shils, *Toward a General Theory of Action,* Cambridge, Mass.: Harvard University Press, 1951, p. 310, n. 4.

even though effort to identify is held at a constantly high level." [23] The success of behavioral identification, Stoke continues, "will be affected by the capacity of the individual to adopt the role." [24] But what is meant by "capacity to adopt the role?" In order to answer this question, an attempt was made to reconceptualize identification in terms of George Herbert Mead's theory of communication.

IDENTIFICATION AND COMMUNICATION

Once it is assumed that identification does not mean internalization of an object, as Freud and many subsequent psychologists thought, but rather movement along a continuum of valenced human relationships, one is readily led to the work of George Herbert Mead. For relationships are predicated on the presence of "Self" and "Other," their mutual interaction and expectations–in other words, the existence of reciprocally defined roles. And roles are defined through communication.

Though uninfluenced by Freud, but like Freud concerned with the development of the Self, Mead found in communication a requisite for identification. It is impossible to present all of Mead's observations on communication here, or to do justice to those of his ideas which are suggestive for the purposes of this study. As the work drawn on here is largely composed of lecture notes by some of his students, the same ideas occur time and again in many different formulations.[25] It is, therefore, by no means easy to select the quotations which best seem to harness the core of his thought.

Two major types, each divisible into two sub-types, may be sorted out of Mead's discussion of cummunication. Only the major types need to concern us. The first type of communication is perhaps best represented by the relationship between mother and baby. The baby may react to a tense mother, without her being aware that she has communicated her feelings to the child. Communication is automatic and unconscious. Behavior as such acts as a signal setting off a response. Soon a child in distress, for instance, does not wait for his mother's comforting acts or words and then respond, but he begins to speak to himself as he has heard his mother speak to him. Mead at times calls this "imitation" which is made possible by the fact that "there is already present in the individual an action like the action of another. . . . We are more or less unconsciously seeing ourselves as others see us. . . . We are unconsciously putting ourselves in the place of others and acting as others act." [26] It is this circuitous process which produces what Mead calls the "sig-

23. Stoke, Stuart M., "An Inquiry into the Concept of Identification," *Journal of Genetic Psychology,* 1950, Vol. 76, p. 177.

24. *Ibid.*, p. 180.

25. Mead, George Herbert, *Mind, Self and Society*. Chicago: University of Chicago Press, 1934.

26. *Ibid.*, pp. 68–9.

nificant symbol." The child plays the part of his mother toward himself, but the response, though significant, is still automatic, unconscious and unintentional. The response within one's self of a symbol (like "dog" or "chair") is "a stimulus to the individual as well as a response. This is what, of course, is involved in what we term the meaning of a thing, or its significance." [27]

The second major type of communication as developed by Mead is characterized by consciousness, an awareness of one's taking the part of another person. The child now consciously plays the part of his father or mother in games, or he may imagine that he is the hero of an adventure story. This, in Mead's terms, is "meaningful conduct." It takes place if the attitude which an individual "calls out in himself can become a stimulus for another act." [28] This process involves communication not in the sense of the first type, but "also an arousal in the individual himself of the response which he is calling out in the other individual, a taking of the role of the other, a tendency to act as the other person acts." [29]

Now, what distinguishes this second type from the first, apart from consciousness, is the *capacity* to anticipate what the response of another person is going to be. This capacity is a function of participation in organized, goal-directed activities—at first games, but later on more functional collaborative activities. The individual must not only take the attitudes of other individuals towards himself and towards one another, but he must also take "their attitudes toward the various phases or aspects of the common social activity or set of social undertakings in which, as members of an organized society or social group, they are all engaged." [30] The activity, then, has a goal, involves others, and is participated in by way of rules or procedures to be followed. In order to reach the goal of the activity, functions must be performed and functional roles must be filled. Communication, then, takes place in terms of the functions to be performed rather than in terms of feelings about particular people involved in the activity. Regardless of one's valued orientations towards the other—whether he is liked or not—it is possible to take his functional role. In other words, taking the role of the other is not so much dependent on identification with the other, but it derives from or is "built in" the unity and structure of "the social process as a whole; and each of the elementary selves of which it is composed reflects the unity and structure of one of the various aspects of that process in which the individual is implicated." [31] The attitude of the whole community or social group Mead refers to as "the generalized other." [32] And it is through the process of "calling out a generalized other" that fully conscious communication with others becomes possible.

27. *Ibid.*, p. 72.
28. *Ibid.*, p. 73.
29. *Ibid.*, p. 73.
30. *Ibid.*, p. 155.
31. *Ibid.*, p. 144.
32. *Ibid.*, p. 154.

Mead's discussion of communication, and particularly of his major types, is suggestive for our analysis of identification. For identification would seem to rest on communication. Unconscious communication, of the first type, should also give rise to a different type of identification than conscious communication. Indeed, though not made explicit, this differentiation between unconscious and conscious communication seems to underlie Parsons and Shils' distinction between identification as "internalization of the values" of the model and identification as "internalization of his specific role." As we have seen, Mead's first type of communication, especially in its later stage, is in many respects similar to the earliest appearance of what in Freudian terminology is called the super-ego, i.e. those norms or values which form a basic part of the emerging personality. Here the most primitive prohibitions or values–such as the distinction between hot and cold, or being a good child or a naughty one–are unconsciously internalized through identification.

Internalization of role, on the other hand, would seem to be based on Mead's second type of communication. Identification takes place not only in terms of unconsciously communicated values, but in terms of a conscious relationship. Since this relationship is one between Self and Other as mutually defined, it serves as the identifying mechanism. Required for identification here is attention to the roles others perform in relation to each other, i.e. the functions they perform as interacting individuals in pursuit of a common objective. Just as communication in terms of others' roles requires capacity to anticipate the others' response, so identification in terms of role is predicated on capacity for such identification.

Capacity for both successful communication and identification in terms of role depends on the degree of actual inter-action that takes place. Such inter-action is severely limited by the particular position which a person occupies in the social structure. A union member is unlikely to be a member of the local country club, or a successful businessman is unlikely to live in a slum tenement house. Inter-action, then, is dependent on such class-relevant variables as occupation, income, or education; it is related to common characteristics rather than common interests. But as common characteristics tend to give rise to common interests, and common interests are a prerequisite for taking the role of the other–i.e. for forming an image of the activity that is required to perform different functions in terms of role–it follows that identification is also dependent on shared characteristics if role performance is to be successful. Without these characteristics the person is *incapable* of taking the role of the other. This type of identification, then, is quite different from simply the sharing of emotional feelings, attitudes or values.

Just as both types of communication continue to operate simultaneously throughout a person's life-time–though the second type becomes increasingly preponderant–so both types of identification play a continuing part in a person's career. They are certainly not mutually exclusive, and one should not expect either type of identification to preclude the other from having an effect on social behavior. *Conduct*–in the sense of actually taking the other's role–should however be more a function of capacity than of personal identification in terms of feelings, attitudes or values.

One should expect that self-identification in terms of class is more likely to be effective when it comes to other identifications or preferences which are predicated on "internalization of values," than when it comes to taking a class-related role in political conduct. Participation in politics, for instance, as a manifestation of role performance, may depend less on identification with a class than on possession of those objective characteristics which are a prerequisite for capacity to imagine and play the role of the other. This does not mean that *only* common characteristics, defined in terms of objective class position, matter in political conduct, but it may suggest why self-identification with class is less effective in political role performance than more attitudinal aspects of political behavior.

CLASS IDENTIFICATION AND POLITICAL ROLES

A number of expectations accompany the role which the democratic citizen should play in the course of a political campaign. He is expected to be interested in the electoral fight, participate in the campaign or, if he does not participate, at least to vote. He is expected to see that there are differences between the parties and care about the outcome of the election. To meet these expectations, he should expose himself to campaign issues and arguments by paying attention to the mass media of communication. Beyond these expectations, the democratic citizen is assumed to feel that his vote counts, and that voting is a moral obligation. He should be a regular voter who takes his role as citizen in earnest from election to election.

In spite of great social pressure to carry out these various aspects of his role as a citizen in a democracy, almost one out of every two Americans fails to register his preferences at the polls. Many studies of voting behavior have suggested that political participation and other facets of the citizen role are a function of people's socio-economic status. That people tend to inter-act with each other in terms of their objective class position, and that such interaction is a prerequisite for capacity to perform successfully class-related political roles, raises the question of whether self-identification with social class makes a difference, *in degree* at least, as far as political role performance is concerned. If it does, one should expect that middle class affiliates will differ from working class consistents by showing better performance, while working class affiliates will differ from middle class consistents by showing worse performance. At the same time, however, the effect of such self-identification should be less than in the case of attitudinal manifestations of political behavior. In other words, the effect of self-identification on political role performance should be attenuated by capacity for such performance.

A number of questions concerning political role were asked by the Survey

Research Center in its 1952 poll. For two of these, participation and exposure to the mass media, detailed tables are presented here; the others will be treated in a summary table. All of the tables show significant differences between affiliates and consistents of both classes. But Class Identification Strength scores suggest the limited and partial effect of identification and may be accepted as indicative of the importance of capacity in political role performance. A separate table summarizes these scores as well as their respective locomotion scores, and contrasts them with those obtained for the relationship between class identification and more attitudinal aspects of political behavior.

Participation in the campaign and the act of voting are probably the most tangible manifestations of political role behavior. The participation scale used in Table 9.2 provides for three degrees of political participation: (a) high: those who voted and also engaged in some other political activity during the campaign; (b) medium: those who voted but did not otherwise participate; and (c) low: those who did not vote. Most evident in Table 9.2 is the fact that there are significant differences between the affiliate groupings and their respective consistent classes. Class Identification Strength scores indicate that the "pull" of identification, though present, is countered by a relative lack of capacity for relevant role performance.

Table 9.2. Class Identification and Participation

	WORKING		MIDDLE	
Participation	*Working* *N = 580*	*Middle* *N = 186*	*Working* *N = 131*	*Middle* *N = 235*
High	22%	28%	30%	49%
Medium	47	53	53	43
Low	31	19	17	8
Total	100%	100%	100%	100%
CIS Index	−9	+9	+13	+41
Tests for:	χ^2	*d/f*	*p*	*T*
WW–WM	10.83	2	< .01	.10
MM–MW	12.04	2	< .01	.14

Attention to the mass media of communication during an electoral campaign may be considered a form of vicarious participation. What, then, is the relative effect of class identification and capacity on this aspect of political role behavior? The "exposure to media" scale divided respondents into three groups: (a) high exposure: those who used three or four sources, of these one or more actively; (b) medium exposure: those who used one or two sources, with active use of at least one; and (c) low exposure: those who used no

Table 9.3. Class Identification and Exposure to Mass Media

	WORKING		MIDDLE	
Exposure	*Working* N = 580	*Middle* N = 186	*Working* N = 131	*Middle* N = 235
High	33%	48%	55%	71%
Medium	27	26	23	14
Low	40	26	22	15
Total	100%	100%	100%	100%
CIS Index	−7	+22	+33	+56
Tests for:	χ^2	*d/f*	*p*	*T*
WW–WM	17 86	2	< .001	.13
MM–WM	10.50	2	< .01	.14

source at all, or made inactive use of any number of sources. Table 9.3 shows an exposure pattern similar to that found in connection with participation. There are significant differences between the affiliated and their respective consistent classes. But the Class Identification Strength score differences are smaller than strong identification would lead one to expect. In other words, capacity for identification to be more effective is lacking.

Similar tests, summarized in Table 9.4, were made in regard to other manifestations of political role behavior. Interest was measured by using the re-

Table 9.4. Class Identification and Political Role Behavior

Relationship between Identification and:	*Tests for*	χ^2	*d/f*	*p*	*T*	*CIS Index*
Interest	WW–WM	26.81	2	< .001	.16	−6 /+29
	MM–MW	22.15	2	< .001	.21	+59/+26
Voting Regularity*	WW–WM	11.42	2	< .01	.11	+68/+59
	MM–WM	20.36	2	< .001	.21	+82/+57
Care for Outcome of Election	WW–WM	8.04	3	< .05	.08	+11+/23
	MM–MW	21.28	3	< .001	.19	+46/+21
Sense of Efficacy	WW–WM	18.31	2	< .001	.13	−4 /+18
	MM–MW	10.2[illegible]	2	< .01	.14	+44/+21
Sense of Citizen Duty	WW–WM	22.46	2	< .001	.14	+23/+50
	MM–MW	3.06	2	< .30	.08	+62/+51

*In connection with voting regularity, the difference between the consistent class groupings is so small that there is no room for meaningful variation in role behavior as a result of class identification. The same was the case in regard to perception of differences between the two parties. In other words, neither the operation of identification nor capacity could be properly isolated and observed.

spondents' own assessment of their interest, the scale distinguishing between: (a) those very interested; (b) those somewhat interested; and (c) those not much interested. The "voting regularity" scale differentiates between: (a) those who had voted in all or most elections since reaching voting age; (b) those who had voted in some elections; and (c) those who had never voted (exclusive of those too young to have ever voted before). Concern with outcome of the election was measured by a four-point scale distinguishing between: (a) those who cared very much; (b) those who cared somewhat; (c) those who didn't care much; and (d) those who didn't care at all. "Sense of efficacy" was measured in terms of a Guttman-type scale which was based on four items which sought to elicit respondents' feelings that one's action can effectively influence the course of political events, i.e. that one's vote counts. Similarly, "sense of citizen duty" was derived from four items, also brought together in a Guttman-type scale, which sought to discover the degree of respondents' acceptance of those obligations which a democratic society expects of its members.[33]

As Table 9.4 indicates, there are, with one exception of working class affiliates on the citizen duty scale, significant differences between the affiliated and consistent classes, suggesting that class identification is not altogether irrelevant in connection with political role performance. But, as in the cases of participation and exposure to the media, the Class Identification Strength scores suggest that identification is countervailed by capacity for effective role behavior. The T values obtained in these tests indicate that the degree of association between class identification and political role behavior, though positive, is uniformly low.

To assess the independent effect of capacity for identification on political role performance, on the one hand, and the relative irrelevance of capacity in regard to attitudinal dimensions of political behavior, one may compare the distance scores yielded by the Index of Class Identification Strength. As it should be expected that the distance between the two consistent classes (WW and MM) is always greater than the distance between an affiliate grouping and its respective consistent class, the more the distance score of the latter (i.e. WW–WM or MM–MW) approximates the distance score of the former, the less partial or limited is the effect of class identification and the less relevant is the capacity factor for identification. In other words, the distance between the two consistent classes yielded by the CIS Index can serve as a standard for measuring the extent of identification by the affiliates as well as the force of capacity.

Table 9.5 reports the distance scores for the relevant pairs of class groupings as well as the differences between these actual distance scores and the "ideal" difference score of zero for a hypothetical "full" identification. For the

33. For more detailed analysis of "political efficacy" and "citizen duty" as well as statistical analysis of the adequacy of these scales, see Campbell, Gurin and Miller, *op. cit.*, pp. 187–9 and 194–5.

purpose of comparison, scores obtained in two attitudinal dimension tests dealing with party identification and demands for government activity in the social welfare field have been included. As the table indicates, the differences in attitudinal manifestations of political behavior are, in general, considerably smaller than those in regard to role aspects of political behavior. This result suggests that capacity for identification is less relevant in connection with attitudes than with roles in political behavior.

Table 9.5. Identification Distance Scores of Class Groupings

	DISTANCE SCORE BETWEEN				
Political Behavior	*WW–MM*	*WW–WM*	*Diff*	*MM–MW*	*Diff*
PARTY IDENTIFICATION	49	40	(9)	35	(14)
GOVT. ACTIVITY DEMANDS	30	24	(6)	23	(7)
Participation	50	18	(32)	23	(22)
Exposure to Media	63	29	(34)	23	(40)
Interest	65	35	(30)	33	(32)
Care for Outcome	35	12	(23)	25	(10)
Sense of Efficacy	48	22	(26)	23	(25)
Citizen Duty	39	27	(12)	11	(28)

Table 9.5 reveals another very interesting pattern. If one compares the difference scores for manisfestations of role performance, a more or less distinct rank order appears to be implicit in these manifestations. For the middle class affiliates, the difference scores are greatest for exposure, participation and interest, somewhat smaller for sense of efficacy and concern over outcome, and smallest for sense of citizen duty. In the case of working class affiliates, exposure and interest also rank among the three greatest difference scores, now joined by sense of citizen duty, while participation shows a somewhat smaller score. This outcome suggests that role manifestations of political behavior differ from attitudinal manifestations in degree rather than in kind, that there is a gradual transition from emotional or personal identification to functional or role identification. The more a given dimension of political behavior is predicated on identification in terms of role, the greater, apparently, is the need for capacity to effectuate behavior in line with identification. In other words, rather than representing a dichotomy, Parsons and Shils' types of identification—"internalization of values" and "internalization of role"—may be considered as mutually interdependent poles of the identification continuum. Our empirical findings, then, support our theoretical considerations, to the effect that both types of identification operate simultaneously, but with more or less relevance for particular aspects of political behavior.

SUMMARY

This study has sought to examine the relationship of identification with social class and political role behavior. Identification with class, in spite of theoretical misgivings, was accepted as an "intervening variable" between objective class position and political behavior, on the assumption that both objective and subjective information about people is better than either alone. However, differences observed between attitudinal and role manifestations of political behavior suggested that class identification as an independent factor affecting political conduct is limited by capacity for identification. Capacity was made dependent, in line with theoretical considerations derived from the work of George Herbert Mead on communication, on people's actual inter-action in the social process. As inter-action is limited by objective class position, identification is more likely to be effective in connection with attitudinal than with role or functional dimensions of political behavior. The latter seem to be more dependent on capacity for identification, capacity depending on objective class position. The data reported on in this study tend to support this hypothesis. Moreover, it appears that rather than being dichotomous opposites, identification in terms of attitudes and identification in terms of role are interdependent ideal-type poles of an identification continuum—both operate simultaneously, but with more or less effect on particular aspects of political behavior.

Chapter 10

The Role of the Representative: Some Empirical Observations on the Theory of Edmund Burke

The problem of representation is central to all discussions of the functions of legislatures or the behavior of legislators. For it is commonly taken for granted that, in democratic political systems, legislatures are both legitimate and authoritative decision-making institutions, and that it is their representative character which makes them authoritative and legitimate. Through the process of representation, presumably, legislatures are empowered to act for the whole body politic and are legitimized. And because, by virtue of representation, they participate in legislation, the represented accept legislative decisions as authoritative. But agreement about the meaning of the term "representation" hardly goes beyond a general consensus regarding the context within which it is appropriately used. The history of political theory is studded with definitions of representation,[1] usually embedded in ideological assumptions and postulates which cannot serve the uses of empirical research without conceptual clarification.[2]

Originally published, with John C. Wahlke, William Buchanan, and LeRoy C. Ferguson, in *The American Political Science Review,* Vol. 53 (September, 1959), pp. 742–56. Reprinted by permission.

1. For a convenient and comprehensive summary of definitions, see John A. Fairlie, "The Nature of Political Representation," this *Review,* Vol. 34 (April-June, 1940), pp. 236–48; 456–66.

2. An effort at conceptual clarification is made by Alfred De Grazia, *Public and Republic—Political Representation in America* (New York, 1951).

I

Many familiar formulations treat representation in a non-functional fashion, viewing it as something valuable in itself, as an ultimate end, and seek to discover or specify its "nature" or "essence." Functional theory, on the other hand, deals with representation from the point of view of the political system as a whole or its component units. Herman Finer, for instance, has suggested that "responsibility is the chief and wider aim, and representativeness merely a convenient means to attain this. . . . The desire for responsible government is paramount; people not merely wish to represent their views, but actually to make and unmake governments." [3] But while functional formulations treat representation as a means for the attainment of some other political objective, failure to test functional propositions by way of empirical research leaves the problems raised by theory in the realm of hypothesis rather than reliable knowledge. In connection with Finer's proposition, for example, there has been little, if any, empirical analysis of the extent to which the represented do, in fact, want to enforce political responsibility, and how capable they are, under modern conditions, of exercising the necessary control. Nevertheless, once relevant concepts are clarified, a functional formulation of representation can open up areas of research which, in turn, may contribute to theoretical cumulation.

The relationship between the representative and the represented is at the core of representational theory. The term "representation" directs attention, first of all, to the attitudes, expectations and behaviors of the represented–to their acceptance of representatives' decisions as legitimate and authoritative for themselves. More particularly, representation concerns not the mere fact that they do accept such decisions, but rather the reasons they have for doing so, their rationalizations of the legitimacy and authority of the decisions made by their representatives.

Sometimes the adjective "representative" denotes nothing more than the publicly approved process by which representatives are to be chosen–as when a distinction is made between a "representative body" (meaning a group of men elected by specific modes of popular election) and a "non-representative body" (meaning a group of men selected by royal or executive appointment, entailed inheritance, or some other non-electoral process). Such usage implies that citizens' attitudes and expectations include, and may extend no farther than, the belief that representatives' decisions must be accepted as legitimate and authoritative *if* the representatives have been selected in the approved manner. In other words, elected officials are called "representatives" primarily because of the way they have been chosen. Even in a looser usage an appointed commission may be approvingly called a body of "representative" citizens, or may be attacked as "unrepresentative," depending on whether its

3. Herman Finer, *The Theory and Practice of Modern Government* (New York, rev. ed., 1949), p. 219.

members might conceivably have been chosen had they been subject to election rather than appointment; and their views will correspondingly be accorded or denied a measure of authority and legitimacy.

But the appropriate process of selecting public decision-makers has never been the really fundamental question for theories of representation. Behind every proposal for altering the method of selecting officials is some assumption, at least, about the effect of such changes on what decision-makers or decision-making institutions do, and how they do it. Proposals for reform must assume or show that the proposed change will bring it about that *what* representatives decide and *the way* they reach decisions is more nearly in accord with expectations and demands of the represented than has been in the case under the system to be reformed. The various defenses of existing systems of selection which postulate "virtual representation" have in common some shading of the belief that the process of selection is not of major significance in determining what representatives do or how they do it, or that decisions made by representatives can be brought in harmony with public expectations, without altering whatever process of selection is being defended by the advocacy of virtual representation.

The relationship between the process of selection of legislators and the modes and consequences of legislative behavior, or the relationship between public expectations and legislative decisions, offer wide and fertile fields for empirical research. Our purpose here, however, is less ambitious than a full-scale investigation of such relationships. It is to eliminate those particular ambiguities in the concept of representation which concern the actions or behavior of representatives, by use of the concept of "role," and to demonstrate the utility of this approach for further research relevant to the theory of representation.

II

A convenient and useful starting point in theoretical clarification is Edmund Burke's theory of representation. For, in following his classic argument, later theorists have literally accepted Burke's formulation and ignored its contextual basis and polemical bias. Burke ingeniously combined two notions which, for analytical purposes, should be kept distinct. In effect, he combined a conception of the *focus* of representation with a conception of the *style* of representation. Parliament, Burke said in a famous passage,[4]

> is not a *congress* of ambassadors from different and hostile interests; which interests each must maintain, as an agent and advocate, against other agents and advocates; but parliament is a *deliberative* assembly of *one* nation, with *one* interest, that of the whole; where, not local purposes, not local prejudices ought to guide but the general good, resulting from the general reason of the whole.

4. In his "Speech to the Electors of Bristol" (1774), *Works*, Vol. II, p. 12.

The sentence indicates that Burke postulated two possible foci of representation: local, necessarily hostile interests, on the one hand; and a national interest, on the other hand. He rejected the former as an improper and advocated the latter as the proper focus of the representative's role. But in doing so, he also linked these foci of representation with particular representational styles. If the legislature is concerned with only one interest, that of the whole, and not with compromise among diverse interests, it follows that the representative cannot and must not be bound by instructions, from whatever source, but must be guided by what Burke called "his unbiased opinion, his mature judgment, his enlightened conscience." Moreover, Burke buttressed his argument by emphasizing the deliberative function of the legislature—presumably in contrast to its representational function. Yet if one rejects his notion of the legislature as only a deliberative body whose representational focus is the whole rather than its constituent parts, the logic of Burke's formulation is no longer necessary or relevant.

Today, many "publics" constitute significant foci of orientation for the representative as he approaches his legislative task. Under the conditions of a plural political and social order, these foci of representation may be other than geographical interests, be they electoral districts or the larger commonwealth. The modern representative faces similar choices concerning the style of his representational role not only *vis-à-vis* his constituency or state and nation, but *vis-à-vis* other clienteles, notably political parties, pressure groups and administrative agencies. From an analytical point of view—though not, of course, from an empirical standpoint—the style of the representative's role is neutral as far as these different foci of representation are concerned. Regardless of his focus of representation—a geographical unit, a party, a pressure group, or an administrative organization—he is not committed to take either the role of free agent, following his own convictions, or the role of delegate, bound by instructions. In other words, Burke's linkage of a particular areal focus of representation with a particular representational style constitutes only a special case in a generic series of empirically viable relationships between possible and different foci of representation and appropriate styles of representation.

Of course, different foci of representation need not be mutually exclusive. They may occur simultaneously, and appropriate role orientations may be held simultaneously. For instance, a party may be so strong in a district that, in the representative's mind, the interests of district and party are identical. Or a pressure group may have such pervasive influence—as, for example, the Farm Bureau in a predominantly agricultural constituency, or the AFL-CIO in a predominantly working class district—that, again, the interests of district and pressure group become identified. Moreover, it is possible that different focal role orientations are activated *seriatim* as circumstances require. In particular, one may assume that on matters of no relevance to the representative's district, roles oriented towards party or lobby as foci of representation may serve as major premises of choice.

The generic extension of Burke's special case, broken down into analytic components, suggests that the focal and stylistic dimensions of representation must be kept separate in empirical research. Burke combined them for polemical reasons: he was writing in opposition to the idea of mandatory representation which had much popular support in the middle of the eighteenth century.[5] The result of this polemical commitment was that the problem of *how* the representative should behave *vis-à-vis* his clienteles became a substantive problem—*what* he should do for the clienteles. But the fact that a representative sees himself as reaching a decision by following his own convictions or judgment does not mean that the content of his decisions is necessarily oriented towards a general rather than a particular interest, just as his acceptance of instructions from a clientele group does not necessarily mean that he is oriented towards a special rather than the public interest. A representative may base his decisions on his own conscience or judgment, but the cause he promotes may be parochial. Or he may follow instructions, but the mandate may be directed towards the realization of the general welfare.

The distinction between the focal and stylistic dimensions of the representative's role allows us to suggest that representation is not concerned with what decisions should be made, but with how decisions are to be made. Now, it is axiomatic that decisions made in institutional contexts, such as legislatures provide, are made in terms of a set of premises which guide the behavior of decision-makers. The notion—explicit in Burke and other traditional formulations—that legislative decisions can be purely rational is not tenable in view of the fact that rationality, while not altogether absent, is invariably bounded by the legislature's institutional environment.[6] One of these boundaries is the representational fabric of the legislature. The representative system provides the representative with some of the assumptions in terms of which he defines his role. The roles he takes, in turn, whether in the focal or stylistic dimensions of representation, provide the premises for decision.

Premises underlying decisions made by legislatures, then, may be of two kinds: (1) they may be premises relevant to the focus of representation; and (2) they may be relevant to the style of representation. With regard to the first kind, for instance, a representative may be guided by premises such as that legislation should benefit either his district or the state, that it should be "liberal" or "conservative," that it should or should not favor special interests, that it should or should not be in performance of his party's campaign pledges, and so on. With regard to the second kind of premises, the representative's choices

5. *Cf.* Samuel H. Beer, "The Representation of Interests in British Government," *The American Political Science Review,* Vol. 51 (Sept. 1957), p. 613, who points out how little general legislation was proposed or enacted in those days.

6. For the conception of "bounded rationality" as well as the notion that roles constitute some of the premises of decision-making behavior, we are indebted to Herbert A. Simon's writings, notably *Models of Man* (New York, 1957). Our own formulations of the concept of role are developed in John C. Wahlke and Heinz Eulau, *Legislative Behavior: A Reader in Theory and Research* (Glencoe, 1959).

may be circumscribed by his stylistic role orientation, whether he sees himself following his own conscience or instructions. In this dimension the premises involved in his decisional behavior refer not to the focus but to the style of his role as representative.

III

The issue of styles of representation–free agency versus mandate–has been confounded by the fact that the enabling source of a representative's power is the electorate of a geographical district. Representation of geographical areas introduces a certain amount of ambiguity into the relationship between representative and represented which is likely to be absent under schemes of proportional or vocational representation.[7] Part of this ambiguity is the widely held expectation, contested by Burke but shared by many citizens and politicians alike, that the representative is a spokesman of the presumed "interests" of the area from which he has been elected. Of course, implicit in this expectation is the assumption that a geographical unit has interests which are distinct and different from those of other units, and which should be represented in public decision-making. This assumption has been challenged on a variety of grounds: that the geographical area as such, as an electoral unit, is artificial; that it cannot and does not generate interests shared by its residents; that it has no unique interests; and so on. Schemes of proportional or vocational representation have been advanced to make possible the representation of allegedly more "natural" interest groupings, such as minority groups, skill groups or economic groups.[8]

The assumption that geographical districts have particular characteristics–such as population attributes and industrial, agricultural or commercial properties–and, hence, unique interests which are, or ought to be, factors influencing the direction of public decisions continues to be shared not only by voters, politicians and others involved in policy-making, but also by scientific students of the political process. It underlies many studies which seek to relate legislative roll-call votes to the socio-economic characteristics of electoral districts,[9] as well as those studies which analyze the socio-economic composition of legislatures.[10]

7. For a perspicacious discussion of ambiguities in representation, see Harold F. Gosnell, *Democracy–The Threshold of Freedom* (New York, 1948), pp. 124–42.

8. Most theories of functional or proportional representation are motivated or supported by tacit and untested assumptions about the relationship of legislators' behavior to the process by which they are selected. This is merely a special case of the general democratic assumption that political responsibility is the mechanisim *par excellence* for bringing legislators' actions in line with the expectations of the represented.

9. See, for instance, Julius Turner, *Party and Constituency: Pressures on Congress* (Baltimore, 1951); or Duncan MacRae, Jr., *Dimensions of Congressional Voting* (Berkeley, 1958).

10. See, for instance, Donald R. Matthews, *The Social Background of Political Decision-Makers* (Garden City, 1954); or Charles S. Hyneman, "Who Makes Our Laws?" *Political Science Quarterly*, Vol. 55 (December, 1940), pp. 556–81.

It is a further assumption of these studies that legislators, having lived in their districts for all or substantial parts of their lives, share the values, beliefs, habits and concerns of the people who elected them and whom they presumably represent. Indeed, a literal interpretation of "represent" is to make something present that is not actually present. But this interpretation is most tenuous under modern conditions. Electoral districts tend to be so heterogeneous in population attributes, so pluralistic in the character of their group life, so diverse in the kinds of values and beliefs held, that whatever measures of central tendency are used to classify a district are more likely to conceal than to reveal its real character. The notion that elections are held as a method to discover persons whose attributes and attitudes mirror those most widely shared by people in their district appears to be of dubious validity.

This does not mean, of course, that the geographical district is dysfunctional from the point of view of maintaining the political system. The very circumstance of heterogeneity in the district tends to free the representative from being readily bound by a mandate, to make for discretion and political responsibility, and to enable him to integrate conflicting demands. The function of representation in modern political systems is not to make the legislature a mathematically exact copy of the electorate.

But the difficulty of finding an identity between representative and represented does not also mean that a representative's point of reference in making decisions cannot be his district. It may or may not be, and whether it is or not is a matter of empirical inquiry. We merely doubt that what orients a representative towards his district rather than some other focus of attention is the similarity between his district's characteristics and his own. We cannot assume, therefore, that even if a representative incorporates in himself the characteristics of his district–which, for argument's sake, may be admitted when he comes from a relatively homogeneous area–he will be more oriented towards the district than a representative who, from the point of view of district characteristics, is a deviant. In fact, the latter may be more concerned with his district and seek to discover its "interests," if they are discoverable, than the former. And if a district interest, so-called, can be specifically singled out, it is more likely to be the interest of a politically salient group in the district than of the district as an undifferentiated entity.

In so far as the district rather than some other unit, such as the entire commonwealth, is at the representative's focus of attention, it is more likely to be a function of political than of demographic or socio-economic variables. The problem is one of discovering under what conditions the representative can afford to disregard the district and still hope to maintain the confidence of his constituents. We might speculate, for instance, that in so far as he cherishes the position of power he holds, he is unlikely to ignore his district. We should expect, therefore, that representatives from districts where competition between the parties is keen are more district-oriented than representatives from one-party districts. Yet, we also know that competitive districts are more likely to be found in the heterogeneous metropolitan areas where district "interests" are difficult to ascertain.[11] In other words, what tends to orient the representative towards his district is likely to be the mechanism of political responsibility effectuated by political competition. District-oriented representatives from metropolitan areas where party competition is strong are, therefore, likely to rely on their own judgment, for a mandate must yield here to discretion to satisfy the demands of political responsibility. Discretion, of course, does not mean that the representative is wholly free to act as he pleases. On the contrary, it means that he will have due regard for all the considerations relevant in the making of legislative decisions. And among these considerations, certainly, the "interests" of his electorate or segments of the electorate, as well as his own estimate of the limits which these interests set to his actions, are important. As Burke admitted,

> it ought to be the happiness and glory of a representative to live in the strictest union, the closest correspondence, and the most unreserved communication with his constituents. Their wishes ought to have great weight with him; their opinion high respect, their business unremitted attention. . . .

Though analytically the foci and the style of the representative's role are distinct, they can be expected to be related empirically in a system of mutually interpenetrating orientations. In other words, just as we need not assume that a commitment to district invariably involves the representative's following instructions from his district (the role orientation of Delegate), or that a commonweal-oriented representative is invariably a free agent (the role orientation of Trustee), so also we need not assume that the foci of a representative's role are invariably unrelated to his representational style. In fact, it is the functionally related network of roles which makes for a representational *system*. We can assume, for instance, that a representative who is highly sensitive to the conflict of pressure groups, but not committed to any one, is more likely to be a Trustee in his representational role than the representative who feels close to a particular group and, consequently, is more likely to be a Delegate. Similarly, we might expect that a representative not strongly attached to a party, but not independent of it, is likely to shift between his own judgment and instructions (the role orientation of Politico).

IV

An opportunity to test the validity of the theoretical distinction here made, between the focus and style of representation, as well as of the representative's role, was afforded in connection with a comparative research project undertaken by the authors during the 1957 sessions of the state legislatures in Cali-

11. See Heinz Eulau, "The Ecological Basis of Party Systems: The Case of Ohio," *Midwest Journal of Political Science,* Vol. I (August, 1957), pp. 125–35.

fornia, New Jersey, Ohio and Tennessee.[12] State legislators in these four states were asked the following question, among others: "How would you describe the job of being a legislator—what are the most important things you should do here?" Of the 474 respondents, 295 gave answers relevant to the stylistic dimension of the representative's role, and 197 of these gave additional answers referring to the areal focus of their role.[13]

Responses concerning the stylistic dimension yielded three major representational role types: Trustee, Delegate, and Politico.[14] These types may be described as follows:

1. *Trustee:* This role finds expression in two major conceptions which may occur separately or jointly. First, a moralistic interpretation: the representative is a free agent, he follows what he considers right or just—his convictions or principles, the dictates of his conscience. Second, a rational conception: he follows his own judgments based on an assessment of the facts in each case, his understanding of the problems involved, his thoughtful appraisal of the sides at issue.

The orientation of Trustee derives not only from a purely normative definition, but is often grounded in conditions which make it functionally necessary. The represented may not have the information to give intelligent instructions; the representative is unable to discover what his clienteles want; preferences remain unexpressed; there is no need for instructions because of a presumed harmony of interests between representative and represented—all of these circumstances may be cited as sources of the role orientation of Trustee.

2. *Delegate:* Just as the Trustee is by no means an empirically pure type, the orientation of Delegate allows for a number of conceptions. All Delegates are, of course, agreed that they should *not* use their independent judgment or convictions as criteria of decision-making. But this does not mean that they feel equally committed to follow instructions, from whatever clientele. Some merely speak of consulting their constituents, though implying that such con-

12. The samples for the four legislatures are 91 per cent in Tennessee, 94 per cent in California and Ohio, and 100 per cent in New Jersey. The four states composing the total sample represent different regions of the country, different ratios of metropolitan and non-metropolitan population, and different degrees of party competition. The interviews, using fixed schedules, uniform in all four states and including both open-ended, focussed-type questions as well as closed, or fixed-answer type questions, averaged about two hours.

13. The reduction in the number of respondents from the total samples is, of course, due to the open-endedness of the question. Hence not all respondents could be used in the construction of the role types as they emerged from representatives' own definitions, and in the analysis.

14. In constructing stylistic and areal-focal role orientation types, the responses to the question were coded in terms of (a) characterization of job; (b) objectives of job; and (c) criteria of decision. Each total answer was broken up into individual statements and coded in terms of manifest content rather than latent meanings, though meaning was taken into consideration in locating manifest statements. Role orientation types were constructed by combining relevant manifest statements which seemed to make for a major orientational dimension. In general, data concerning criteria of decision yielded the stylistic orientation, and data concerning the objectives of the job yielded the areal orientation.

sultation will have a mandatory effect on their behavior. Others frankly acknowledge their direct dependence on instructions and accept them as a necessary or desirable premise for their decisions. Some may even follow instructions counter to their own judgment or principles. In other words, the possibility of conflict in role orientations is clearly envisaged and resolved in favor of subordinating one's independence to what is considered a superior authority.

3. *Politico:* The classical dichotomization of the concept of representation in terms of free agency and mandate was unlikely to exhaust the possibilities of representational styles. Depending on circumstances, a representative may hold the Trustee orientation at one time, and the Delegate orientation at another time. Or he might seek to reconcile both in terms of a third. One can think of representation as a continuum, with the Trustee and Delegate orientations as poles, and a midpoint where the orientations tend to overlap and, within a range, give rise to a third role. Within this middle range the roles may be taken simultaneously, possibly making for conflict, or they may be taken serially, one after another as conditions call for.

Because the data do not permit sharp discrimination between the two possibilities, we shall speak of representatives who express both orientations, either simultaneously or serially, as Politicos. In general, then, the Politico as a representational role type differs from both the Trustee and the Delegate in that he is more sensitive to conflicting alternatives in role assumption, more flexible in the way he resolves the conflict of alternatives, and less dogmatic in his representational style as it is relevant to his decision-making behavior.

The spell of the Burkean formulation on the interpretation of representation tended to create reactions which, it seems, are almost as arbitrary as Burke's formula itself. In particular, the functional notion, itself quite realistic under modern conditions, that the legislature is an agency for the coordination and integration of diverse social, economic and political interests makes apparent the simple-mindedness of Burke's theory, now as then. Carl J. Friedrich, for instance, has pointed out that "the pious formula that representatives are not bound by mandate, that they are subject only to their conscience and are supposed to serve the common weal, which is repeated in so many European constitutions, while significant as a norm, may lead to differentiating as well as to integrating results." [15] Yet, in concentrating on the multiplicity of potential representational foci, Friedrich went too far in his rejection of Burke. For, once the distinction is made between the style of the representative's role and its focus, Burke's "pious formula" is still relevant. Both the focus and the style are likely to be influenced by the character of politics at a given time and by the demands of contemporary political circumstances on the representative as a decision-maker. Functional analysis cannot limit itself to the foci of representation alone, but must also pay attention to those political requirements which may be relevant to the representative's style.

15. *Consttutional Government and Democracy* (Boston, rev. ed., 1950), p. 297.

Our hypothesis may be stated as follows: the exigencies of modern government, even on the relatively low level of state government, are exceedingly complex. Taxation and finance, education and public welfare, legal reform, licensing and regulatory problems, transportation, and so on, are topics more often than not, beyond the comprehension of the average citizen. Unable to understand their problems and helpless to cope with them, people are likely to entrust the affairs of government to the elected representatives who, presumably, are better informed than their constituents. People may pay lip service to the notion that a representative should *not* use his independent judgment,[16] but in fact they are unable, or do not care, to give him instructions as may once have been possible when the tasks of government were comparatively simpler. It is likely, therefore, that the representative has become less and less a Delegate and more and more a Trustee as the business of government has become more and more intricate and technical. Rather than being a "pious formula," the role orientation of Trustee may be a functional necessity, and one should expect it to be held by state legislators more frequently than that of Politico, and the latter more frequently than that of Delegate.

Table 10.1. Distribution of Representational Role Orientations in Four States

Representational Role Orientation	*Calif. (N = 49)*	*N.J. (N = 54)*	*Ohio (N = 114)*	*Tenn. (N = 78)*	*Total (N = 295)*
Trustee	55%	61%	56%	81%	63%
Politico	25	22	29	13	23
Delegate	20	17	15	6	14
Total	100%	100%	100%	100%	100%

A test of this general proposition is possible by way of comparative analysis of the distribution of representational role styles in the four states. As Table 10.1 indicates the role orientation of Trustee is held by a greater number of legislators than that of either Politico or Delegate. In all four states it appears more frequently, and significantly more frequently, than the other two. More-

16. In the years before the second World War, public opinion polls several times sampled expectations in this regard. Relevant poll questions were: (1) Do you believe that a Congressman should vote on any question as the majority of his constituents desire or vote according to his own judgment? (2) Should members of Congress vote according to their own best judgment or according to the way the people in their district feel? (3) In cases when a Congressman's opinion is different from that of the majority of the people in his district, do you think he should usually vote according to his own best judgment, or according to the way the majority of his district feels? In three of four polls, 61, 63 and 66 per cent, respectively, of the respondents said the Congressman should vote the way people feel. In the fourth poll, only 37 per cent gave this answer. See Hadley Cantril, Ed., *Public Opinion, 1935–1946* (Princeton, 1951), p. 133.

over, the Politico appears somewhat more frequently in all states than the Delegate.

The Trustee orientation appears significantly more frequently in Tennessee than in the other three states, a fact that seems to contradict the proposition that the orientation of Trustee varies with the complexity of governmental affairs. As Tennessee is less urbanized and industrialized than the other states, one should expect Tennessee legislators to be less often Trustees and more often Delegates than legislators in California, New Jersey or Ohio. But it may also be that "complexity" is a function of perceptions, regardless of the real situation. If so, then to Tennesseans the relatively less complex character of socio-economic life may appear more complex than it actually is, compared with the other states. The more frequent appearance of the Trustee orientation there may only be symptomatic of an even greater feeling of helplessness and inefficacy on the part of people *vis-à-vis* governmental problems, as it is perceived by state representatives. Such perceptions may be a reflection of the lower educational level in Tennessee; but to demonstrate this is beyond the limits of this analysis.[17]

V

If, as suggested earlier, a representative's areal-focal orientation does not automatically derive from ascertainable district interests or from personal characteristics he may share with his constituents, the question arises where such orientations do come from, and how they intrude on the representative's conception of his role. For the purposes of this study, it was possible to delineate three areal-focal orientations which may be described as follows:

1. *District-orientation:* District-oriented representatives had essentially two alternatives: either they could simply mention their districts or counties as being relevant in their conception of their jobs, or they could explicitly place their districts as being above the state as an important factor in their legislative behavior. Among the former, the most frequent responses suggested that it is the representative's job to take care of his district's needs and pass legislation which will benefit his district or county. Others emphasized the policy problems involved in legislation and the necessity to protect what they considered district interests from the policy point of view. Or the emphasis was on the services which these representatives think they are expected to render for their district. Another group of district-oriented representatives specifically pointed to the importance of placing the interests of their district above those of the state, though they usually admitted that state concerns should also be given consideration.

17. As the Trustee orientation includes responses stressing traditional moral values, it might be assumed that these virtues—such as following one's conscience or what one feels to be "right"—are more valued in rural Tennessee than in the three more urbanized states. But inspection of the frequency with which this attitude appears in Tennessee as against the other states does not reveal significantly different distributions of relevant responses: California—18 per cent; New Jersey—8 per cent; Ohio—28 per cent; and Tennessee—23 per cent.

2. *State-orientation:* As in the case of the district-oriented respondents, state-oriented representatives may either mention the state alone as the salient focus, or they may also mention the district, but clearly tend to place state above district. Some emphasized the need of state policy or state programs as an overriding consideration. A second group pointed to both state and district as relevant foci, but tended to give the benefit of doubt to the state. Finally, some state-oriented representatives explicitly emphasized the desirability of overcoming parochial considerations in favor of the state.

3. *District-and-state-orientation:* A third major group of respondents who spontaneously concerned themselves with the areal focus of their role mentioned both district and state, but, apparently, did not envisage a possibility of conflict and thought that they could attend to both foci without undue difficulty. Yet, the generality of the responses given in this connection may be deceptive, and coding them under this rubric may have been somewhat arbitrary in a number of cases. Though the actual language used tended in the direction of the state as the focus of role orientation, the tone often appeared to be more indicative of a latent district orientation. One should expect these hyphenated representatives to resemble district- more than state-oriented representatives.

Areal role orientations may be assumed to be a function of the dynamics of the democratic political system with its emphasis on the responsibility of the representatives to the represented. Political responsibility—a set of relationships in which the elected are sensitive to the power of the electors over them, and in which the elected are aware of the sanctions which make responsibility a reality—is predicated on the existence of a competitive political system where constituents have a genuine choice, *i.e.*, where the representatives are periodically confronted with the real possibility of removal from office. The sanction of removal inherent in a competitive party system serves to focus representatives' attention on their district rather than the state as the crucial point of reference. Representatives from competitive areas are more likely to be district-oriented than representatives from one-party areas, while representatives from one-party areas are more likely to be state-oriented than those from competitive areas.

An initial, though crude, test of this hypothesis is possible by examining the distribution of areal role orientations in the four states. Tennessee representatives might be expected to be less district-oriented than representatives in the other states, in view of the predominant one-party character of Tennessee politics. As Table 10.2 indicates, the data support this hypothesis. Though the percentage differences are small and statistically not significant, except in the California-Tennessee contrast, only 21 per cent of the Tennessee representatives are district-oriented as against 35 per cent in California, 27 per cent in New Jersey, and 28 per cent in Ohio. But the most noticeable aspect of Table 10.2 is the fact that Tennessee representatives in significantly greater proportion failed to express themselves spontaneously in this connection. Why this is

Table 10.2. Distribution of Areal Role Orientations in Four States

Areal Role Orientation	*Calif. (N = 113)*	*N.J. (N = 79)*	*Ohio (N = 162)*	*Tenn. (N = 120)*	*Total (N = 474)*
District	35%	27%	28%	21%	27%
District-and-State	14	28	25	8	19
State	20	14	16	9	15
No mention	31	31	31	62	39
Total	100%	100%	100%	100%	100%

so can, at this point, be only a matter of speculation. Tennessee representatives may take whatever areal foci they have so much for granted that they feel no need to mention them, or they may simply be less articulate than representatives elsewhere. Finally, while there is a somewhat sharper differentiation between district and state role orientations in California than in New Jersey and Ohio (where the combined category figures more prominently), relatively few representatives in all states mentioned the state alone as the focus of their areal orientation.

*Table 10.3. Political Character of Electoral Districts and Areal Role Orientations in Three States**

	POLITICAL CHARACTER OF DISTRICT		
Areal Role Orientation	*Competitive (N = 72)*	*Semi-competitive (N = 77)*	*One-party (N = 96)*
District	53%	48%	33%
District-and-State	28	34	33
State	19	18	34
Total	100%	100%	100%

*California, New Jersey and Ohio. "Non-respondents" on the areal dimension have been omitted.

A more severe test of the hypothesis is possible by relating areal role orientations to the political character of representatives' home districts. Because party competition as an independent variable has no room for operation in predominantly one-party Tennessee,[18] Table 10.3 presents the combined data for California, New Jersey and Ohio alone.[19] As Table 10.3 shows, 53 per

18. Of the 46 Tennessee respondents who mentioned an areal orientation, only four came from competitive and five from semi-competitive districts.

19. Competition in district was severally defined in the four states on the basis of past election returns. Space limitations prevent us from specifying the criteria here. They may be obtained from the authors.

cent of the representatives from competitive districts were district-oriented, while only 33 per cent of those from one-party districts were so classified. On the other hand, one-party district representatives held in significantly greater proportion a state orientation than those from competitive districts.[20] The data support the hypothesis that areal orientation varies with the political character of the district in which representatives are elected.[21]

VI

The analytical distinction between the foci and the style of representation is helpful in dissecting the representative's role. Actual behavior is not a function of discrete role orientations, however, but of a system of such orientations. It is the network of interpenetrating roles which gives pattern and coherence to the representational process. It is essential, therefore, to relate areal and stylistic role orientations to each other in terms of significant hypotheses about conditions of their co-variation in the representational system.

It has been suggested earlier that, analytically, stylistic role orientations are neutral. What correlation may be found empirically, therefore, should depend on some crucial attribute in the independent variable—in this connection the areal role orientation. It may be suggested that this crucial attribute is the condition of effective political responsibility. In so far as they differ, district-oriented representatives are ultimately responsible to their constituents, while state-oriented representatives are not responsible to an equivalent state-wide constituency. The state-oriented representative cannot point to a state-wide clientele from which he could possibly receive a mandate.[22] Hence the hypothesis may be advanced that state-oriented representatives are more likely to be Trustees than district-oriented representatives, whereas the latter are

20. $\chi^2 = 9.238$ for the entire array, where $d.f. = 4$, $p \geqslant .05$. If the middle categories are omitted and only competitive and one-party districts are compared with respect to state and district orientation alone, $\chi^2 = 7.12$; $d.f. = 1$; $p < .01$.

21. However, this finding may be spurious. It might be less a function of the political character of the district than of its ecological character. Competitive districts are, more often than not, located in metropolitan areas, while one-party districts are more frequent in non-metropolitan areas. It seemed advisable, therefore, to control the districts' political character by their ecological character. For this purpose, the districts were divided on the basis of the 1950 Census specifications. The hypothesis concerning the relationship between political character of district and areal orientation was clearly maintained in both metropolitan and non-metropolitan districts. However, while the pattern proved similar in both ecological categories, a greater proportion of district-and-state-oriented representatives appeared in the non-metropolitan than in the metropolitan areas, suggesting a pull towards greater dichotomization of areal orientations in the metropolitan environment. In view of the intimate connection in industrialized states between metropolitan and state-wide problems, this result is not surprising. It seems that the state is more salient as a focus of attention for representatives from metropolitan districts (no matter what their political character) than from non-metropolitan districts.

22. He might, of course, receive instructions from a state-wide clientele such as a pressure group or political party, but these constitute other dimensions of his attention foci.

more likely to be Delegates than the former. As Table 10.4 demonstrates, this is in fact the case. While 84 per cent of the state-oriented representatives are Trustees, only 37 per cent of the district-oriented and 55 per cent of the district-and-state-oriented representatives are so. And while 36 per cent of the district-oriented representatives are Delegates, only 8 per cent of the district-and-state-oriented and none of the state-oriented hold a mandatory view of their representational role.

*Table 10.4. Areal-Focal and Representational Role Orientations in Four States**

Representational Role Orientation	District-oriented (N = 89)	State-District-oriented (N = 64)	State-oriented (N = 44)
Trustee	37%	55%	84%
Delegate	36	8	—
Politico	27	37	16
Total	100%	100%	100%

* χ^2 for the entire array = 37.759; $d.f. = 4$; $p < .001$.

Moreover, Table 10.4 supports some corollary hypotheses. In the first place, because a representative is district-oriented, he need not be a Delegate any more frequently than a Trustee. This simply means that though a representative may clearly have his district at his focus of attention, he may nevertheless act on behalf of the district, in his own conception, as a free agent. Such a representative will say that he knows and understands what the district needs and wants, and he rejects the notion that anybody in the district can tell him what to do. As Table 10.4 shows, among the district-oriented representatives, almost equal proportions, 37 per cent and 36 per cent respectively, are Trustees and Delegates. On the other hand, state-oriented representatives are more likely to be Trustees than anything else. This hypothesis is based on the assumption that the state-oriented representatives do not and cannot recognize a state-wide areal clientele which could give them instructions. As Table 10.4 indicates, none of the state-oriented representatives is a Delegate, and only 16 per cent are Politicos.

Finally, if the representative's areal focus is both his district and the state, one should expect that he will take the role of Politico more frequently than either the district- or the state-oriented representative. For, because he stresses both foci, he is likely to be subject to cross-pressures: as a district-oriented representative he will take the role of Delegate at least as frequently as that of Trustee; as a state-oriented representative he will take the role of Trustee more frequently than any other. We should expect, therefore, that this representative will not only be a Politico more frequently than the other two areal-orientational types, but also that he will take the Trustee role more frequently than the Delegate role. Both hypotheses find support in the data reported in Table 10.4. While the differences are small, 37 per cent of the district-and-state-oriented representatives are Politicos, while only 16 per cent and 27 per cent of the other two groups admit to this representational style. Moreover, a majority are also Trustees, while only 8 per cent are Delegates—evidence of the differential effect of areal role orientations on the particular stylistic roles which seem most appropriate.

This analysis supports the notion that the areal-focal and stylistic dimensions of representation give rise to role orientations which, though analytically distinct, constitute a role system, and that this system gives the process of representation both its structure and its function.

Chapter 11

Occupational Mobility and Political Career

Recruits for elective public office in the United States are largely drawn from occupations relatively high in the occupational status scale.[1] This does not prove, as Marxists would have it, that there is a conspiracy to control the governmental apparatus in the interest of a ruling class. There are more simple and plausible explanations. In the first place, the expenses involved in seeking elective office are so high and the rewards so small that only those financially capable can afford the necessary sacrifices. Second, the amount of time required for holding public office, even if it does not mean full-time service, is so great that only occupationally "expendable" persons may be available for political recruitment. Third, the insecurity accompanying elective office is so high that only those who can readily return to their private occupations will venture into politics. Finally, the politician's role, in the electoral process as well as in elective office, calls for considerable communicative skills which, in part at least, can only be acquired in the course of preparation for and practice in a private occupation. The requisites of a political career are quite obviously related to the kind of occupation pursued by a person in his private life.

There is a reciprocal function of the political career for private occupations as well. Just those individuals whose private pursuits qualify them for public office may also derive advantages from political status for their private occupations. This is particularly true of the legal profession, but it is also true of

Originally published, with David Koff, in *Western Political Quarterly,* Vol. 15 (September, 1962), pp. 507–21. Reprinted by permission.

1. This statement hardly needs documentation. For recent bibliographical references, see Dwaine Marvick (Ed.), *Political Decision-Makers: Recruitment and Performance* (Glencoe: Free Press, 1961), pp. 334–43.

persons employed in real estate, insurance, and retail trades.[2] The experience and publicity of public office, the wide contacts made possible by the political occupation, and the actual influence on public policy that may be exerted, are likely to benefit some individuals in their private vocations. Considerations of this sort undoubtedly attract certain people to politics (though the politician's own stock-in-trade appeal to "public service" cannot be written off simply as an altogether empty formula).

Of all the choices an individual makes in the course of a lifetime, that of occupation is probably more far-reaching than any other. It is not only likely to determine how he makes a living, but, as Morris Rosenberg has pointed out, "the individual who makes an occupational choice also commits himself to a certain pattern of thought and behavior for years to come. In many cases, if the role is sufficiently internalized, it may influence his entire personality structure." [3] But the political career is not ordinarily pursued in the manner of most occupations. Most politicians have achieved some standing in the private occupational world before going into politics. It is the private occupation, therefore, rather than his political career, which probably reflects the politician's attitudes and values.[4]

Politics as a vocation and private occupation are interdependent, then, not only in very practical respects, but also in terms of a potential harmony of attitudes and values. If this be so, the question may be asked whether politicians for whom the private occupational choice represented an "advance" over the occupational status of their fathers differ in their political careers from those whose occupational choice did not involve a drastic change from parental values. Although occupational mobility may be upward as well as downward, not many politicians are likely to be downwardly mobile. If private occupational choice makes a difference, therefore, it should be largely one between upwardly mobile politicians and those whom we might call "status-stable."

The question may be reformulated: if private occupation as currently held by a politician is a source of his public attitudes and values, is occupational mobility an additional factor in shaping the political career? When an individual moves to a position on the scale of occupations higher than that held by his father, it may reflect an orientation towards the rewards of the higher occupation somewhat different from that of those who are occupationally status-stable. And if this be so, does it also influence his public career? We may

2. For the role of the legal profession, see David R. Derge, "The Lawyer as Decision-Maker in the American State Legislature," *Journal of Politics,* 21 (August 1959), 408–33, and the literature cited there. For other occupations, see the older study by Charles S. Hyneman, "Who Makes Our Laws?" in John C. Wahlke and Heinz Eulau (Ed.), *Legislative Behavior* (Glencoe: Free Press, 1959), pp. 254–65.

3. Morris Rosenberg, *Occupations and Values* (Glencoe: Free Press, 1957), p. 2.

4. The pervasive influence of occupational competence on the specializing behavior of politicians is discussed by William Buchanan, Heinz Eulau, LeRoy C. Ferguson, and John C. Wahlke, "The Legislator as Specialist," *Western Political Quarterly,* 13 (September 1960), 636–51.

suggest that the reciprocal relationship between public and private occupation is accentuated among those who in private life are upwardly mobile.

But one might also entertain another view: precisely because public and private occupational attitudes and values are interdependent, occupational mobility as such will not make a difference in how a person relates himself to politics once higher private status has been attained. Although status-striving occurs in the political world as much as in the private, a finding that mobility patterns in one are not related to mobility patterns in the other would suggest that political advance is not an avenue to power and prestige in the private sphere. A finding of this kind would tell us as much about the functional quality of politics in American life as would a positive result.

RESEARCH DESIGN: INTERVIEW, SAMPLE, INDEX AND CONTEXT

This study investigates the effect, if any, of occupational mobility and stability on the career perspectives of American state legislators. Though many studies have been made of the relationship between occupation and political behavior, none, as far as we know, has been concerned with the effect of mobility on political careers. The possibility of doing this study was given in connection with a larger project of research on legislative roles.[5] During the legislative sessions of 1957, 100 per cent of the New Jersey legislators, 94 per cent of those of Ohio and California, and 91 per cent of the Tennessee legislators were interviewed. Of the total of 474 original respondents, only 325 could serve the purposes of this study, either because proper occupational classification of the legislators or their fathers was impossible; or because, in the case of legislators and their fathers classified as farmers, it was impossible to specify a meaningful mobility pattern.

In the course of the interview, the legislators were asked the following questions:

1. How did you become interested in politics? What is your earliest recollection of being interested in it?
2. What governmental or party positions—local, state, or federal—had you held before going into the legislature?
3. Just how did it come about that you became a legislator?
4. Do you expect to continue to run for the legislature?
5. Are there any other political or governmental positions—local, state, or federal—which you would like to seek?

5. The data on which this analysis is based were collected as part of the State Legislative Research Project. For a full report on this project, see John C. Wahlke, Heinz Eulau, William Buchanan and LeRoy C. Ferguson, *The Legislative System: Explorations in Legislative Behavior* (New York: Wiley, 1962). The Project is not responsible for the analysis reported here.

The open-ended character of some of these questions makes it mandatory to consider the results of this study as suggestive rather than definitive. While open-ended questions have the advantage of leading to spontaneous and widely ranging responses, and of allowing the respondent himself to formulate or "structure" the topic under investigation, there are certain drawbacks that limit their usefulness for systematic treatment. For instance, many respondents gave more than one answer, thus preventing the possibility of assigning priorities within a particular response pattern. Secondly, the respondents differed a great deal in a number of personal characteristics significant in answering open-ended questions. A few were suspicious of the interview and gave minimum, if not evasive, answers. Others were more candid. Some were genuinely pressed for time and failed to elaborate as fully as those who were willing to devote a great deal of time to the interview. Still others—especially those with relatively little education—were unable to articulate answers to questions about which they had evidently thought little prior to the interview. Fluctuations in mood, in attitude toward the interview, in verbal facility, or in self-consciousness lent considerable variability to the answer patterns.

These differences are inherent in the open-ended interview question and in the interview situation. They do not allow us to make categorical statements about possible distributions in answers, which we might have found if only direct, closed questions had been asked. For instance, the fact that a certain proportion of the respondents mentioned their family as the source of their earliest political interest does not mean that others, who did not mention this, were not influenced by their family or, on second thought, might not have recalled the family as a source.

Because of the heterogeneity of answer-patterns, we used as the base for computing percentages only those respondents whose answers could be coded in a particular category. As we are unable to ascertain whether these "effective" respondents constitute a random sample of all possible respondents, i.e., of all those interviewed, we have not subjected the distributions to the familiar tests of statistical significance. For tests of statistical significance, in experimental as well as in survey research, are based on the assumption that the data come from a random sample of the population which is analyzed. Random sampling is essential for significance-testing precisely because not all factors of possible relevance are controlled. This is, of course, an overstatement of the sampling requirement, for *all* factors are never controlled even in carefully designed experiments. But we can certainly assume that in this study not all factors of possible relevance were even considered due to its exploratory character. There are other reasons for not applying statistical tests to the data, but only one further consideration will be mentioned here because it seems particularly critical in the present case.

Though the analysis was undertaken with theoretical notions in mind, an exploratory study of this kind cannot formulate in advance all the hypotheses for which data may be available. In fact, even if there are a priori hypotheses, they are likely to be modified once initial tabulations are examined, and further hypotheses are developed on inspection of the data. But if hypotheses are adjusted or newly proposed after the data have been looked at, it is certainly unnecessary to test such *post facto* hypotheses for statistical significance of the differences or relations between variables which have been discovered by inspection. The process is circular: what is to be proven has already been proved. This procedure gives a purely spurious impression of validity. It in no way tells us anything significant about the real distribution of the differences or relations in the population. In other words, what may be "statistically significant" need not necessarily be "socially significant," and what may be "statistically insignificant" may yet be very suggestive.

That, as a group, state legislators are occupationally highly mobile appears from the aggregated comparisons of fathers' and sons' occupations presented in Table 11.1. There were two-and-a-half times as many professionals among the legislators as among their fathers; but also five times as many "middle" or "lower" occupations among the fathers as among the respondents. In fact, the three lowest status categories disappear completely from the aggregate of legislators.

Table 11.1. Fathers' and Sons' Occupational Status (in percentages)

Occupational Status (N = 325)	*Fathers*	*Sons*
Professional	24	56
Managerial	40	37
Clerical/Sales	7	6
Craftsman	7	1
Skilled labor	14	–
Service	3	–
Unskilled	5	–
Total	100	100

The basic instrument employed in this analysis is an occupational status index or scale. The scale is a condensed version of a generally accepted occupational status rating device.[6] Although the rank order of the scale is somewhat arbitrary, there are nevertheless valid reasons—in terms of income, education, and prestige ratings—to support the order. Moreover, in order to allow for relative instability in ordering which may exist between neighboring ranks, upward mobility was defined operationally as involving two or more steps on the scale rather than a single step. Table 11.2 presents the breakdown among the seven occupational status groups. It yields a group of 105 "mobile" and

6. See Natalie Rogoff, *Recent Trends in Occupational Mobility* (Glencoe: Free Press, 1953), pp. 19–42.

Table 11.2. Occupational Mobility Patterns of 325 State Legislators

	RESPONDENT					
Father	(1)	(2)	(3)	(4)	(5)	
Professional (1)	49	28	1	–	–	(78)
Managerial (2)	62	59	6	1	–	(128)
Clerical/Sales (3)	15	7	1	–	–	(23)
Craftsman (4)	15	6	2	1	–	(24)
Skilled labor (5)	27	12	5	1	2	(47)
Service (6)	6	2	–	–	–	(8)
Unskilled (7)	6	6	6	1	1	(17)
	(180)	(120)	(18)	(4)	(3)	325

220 "status-stable" legislators.[7] The mobility index does not differentiate between levels of origin and levels of attainment. In other words, a legislator whose father was an unskilled worker, and who is a craftsman, is assumed to have advanced as much as one whose father was a craftsman, and who has become a professional. This may be a weakness in the interpretative value of the index, but it is alleviated by the fact that only very few cases involve movement from the two lowest to the two highest categories; and a move from skilled labor to clerical is more comparable to a move from clerical to professional status, but still not equivalent.

There is reason to assume that occupational mobility will have different consequences for a political career in different political contexts. Insofar as occupational mobility implies a desire to advance, it may be surmised that a political career in a competitive context is more attractive to mobile than to status-stable individuals. Having overcome competitive obstacles in private life, the mobile person will be less inclined than the status-stable individual to avoid competitive political situations. We should expect, therefore, that more mobiles than status-stables will be found in competitive environments.

In terms of an index of party competition in state legislative district, New Jersey was classified as the most competitive of the four states, followed by Ohio, California, and Tennessee, in that order.[8] New Jersey's and Ohio's legislatures included 37 and 38 per cent mobiles, respectively; California, 29 per

7. The group of 220 "status-stable" legislators, as Table 11.2 shows, includes eight apparently "downwardly-mobile" respondents. However, the meaning of "downward mobility" in this connection is such that we seem justified in treating the eight as status-stable. Seven of them held clerical or sales jobs, while they reported their fathers as having been in professional or managerial occupations. One respondent, classified as a craftsman, reported his father as managerial. But as these classifications are ambiguous and probably conceal as much difference within as they reveal differences between categories, the inclusion of the eight in the status-stable group is unlikely to distort the results.

8. Party competition in district was severally defined in the four states on the basis of past election returns. Space limitations prevent us from specifying the criteria here. For a full discussion of the index, see Wahlke and others, *op cit.*, Appendix 2.1.

cent; and Tennessee, only 22 per cent. The relationship also appears, as in Table 11.3, if we compare the proportions of mobile and status-stable legislators from different types of constituencies, regardless of state. The data suggest that competitive political situations may be more congenial to mobile than to status-stable legislators, and that there may be some relationship, if only a tenuous one, between the type of person who advances occupationally and the type who enters politics in a competitive context. Yet the differences, either by state or by district, are not large enough to be more than suggestive. For this reason, as well as to avoid unduly small figures if the data were handled on a state-by-state basis, we shall combine them in the analysis.

Table 11.3. Mobile and Status-Stable Legislators, by Competition in District (in percentages)

Type of District	*Mobiles (N = 105)*	*Status-Stables (N = 220)*
Competitive	33	25
Semi-competitive	27	28
One-party	40	47
Total	100	100

ENTRY INTO POLITICS

A political career begins even before the would-be politician actively enters the political arena. A variety of influences may stimulate a political career.[9] We might expect, therefore, that mobiles will attribute their earliest interest in politics to influences different from those of status-stables. Indeed, asked to recall the sources of their earliest concern with politics, mobiles and status-stables differ in their recollections. And the differences are quite plausible—initial indications of the "style" which mobiles and status-stables may bring to politics. As Table 11.4 shows, the most noticeable difference occurs in the mentioning of primary groups—a category which includes the family as the by far most frequently mentioned source of earliest political interest. While over a half of the status-stables recalled this source, somewhat less than two-fifths of the mobiles did likewise. This result is not surprising if it is recalled that all of the mobiles had fathers in occupations ranked third or below. Politics is less cultivated in lower- than in upper-class families; the family is too much involved in making a living to concern itself with politics or to engage in political activity.

As basic attitudes, including political ones, are formed early in life, and

9. See Heinz Eulau, William Buchanan, LeRoy C. Ferguson, and John C. Wahlke, "The Political Socialization of American State Legislators," *Midwest Journal of Political Science,* 3 (May 1959), 188–206.

Table 11.4. Major Sources of Political Interest (in percentages)

Major Sources	*Mobiles (N = 101)*	*Status-Stables (N = 207)*
Primary groups	38	52
Participation	63	54
Events/conditions	26	28
Predispositions	47	55
Beliefs	7	3

especially in the family context, it is also understandable that status-stables mentioned "predispositions" in greater proportion than did the mobiles. Mobiles probably become involved in politics later in life than status-stables and develop a political commitment at a later date. On the other hand, mobiles mentioned "participation" of some kind in politics or civic affairs more frequently as a source of early interest. This, too, is plausible. The mobile person finds himself engaged in some public activity, and this activity stimulates an interest in politics.

A somewhat similar pattern was found in responses to a question asking the legislators just what clinched their decision to go into active politics. While differences between mobiles and status-stables were very small or nonexistent in most categories, 10 per cent of the status-stables but only 3 per cent of the mobiles mentioned their family in this connection. On the other hand, 21 per cent of the mobiles but only 14 per cent of the status-stables reported the political party as a source of decision. Mobiles, we noted earlier, are more prepared than status-stables to embark on a political career in areas where party competition is keen. In such areas the party is a necessary vehicle of political advance. By its very nature it is an "open" organization which welcomes "established" as much as "mobile" individuals who promise to be winning candidates, and it does so without inquiring into the candidate's social pedigree.

A number of respondents among both mobiles and status-stables, referred to what we may call the "personal context" of their decision to enter politics, circumstances which seemed to them important enough to recall. As appears in Table 11.5, more status-stable legislators tended to mention "general opportunity" or specific "opportunities" than did the mobiles. Opportunity, of course, means different things to different people; to some, it may imply merely a chance to succeed; to others, it may mean a chance to demonstrate skills and ability as a means to success. To most legislators it meant that they had a good chance to win without too much difficulty—that no opposition existed, or that the incumbent had died and left the position vacant. These situations, it seems, are particularly to the liking of status-stables. Although in actuality the situations may have been equally assured for mobiles, they do not seem to accept that assuredness as a critical aspect of the decisional context.

Table 11.5. Personal Context of Decision to Enter Politics (in percentages)*

Context	*Mobiles (N = 42)*	*Status-Stables (N = 86)*
General opportunity (had support, chance to win, etc.)	7	20
Specific opportunity (incumbent died, no opposition, etc.)	38	54
Opportunity to combine employment with politics	24	22
Reputation from other pursuit	14	15
Family conditions favorable	7	3
Nobody else available for job	7	9

*Percentages total more than 100 since more than one response was possible.

Respondents also volunteered a number of "motivational" reasons for their decision to enter politics. Although the number giving explicitly "selfish" reasons was small and not different for the two occupational status groups (17 per cent for the mobiles and 19 per cent for the status-tables), 44 per cent of the mobiles expected some kind of "gain" from combining legislative service with their private occupation, while only 10 per cent of the status-stables expressed this consideration. However, the responses in the "selfish" category were too ambiguous to serve much analytical use. Moreover, it is hazardous to read too much into the "selfish" response patterns without simultaneously inspecting the "altruistic" reasons that were given. Here, as may be seen in

Table 11.6. Altruistic "Reasons" for Decision to Enter Politics (in percentages)*

Reasons	*Mobiles (N = 50)*	*Status-Stables (N = 88)*
To serve (general: job to do; accomplish things; etc.)	34	48
To serve (solve a special problem)	12	17
To serve people of district	12	11
To represent views of business	4	2
To represent views of labor	12	2
To represent views of ethnic or religious group	8	–
To fight for ideals (stop socialism in government; fight graft and corruption; etc.)	16	32
To be useful politically (help ticket; build up party; support governor; etc.)	8	3

*Percentages total more than 100 since more than one response was possible.

Table 11.6, the status-stables inclined more towards emphasizing the "service" motive and a "politics of ideals" than the mobiles did. Somewhat more of the latter, in turn, stressed reasons of a "representational" quality. The data are difficult to interpret, but it would seem that status-stables are less "group-bound" and view legislative service in more general terms. They apparently can do so precisely because, unlike the mobiles, they are presumably less concerned with status. Mobiles, on the other hand, may take the "representational" stance because they feel that they must maintain their position of "achievement" in the eyes of the group in which they originated or into which they have moved. Having moved up from low-status background, mobiles may maintain an interest in "underprivileged" groups and at the same time affirm their new belongingness in the group into which they have moved. This interpretation is in accord with another finding, reported below, that mobiles tend to hold ideological views which reflect their relatively low origins.

POLITICAL EXPERIENCE AND ROLES

If occupational mobility patterns are carrying over into the political world, we should expect that mobiles have a more difficult task in boarding the political escalator than status-stables. The latter have an initial advantage in coming from high occupational backgrounds. Without making any assumptions about a "typical" political career–such as that political mobility is necessarily from "lower" to "higher" positions–it is likely that mobiles will begin their political careers at lower levels from which they "advance" to higher levels, very much as they have moved in the private occupational sphere. In the case of mobiles, the competence and skills necessary for political office may have to be acquired as a result of political activity itself, while status-stables may have had an opportunity to acquire them elsewhere–in home or school, preparing them for entry into public service at higher levels or positions.

Although the differences between mobiles and status-stables are far from convincing as proof in this respect, they reveal tendencies in the expected direction. Table 11.7 reports legislators' governmental experience prior to their state legislative service. In the first place, it appears, though the difference is very small indeed, that more status-stables than mobiles had no previous governmental experience at all. Second, and here the data are more satisfactory, more mobiles than status-stables held governmental office at the local level, while more status-stables had occupied state or even federal positions before running for the legislature. Apparently, the political career is somewhat longer and more arduous for mobiles than it is for status-stables.

The data are again less convincing if it comes to the status of the positions held at different levels. Almost equal proportions of both groups—44 per cent in the case of status-stables, 47 per cent in the case of mobiles—held "high" positions; and 28 and 26 per cent, respectively, held "low" positions. Only "middle" positions were held by a greater proportion of status-stables (55 per

Table 11.7. Previous Government Experience: Level (in percentages)

Level of Experience	*Mobiles (N = 105)*	*Status-Stables (N = 220)*
No previous experience	46	50
Previous experience	54	50
Total	100	100
Previous experience*	(N = 57)	(N = 110)
Local	93	82
State	19	24
National	6	14

*Percentages total more than 100 since a respondent could have had experience on more than one level.

cent) than of mobiles (42 per cent). The data are difficult to interpret because contrary interpretations are possible. On the one hand, we might expect that status-stables, having the advantage of status "from birth," so to speak, would be more likely to have filled "high" positions than the mobiles. On the other hand, mobiles—presumably motivated to advance themselves in the political arena as they have already moved up in the private occupational world—might also be found in "high" positions (as almost half of them actually were). In the face of both interpretations, the data are necessarily inconclusive.

But status-stables seem to have a considerable jump on mobiles in occupying legislative or party offices in the legislature itself. Though the difference between mobiles and status-stables holding any such office is small (36 per cent as against 39 per cent), about three-fourths of available positions were occupied by status-stables (partly a function of there being more than twice as many of them than of mobiles; partly, in all probability, because many of the

Table 11.8. Legislative Offices held by Mobiles and Status-Stables (in percentages)

Held by	*Major**	*Chairmanship*	*Important Committee†*
Status-stables	76	71	74
Mobiles	24	29	26
Total	100	100	100
Number of Offices	(21)	(85)	(73)

*Speaker; president; speaker or president pro tem; majority or minority floor leaders and assistant floor leaders; chairmen of Rules, Conference, Reference, Calendar committees.
†Members of Rules, Reference, Conference, Calendar committees; Legislative Service or similar commissions.

status-stables come from one-party areas, with resulting tenure of office and seniority). On the other hand, those mobiles who have reached these positions may be said to have brought their occupational status into balance with political status.

In general, once they have won a legislative seat, we should not expect mobiles to differ in a significant way from status-stables in political role-taking. Regardless of whether they confront such important political "others" as fellow legislators, constituents or lobbyists, mobiles and status-stables should exhibit very much the same orientations and behavior.[10] And our data, not reported here, do not show even tendentious differences. Similarly, we found little difference in mobiles' and status-stables' "sense of efficacy," the feeling that they are "in control" of the legislative situation and of their duties as legislators. Only 23 per cent of the status-stables and 27 per cent of the mobiles scored "low" in sense of legislative efficacy.

On the other hand the "style" involved in legislators' role-taking and behavior–the attitudinal stance they demonstrate–may yet reveal differences between mobiles and status-stables symptomatic of their different social origins. In the first place, as we noted earlier, mobiles seem to be somewhat more committed to and involved in the political party as a vehicle of political mobility. In fact, it appears that mobiles are somewhat more partisan in attitude than are the status-stables, scoring +25 as against +17 on a simple partisanship index. Second, in view of the fact, reported above, that mobiles were especially sensitive to groups in deciding to seek a political career, we might expect that in their "representational style" mobiles will be more likely to see themselves as "delegates" rather than "free agents" or "trustees." Indeed, 21 per cent of the mobiles as against only 13 per cent of the status-stables were classified as "delegates." [11] Third, as mobiles come from humble social origins, we might expect them to be "liberal" in ideological orientation to a greater extent than the status-stables. As Table 11.9 shows, though the differences are small, the proportions tend in the expected direction: more of the mobiles than of the status-stables are "liberal," and more of the status-stables than of the mobiles are conservative." [12]

These results coincide with those reported by Maccoby and her associates in

10. Ths is so because, on theoretical grounds, political roles and behavior in the performance of these roles are functions of current interpersonal relations rather than of previously learned attitudes or values. See John C. Wahlke, William Buchanan, Heinz Eulau, and LeRoy C. Ferguson, "American State Legislator's Role Orientations Toward Pressure Groups," *Journal of Politics,* 22 (May 1960), 203–27.

11. On the notion of "representational style" (as against "representational focus"), see Heinz Eulau, John C. Wahlke, William Buchanan, and LeRoy C. Ferguson, "The Role of the Representative: Some Empirical Observations on the Theory of Edmund Burke," *American Political Science Review*, 53 (September 1959), 742–56.

12. This scale must be treated with some caution. It consists of only three items, hardly enough to cope with a complex attitudinal syndrome. Yet, the scale yielded a coefficient of reproducibility of .924, well within Guttman's standard of acceptability.

Table 11.9. Ideological Orientation of Mobiles and Status-Stables (in percentages)

Ideology	*Mobiles (N = 103)*	*Status-Stables (N = 215)*
Strongly conservative	14	16
Conservative	16	23
Liberal	31	28
Strongly liberal	39	33
Total	100	100

a study of young adults.[13] These researchers found that young, upwardly mobile people tend to adopt the behavior patterns of the class into which they have moved. Mobile legislators, we found, play various legislative roles in very much the same way as do status-stables. On the other hand, Maccoby and associates also found that upwardly mobile young people retain most of their original group's ideology. Similarly, we found that in their ideology mobile legislators tend to reflect their social origins in being somewhat more "liberal" than those legislators whose current status and social background are the same.

CAREER EXPECTATIONS AND ASPIRATIONS

"Subjectively," Everett C. Hughes once observed, "a career is the moving perspective in which the person sees his life as a whole and interprets the meaning of his various attributes, actions, and the things which happen to him." [14] Mobile and status-stable legislators should envisage their political future somewhat differently. An intention to continue in politics–whether in the same position or another–may be indicative of satisfaction or dissatisfaction with the political career, especially as it affects the legislator's private occupation. We might speculate that status-stable individuals would be more cautious in anticipating the future, and that they would be more inclined than mobiles to give politics up if they sense possible conflict between their occupational and political careers. Mobile individuals, on the other hand, having taken an initially more hazardous plunge into politics, presumably in anticipation that politics would further advance them in status and prestige, might be expected to be more certain about their political intentions and to be more involved in the political career.

Legislators were asked whether they planned to run again for their legislative seat. Their responses give tentative support to our speculation. Eight per cent more of the status-stable than of the mobile legislators (28 and 20 per

13. See Eleanor E. Maccoby, Richard E. Matthews, and Alton S. Morton, "Youth and Political Change," in Heinz Eulau, Samuel J. Eldersveld, and Morris Janowitz (Eds.), *Political Behavior* (Glencoe: Free Press, 1956), pp. 299–307.

14. Everett C. Hughes, *Men and Their Work* (Glencoe: Free Press, 1958), p. 63.

cent, respectively), gave an ambiguous response, while more of the mobiles gave either a clear "yes" (65 as against 60 per cent) or a clear "no" (15 as against 12 per cent) answer. Apparently, a sizable majority of all legislators have a positive expectation to continue in their current political office. But a few more of the mobiles also have a negative attitude toward continued incumbency. Examination of the "reasons" given by either group may shed some light on these reactions.

In regard to reasons *for* running again, there were few important differences between the two groups. The most frequent reason given, by both mobiles and status-stables, was "personal involvement" in politics and legislative work, but it was given by slightly more of the mobiles than of the status-stables (64 as against 59 per cent of those giving reasons). Status-stables mention "service to the public" somewhat more frequently (35 as against 29 per cent) as well as "personal reasons" (12 as against 3 per cent), which include references to the state of one's own business. More revealing are the reasons *against* running again. As Table 11.10 shows, prominent among the reasons given by mobiles was "power"–the respondent felt that running again would show lack of ambition, or he indicated that he would run for higher office. Mobiles, too, were more sensitive to "political contingencies"–particular conditions that might affect their political career. Status-stables, on the other hand, again stressed "personal reasons"–family, age, or health–and "job demands"–that legislative work is too arduous and time-consuming. It would seem that certain attitudes towards life formed in the course of the private career are transferred to the political arena: mobiles are somewhat more involved in politics and

Table 11.10. Reasons against Running Again (in percentages)*

Reasons	*Mobiles (N = 32)*	*Status-Stables (N = 74)*
Power (running for higher office; running again shows lack of ambition; etc.)	31	18
Political contingencies	19	11
Personal (family; age; health)	9	19
Job demands (too much time; etc.)	9	23
Economic (business suffers; costs too much; etc.)	22	27
Length of service (long enough)	16	19
Personal inadequancy (uncomfortable in politics; etc.)	6	9
Ethics (might lose principles by staying; etc.)	—	3
Boredom (job too routine; etc.)	3	5

*Percentages total more than 100 since more than one response was possible.

politically more sensitive and ambitious, while status-stables are more cautious in committing themselves to politics and appraise their continued stay in politics in terms of its consequences for various aspects of their private lives.

The legislators were also asked whether they would like to seek any other political or governmental job—local, state, or federal. The data show that equal proportions of mobiles and status-stables (41 per cent each) were planning to seek another office, but somewhat more of the mobiles definitely rejected a career beyond the state legislature (37 per cent as against 32 per cent of the status-stables). This result is somewhat surprising, for we might expect just the opposite—that, as a group, mobiles would be politically more aspiring than they seem to be. It may be, however, that the mobiles actually consist of two subgroups—a group which, on having reached what may appear to them a sufficiently high political status—that of state legislator, is satisfied with consummating this achievement; and another group, still dissatisfied and still ambitious. That this may be the case appears from inspection of Table 11.11. Among the mobiles intending to run for another office, 10 per cent more than among the status-stables chose federal office—mostly the Congress—as the goal of their aspirations. Status-stable legislators, on the other hand, were more willing to settle for another office on local or state levels.

Table 11.11. Level of Aspiration (in percentages)*

Level	*Mobiles (N = 55)*	*Status-Stables (N = 126)*
Federal	56	46
State	40	42
Local	18	24
Other	13	10

*Percentages total more than 100 since more than one response was possible.

Interestingly, in giving "reasons" for seeking another office, the mobile legislators were somewhat less inclined than the status-stables to ascribe their intention to ambition or a desire for further advancement (46 as against 52 per cent). Why this is so is difficult to say. It may be that these "unsatisfied" mobiles are unable or unwilling to articulate their own ambitions; or it may be that the status-stables in this politically aspiring group do not perceive the state legislature as congruent in prestige with their status in private life. But this is speculation; the data themselves are silent.

Reasons given for *not* seeking another office further support the supposition that mobile legislators may be of two types. As Table 11.12 shows, more than half of the non-aspiring mobiles stated that they preferred the state legislature where they were doing a good job or enjoyed the friendships they had made. Moreover, of this group of mobiles, as many as 38 per cent indicated they had no further political aspirations for business or occupational reasons—that they could not see a way of combining another political job with their private career. Moreover, as Table 11.12 shows, they differed in these respects quite considerably from the non-aspiring status-stables who tended more to emphasize political difficulties in their way to further office, personal matters and so on, or who frankly admitted to having no political aspirations. But in some respects the non-aspiring mobiles are similar to status-stables—those status-stables who were not even willing to run for their current state legislative seat again (see Table 11.10). It looks as if the same problem—possible conflict between public and private career—is faced by some mobiles and some status-stables at different critical stages of personal development. Status-stables face the problem of conflict earlier than mobiles. Some of the latter, having advanced occupationally, seem to look on their state legislative job as a satisfactory equivalent in the public sphere of their status in the private occupational world, but they are not prepared to risk further ventures into politics which may threaten their occupational status. Other mobiles, however, are ready to undertake just that risk and are looking to other political office as another step in their drive for status and prestige. In that respect they are very similar to those status-stables who, we noted earlier, are quite frank in stating their aspirations for higher political office.

Table 11.12. Reasons for Not Seeking Other Office (in percentages)*

Reasons	*Mobiles (N = 24)*	*Status-Stables (N = 44)*
Preference for state legislature	54	36
Business or occupation	38	9
Political difficulties seen	–	16
Non-political (no aspirations)	8	27
Personal (age; health; etc.)	4	18
Family considerations	8	5
Political (must maintain local standing; power)	4	5

*Percentages total more than 100 since more than one response was possible.

CONCLUSION

The data reported in this analysis are in many respects unsatisfactory—not because they are "bad" data as such, but because statements about the consequences of occupational mobility for political recruitment and careers must be considered highly tentative. Many of the differences in the response patterns of occupationally mobile and status-stable legislators are so small that they can be meaningfully interpreted only with great caution. Yet, we noted a number of plausible differences and tendencies which suggest that occupational mobility engenders values and orientations which seem to carry over into the political sphere. It appears that mobile individuals make more of a career out of political office-holding than do occupationally status-stable individuals.

When they first come to politics, mobile politicians tend to be more oriented toward their occupational success than do status-stable politicians. Mobiles seem to look initially at opportunities outside their occupation in terms of the benefits these opportunites may have for their occupation; status-stables tend to be less occupation-conscious, looking upon the rewards of legislative service in direct personal terms rather than perceiving these rewards in terms of their effect on their private occupation. Mobiles, having acquired status in the private sphere, may for some time consciously, and for some time subconsciously, tend to evaluate the effects of their political standing on their private status standing; whereas the status-stables, being presumably less concerned with status, will consider the implications of their political career in more generalized terms.

Their social origins seem to sensitize the mobiles to aspects of the political professional's role which status-stables are likely to ignore. Precisely because they are less concerned with problems arising out of the condition of occupational mobility, status-stables can afford to be less committed to partisanship, a popular representational style, or a more socially-conscious set of political ideas. On the other hand, there seems to be a latent function in the mobiles' tendency to accentuate these values: having emancipated themselves from lower occupational status and moved into higher status positions, the mobiles may find in their background a psychologically more secure point of orientational reference than in the occupational status group into which they have moved.

The data on occupational mobility and career expectations and aspirations suggest that, in due course, there may be a subtle shift in mobiles' attitudes towards politics. The relationship between occupational and political mobility is intricate and difficult to disentangle, but it tends to become more reciprocal. In general, it seems that once committed to politics, the mobiles are more prepared to take the risks of elective office-holding than do the status-stables, that they are more involved in the political game, and that they now tend to be less occupation- or business-bound than status-stables. From a functional point of view it may be that a democratic politics needs both types of politicians—mobiles and status-stables—each of whom brings to politics characteristic values and orientations rooted in the private occupational sphere. It is in this respect that occupational mobility or stability seem to be further factors in influencing the quality of political life.

Chapter 12

Political Socialization and Political Roles

Political socialization theory frequently stresses that adult political behavior is little more than an elaboration of patterns rooted in childhood experiences. It is assumed that early political socialization is more "basic" than later learning experiences and that the patterns formed as a result of childhood socialization can be dislodged only under unusual circumstances.[1] This assumption leads to a developmental or sequential theory of political socialization. Events or experiences of one stage determine what type of behavior will be manifest at later stages.

That students of the political career might be intrigued by this proposition is obvious. Social scientists who wish to explain why politicians behave as they do are plagued by the task of discovering what pressures operate on the politi-

Originally published, with Kenneth Prewitt and Betty H. Zisk, in *Public Opinion Quarterly*, Vol. 30 (Winter, 1966–67), pp. 569–82. Reprinted by permission.

1. The cultural anthropologists have argued this point quite persuasively. See the general discussion in Robert LeVine, "Political Socialization and Culture Change," in Clifford Geertz, Ed., *Old Societies and New States*, New York, Free Press of Glencoe, 1963, pp. 280–303. Citing cultural anthropologists, linguists, and social psychologists, Professor LeVine writes that early learned attitudes and values are resistant to change. The general proposition is partially supported with data on the political attitudes of children as reported in the work of Greenstein and of Hess and Easton. See Fred I. Greenstein, "The Benevolent Leader: Children's Images of Political Authority," *American Political Science Review*, Vol. 54, 1960, pp. 934–943; and Robert D. Hess and David Easton, "The Child's Changing Image of the President," *Public Opinion Quarterly*, Vol. 24, 1960, pp. 632–644. Hyman has suggested an important general modification to the hypothesis. He writes that different aspects of political orientations have different growth curves; for instance, though party affiliation is well established in early life, political ideology tends to emerge in response to factors present in the political socialization experiences of adults. Herbert Hyman, *Political Socialization*, Glencoe, Free Press, 1959, pp. 46–47.

cian and in what proportions. If a major factor accounting for adult political behavior is predispositions brought to the adult role from prior experiences and if this is as true for elected politicians as for any other adult, then we can explain aspects of the incumbent politician's behavior with evidence about his past. The research question can be posed as follows: Are the differences between how elected officials perform their tasks rooted in different kinds of pre-incumbent experiences?

Evidence on 421 state legislators from 4 states and 129 city councilmen from 23 cities composes a sample suitable for our purposes. Both these sets of elected officials include incumbents of two types: (1) those who report that their interest in public affairs began during their childhood years, and (2) those who report that their interest was deferred until adulthood. In addition, both legislators and councilmen are members of formalized political institutions that require the performance of certain duties, but each institutional setting allows for alternative ways of performing these duties. Within each group of officeholders there are differences with respect to pre-incumbent experiences and differences with respect to incumbent role orientations.

METHODOLOGICAL NOTES

This is a study of data collected on two quite different levels of American government—the level of partisan state legislatures and of nonpartisan local city councils. For the purpose of this analysis, data from different jurisdictions on each of these levels are aggregated. That this aggregation does not do violence to contextual considerations is demonstrated by the fact that the independent variable, time of initial interest in public affairs, is evenly distributed across jurisdictional boundaries on the state level as well as on the local level (see Table 12.1).

Table 12.1. Time of Initial Interest in Public Affairs Related to State Boundaries (in percentages)

	STATE				
Time	*California (N = 110)*	*New Jersey (N = 57)*	*Ohio (N = 150)*	*Tennessee (N = 98)*	*Councils (Aggregated)* (N = 129)*
Pre-adult	64	60	64	61	54
Adult	36	40	36	39	46
	100	100	100	100	100

*The breakdown by individual city is not presented. The small *N*'s per city make the percentages fairly meaningless. We have satisfied ourselves that the ordering variable is not related to any particular grouping of cities that might have a bearing on the data presented in the following tables.

And, as Table 12.2 demonstrates, for the partisan state legislators, their party identities are equally unrelated to the time factor.

We might note parenthetically here that the focus is not on comparing legislators with councilmen. The theory is concerned with comparing those who were first exposed to public affairs as children with those who were not exposed until adulthood. However, analysis of data collected at different levels of American government does serve as a basis for appraising the validity of inference about the relationships in which we are interested. If a given relationship is consistent for both the partisan state legislators and the nonpartisan city councilmen, we can assume that factors other than the specific institutional context are at work. In this sense, we can think of either level of government as serving as an independent check on the relationships found at the other.

Table 12.2. Time of Initial Interest in Public Affairs Related to Party Affiliation (in percentages)

	PARTY AFFILIATION	
Time	*Democratic (N = 204)*	*Republican (N = 217)*
Pre-adult	65	61
Adult	35	39
	100	100

We shall ignore certain differences that do occur between councilmen and legislators. These differences make theoretical sense–state legislators tend to respond in slightly more "politicized" fashion than do the councilmen. Interpretation of these data is a different task; our interest is in the ways in which early-socialized politicians systematically differ from their adult-socialized colleagues, irrespective of the level and institutional context.

One further methodological note is in order. The data reported here are recall data. Such information is, at best, incomplete and may be inaccurate. As with any study relying on recall data, we can only rest our case on the assumption that constant interpretations and reinterpretations of the past, however inaccurate as representations of some objective reality, take place in a context meaningful to the individual. What are the perceptually relevant aspects of the past is the question to be answered. For example, it is not to be determined which respondents had politically active families but which respondents think of their families as having been politically active. It is the politician's account of his history and not the historian's that we seek. In this sense, inaccurate recall data would be information that distorted the respondent's *image* of his past; we have no grounds for believing that respondents chose deliberately to conceal or distort what was important to them in their political history.

THE INDEPENDENT VARIABLE

Table 12.3 presents the distribution on time of initial interest in public affairs recalled by the state legislators[2] and the city councilmen.[3] For analytic purposes the respondents are divided into (1) those who date their initial interest in public affairs during college or the equivalent period, or before, and (2) those who report adult political socialization experiences.

Table 12.3 Time of Initial Interest in Public Affairs (in percentages)

Time Recalled	*State Legislators (N = 421)*	*City Councilmen (N = 129)*
Childhood or grammar school	38	22
Adolescence or high school	15	17
College or equivalent period	11	15
After college or equivalent period	16	33
At time of entry into public life	20	12
	100	99[a]

[a]Due to rounding.

As used here, "political socialization" refers to the set of experiences that usher an individual into the general political world. Other persons, groups, and situational events are the more important agents performing this function. We classify the respondent in this study according to the chronological point in his life at which he dates his *initial* introduction to public affairs. No assumption is made that political socialization stops there; obviously, exposure to political images and concerns is a process continuing throughout the political career. Though it is a bit arbitrary to usurp the word "socialization" to designate the

2. The series of questions asked the state legislators that produced the information reported in Tables 12.3 to 12.6 was as follows: "How did you become interested in politics? For example, what is your earliest recollection of being interested in it? What other members of your family or close relatives held public or political office before you yourself did?"

3. To elicit the data reported in Tables 12.3 to 12.6, councilmen were asked the following series of questions: "If you can think back as far as you can, how did you become interested in government or public affairs? For instance, what is your earliest recollection of being interested? As far as you recall, was there any particular situation that stimulated your earliest interest in government? Were there any particular persons who made you get interested in government at this time? (If yes) Who were these persons? How about your family? Were government and public affairs ever discussed? Speaking of your family, were any of your family members active in community affairs or politics?"

starting point, it is relevant to ask when the process originated and to inquire into factors associated with different starting points.

TIME OF INITIAL INTEREST AND SOCIALIZATION EXPERIENCES

The first task is to determine whether time of initial exposure to the political world has a bearing on the images acquired about political matters. It makes no theoretical sense to use time of initial interest as an independent variable unless we can demonstrate that the point in the politician's life when he first acquired political information and images has a bearing on what types of thoughts he had about the political world. Not unexpectedly, whether the incumbent politician reported childhood or adult interest in public affairs is strongly and consistently related to important factors about the socialization experience. Both legislators and councilmen who date their interest early in life systematically differ from their colleagues with respect to their socialization experiences and their predispositions associated with earliest interest.

Whether or not there is a politically active family in the background is strongly related to time of initial political socialization. Better than half (52 per cent) of the legislators and nearly half of the councilmen (45 per cent) who note early interest report family political activity. This compares with 7 and 18 per cent, respectively, of their colleagues who perceive adult experiences as first ushering them into the political world. Though the finding is expected, its theoretical importance should not be underestimated. Growing up in a politically involved family provides opportunities for learning about politics in an intimate setting. Impressionable youth attributes significance to parental interests, especially when conversations are reinforced with examples of adult behavior. Survey studies have firmly established the link between parental politics and partisan loyalties of offspring. Thus, in spite of arguments about the low salience of politics in most American families, family-learned orientations do stick. More than party ties are involved in the political socialization experiences of these respondents. The politician who was "born into a political family" or who "just grew up in politics" attributes his political involvement to a long-standing consciousness about political issues. He is informed of the serious as well as pleasurable aspects of political life. The interview protocols amply support the general point that images of the political world conveyed via personally involved families produce more than casual commitment on the part of offspring.

This information about family activity can be supplemented with data on other types of persons and activities that usher people into the political world. Table 12.4 presents strong evidence that pre-adult political socialization is associated with a different pattern of events than deferred socialization. It is obvious that the group context varies with the time in one's life when he

Table 12.4. Socialization Experiences and Time of Socialization (in percentages)

	TIME OF SOCIALIZATION			
	PRE-ADULT		ADULT	
Experiences	*Legislators (N = 147)*	*Councilmen (N = 70)*	*Legislators (N = 86)*	*Councilmen (N = 59)*
Study of politics in school	38	47	5	7
Participation in school politics	17	31		3
Political activities: campaigning, partisan and nonpartisan work	48	31	47	39
Nonpolitical activities: civic, vocational, religious groups	18	14	60	63

NOTE: Percentages total more than 100 since some respondents gave more than one answer.

initially encounters political symbols and concerns. Studies of career patterns in the professions have illustrated how social groups nourish ambitions and provide definitions and directions for the career aspirant.[4] The logic of this position is persuasively supported with reference group theory, which points out that the cues picked up from others determine how we view the world and our place in it. Following this line of reasoning, we view it as important to identify the setting of a respondent's initial introduction to the political world.

The educational context as a stimulant to political interest sets the early entrants apart from the late-comers to the political world. The interview schedules are rich with quotations attesting to the "inspirational" nature of the educational experience. One respondent followed up his classroom interest "by making a habit of attending city council meetings every Monday night." Others were so absorbed by their new interest that they have maintained life-long contact with the teacher first responsible for their political introduction.

The other sizable break in Table 12.4 demonstrates that those who became interested in politics as adults view civic and related activities as responsible for their introduction to public life in much greater proportions than do their colleagues who became interested when young. A word is in order about this coding category. It is not presumed that activities coded "nonpolitical" are entirely removed from the political world. In fact, the opposite is being implic-

4. See Oswald Hall, "The Stages of a Medical Career," in E. G. Jaco, Ed., *Patients, Physicians, and Illness: Behaviorial Science and Medicine,* Glencoe, Free Press, 1958, pp. 289–300, and Patricia Kendall and Robert Merton, "Medical Education as Social Process," in *ibid,* pp. 321–350.

itly argued. That such activities so often usher persons into public life strongly suggests that they are the functional equivalents of specifically political activities. What *is* clear from reading the protocols is that in the minds of the respondents certain experiences were not political. Civic affairs, community work, occupational and professional contacts, were the more frequently cited experiences. Approximately three-fifths of both legislators and councilmen who came to politics as adults mention activities which, though tangential, are not part of the formal governmental world. Fewer than one-fifth of their colleagues make such claims. Many of the former group mentioned their community contacts to explain how public office is simply an extension of their civic obligations: "This is actually an extension of my activities in the community. . . . It is only a short step from service clubs, civic progress . . . to public office." What is missing from the political socialization experiences of these respondents is the glamour and drama associated with the political world for those who report earlier socialization. Of course, all who came to politics early did not report colorful accounts of their socialization, nor did persons moving into the political arena as adults always describe a prosaic involvement. But there is a strong tendency for different images and experiences to be associated with different time periods of interest. This follows from the socialization agents involved. Business associates at a luncheon are likely to convey images of the political world that bear little resemblance to pictures drawn by a volatile family member or a teacher bent on stimulating excitement. And, irrespective of the images drawn, the lawyer or businessman in his thirties certainly absorbs different cues from those absorbed by the adolescent or college student.

The work on general political socialization has identified how particular events or conditions may arouse latent political interest. In response to our open-ended questioning, slightly more than a quarter (27 per cent) of the legislators and 60 per cent of the councilmen reported that a specific event or condition was instrumental in awakening their political concern. Presidential campaigns, economic crises, and wars have received the most attention in survey work; to such global events, we can add that local conditions or issues often serve as lubricants to political involvement. The limited number of responses prohibits pushing the data very far, but ordering the responses by time of initial interest does reveal sizable differences. Those drawn to politics in youth were likely to recall campaigns or colorful political figures (Table 12.5). In particular, the excitement and turbulence of the presidential campaign whetted their appetites for things political. Persons who recalled local conditions or issues (overwhelmingly the latecomers) characterized events associated with their political introduction in much more pedestrian and pragmatic terms. These are men who entered public life to solve an immediate problem: "Well, I was driving the school bus, and there were muddy roads . . ." or "I was against the dog leash law."

Though we are concerned not with the "why" of political involvement but with the conditions associated with socialization, 27 per cent of the legislators

Table 12.5. Particular Events and Time of Initial Socialization (in percentages)

	TIME OF SOCIALIZATION			
	PRE-ADULT		ADULT	
Event	*Legislators (N = 73)*	*Councilmen (N = 49)*	*Legislators (N = 42)*	*Councilmen (N = 29)*
Presidential, gubernatorial, senatorial campaigns or administrations	83	57	31	8
Crisis events, wars, or the depression	12	14	26	14
Local conditions or issues	8	29	52	82

NOTE: Percentages may total more than 100 since some respondents gave more than one answer.

and 75 per cent of the councilmen gave "motivational" answers to the open-ended question probing into earliest political interest. Table 12.6, which reports this information, further illustrates that different factors are associated with early vs. late political socialization.

Well over half (62 per cent) of the legislators attracted to politics in youth and nearly half (44 per cent) of their counterparts at the local level mention specifically political kinds of predisposition. In particular, they select a practicing politician as an ego-ideal: "When I was young I admired a Congressman by the name of. . . ." Though the more normal pattern for American youth is to select their ego-ideals from the world of sports or the cinema, it is not surprising that a few seize on political personalities and, important for our

Table 12.6. Predispositions and Time of Initial Socialization (in percentages)

	TIME OF SOCIALIZATION			
	PRE-ADULT		ADULT	
Predisposition	*Legislators (N = 63)*	*Councilmen (N = 51)*	*Legislators (N = 50)*	*Councilmen (N = 46)*
Admiration for politicians	48	42	6	13
Ambition for political power	14	2	8	
Sense of indignation	9	26	32	37
Sense of obligation	25	24	44	35
Other (desire for sociability, etc.)	5	8	10	22

NOTE: Percentages may total more than 100 since some respondents gave more than one answer.

purposes, they turn up in samples of elected politicians. It is reasonable to suggest that such identifications have an impact on early political awareness and could well produce tenuous psychological relations with the political world that are missing for those socialized into politics as adults.

Indignation as a predisposition is cited more frequently in the responses of those socialized as adults than in the answers of the youthful deciders. Dissatisfaction with both specific incumbents and general situations is articulated in pragmatic terms. The diffuse identification with the political world produced by the events associated with early political interest is absent from the socialization experiences of most late-comers. We are reluctant to make too much of these responses, although they are quite consistent with information presented in Tables 12.4 and 12.5. When the information sources are business associates rather than school teachers and when the stimulating event is a local problem rather than a Presidential campaign, it is not surprising that predispositions are narrowly defined.

We can now return to the question of this section: Are different sets of experiences associated with beginning a political career as a youth rather than as an adult? The answer is, of course, yes. For both legislators and councilmen, the evidence consistently points to patterns of experience associated with specific time of socialization. Those politically sensitive in youth report a different set of persons as the source of their interest, different activities as the channel to political awareness, different events and conditions associated with the socialization stage, and a different range of predispositions from their colleagues who were not politically stirred in youth. Those politicized early recalled events and experiences that generally bespoke of personalized, dramatic, and diffuse socialization experiences. Those socialized as adults were less personally involved. Pragmatism, specificity, and casualness accompanied their initial political introductions.

TIME OF INITIAL INTEREST IN PUBLIC AFFAIRS AND INCUMBENT ORIENTATIONS

It is to be expected that time of political socialization is related to a considerable range of factors associated with initial political exposure. The youth lives in a world different from that of the adult. The youth and the adult receive and respond to different messages and form political images accordingly. Since we have incumbents who date their careers from childhood or adolescence and others who date theirs from their more recent past, we have the categories that permit us to examine the research question: Is there a relationship between the nature of an incumbent's initial political socialization and how he views his incumbent duties? Do events and images associated with an early career stage restrict the choices made at a later stage? If so, the two categories of respondents—those politically socialized in youth and those politically socialized as adults—should behave quite differently as public officeholders.

The authors of *The Legislative System* identified several major role-orientations held by their respondents.[5] They asked legislators about their constituency relationships ("representational role-orientations"),[6] about their stance toward groups ("group role-orientation"),[7] and what self-expectations they had with respect to performance of legislative duties ("purposive role-orientation").[8] The city councilmen were classified according to the same or functionally equivalent measures. Table 12.7 presents the results.

In addition to these role-orientations, legislators and councilmen were asked about their sense of legislative efficacy. A scale was designed to measure how skillful and adept they considered themselves in legislative politics (see Table 12.8).[9]

Tables 12.7 and 12.8 testify to a consistent *lack* of relationship between initial socialization into politics and incumbent orientations. There are thirteen different dependent categories presented in these tables. In no case does the percentage difference between state legislators who came to politics early and legislators who report adult socialization exceed 7 per cent. This is amazing

5. John C. Wahlke, Heinz Eulau, William Buchanan, and LeRoy C. Ferguson, *The Legislative System: Explorations in Legislative Behavior,* New York, Wiley, 1962, Chaps. 11, 12, and 14.

6. Representational role-orientations is a typology constructed from questions probing how the politician feels he should carry out his representational duties. Following the clue of Edmund Burke, officials who follow the dictates of their own conscience are called "trustees"; those who follow the instructions of their constituency are called "delegates"; to handle respondents who combine characteristics of the trustee and the delegate when making a decision, a third type was added to Burke's classification—the "politico." The major question producing this typology was, "How would you describe the job of being a legislator (councilman)—what are the most important things you should do here?"

7. Group role-orientations are the attitudes and perceptions held by the councilmen and legislators toward the activities of interest groups in legislative politics. The typology is self-evident; facilitators respond to, even seek out, spokesmen for collective interests, neutrals occupy a more cautious but not necessarily hostile spot, and resisters view themselves as rejecting group demands. The construction of this typology is too detailed for reporting here. For the construction of the legislator classification, see pp. 468–470 in *The Legislative System.* A somewhat different typology has been constructed for the city councilmen; however, for our purpose, it is a functional equivalent. City councilmen have been called pluralists, tolerants, and antagonists (see Betty H. Zisk, Heinz Eulau, and Kenneth Prewitt, "City Councilmen and 'The Group Struggle': A Typology of Legislators' Role Orientations," *Journal of Politics,* Vol. 27 August 1965, pp. 618–646).

8. Purposive role-orientations refer to how the politician formulates his job as lawmaker. The inventor emphasizes policy initiation and innovative solutions to community problems. A broker primarily defines his function as compromising, arbitrating, and integrating differences brought to the council or legislature. The tribune emphasizes the necessity of expressing the will of the people. And the ritualist stresses the mechanisms of the legislative process and the mechanics of the legislator's job.

9. Scores of legislative efficacy were constructed from the following scale items: "There is so little time during a session to study all the bills that sometimes I don't know what I'm voting for or against." "Many of the bills are so detailed and technical that I have trouble understanding them." "So many groups want so many different things that it is often difficult to know what stand to take." "My district includes so many different kinds of people that I often don't know just what the people there want me to do.' Items asked of the city councilmen were slightly revised to make sense in the council setting.

Table 12.7. Role Orientations and Time of Initial Socialization (in percentages)

	TIME OF SOCIALIZATION			
	PRE-ADULT		ADULT	
Role-orientation	*Legislators*	*Councilmen*	*Legislators*	*Councilmen*
Representative:				
Trustee	67	70	74	54
Delegate	16	3	12	16
Politico	18	28	14	31
Total per cent	101[a]	101[a]	100	101[a]
Total (*N*)	(154)	(68)	(85)	(59)
Group:[b]				
Facilitator (pluralist)	40	48	34	38
Neutral (tolerant)	33	38	39	49
Resister (antagonist)	27	14	27	14
Total per cent	100	100	100	101[a]
Total (*N*)	(245)	(64)	(151)	(51)
Purposive:[c]				
Inventor	33	31	35	31
Broker	32	40	33	47
Tribune	50	27	50	24
Ritualist	16	47	15	36
Total (*N*)	(264)	(67)	(155)	(59)

[a]Due to rounding.
[b]Typologies for councilmen in parentheses.
[c]Percentages may total more than 100 since some respondents gave more than one answer.

Table 12.8. Sense of Legislative Efficacy and Time of Initial Socialization (in percentages)

	TIME OF SOCIALIZATION			
	PRE-ADULT		ADULT	
Efficacy Score	*Legislators (N = 259)*	*Councilmen (N = 58)*	*Legislators (N = 153)*	*Councilmen (N = 49)*
High	37	28	33	39
Medium	37	38	43	34
Low	26	34	24	27
Total	100	100	100	100

indifference of the dependent items to the "ordering" power of the time variable. Lack of differences between the two groups of councilmen is less striking but nevertheless apparent. The "greater" differences among councilmen may be due to instability caused by the smaller number or it may be due to institutional differences. If the former, additional data (currently being collected) will stabilize the percentages and wash out seeming differences; if the latter, we will have to revise the theory and take into account the effect of local-state differences.

CONCLUSION

At this juncture of the research, we rest our interpretation on the following conclusions:

1. Time of initial political socialization is indicative of a considerable range of early political experiences. Among both councilmen and legislators, explicit political awareness in youth sets one apart from colleagues with respect to personal contacts, images formed, global and particular events, and predispositions associated with the socialization experience.

It is not inconsistent with much current writing to presume that such different syndromes of experiences would produce different orientations toward political duties and problems. However:

2. Early political socialization is apparently unrelated to major aspects of incumbent orientation. Differences in orientations toward significant actors in the legislative arena and differences in self-evaluations are not rooted in experiences associated with the genesis of the political career.

When people fail to behave as a hypothesis says they should behave, the social investigator may argue his findings from two perspectives. Blame may be laid to his data, sample, or indicators—a methodological rationale; or his initial proposition may be called into question—a theoretical rationale. We have opted for the latter alternative and will reason that the developmental hypothesis is not applicable to the careers of elected politicians.

But first, why reject a methodological reason? The question is particularly relevant because the study has one obvious methodological difficulty. Since our definition of earliest political exposure, and the data collected, stress the capacity of the officeholders to recall and articulate the politically relevant events in their backgrounds, we necessarily tap their manifest political socialization. It is possible that more discriminating questions and more sensitive indicators would identify latent political socialization as well, and that a typology based on such information *would* correlate with incumbent orientations. Whatever merit there may be in this argument, the fact remains that time of their initial political awareness did serve as a useful indicator of how legislators and councilmen were socialized into an active political interest. Tables 12.4 through 12.6 demonstrate that time does elicit information about manifest political socialization, and Tables 12.7 and 12.8 present evidence that such experiences are unrelated to incumbent political orientations. Thus it is evident that the two distinct categories of early career experiences do not relate systematically to later career orientations.

The developmental hypothesis argues that early learned political images have a bearing on subsequent political behavior. Adapted to the study of political careers, this proposition reads: Early career experiences have a bearing on incumbent political orientations. Our data suggest this is not the case. A counter-hypothesis can be suggested: Intervening between initial political socialization and incumbent behavior are political experiences that condition subsequent behavior irrespective of factors associated with initial socialization.[10] These experiences interrupt the career sequence and retard or even reverse patterns formed during earlier stages. Recruitment and induction experiences may be of this kind; such experiences are closer in time and in kind to those of the incumbent officeholder. They serve as guidelines for the incumbents's present behavior. In addition, institutional considerations and pressures undoubtedly provide direction as the officeholder relates to his constituency, his party, or his interest groups; and his interactions within the legislative or council setting may be the primary factor accounting for how he evaluates his own performance.

These notions, however, are a topic for another analysis. We can briefly restate the findings and the argument: Early political experiences, especially those associated with childhood and adolescence, though they may be vividly recalled, are not crucial determinants of the behavior of American state legislators and city councilmen as they respond to official duties. It is likely that other more relevant events intervene and other more pressing demands provide the guidelines that structure the orientations of political officeholders to their tasks.

10. See Kenneth Prewitt, "Career Patterns of Local Elected Officials," paper presented at American Political Science Association Meeting, Chicago, Illinois, Sept. 9–12, 1964.

Part IV

Accent on Analysis: Structures

Chapter 13

The Ecological Basis of Party Systems

This is an analysis of the relationship between the ecological structure of Ohio's eighty-eight counties and the structure of their party systems, as reflected in the vote for the Ohio House of Representatives over a period of six elections, from 1946 to 1956.

PROBLEM

A viable democratic political system, as any social system, has to meet certain internal-structural requisites that can be shown to be functional for achieving the goals of the system. Among the goals of a democratic political system are the continuing crystallization, institutionalization and resolution of social, economic and other conflicts. These goals are mutually interdependent. If conflicts remain uncrystallized, they are unlikely to be institutionalized; and if they are not institutionalized, they are likely to remain unsolved. The political system will be characterized by tensions making for basic political instability.

Among the structural requisites of a stable democratic system is the existence of political parties which, by competing for public support on reasonably even terms, serve as agents of conflict crystallization and institutionalization and, through bargaining and compromise, contribute to the resolution of conflicts of interest. Competitive parties are, therefore, structural requisites of the democratic political system in that they facilitate the achievement of some of its goals, notably the crystallization, institutionalization and resolution of conflicts.

Reprinted from *Midwest Journal of Political Science,* Vol. 1 (August, 1957), pp. 125–35, by permission of the Wayne State University Press.

But a political system is not a closed system. It functions within a series of environments which tend to condition its structure. One might mention the prevailing system of class relations, the economic system, the cultural or value system, and so on. Of such environmental systems, the ecological system, i.e., the pattern of the residential distribution of the population, has long been recognized as a major conditioning factor, but the precise relationship between the structure of the ecological system and the structure of the party system has not been widely explored. In his recent *American State Politics* (1956), V. O. Key, Jr. perceptibly analyzed the effect of metropolitan and rural environments on the fortunes of the political parties in sundry states, but he was not primarily concerned with an analysis of the relationship between the structure of the ecological system as an external determinant and the structure of the party system as an internal determinant of the political system.

HYPOTHESIS

It is a most general hypothesis of this study that there is a direct relationship between the character of an area's ecological structure and the structure of its party system. In particular, the hypothesis is entertained that urban structures are conducive to the existence of competitive party systems and that there is a progressive transition to semi-competitive and non-competitive (one party) systems as areas are located along an urban-rural ecological continuum. If this hypothesis can be supported, one may speculate that increasing urbanization, especially the expansion of metropolitan areas, is favorable to the extension of a competitive party politics as a structural requisite of the democratic political system.

THEORY

Underlying the hypothesis are some broad theoretical notions about factors in the urban environment which are conducive to a competitive party system. Without reviewing here the large and often controversial literature of urban sociology, it may be suggested that competitive attitudes, orientations and practices are functions of such major ecological variables as the size, density and heterogeneity of urban aggregates. In particular, the city, in contrast to the open country, is characterized by a greater range of individual variations, a more pervasive segmentalization of human relationship making for membership in widely divergent groups as well as for divided allegiances, a more complicated class structure and heightened social and physical mobility, a greater division of labor and more intense economic rivalry, a wider range of ideas and more secular attitudes. This kind of environment is likely to be more favorable to the development of competitive parties than small town or rural environments where social relationships are more limited and limiting, where sacred values and traditional behavior patterns are cherished, where social and ideological differences are less tolerated, where group memberships are concentric rather than tangential, and so on. In such environments semi-competitive or non-competitive party systems are more likely to predominate.

These theoretical considerations are not meant to imply that the city, as some sociologists have held, is an undifferentiated mass of people characterized by anonymity, impersonality, standardization, or disorganization, as opposed to the country with its presumed friendliness, community spirit, spontaneity of association and mutual aid. Such differentiation does violence to the continuing assimilation of city and country which has been the outstanding feature of ecological development in the United States during the past sixty years or so. "Urban" and "rural," then, are used here as convenient shorthand phrases to denote ecological differences, on the assumption that, in spite of the assimilation process, "rurbanization" has not as yet gone far enough to eliminate all distinctions between city and country. Urban and rural are not to be construed, therefore, as ideal types, but as two poles of a continuum which does not permit radically discontinuous variations as one moves from one end to the other but makes for variations nonetheless.

In order to proceed with the analysis, Ohio's eighty-eight counties had to be classified in terms of their (a) ecological structure, (b) structure of party system, and (c) party dominance. In the following we shall briefly summarize the main steps taken in the preparatory stage of the analysis.

Ecological Structure

The nature of a person's place of residence is an easily available and tangible index of the ecological structure of a county. The United States Census divides the population into three main categories: urban, rural non-farm, and rural. For the purposes of this study the urban and rural non-farm categories were combined, on the assumption that due to "rurbanization" non-farm people outside urban areas have attitudes and orientations closer to those of urban than of farm people. In order to test the reliability, if not the theoretical validity, of the combined category as an index of urban structure, it was correlated with other indices of urban and rural differentiation available in the Census. The combined urban and rural non-farm category should correlate highly and positively, for instance, with indices of size, density and heterogeneity of population, as well as with some other relevant demographic characteristics, and it should correlate highly and negatively with rural characteristics. Table 13.1 presents the correlation coefficients, based on 1950 Census data.

Table 13.1 indicates that, as expected, very high correlations were obtained between the combined index of urban and rural non-farm residence and the two measures of size and density. The coefficients for the heterogeneity factors vary—that for percent foreign-born being reasonably high, that for percent

Table 13.1. Correlation Coefficients for Urban and Rural Non-Farm Residence, and Selected Ecological and Demographic Characteristics of 88 Ohio Counties, 1950 Census Data

Factor	Census Category	Rho
Density	Population per square mile	+.95
Size	Total population	+.93
Heterogeneity	Percent foreign-born	+.68
	Percent non-white	+.49
Employment	Percent in manufacturing	+.73
	Percent in agriculture	−.96
Income	Median family income	+.76
	Percent with less than $2,000	−.77

non-white only moderately high, but both are satisfactory. The high positive and negative coefficients for employment in manufacturing and agriculture, respectively, as well as the income coefficients, further support the discriminatory reliability of the residence criterion as an ecological index.

However, in order to refine the urban category, a further distinction was made between counties located in metropolitan areas, as defined by the Census, and those not within metropolitan areas, but with urban aggregates of 2,500 population or more. Application of these criteria yielded five major ecological categories ranging from "metro" to "rural." The description of these categories and the distribution of the eighty-eight Ohio counties by these categories are found in Table 13.2.

Table 13.2. Distribution of 88 Ohio Counties by Major Ecological Categories

Category	Description	*N*	Percent
Metro	All counties in standard metropolitan areas	17	19
Urban	All counties with urban aggregates of 2,500+ population and a ratio of urban and rural non-farm population of more than 80%	10	11
Urban-Rurban	All counties with urban aggregates of 2,500+ population and a ratio of urban and rural non-farm population of 70–80%	31	35
Rural-Rurban	All counties with urban aggregates of 2,500+ population and a ratio of urban and rural non-farm population of less than 70%	19	22
Rural	All counties *without* an urban aggregate of 2,500+ population	11	13
	Total	88	100

Political Structure

County election data for the Ohio House of Representatives from 1946 to 1956 were analyzed to determine the structure of the party systems in the eighty-eight Ohio counties which also serve as election districts. During this period, the Democrats organized the House only in 1948. The election of 1946 was chosen as the starting point of the series as it marked the first "normal" post-war contest.

As a number of counties are multi-member districts, i.e., more than one contest takes place in any one election, the total number of contests in the six elections since 1946 was used as an initial device to classify the counties in terms of competition between the two major parties. A competitive party system district was defined as one in which one of the two parties has won at least 25 percent, or more, of *all* the *contests* in the six elections. On this basis, only sixteen counties, or 18 percent of eighty-eight counties, could be classified as "competitive."

Inspection of the data suggested that in some counties where it had won less than 25 percent of the contests, or none at all, the second party was nevertheless able to stimulate reasonably strong opposition to the dominant party—opposition effective enough to win a contest occasionally, and to keep the dominant party on its toes. It seemed feasible, therefore, to divide the counties not classified as competitive into two categories: (1) semi-competitive, and (2) non-competitive (or one-party) systems.

A semi-competitive system was defined as one where the second party, though winning less than 25 percent of the contests, or none, had won 40 percent or more of the popular two-party vote in *at least four* of the *elections* held between 1946 and 1956. For this purpose, the vote cast in individual contests in multi-member districts was averaged, and the mean vote cast for all party candidates was used as the percentage index. On this basis, another twenty-four counties, or 28 percent of the total, could be classified as semi-competitive.

The residue of counties, forty-eight in all, are the non-competitive (one-party system) districts, where the second party has won less than 25 percent

Table 13.3. Distribution of Different Party Systems in 88 Ohio Counties, Based on 1946–1956 Election Data for the House of Representatives

Character of Party System	*N*	Percent
Competive	16	18
Semi-competitive	24	28
Non-competitive	48	54
Total	88	100

of the contests, or none, and over 40 percent of the vote in *less than four* of the elections since 1946. Table 13.3 summarizes the data.

Party Dominance

For purposes of "control" to be applied in the analysis, it was necessary to define "party dominance" in semi-competitive and non-competitive party systems. A county or district was considered "dominated" by a party if that party had won 75 percent or more of the total number of contests in the period 1946–1956. As Table 13.4 indicates, the Republican party is overwhelmingly dominant through time in the non-competitive as well as in the semi-competitive counties.

Table 13.4. Party Dominance in Semi-Competitive and Non-Competitive Election Districts for the Ohio House of Representatives, 1946–1956

Party Dominance		*N*	Percent
Semi-competitive party systems			
Republicans dominant		21	88
Democrats dominant		3	12
	Total	24	100
Non-competitive party systems			
Republicans dominant		43	90
Democrats dominant		5	10
	Total	48	100

Analysis

On the basis of the foregoing classifications, a first step in the analysis of the relationship between ecological structure and party-system structure was a complete cross-tabulation of the eighty-eight counties. Table 13.5 presents the results. Most evident is the marked difference between the metropolitan and the four other ecological areas with respect to party competition. Surprisingly, only one of the ten counties classified as urban turned out to have a competitive party system. But none of the rural counties fell into the competitive system category. On the other hand, both metropolitan and urban counties differ significantly from the urban-rurban and rural-rurban counties in the semi-competitive classification. The relatively large percentage of semi-competitive party systems found in the rural counties is partly due to the absence of competitive party systems in that category, but it is also due to the fact that in some scattered counties in the southern part of the state the Democratic

Table 13.5. Ecological and Party-System Structure of Ohio Counties, Derived from 1950 Census Data and Election Results for the Ohio House of Representatives, 1946–1956

	IN PERCENTAGES				
Character of Party System	*Metro N = 17*	*Urban N = 10*	*Urban-Rurban N = 31*	*Rural-Rurban N = 19*	*Rural N = 11*
Competitive	41	10	16	16	0
Semi-competitive	41	50	19	5	45
Non-competitive	18	40	65	79	55
Total	100	100	100	100	100

party has been able to maintain a certain degree of traditional electoral strength. With regard to non-competitive or one-party systems, the progression increases systematically from the metropolitan structures to the rural-rurban structures, declining slightly in the rural structures due to the relatively strong showing of semi-competitive systems in these rural counties.

Table 13.5 suggests that it may be permissible, without doing violence to the data, to combine the urban-rurban and rural-rurban ecological categories into a single rurban category. Table 13.6 presents the re-classification. The table indicates more clearly that some kind of party competition, either of the complete or modified kind, is a quality of metropolitan and urban ecological areas, while non-competitive party systems are predominantly small town and rural phenomena. It may be interesting to note in this connection that the mean size of the largest town in the urban counties is 27,233 ± 10,800, in the urban-rurban counties only 12,081 ± 6,500, and in the rural-rurban counties a mere 6,088 ± 874. In other words, these ecological areas differ not only with respect to the size of their largest urban centers, but, as the standard deviations show, the range of variation declines progressively, suggesting the greater homogeneity at the small town end of the urban-rural continuum. The

Table 13.6 Revised Ecological and Party-System Structure of Ohio Counties

	IN PERCENTAGES			
Character of Party System	*Metro N = 17*	*Urban N = 10*	*Rurban N = 50*	*Rural N = 11*
Competitive	41	10	16	0
Semi-competitive	41	50	14	45
Non-competitive	18	40	70	55
Total	100	100	100	100

table points up the small town basis of one party systems in Ohio, while inroads into the rigidity of one party politics are most noticeable in the large percentage of semi-competitive party systems in the urban ecological areas (a pattern disturbed only in the rural category, as explained already). If, as in Table 13.7, one disregards the difference between competitive and semi-competitive party systems, the relationship between ecological structure and party competition is even more evident. In fact, the table would seem to justify a recombination of the ecological categories into two single categories, a metropolitan-urban and a rurban-rural classification. Table 13.8 presents the data.

Table 13.7. Further Revision of Ecological and Party-System Structures, Ohio

	IN PERCENTAGES			
Character of Party System	*Metro N = 17*	*Urban N = 10*	*Rurban N = 50*	*Rural N = 11*
Competitive & Semi-competitive	82	60	30	45
Non-competitive	18	40	70	55
Total	100	100	100	100

Table 13.8. Ecological and Party-System Structures Dichotomized, Ohio

	IN PERCENTAGES	
Character of Party System	*Metro-Urban N = 27*	*Rurban-Rural N = 61*
Competitive & Semi-competitive	74	33
Non-competitive	26	67
Total	100	100

Non-competitive or one-party systems now appear even more clearly as correlates of small-town and rural ecological structures, while some form of party competition appears to predominate in the metropolitan and medium-size urban areas.

However, in spite of the clear nature of the demonstrated relationship, it might be argued that the connection between ecological structure and party system structure is spurious, particularly in the semi-competitive and non-competitive counties. Could it be, for instance, that the predominance of one party systems in the non-metropolitan counties is a function of the overwhelming strength of the Republican party in the state as a whole? In order to deal with the party factor, it seemed advisable to control the urban and rurban areas by party dominance. Unfortunately, the number of such counties in which the Democratic party predominates is so small (four in all) that the data cannot be properly assessed, though they move in the expected direction. However, if the ecological categories are controlled by Republican dominance, the small town basis of non-competitive party systems in these counties is evident. As Table 13.9 shows, while the eight Republican-dominated urban

Table 13.9. Party Systems in Urban and Rurban Counties, Ohio, Controlled by Party Dominance

	IN PERCENTAGES			
Character of Party System	*Democrats Urban N = 1*	*Dominant Rurban N = 3*	*Republicans Urban N = 8*	*Dominant Rurban N = 39*
Semi-competitive	100	0	50	18
Non-competitive	0	100	50	82
Total	100	100	100	100

counties are equally split between semi-competitive and non-competitive party systems, one party systems are overwhelmingly present in the rurban environments where 82 percent of the Republican-dominated counties have no competitive systems of any kind.

CONCLUSION

The data presented in the analysis seem to support the hypothesis that there is a direct relationship between the ecological structure of the counties which serve as election districts for the Ohio House of Representatives and the structure of the party systems in these counties. Competitive party systems, either truly competitive or semi-competitive seem to be functionally related to metropolitan and urban ecological structures, while non-competitive or one-party systems seem to be functionally related to small town and rural ecological structures. Increasing urbanization would seem to be conducive to the further development of a competitive party system as a structural requisite of the democratic political system.

POSTSCRIPT

The study had an interesting post-publication history. In 1960, David Gold and John R. Schmidhauser published an analysis "designed to test the validity of Eulau's *specific* hypothesis in the case of the 99 counties of Iowa during the same period chosen by him." They concluded: "Contrary to the Eulau hypothesis, the Iowa data indicate that . . . there was *not* a simple positive association between the degree of urbanization and the intensity of party competition." [1] But in 1963, Phillips Cutright examined the relationship between urbanization and party competition in as many as ten states: "The primary stimulus for this research stems from the apparently contradictory findings of Gold and Schmidhauser in their study of Iowa and the Ohio case as presented by Eulau." Cutright concluded that his data support Eulau's hypothesis that "urbanization is positively associated with competitive party politics." [2] The measurement problems involved in this "controversy" were later discussed by Kenneth Janda in another connection.[3]

1. David Gold and John R. Schmidhauser, "Urbanization and Party Competition: The Case of Iowa," *Midwest Journal of Political Science,* Vol. 4 (February, 1960), pp. 62–75.

2. Phillips Cutright, "Urbanization and Competitive Party Politics," *Journal of Politics,* Vol. 25 (August, 1963), pp. 552–64.

3. See Kenneth Janda, *Data Processing: Applications to Political Research* (Evanston: Northwestern University Press, 1965), pp. 175–78.

Chapter 14

Bases of Authority in Legislative Bodies: A Comparative Analysis

Authority relations are usually treated as characteristic properties of administrative or bureaucratic organizations. Though formally structured as hierarchies of superordination and subordination, authority relations in such organizations represent perplexing analytical problems involving both the identification of authority and its measurement.[1] The task of analysis is compounded in legislative bodies, where those in high formal office--presidents, speakers, and floor leaders--are either *elected* to their positions or *succeed* to office as a consequence of political manipulations which often elude the outside observer.

Little is known about authority relations in legislative bodies. There is a great deal of anecdotal information about the dictatorial speaker--"Uncle Joe" Cannon (Speaker of the U.S. House of Representatives, 1903–1911) is the prototype--or about the arbitrary committee chairman who pigeonholes whatever bills he dislikes. More systematic efforts to identify and measure power in legislative institutions through study of roll-call votes have proved difficult.[2] In the Congress, there seems to be a close congruence between for-

Originally published in *Administrative Science Quarterly*, Vol. 7 (December, 1962), pp. 309–21. Reprinted by permission.

1. See Robert L. Peabody, Perceptions of Organizational Authority: A Comparative Analysis, *Administrative Science Quarterly*, 6 (1962), 461–482.

2. See Robert A. Dahl, The Concept of Power, *Behavioral Science*, 2 (1957), 201–215; Duncan MacRae, Jr., and Hugh D. Price, Scale Positions and "Power" in the Senate, *Behavioral Science*, 4 (1959), 212–218.

mal and informal leadership, but the question–what makes for the acceptance of authority?–remains unanswered.[3]

There is reason to believe that the degree to which the decisions of legislative leaders are accepted depends on certain "values" that serve as bases of authority being attributed to them by the rank-and-file membership.[4] Presumably, legislators are not equally credited by their peers with skill, knowledge, respect, or affection, to name just a few of such values. In so far as legislative leaders have some of these characteristics attributed to them more frequently than other legislators, their authority may be said to be rooted in such value attributions. Of course, this does not answer an important question: Do men come into positions of legislative leadership because such characteristics are attributed to them to a higher degree than to other members, or is the greater attribution of these values to them partly the result of their occupying offices invested with formal authority? Whatever the answer to this question, one should expect that the authority of legislative leaders–acceptance of their decisions–is likely to depend on their being *attributed* values to a high degree.

THREE VALUES

Hypothetically speaking, in every legislative body authority is likely to be based on respect. Respect is a value which may be attributed unevenly: some men are given more deference than others. In legislatures, distinguished as they are from administrative structures by a strong egalitarian ethos ("each man's vote counts alike here"), respect arises out of those informal norms of behavior, "rules of the game," in terms of which legislators regulate each other's conduct [5] and which are enforced by both positive and negative incentives. Those who fail to conform are variously ostracized, censured, or punished, and they are not likely to enjoy respect. Those who excel in playing by the rules are given respect and are rewarded: their bills will have a better chance of being passed: they may be appointed to committee chairmanships; or they may be elected to positions of leadership.

The egalitarian milieu of legislative bodies, the camaraderie that comes with close personal contact, involvement in the common task, and pride in electoral survival make it easy to develop friendships (which, in bureaucratic organizations, are restricted by the status system: only those on the same level in the hierarchy, or in adjacent status positions, come into close contact in their work

3. See David B. Truman, *The Congressional Party* (New York, 1959), pp. 94–144, 193–246.

4. This formulation is indebted to, though it also deviates from, Harold D. Lasswell's propositions about the functions of values in politics. See, for instance, Harold D. Lasswell and Abraham Kaplan, *Power and Society* (New Haven, 1950), pp. 55–62, 133–136.

5. This has been most intensively studied in the U. S. Senate. See Donald R. Matthews, *U.S. Senators and Their World* (Chapel Hill, N.C., 1960), pp. 92–177; Ralph K. Huitt, The Morse Committee Assignment Controvery: A Case Study in Senate Norms, *American Political Science Review*, 51 (1957), 313–329.

and associate with each other in informal settings). Friendship is a strong bond in politics, and the affections of friendship carry over into the business of lawmaking. In every legislature there are more or less cohesive groups of friends and cliques, often related to each other through overlapping memberships or secondary contacts.[6] Again, as with respect, attributions of affection are likely to be unevenly distributed. Some legislators are more widely chosen as friends than others.

Legislatures, like administrative organizations, develop and cultivate a specialization of labor in dealing with particular subjects, which has been institutionalized in the creation of standing committees. But a legislator also shows a degree of expertise that is independent of his committee assignments and that is rooted in his personal skill and training. Regardless of the committees to which they belong, some legislators are recognized as more expert than others in particular subjects by their colleagues.[7]

VALUES IN EIGHT CHAMBERS

This analysis deals with the distribution of these three values—respect, affection, and expertise—in eight chambers of four American state legislatures—those of California, New Jersey, Ohio, and Tennessee.[8] The main hypothesis of this analysis is that a greater degree of respect, affection, and expertise is attributed to legislative leaders than to rank-and-file members. If it should be found that the leaders do not differ from other legislators or, perhaps, rank below them in the values ascribed to them, it may be assumed that, unless other bases are available, their authority rests on fragile foundations. Moreover, it may be possible to identify a reserve of highly ranked legislators among the rank and file from which future leaders can be recruited.

The data on which the analysis is based were collected in an interview survey of 474 legislators in eight legislative chambers during the 1957 sessions.[9] In the course of the interview, all legislators in the sample were asked

6. See Samuel C. Patterson, Patterns of Personal Relations in A Legislative Group, *Public Opinion Quarterly,* 23 (1959), 101–118.

7. See William Buchanan, Heinz Eulau, LeRoy C. Ferguson, and John C. Wahlke, The Legislator as Specialist, *Western Political Quarterly* 13 (1960), 636–651.

8. The data used in this article were collected as part of the State Legislative Research Project. For a full report of this project, see John C. Wahlke, Heinz Eulau, William Buchanan, and LeRoy C. Ferguson, *The Legislative System: Explorations in Legislative Behavior* (New York, 1962). The preparation of this analysis was made possible by a grant from the Political Behavior Committee of the Social Science Research Council and a subsidy from the Public Affairs Committee of Stanford University to Richard Duncan, who prepared a preliminary analysis of the data. None of the organizations mentioned is responsible for the analysis.

9. In California and Ohio, 94 per cent were interviewed; in Tennessee, 91 per cent; and in New Jersey, 100 per cent. For a short report on technical aspects of the project, see John C. Wahlke, Heinz Eulau, William Buchanan, and LeRoy C. Ferguson, The Annals of Research: A Case of Collaboration in Comparative Study of Legislative Behavior, *American Behavioral Scientist,* 4 (May 1961), 3–9.

a series of questions: Whom did they consider the "most widely respected" among their colleagues? Whom did they consider their "closest personal friends?" Whom did they consider "particularly expert in their respective fields?"

In order to compare any one legislator with all others in terms of the number of nominations he received, it was necessary to develop a standard of comparison. This standard was likely to vary from one set of value atltributions to the next as a function of the number of choices requested—four or five in the case of respect, five or six in the case of expertise, and an unspecified number in the case of affection (though most nominations here usually varied from none to six). As the actual number of choices could also vary within each set from one respondent to the next, the standard had to be some measure of central tendency. Therefore, the total number of nominations in any one set was divided by the number of *potential* recipients—that is, the total number of members in a chamber. This was done on the assumption that if all actual choices were, by chance, equally distributed among all the members, the resulting hypothetical frequency of choices could serve as a standard in terms of which actual nominations could be ordered. For instance, the total number of nominations for respect in the Ohio House were 655. This figure was divided by 139, the number of members. Had the nominations been equally distributed by chance, each member would have received 4.71 choices. This hypothetical standard may serve two purposes: first, to compare the eight chambers as wholes or any subgroup in a chamber, such as the leaders and rank-and-file members; and second, to place any one member as falling above or below the standard. Table 14.1 presents the hypothetical frequencies (*hf*) for the three sets of value nominations.

Table 14.1. Hypothetical Frequencies of Nominations

	HOUSE				SENATE			
Value	Calif.	N.J.	Ohio	Tenn.	Calif.	N.J.	Ohio	Tenn.
Respect	3.26	4.26	4.71	4.12	2.58	3.56	4.40	3.18
Affection	3.90	3.05	3.93	4.40	3.05	3.52	3.24	3.30
Expertise	4.96	4.94	4.62	2.62	4.00	3.52	4.95	3.60

The fluctuations within each set from chamber to chamber are probably symptomatic of different degrees of importance attached to the values of respect, affection, and expertise in the different chambers. Respect, for instance, seemed to be attributed to members more frequently in the Ohio House ($hf = 4.71$) than in the California Senate ($hf = 2.58$). Affection seemed more difficult to secure in the New Jersey House or California Senate (both with $hf = 3.05$) than in the Tennessee House ($hf = 4.40$). Expertise was less commonly attributed to members of the Tennessee House (*hf* = 2.62) than of the California House (*hf* = 4.96).

THE RANK AND FILE

How are the attributions of respect, affection, and expertise distributed among the rank-and-file memberships of the eight chambers? Table 14.2 shows the

Table 14.2. Distribution of Rank and File (in percentages)

	HOUSE				SENATE			
Nominations regarding:	Calif. (*N* = 74)	N.J. (*N* = 52)	Ohio (*N* = 136)	Tenn. (*N* = 96)	Calif. (*N* = 39)	N.J. (*N* = 18)	Ohio (*N* = 32)	Tenn. (*N* = 29)
Respect								
Above *hf*	23	27	18	22	26	28	25	21
Equal *hf*	4	4	1	8	10	5	3	10
Below *hf*	43	33	42	35	38	56	53	31
Zero (not named)	30	36	39	35	26	11	19	38
Affection								
Above *hf*	28	29	30	35	31	33	34	34
Equal *hf*	14	19	15	16	18	22	19	14
Below *hf*	51	42	48	47	38	28	44	38
Zero (not named)	7	10	7	2	13	17	3	14
Expertise								
Above *hf*	28	25	20	21	31	33	37	24
Equal *hf*	2	4	1	3	8	17	3	7
Below *hf*	23	25	27	22	28	17	22	28
Zero (not named)	47	46	52	54	33	33	38	41

distributions in terms of the hypothetical frequency. It shows that the distributions do not follow a sharply pyramidal form, though the "above hypothetical frequency" groupings in no case include much more than a third of the rank and file. The largest high-ranking grouping is found in the expertise set of the Ohio Senate (37 per cent), and the most exclusive high-ranking grouping characterizes the attribution or respect in the Ohio House (18 per cent).

In general, Table 14.2 shows that the distribution of value attribution tends to be very similar in these eight legislative chambers. For instance, in the high-ranking groupings the range for respect is quite small, from 18 per cent in the large Ohio House to 28 per cent in the small New Jersey Senate. Although attribution of respect, as noted in Table 14.1, is frequent in the Ohio House, it is evidently difficult for individual members to reach a high ranking. Indeed, in the three large chambers—the Ohio House as well as the California and Tennessee Houses—inclusion in the "above" high-frequency grouping is more difficult to attain than it is in the small chambers (with the exception of the Tennessee Senate). It is plausible that there should be a relationship between the size of a chamber and the frequency with which respect is attributed: the larger a group is, the more difficult it is for an individual to be recognized as deserving respect.

Similarly, the range in the "above" high-frequency groupings for affection is very narrow, from 28 per cent in the California House to 35 per cent in the Tennessee House—a difference of only 7 per cent. Affection seems to be attributed more frequently, however, than respect, as Table 14.2 shows.

The expertise nominations show a partly similar, partly different pattern. The difference lies in the relatively wide range of the proportions of legislators in the "above" groupings—from 37 per cent in the Ohio Senate to only 20 per cent in the Ohio House. The similarity lies in the apparent relationship between size of chamber and expertise attributions. As in the case of respect, nominations of expertise are made more frequently in the smaller than in the larger chambers.

A more convenient way to examine the similarities and differences between chambers and value sets is to score a legislator's total nominations with reference to the hypothetical frequency standard. For this purpose, a legislator above the *hf* standard was given a score of 3; a legislator whose actual nominations ware equal to the *hf* criterion was given a score of 2; a legislator falling below the standard a score of 1; and a legislator with no nominations a score of zero. The individual scores so obtained were averaged for each value set in each chamber, yielding a simple index also ranging from three to zero.

Table 14.3. Value Indexes for Rank and File

	HOUSE				SENATE			
Value	Calif.	N.J.	Ohio	Tenn.	Calif.	N.J.	Ohio	Tenn.
Respect	1.20	1.21	1.01	1.17	1.36	1.50	1.53	1.14
Affection	1.64	1.67	1.66	1.85	1.67	1.72	1.84	1.69
Expertise	1.11	1.07	.90	.91	1.36	1.50	1.41	1.14

Table 14.3 presents the index figures so obtained for the rank and file of the eight chambers. The averaged scores, it appears, fall in a range (from .90 to 1.85) below the index figure of two which should be attained if all nominations were equally distributed by chance among all potential recipients. Moreover, it appears more clearly from Table 14.3 that in all four legislatures (except for Tennessee in regard to respect and affection), value nominations are somewhat more widely shared in the smaller than in the larger chambers.

The differences are small, but the general pattern in elective bodies such as legislatures suggests that the concentration of value attributions at the top of an institutional structure may be more characteristic of larger than of smaller organizations.

COMPARISON OF LEADERSHIP AND MEMBERSHIP

Whatever ideas one may entertain about the "natural history" of value attributions–whether they occurred before or after a legislator moved into a position of formal leadership–it can be assumed that in order to make effective use of the office more is needed than sheer incumbency. One should expect, therefore, that leaders as a group should receive more value nominations than the aggregate of rank-and-file members. However, each of the three values may not be equally relevant for effective authority. For instance, respect is probably more critical than affection or expertise in a leader's ability to have his decisions accepted. Without respect, leaders may not stay in office very long, no matter how many nominations they may receive in regard to values such as affection or expertise. In fact, expertise may be least relevant in this connection. It may even constitute a handicap because legislative leaders are expected to be "generalists" rather than specialists. We should anticipate, therefore, that the leadership cadres in the eight chambers will differ most from the rank and file in the share of respect they receive, less so in the share of affection, and least in the share of expertise attributions. Table 14.4 presents the results.

Table 14.4. Comparison of Leaders and Members

	HOUSE				SENATE			
	Calif.	N.J.	Ohio	Tenn.	Calif.	N.J.	Ohio	Tenn.
Respect								
Leaders	2.16	1.50	3.00	3.00	3.00	1.67	3.00	3.00
Members	1.20	1.21	1.01	1.17	1.36	1.50	1.53	1.14
Difference	.96	.29	1.99	1.83	1.64	.17	1.47	1.86
Affection								
Leaders	2.67	2.00	3.00	3.00	3.00	1.33	2.50	3.00
Members	1.64	1.67	1.66	1.85	1.67	1.72	1.84	1.69
Difference	1.03	.33	1.34	1.15	1.33	–.39	.66	1.31
Expertise								
Leaders	1.50	1.17	2.33	2.33	1.00	.67	1.00	2.00
Members	1.11	1.07	.90	.91	1.36	1.50	1.41	1.14
Difference	.39	.10	1.43	1.42	–.36	–.83	–.41	.86

Altogether, there were 28 leaders in the high-level offices of the eight chambers, including speakers, presidents pro tem, and party floor leaders. In general, as Table 14.4 shows, if New Jersey is excluded, our expectations are met. Leaders differ most from members in the degree to which they are respected, then in the degree of affection shown them, and finally in the expertise attributed to them. We note one persistent exception, however, in both New Jersey chambers. Though given more respect than the members, the New Jersey leaders differ little from the members, and the differences are considerably smaller than in the other three states. In regard to affection, New Jersey Senate members actually were favored with affection more frequently than the leaders, and in the House the difference, though favorable to the leaders, is again much smaller than in the other three legislatures. In expertise also, New Jersey leaders were not credited with expertise more frequently than members.

There is a very simple explanation for the New Jersey results. In the small New Jersey chambers, all crucial procedural as well as substantive decisions are made by the majority party caucus as a body. In both chambers members of the majority party are rotated in and out of the speakership and other offices each session. Many of the members in any one session are, therefore, former speakers or former floor leaders, and they may be more influential than the incumbent officers. The wider distribution of value attributions in the data accurately mirrors these formal institutional arrangements in the New Jersey legislature. Indeed, the "deviant case" of New Jersey provides a good test of both the hypothesis and the reliability of the three value measures used in the analysis.

The results of Table 14.4 also suggest that expertise is not necessarily a value that serves as a base of authority. In five of the eight chambers, the differences in expertise attributions between leaders and members are either negative or very low, and in the two chambers where the difference is relatively large (the Ohio and Tennessee Houses), it is mainly due to the very low attributions given to the members. In the case of Tennessee, there is another simple institutional explanation. Tennessee legislative leaders, unlike those in the other states, are directly involved not only in the procedural but also in the substantive aspects of legislation. The floor leaders continually intervene in debates, either for or against bills, and they must have more than casual acquaintance with the content of legislation. The finding that they are named experts more than leaders in most of the other chambers seems to reflect this institutional procedure.

It is important to keep in mind that we are dealing here with aggregates of leaders rather than with individuals. In reality, there exist, of course, differences in the value attributions given to individual leaders as well. Some were nominated much more frequently than others with regard to any one of the values, but, in general, it seems that formal leaders in legislative bodies are attributed respect and affection more frequently than the rank and file. In attributions of expertise, the leaders differ much less from the membership. In fact, they do not seem to be expected to excel in a particular specialty. Moreover, as we shall see in the next section, there are among the rank and file a number of members who compare favorably with the leadership in regard to the number of nominations they receive for respect and affection.

COMPARISON OF LEADERS AND CHALLENGERS

By using the hypothetical frequency standard for respect and affection, it is possible to identify those members among the rank and file who seem to "challenge" the formal leaders. These challengers may either constitute a reserve from which future leaders will be recruited by co-optation into the incumbent leadership, or they may constitute a counterelite that threatens the present leadership. Whatever the case may be, the challengers seem to be important "informal leaders" at the immediate periphery of the formal authority nucleus. They are operationally defined as those members whose nominations with regard both to respect and affection are above the hypothetical frequency standard. Their proportions in the eight chambers are shown below.

State and chamber	*% challengers*
Ohio Senate	9
California Senate	10
Ohio House	11
Tennessee Senate	14
Tennessee House	17
New Jersey House	17
California House	19
New Jersey Senate	22

These distributions partly confirm what is already known about the various chambers. Why the two New Jersey chambers should produce relatively large numbers of challengers has already been suggested. The relatively high proportion of challengers in the California House becomes plausible if it is recalled that, at least as late as 1957, when the study was made, party discipline was lax in the California House, where both parties consisted of fluid factions and where the speaker attained office by mobilizing a bipartisan coalition in his support. Factionalism, too, is likely to account for the relatively high proportion of challengers in the Tennessee chambers.

In order to be able to make a meaningful comparison, the indexes of leaders and challengers were scored by the procedure described earlier, with the difference that the hypothetical frequency standard was recomputed for the leaders and challengers alone. (That is, leaders' and challengers' nominations were divided by their total number, now excluding all others). Table 14.5 presents the results.

In general, comparison of the differences between the two groups shows

Table 14.5. Comparison of Leaders and Challengers

	HOUSE				SENATE			
	Calif.	N.J.	Ohio	Tenn.	Calif.	N.J.	Ohio	Tenn.
Respect								
Leaders	2.17	1.67	2.33	2.33	3.00	1.00	3.00	1.75
Challengers	1.71	2.10	1.53	1.19	1.75	2.76	1.33	1.00
Difference	.46	–.43	.80	1.14	1.25	–1.76	1.67	.75
Affection								
Leaders	2.00	1.33	2.33	3.00	1.00	1.00	2.00	2.00
Challengers	1.64	2.10	1.93	1.75	2.00	2.76	1.00	1.75
Difference	.36	–.77	.40	1.25	–1.00	–1.76	1.00	.25

that the formal leaders maintain their advantage over the challengers. However, in most of the positive advantages the margin is narrow. In regard to respect attributions, the New Jersey leaders in both chambers, now, not unexpectedly, come out second best; but California House leaders, too, do not have a large advantage over their challengers. In regard to affection nominations, the differences are even smaller—the largest difference being 1.25 in the Tennessee House.

It would seem, then, that what facilitates occupancy of formal leadership positions in legislative bodies and gives support to the exercise of authority, more than anything else, is the respect given the incumbents of high offices by their fellow legislators. This is plausible: leaders, more than other members of a legislature, are expected to play by the rules of the game, and they are rewarded for doing so by being given respect by more of the other members than the rank and file or the group identified as challengers. Respect is probably the most distinguishing value at the base of authority in legislative bodies. Without it, authority is likely to be weak and impotent.

CONCLUSION

Incumbents of high formal positions in legislative bodies are attributed certain values like respect or affection more frequently than the rank and file or those members who vie with them for these values—the challengers. The data presented in the analysis cannot tell us whether high position in the legislature's informal authority structure is cause or consequence of occupancy of high formal office. They do suggest, however, that their being attributed certain values more frequently than other members is perhaps a necessary, though not a sufficient, condition for the effective exercise of leaders' authority. We may infer that as long as formal leaders are able to stay ahead of the rank-and-file members as well as of the challengers in respect attributions, they are likely to maintain their position in the structure of authority. It would seem that the attribution of values is in part facilitated by the institutional arrangements of a legislative body, but neither this alone nor formal office alone seem sufficient for effective legislative authority. Both seem to be required to generate the degree of authority without which human organizations—even such relatively democratic and egalitarian groups as legislative bodies—cannot effectively function as decision-making agencies.

Chapter 15

Policy Maps of City Councils and Policy Outcomes: A Developmental Analysis

THE PROBLEM

In spite of common challenges stemming from the common environment shared by all cities in a metropolitan region, continued and even increasing social and economic differentiation among and within cities rather than homogenization and integration are the most significant features of the contemporary metropolitan scene.[1] Cities within the same metropolitan region are not only maintaining but also developing distinct and unique "public life styles." [2] Urban sociology and urban geography have raised a multitude of questions and given a multitude of answers in seeking to account for the fact that cities facing basically similar challenges from the environment react so differently to these challenges. Most relevant research deals with the problem

Originally published, with Robert Eyestone, in *The American Political Science Review*, Vol. 62 (March, 1968), pp. 124–43. Reprinted by permission.

1. See, for instance, the recent work by Oliver P. Williams et al., *Suburban Differences and Metropolitan Policies: A Philadelphia Story* (Philadelphia: University of Pennsylvania Press, 1965).

2. Oliver P. Williams in a recent paper has argued that metropolitan regions are collections of small groups of residents and the economic superstructures necessary to sustain them. Each group is characterized by the choice of a distinctive life style, and because members of the various groups wish to live in congenial environments they tend to be found in similar locations throughout the region. Precisely where they are located is a matter of economics and the remnants of past land uses in the regions, but the fact of congeniality is a major cause of similarity in location choice. See "A Framework for Metropolitan Political Analysis," prepared for the Conference on Comparative Research in Community Politics, held at Athens, Georgia, November 16-19, 1966.

of differentiation and its effects on the development of cities in terms of historical settlement patterns, economic location and growth, or geographical space distribution.[3]

But differences in municipal life styles may also be the result of differences in public policies deliberately pursued by local governments in the metropolitan area. If this is so, the common pressures from the environment are evidently interpreted differently in the process of public decision-making that seeks to cope with them. It would seem, then, that metropolitan cities are in different stages of policy development. Leaving aside momentarily the meaning of "stages of policy development," we can ask a number of questions that may shed light on the relationship between environmental pressures and public policies designed to meet these pressures. If cities are in different stages of policy development, how can the stages be identified? Is policy development linear and "progressive," or is it reversible? Do the stages of policy development in fact correspond to relevant conditions of the environment? But if there are no differences in environmental challenges, what makes for arrested development in one city, while a similarly challenged city takes off or another is highly developed? On the other hand, if cities are in different stages of development, is it due to their possessing uneven resource capabilities by which environmental problems can be solved? But how can one explain why cities with equal resources adopt quite different public policies? What is the character of the policies designed to meet environmental challenges? Are they attempts to adjust the city to the changing environment, or are they attempts to control the environment, or both?

Questions like these in turn direct our attention to the need for exploring the policy perspectives of urban decision-makers. How do municipal policy-makers perceive their community's environment and problems stemming from environmental conditions? What are their short-term policy positions, and what are their long-range policy images of the future? Are their perceptions of problems, policy orientations and expectations related to the city's stage of policy development? And if this is the case, what are we to make of the relationship from a theoretical point of view? Although we do not propose to deal with all of these questions, it seems to us that they provide the cutting edge of an empirical theory of urban public policy.

THE PROJECT

This study of the policy maps of city councils in relationship to city policy development is part of a much larger project on municipal legislative bodies conducted in the ninety-odd cities of the San Francisco Bay metropolitan region since 1964.

3. See for instance, F. Stuart Chapin, Jr. and Shirley F. Weiss (Eds.), *Urban Growth Dynamics* (New York: John Wiley & Sons, 1962); Wilbur R. Thompson, *A Preface to Urban Economics* (Baltimore: Johns Hopkins University Press, 1965); the relevant literature is legion.

The data used in this report come from the following sources: (a) city size, density and growth data from the 1960 and 1965 Censuses of Population; (b) city per capita assessed valuation data and expenditure data for planning and amenities from the *Annual Report of Financial Transactions concerning Cities of California,* for the fiscal years 1958–1959 to 1965–1966, published by the State Controller; and (c) data concerning council policy maps from interviews with city councilmen conducted in 1966 and 1967.

The interviews, using both open-ended and closed questions, averaged about three hours in length. In addition, councilmen were asked, at the end of each interview, to fill out a written questionnaire. Interviews were held, as the tabulation below shows, in 89 cities located in eight counties around the San Francisco Bay. Two councils refused to cooperate altogether, and in four others not enough councilmen were interviewed to permit analysis at the council level. Inadequate budget data in the case of six cities incorporated after 1959 further reduced the number of councils available for this analysis to 77. One city, incorporated after interviewing had begun, has been excluded from the study as has been the city-county of San Francisco because its Board of Supervisors is a much more professionalized legislative body than the other councils of the region.

	Number of Councils	*Number of Councilmen*
Interview targets	89	488
Access refused	– 2	– 10
	87	478
Deficient council data	– 4	– 12
	83 (93%)	466
Interview refusals		– 31
		435 (89%)
No budget data available for analysis	– 6	
	77 (87%)	

THE MODEL

The model guiding the analysis is a partial one, and we shall not be dealing in the analysis with all of its relevant empirical components.[4] The model pre-

4. More complete studies, using multiple correlation and regression analyses, will appear in forthcoming publications of the City Council Research Project. But see also our earlier report: Robert Eyestone and Heinz Eulau, "City Councils and Policy Outcomes: Development Profiles," in James Q. Wilson (Ed.), *City Politics and Public Policy* (New York: John Wiley & Sons, 1968).

dicts city policy development as a response to external and internal features of the urban environment. The external features include, but are not exhausted by, city size, density and growth as the most immediate symptoms of common challenges from the environment, as well as city resources as environmental constraints on policy outcomes. The internal features include, but are not exhausted by, the demands for certain policies made by individuals and groups as well as the policy orientations which local decision-makers themselves bring to or formulate in the course of the policy-making process. The model seeks to order these component variables and relate them to each other in a theoretically meaningful manner.

The model assumes that city size, density and growth as well as resources are antecedent variables; that individual or group demands and decision-makers' policy orientations are intervening variables; and that policy outcomes and resultant stages of policy development are consequent variables. Of course, in empirical reality neither city size, density or growth nor city resources are truly independent precisely because public policies may be designed to control the city's environment or increase its resources. But for the purpose of short-term analysis we can assume these variables to be independent.

Although we shall not deal with individual or group demands in this paper, they are likely to be related to the city's demographic features. For instance, the larger a city's population, the more and the more diverse demands are likely to be made on policy-makers (and, moreover, the more and more diverse demands for policies coping with problems stemming from environmental challenges are likely to be made). On the other hand, decision-makers' policy orientations should be independent of environmental variables, though they are likely to be related to the policy preferences of individuals or groups that are not independent of pressures from the environment.

Policy outcomes are assumed to follow each other in a characteristic sequence that constitutes the city's policy development. These outcomes are responses to environmental challenges, such as those occasioned by high population density or a high growth rate. Moreover, they are indicative of policy-makers' willingness to utilize city resources. Changes in city size or density due to growth as well as in resource capability bring about changes in policy outcomes that move the city along from one stage to another in the developmental process. The process of policy development need not be uni-directional; at least temporary reversals are possible.

Environmental challenges may or may not be perceived by policy-makers as "problems" requiring action. Even if problems are not perceived and no action is taken, there is a policy that is reflected in policy outcomes. Policy-makers' sensitivity to environmental challenges is influenced by the demands that are made on them as well as by their own policy preferences and policy images. Therefore, city policy development is not only due to changes in the environment but is mediated by policy-makers' orientations to action. For instance, whether or not resources are mobilized for development depends to a large extent on demands made on government as well as on the policy preferences of policy-makers.

However, policy-makers' perceptions of problems, policy positions and policy images—their "policy maps," so to speak—are themselves not independent of policy development. Because policy development is cumulative in that past policy outcomes constrain current policy proposals—what is feasible and what is not—policy maps are likely to be formulated, consciously or unconsciously, within the restrictive context of the stage of development in which a city is momentarily located. In other words, policy-makers cannot do as they please. The model assumes, therefore, that decision-makers' policy maps reflect as well as shape policy development.

Not all the propositions that can be derived from the model will be tested in this study. We present the model to give direction to the analysis. Particular hypotheses derived from the model will be introduced as we proceed. Our major objective is to demonstrate the utility of the typology of policy development that we construct from city budget data as indicators of policy outcomes and, indirectly, of public policy.

THE CONCEPTS AND MEASURES

1. *Policy and policy outcomes.*

"Policy" is defined as the relationship of a governmental unit to its environment. It finds expression in general programs and specific decisions, or in policy declarations of decision-makers. But because a policy need not be declared to be a policy, analysis cannot rely on manifest statements or overt decisions alone but must concern itself with policy outcomes. By policy outcomes we mean the concrete manifestations of policy—revenues, expenditures, regulations, court decisions, the exertion of police power, and so on. Policy outcomes, then, reflect the orientations of policy-makers, regardless of whether or not a conscious decision has been made. On the other hand, because policy outcomes may at times represent unanticipated results not intended by policy-makers, policy analysis cannot altogether ignore policy declarations. In fact, the relationship between policy intentions and policy outcomes challenges the analyst of public policy.

To develop our concept of policy further, we conceive of public policy as a response of government to challenges or pressures from the physical and social environment. Changes in public policy either adjust or adapt the political system to environmental changes, or they bring about changes in the environment. Which course of action is chosen depends on a multitude of factors—the structure of the political system, its human and physical capabilities, the degree of mass or elite involvement in the political process, the vitality of private associations making public demands; and, last but not least, the perceptions, preferences and orientations of policy-makers.

The problematics of policy-making arise out of the relationship between changes in the environment that require some response, the ways in which these changes are experienced as challenges by decision-makers, and the values that decision-makers may seek in formulating policy. Policy, then, is a response to environmental pressures, both physical and social, as well as anticipation of a future state of affairs. If this is the case, a change in policy is both causal and purposive: it is "caused" by environmental challenges, but it is also directed toward a goal and shaped by a purpose. The tension arising out of the simultaneous impact of causal and purposive "forcings" is a basic dilemma in the scientific study of politics.

Analysis of policy outcomes through time requires a classification of policies.[5] We distinguish between "adaptive" and "control" policies. The measure used as an indicator of an adaptive policy is the percentage of *total* government expenses spent for health, libraries, parks, and recreation.[6] These major accounting categories used to report expenditures presumably include the major amenities offered by cities. A "high amenities" city differs from a city with a traditional services orientation in that it spends less of city income for fire and police services or public works.[7]

The measure used to indicate a city's control policy is the percentage of all *general* government expenses spent by the planning commission. *General* government expenses include essentially all administrative expenses and salaries *not* included under fire, police or recreation categories, and so on.[8]

2. *Policy development and its measurement.*

Policy outcomes are responses to changes and challenges in the environment. Policy development refers to a set of policy outcomes that follow each other

5. Much classificatory activity, in the field of public policy analysis as elsewhere, is a game. Either the inventors of classifications and typologies do not make it clear just what analytical purpose the classification is to serve, or they may even imply that by having a classificaton they have explained something. We make this point to have it understood that we are not interested in justifying or defending the particular typology of policy development that we have constructed, but in examining its utility in the analysis at hand.

6. Since education and public welfare policies are not made at the city level in California, we cannot use expenditures in these areas as measures of policy outcomes.

7. The amenities measure is an attempt to tap Williams' and Adrian's concept of amenities. See Oliver P. Williams and Charles R. Adrian, *Four Cities: A Study in Comparative Policy Making* (Philadelphia: University of Pennsylvania Press, 1963), pp. 198–225.

8. Expenses by the planning commission include both expenses and outlays, therefore encompassing the range of items from paper supplies to salaries of full-time city planners to special outside studies commissioned by the city planning commission. California State law requires every city to have a planning commission, but this body may be, and frequently is, a standing committee of citizens appointed by the city council and incurring no expenses charged against the city. Therefore, the actual dollar amount spent by the planning commission would seem to be a good indicator of the extent of a city's commitment to the idea of planning as a way to control the environment. General government expenses are used as the percentage base rather than total government expenses in order to make planning definitionally independent of amenity expenditures.

sequentially through time. If the annual outcomes are similar, we speak of the resulting profile as a *stage* of policy development. Three stages will be identified: *retarded, transitional,* and *advanced.*[9] The median of medians for all cities with respect to planning and amenities expenditures over a period of eight years serves as the criterion of similar or dissimilar outcomes.

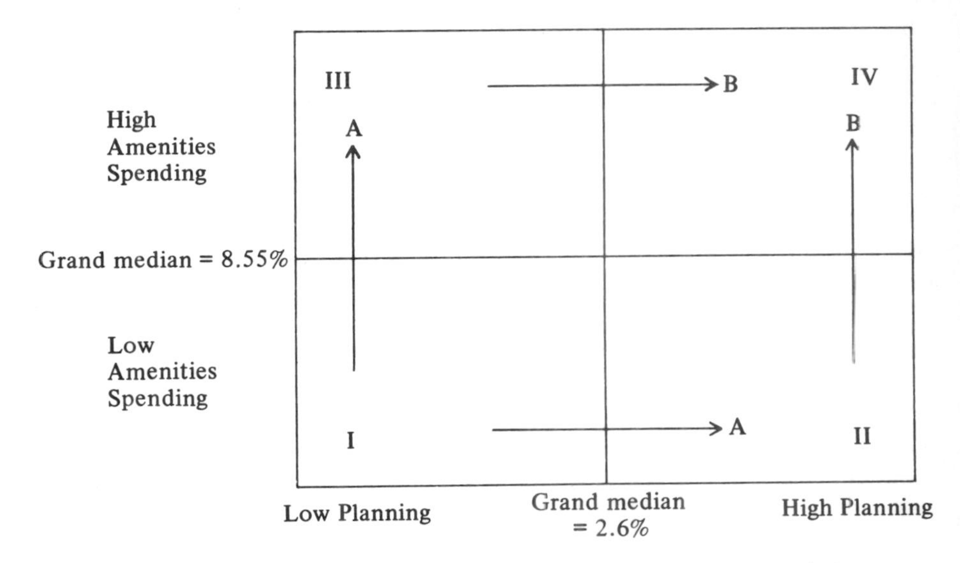

FIGURE 15.1. Categories of policy outcomes over eight-year period.

The definition of a set of sequential and similar outcomes as a stage presupposes continuity and stability. But the conception of development implies that one stage may, sooner or later, be followed by a new stage. It is unlikely that one stage will suddenly yield to another. Not only may development revert; even if development is "progressive," the transformation from one stage to the next may involve a series of dissimilar outcomes—some outcomes characteristic of an earlier stage, others characteristic of a later stage. If this occurs, an eight-year profile cannot easily be assigned to one stage or another. Put differently, we cannot easily predict whether the system will remain in the earlier stage or move into a later stage.

9. It is important to keep in mind that while we are using categories reminiscent of such concepts as "traditional," "transitional" and "modern" used in the literature of comparative politics, our observations cover only a small segment of that part of the historical developmental process usually called "modern". It is all the more significant that, even within this small part, we can locate cities in clearly different stages of policy development. This suggests that a concept like "modern" disguises a great deal of the variance that more microscopic analysis can reveal. The point is that our stages "correspond" only analytically to similarly conceived stages used in the long-term analysis of national development.

To cope with this possibility, we define a set of sequential but dissimilar policy outcomes as a *phase* of development. The notion of phase suggests that the sequence is less clearly bounded and, perhaps, of shorter duration than a stage. As we are constructing three stages of development, we must provide for two phases—an *emergent* phase that indicates movement from the retarded to the transitional stage, and a *maturing* phase that is located between the transitional and advanced stages.

Figure 15.1 illustrates how annual policy outcomes are assigned to a stage or phase of policy development. If planning and amenities expenditures fall below the grand medians in every year of the eight-year sequence, the profile is classified as *retarded* (cell I); if one or the other type of expenditures falls above the grand medians, the profile is designated as transitional (cells II and III); and if both planning and amenities expenditures are above the medians in all eight years, the profile is being assigned to the *advanced* stage of development (cell IV). If during the eight-year sequence expenditures move across the median lines, the profiles represent phases of development: outcomes moving from cell I to cells II or III (arrows A) are classified as *emergent;* those moving from cells I, II or III into cell IV (arrows B) are designated as *maturing.*

Table 15.1. Developmental Typology of City Policy Profiles With Opportunities for Change and Reversals

Development Type	*Cities* *N =*	*Opportunities* *N =*	NUMBER OF REVERSALS *(1)*	*(2)*	*(3)*	*(4)*	REVERSALS *N =*	*% =*
Retarded	11	76	7	2			11	14
Emergent	14	98	5	5	1		18	18
Transitional	26	182	9	6		1	25	14
Maturing	15	104	5	6	1		20	19
Advanced	16	112	4	1			6	5
	82	572	30	20	2	1	80	14

Cases of "reversals" for which the model does not provide are being assigned to stages or phases of development in such a way that "reversal errors" are reduced as much as possible. This involves informed but hopefully not arbitrary assignment decisions.[10] We are satisfied that the reversals are not sufficient to invalidate the typology of policy development. As Table 15.1 shows, for the 82 cities whose policy profiles can be identified over an eight-

10. For a more detailed discussion of how the development typology was constructed and cities assigned to a stage or phase of policy development, see Eyestone and Eulau in Wilson, *op. cit.*

year period, there were 572 opportunities for change in annual outcomes.[11] Of these opportunities eighty, or fourteen per cent, represented reversals from one year to the next. In the other 86 per cent of opportunities, there either was no change, that is, all outcomes remained in the same stage over all eight years; or change occurred in the hypothesized ("progressive") direction. Reversals in stable stage cities are due, of course, to the assignment of some "impure" cases where reversals seem to be only temporary deviations from the regular pattern.

A validity test. In order to test the validity of the typological constructs and the underlying assumptions, we can divide the eight-year period into two four-year periods and assign each period's profile to either a stage or phase of policy development. Cross-tabulation permits us to inspect the internal movement of the policy profiles from one period to the next. If our assumptions and assignments are reasonably valid, we should be able to predict, from knowledge of a profile's location on the development scale in the first four-year period, where it will be located in the second four-year period. We predict that cities in a stage of development are less likely to move than cities in a phase of development. We also predict that when there is movement, it is more likely to be in the hypothesized "progressive" direction than in a reversed direction. Table 15.2 presents the results.

Table 15.2. Policy Development of Cities in Developmental Sequence From 1958–61 to 1962–65

	STATE OF DEVELOPMENT IN 1962–65				
State of Development in 1958–61	*Retarded N = 11*	*Emergent N = 14*	*Transitional N = 26*	*Maturing N = 15*	*Advanced N = 16*
Retarded $N = 16$	6	9			1
Emergent $N = 16$	4	2	7	3	
Transitional $N = 24$	1	3	14	5	1
Maturing $N = 16$			5	7	4
Advanced $N = 10$					10

It is readily evident that, with some exceptions, both predictions are supported by the data. Of the 50 cities in stages of development during the 1958-1961 period, thirty or 60 per cent remained in the same stage during the following 1962-1965 period; but of the 32 cities in a phase of development during the earlier period, only nine or 28 per cent remained there in the later

11. This calculation is made as follows: over eight years, each city's annual outcomes could change seven times. This would make for 82×7, or 574 opportunities for all cities. However, as we missed data for the first fiscal year in two cities, we must deduct two opportunities, giving us the 572 figure.

period. If we consider the direction of movements, it appears that of the 20 cities in stages during the earlier period that did move, sixteen or 80 per cent advanced in the expected direction. But this result is, of course, largely a function of the boundaries set to the typology: retarded cities can only move forward and advanced cities can only move backward. More significant, therefore, is the fact that none of the advanced cities reverted, suggesting that once this plateau is reached, institutionalization of policies makes reversal unlikely; and the further fact that of the ten transitional cities that did move, six moved forward and four backward. Similarly, of the 14 emergent cities that moved, ten or 71 per cent moved forward as expected and only four returned to the retarded stage in the later period; but of the nine moving maturing cities, a bare majority of five reverted to the transitional stage. Of course, these results, whether "favorable" or not from the developmental standpoint, may be influenced by the original data. Some policy outcomes as measured are in some cases very close to the median of medians cutting point that serves as the criterion for assignment, so that we may be dealing here with errors over which we have no control. Nevertheless, we believe that the weight of the evidence is sufficient to warrant our interpretation of Table 15.2. It is also noteworthy that few of the movements, either forward or backward, exceed one step at a time. Of the 26 cities moving forward and having an opportunity to do so by *more* than one step (i.e., those retarded, emergent and transitional in the first period), twenty-one or 81 per cent moved one step only; and of the nine cities moving backward and having an opportunity for more moves (i.e., those transitional and maturing in the first period), all but one reverted only one step.

Reversed development is an empirical fact of life. While stages of development as conceived by historians are inevitably consecutive and irreversible, policy development is in fact reversible. Although we assume that in general stages and phases follow each other in "progressive" order, an assumption that the results of Table 15.2 certainly do not falsify, no rigid assumptions need or should be made about the direction of change. Policy is the creation of men and can be changed by men, within certain constraints imposed by environmental necessities, in whatever direction they prefer. Otherwise the concept of policy would make little sense.

3. *Resource capability.*

A city's resource capabilities can be measured in a variety of ways. Ideally, we would like to think of resource capability as the maximum amount of income a city can expect annually when serious efforts are made to tap all possible income sources, including current revenues from taxes, borrowed funds, grants in aid, or income from utilities, and so on. However, we have no way to determine whether such efforts have been made. Moreover, were we to use the readily available city income figures as a measure of resource capability, the measure would contravene our assumption that some cities are more pressed for revenue than others. Nor can we use a measure equivalent to per capita gross national product that is used in the comparative study of nations.[12] For a high proportion of the production of any city crosses city boundaries and is not available to support local government expenditures. Needed is a measure of the wealth remaining wholly within city limits and available to local taxation or such state taxation as is refundable to the city.

The measure we are using is, therefore, total assessed valuation per capita subject to local taxation for fiscal 1965–1966, as determined by the California State Board of Equalization. In using this measure we assume that wealth in the form of private, commercial and industrial property will be a potential source of revenue, and that per capita assessed valuation is a rough indicator of a city's resource capability.[13] A city will hesitate to institute new programs or expand old ones if it has a low level of assessed valuation per capita, but may be more inclined to do so if it has a high level of valuation.

4. *Policy maps.*

Policy, we must remember, is a theoretical concept imposed on observed reality. Regardless of whether specific decisions have been deliberately made or not, what we observe are policy outcomes from which city policy is inferred. If, as we shall suggest, policy outcomes as summarized in the typology of policy development are positively related to indicators of what we may consider environmental challenges, the presumption that the policy was intended to meet the pressures of the environment is strong, but it is only a presumption. And because it is only a presumption, the investigation of policy-makers' "policy maps" becomes an important component of policy analysis.

What do we mean by "policy map"? In the first place, we assume that if policy is a response to environmental challenges, these challenges will have been perceived by policy-makers. They may choose, consciously or unconsciously, not to act, but such non-action is also a response that will be reflected in policy outcomes. By being perceived the environmental challenges become "problems" or "policy issues." In order to tap this facet of the policy map, we asked this question:

Mr. Councilman, before talking about your work as a councilman and the work of the council itself, we would like to ask you about some of the problems facing this community. In your opinion, what are the two most pressing problems here in (city)?

12. For a discussion of system capabilities, see Gabriel A. Almond, "A Developmental Approach to Political Systems," *World Politics*, 17 (January, 1965), 195–203.

13. Assessed valuation includes private houses and property, commercial property and industrial property. From private property a city derives personal property revenues and a portion of state income tax revenues; from commercial property it receives property and sales tax revenues; and from industrial property it gets property tax revenues.

The policy map consists, secondly, of the policy-maker's recommendations for action or "policy positions"—those preferences that he either brings into the policy-making situation or evolves in the course of decision-making. Again, his not consciously entertaining a policy position on an issue is yet to be considered a policy orientation and a component of his policy map. We therefore asked this question:[14]

Now, looking toward the future, what one community-wide improvement, in your opinion, does this city "need most" to be attractive to its citizens?

Finally, we assume that the policy map includes the policy-maker's "ends-in-view" or values—those hopes and expectations concerning the future which policy decisions are to bring about. The following question was designed to yield what one may think of as the "policy image":

Now, taking the broadest view possible, how do you see (city) in the future? I mean, what kind of a city would you personally like (city) to be in the next twenty-five years?

Whether these three components of the policy map constitute a consistent whole, a "perspective" as Harold Lasswell would call it,[15] is an empirical question not central to the present study, but one we shall speculate about in the conclusion. Needless to say, perhaps, knowledge of the policy map does not permit prediction about the outcome of decision-making on any particular policy issue. But we proceed on the assumption that policy maps represent important linkages between environmental challenges and public policies.

5. *Units of analysis and interpretation.*

Although the data on policy maps come from interviews with individuals, our analysis uses councils as the units of analysis. Decision-making by legislative bodies is a collective act. Not the individual councilman but the council, as a whole under the majority rule, is the effective policy-maker. Past research on legislatures, following in the wake of voting studies, has analyzed the behavior of individuals *in* the legislature in order to make statements about the behavior *of* legislatures. This procedure presents serious problems of inference. Because policy outcomes as measured by budget data are due to collective decisions (or non-decisions), the legislative group rather than the individual legislator is the more viable unit of analysis. Council perceptions, positions

14. This is not the only question we asked in this connection. For instance, we also asked a great many closed "agree-disagree" questions some of which we used in the earlier analysis, in Wilson, *op cit.*

15. See Harold D. Lasswell and Abraham Kaplan, *Power and Society: A Framework for Political Inquiry* (New Haven: Yale University Press, 1950), p. 25.

or images are therefore constructed or reconstructed from data about individuals or provided by individuals, permitting us to make statements about city councils and not about city councilmen. We shall report the rules followed in this procedure in the text or footnotes.[16] This type of analysis is of course made possible by the relatively large (though for satisfactory statistical purposes still all too small) number of legislative groups being investigated. As far as we know, no similar type of analysis using as many as eighty or so units has ever been undertaken in the comparative study of legislative bodies.

In reading and interpreting the tables, a number of methodological considerations must be kept in mind. In the first place, we are dealing with data that come from truly independent sources—the federal Census reporting population characteristics, city budgets reporting financial allocations, and interviews with city councilmen. These different kinds of data are used to construct quite different properties of the units—city councils—that we are observing. The Census yields data that are best interpreted as representing the council's "contextual" properties; the budget data are representative, in a very direct sense, of the council's "emergent" properties; and the interview data provide the basis for "aggregate" properties.[17] To relate properties as diverse as these is extraordinarily difficult. But for this reason one cannot simply write off even modest relationships between variables as not significant.

Second, the typology of policy development that serves as our major device for ordering the data is not a simple continuum. While the five types constitute an ordinal ranking on a scale from "more developed" to "less developed," they also represent qualitative differences associated with different levels of development. In other words, a city's movement from one stage into another may be due to structural changes in causal factors rather than simple gradual increases. This means that variables related to city policy development may well exhibit sharp changes at certain points in the developmental sequence rather than incremental changes from one stage to another. For instance, a council's orientation to action may change radically after it has left the retarded stage and entered the emergent phase and then not change at all. Also, variables need not change monotonically across the five developmental types. Development may be related, for instance, to city growth in the early stages or

16. This is not the place to discuss the methodological problems and procedures involved in "stepping up" the data from the level of the individual (micro-analysis) to the level of the group (macro-analysis). Suffice it to say that our empirical results justify the viability of the procedures, although we would be the first to admit that many technical problems remain to be solved.

17. Paul F. Lazarsfeld has written in many places about the variety of "group properties" that need to be distinguished in analysis lest errors of inference be made. See, for instance, Paul F. Lazarsfeld, "Evidence and Inference in Social Research," in Daniel Lerner (Ed.), *Evidence and Inference* (New York: The Free Press, 1959), pp. 117–125; or Paul F. Lazarsfeld and Herbert Menzel, "On the Relation between Individual and Collective Properties," in Amitai Etzioni, *Complex Organizations* (New York: Holt, Rinehart and Winston, 1961), pp. 422–440. We are not dealing with the global, structural or relational properties of councils in this analysis.

phases but may decline in the advanced cities. Or cities at the three intermediate levels of policy development may show characteristics not shared by the least and most developed cities. Or cities in the two phases of development may be more similar to each other than to cities in the immediate neighboring stages.

Finally, we are less impressed by "significant differences" in a statistical sense that we might find than by patterns in the distribution of the data that make theoretical sense. The small number of cases also makes difficult the controlling of one variable by another that is so necessary if spurious relationships and false interpretations are to be avoided. We have used the control technique in relating resource capability to policy development, but we have not done so with the interview data, largely because the frequencies of cases in particular cells of the tables would be greatly strained by the procedure. This makes it all the more necessary to view each table not as an isolated entity unrelated to any other table. Rather, it is the weight of all the tables inspected simultaneously that must be considered in making inferences or drawing conclusions.

THE ANALYSIS

1. *Environmental challenges and policy development.*

City size, density and growth rate are direct indicators of challenges from the environment that every city faces. They bring in their wake problems that the city council may seek to solve through policies that adapt the city to the environment or that control environmental pressures. As the typology of city policy development is built on outcomes that reflect such policies, it follows:

Hypothesis 1a: The larger a city's size, the more developed is city policy likely to be.

Hypothesis 1b: The greater a city's density, the more developed is city policy likely to be.

Hypothesis 1c: The greater a city's growth, the more developed is city policy likely to be.

Table 15.3 shows that the three hypotheses are not falsified by the data. Moreover, the data show a pattern of policy development that, with two exceptions, is highly linear. We have no explanation for the deviation from the pattern of the transitional cities in the low density category. With regard to growth we note, as we perhaps might have expected, a levelling-off of the effect of growth in the advanced stage, the terminus of development. Apparently, once policy development has reached the advanced stage, growth is likely to be marginal in its effect on city policy.

The data suggest that city councils adopt policies which are congruent with needs rooted in pressures from the environment. Whatever the declared policy

*Table 15.3. Relationships Between City Size, Density and Growth and Policy Development**

	POLICY DEVELOPMENT				
	Retarded *N = 11*	*Emergent* *N = 14*	*Transitional* *N = 26*	*Maturing* *N = 15*	*Advanced* *N = 16*
Population Size					
<10,000	82%	79%	35%	13%	0%
10–50,000	18	21	46	67	44
>50,000	0	0	19	20	56
	100%	100%	100%	100%	100%
Density					
<2,000	73%	58%	19%	41%	0%
2–4,000	18	28	50	26	44
>4,000	9	14	31	33	56
	100%	100%	100%	100%	100%
Growth Rate					
<10%	54%	36%	43%	13%	19%
10–50%	46	49	39	47	62
>50%	0	14	19	40	19
	100%	99%	101%	100%	100%

*Size and density data for 1965; growth rate for 1960–65.

objectives of city fathers, they tend to follow policies that either adapt the city to or seek to control the environment.

2. *Resource capability and policy development.*

The resources available to a city government are an important constraint on the expenditures it can make and the policies it can follow. Resource capability is largely an objectively limiting factor, but it is also subjective in that its limiting effect is interpreted by the city council before it becomes a factor in the policy-making process. For instance, the council estimates how high a tax rate city residents are willing to approve. High resource capability is necessary for policy development, but it is not sufficient. Nevertheless, we hypothesize:

Hypothesis 2: The higher a city's resource capability, the more developed is city policy likely to be.

Table 15.4, Part A, shows that there is no support for the hypothesis. In fact, more of the retarded cities seem to have high resource capability than any

Table 15.4. Relationship Between City Resource Capability and Policy Development

	POLICY DEVELOPMENT				
Assessed Valuation Per Capita	*Retarded* N = 11	*Emergent* N = 14	*Transitional* N = 26	*Maturing* N = 15	*Advanced* N = 16
Part A					
>$2,600	54%	28%	38%	33%	44%
$1,700–2,600	18	44	24	47	25
<1,700	27	28	38	20	31
	99%	100%	100%	100%	100%
Part B					
Size <25,000					
<$1,700	27%	28%	24%	13%	6%
>$1,700	73	72	39	54	6
Size >25,000					
<$1,700	—	—	15	7	25
>$1,700	—	—	23	27	62
	100%	100%	101%	101%	99%
Density					
<2,000					
<$1,700	9%	14%	0%	7%	0%
>$1,700	63	44	19	33	0
>2,000					
<$1,700	19	14	38	13	32
>$1,700	9	28	43	47	68
	100%	100%	100%	100%	100%
Growth					
10%					
<$1,700	9%	0%	19%	0%	6%
>$1,700	46	36	23	13	13
>10%					
<$1,700	18	28	19	20	25
>$1,700	27	36	39	67	56
	100%	100%	100%	100%	100%

of the other cities in various stages or phases of development. However, the distributions may be misleading. As we suggested, policy development is dependent on policy-makers' willingness to mobilize resources, and their willingness to do so may depend on the intensity of pressures from the environment *regardless* of available resources. Therefore, one must control the relationship between resource capability and policy development by such indicators of environmental challenges as size, density or growth rate. Table 15.4, B, reports the findings.

In the smaller cities, presumably less subject to environmental challenges, fewer of the more developed than of the less developed cities are low in resource capability, just as hypothesized; but development also declines in cities of the same size with high capability, counter to the hypothesis. In the larger cities, on the other hand, resource capability is highly related to policy development in the advanced stage.

Controls for density reveal the same pattern even more distinctly. In the low density, high capability cities policy development declines, counter to the hypothesis; but in the densely populated cities high resource capability is related to policy development across the continuum in linear order.

Finally, if resource capability is controlled by growth rate, the developmental process clearly follows the hypothesized pattern only in the high growth cities with high assessed valuation (and again in linear fashion except for levelling off in the advanced stage). The data do not permit us to say anything about the slow-growing, low capability cities; but in the slow-growth, high capability and the high growth, low capability cities Hypothesis 2 is clearly falsified.

Policy-makers evidently respond to environmental pressures less in terms of the resources that are available than in terms of their willingness to mobilize these resources. It is for this reason that inquiry into policy-makers' perceptions of city problems, policy positions and policy images becomes an important part of policy analysis.

3. *Problem perceptions and policy development.*

Environmental challenges are not self-evident. They become evident only if and when they give rise to "problems" that come to the attention of policy-makers. The perception of a problem means that traditional ways of doing things–policies–are inadequate or at the very least that their adequacy is in question. It is through the perception of problems, then, that the policy process is set in motion. But, if policy-makers do not respond to problems generated by environmental challenges, either by not perceiving them or not acting upon them, this does not mean that there is no policy. It simply means that prevailing policy continues.

In collegial bodies like legislatures or councils a problem is a problem if the members *between them* are aware of the problem, but it is not necessary for all or even most of the members to perceive it. Different members have access to different aspects of the environment. Because of varied membership elected collegial bodies can be more sensitive to the environment than administrative hierarchical organizations. "Problem diversity" therefore refers to the absolute number of different problems articulated by a council, adjusted for comparison across councils by the total number of mentions in each council.[18] Because as we have seen, the more developed cities face more severe environmental challenges, we formulate:

Hypothesis 3: The more diverse the problems perceived by a council, the more developed is city policy likely to be.

Table 15.5. Relationship Between Problem Diversity and Policy Development

Diversity Score Quartile	POLICY DEVELOPMENT				
	Retarded N = 9	*Emergent N = 12*	*Transitional N = 25*	*Maturing N = 15*	*Advanced N = 16*
I. (Most)	45%	33%	20%	27%	6%
II.	22	17	28	20	44
III.	22	33	28	13	31
IV. (Least)	11	17	24	40	19
	100%	100%	100%	100%	100%
Index	+34	+16	−4	−13	−13

Table 15.5 shows that this hypothesis is falsified by the data. In fact, problem diversity is greatest among the councils of the retarded cities where one might least expect it and declines almost linearly in the following stages and phases, though there is some levelling off at the more developed end of the development continuum.

How can one interpret this finding? One plausible answer is that policy develops in response to few but intensively felt problems, while a multitude of minor problems that are not critical do not stimulate the policy process. If this is so, we should expect that problems are more "visible" to the council as a whole in the more developed than in the less developed cities. A measure of "problem visibility" must take account not only of the absolute number of

18. That is, the absolute number of individual problems named was divided by all problem responses made in a council. The resulting scores, that could range from zero to one, were rank-ordered and divided into the quartile ranges used in the analysis.

problems that are articulated, but also of the number of councilmen who articulate any one problem.[19] We postulate:

Hypothesis 4: The more visible problems are to the council, the more developed is city policy likely to be.

Table 15.6. Relationship Between Problem Visibility and Policy Development

Visibility Score Quartile	POLICY DEVELOPMENT				
	Retarded $N = 9$	*Emergent* $N = 12$	*Transitional* $N = 25$	*Maturing* $N = 15$	*Advanced* $N = 16$
I. (High)	22%	17%	28%	40%	12%
II.	11	33	24	13	45
III.	0	25	36	20	31
IV. (Low)	67	25	12	27	12
	100%	100%	100%	100%	100%
Index	−45	−8	+16	+13	0

Table 15.6 tends to support the hypothesis, although there is some dropping-off at the advanced stage. One might expect this because, as the very concept "advanced" suggests, a council in this stage of policy development is likely to have the challenges stemming from the environment well in hand. As a result, not only are fewer problems perceived in this stage, but the few problems are so self-evident that, though of great urgency, they fail to stand out as particularly visible.

Problem visibility may be thought of as setting the council's legislative agenda. The more visible a problem, the more likely it is to be considered by the council. But the visibility is at most a necessary and not a sufficient condition for legislative action. In order to act, the council must in fact be agreed that the problem is a problem. We therefore measure the degree of council agreement on the single most visible problem as well as council agreement on the general policy area that seems most problematic.[20] We propose:

19. That is, the number of problems named was multiplied by the number of respondents and divided by all responses squared. The resulting score was subtracted from one to rank-order the councils from high to low. The formula then is: $1 - NP \times NR/r^2$, where NP = number of problems, NR = number of respondents, and r = number of total responses.

20. The measure of agreement on a single problem is simply the proportion of councilmen among all respondents who mentioned the most frequent problem. For the measure of problem area agreement, the number of responses in the area receiving the most responses was divided by the number of responses in all areas. Five "problem areas" were provided for classification of individual problems: Services and Utilities, Amenities, Promotion and Development, Social and Remedial Problems, and Governmental and Intergovernmental Problems.

Hypothesis 5: The more agreement on the single most visible problem, the more developed is city policy likely to be.

Hypothesis 6: The more agreement on the most visible problem area, the more developed is city policy likely to be.

Table 15.7. Relationship Between Agreement on Specific Problem and General Problem Area and Policy Development

	POLICY DEVELOPMENT				
Single Problem Agreement	*Retarded* N = 9	*Emergent* N = 12	*Transitional* N = 25	*Maturing* N = 15	*Advanced* N = 16
67–100%	22%	50%	36%	47%	43%
51–66%	45	25	32	20	43
50–50%	33	25	32	33	13
	100%	100%	100%	100%	99%
Index	−11	+25	+4	+14	+30
Problem Area Agreement					
67–100%	33%	17%	32%	13%	37%
51–66%	0	8	16	54	13
0–50%	67	75	25	33	50
	100%	100%	100%	100%	100%
Index	−34	−58	−20	−20	−13

Table 15.7 tends to support these hypotheses, but we note an interesting deviation from the expected patterns in the cities of the emergent phase. While on the single problem measure more councils in the emergent phase reveal high agreement, these councils are least agreed on the general area of problems facing their cities. We can only speculate on these results. It may be that being in the emergent phase is, on the one hand, a disorienting condition that makes it difficult to achieve agreement on the general area of problems that require action; but that, precisely because of this condition, high agreement can be reached on the single most urgent problem. However, we also note that all councils, regardless of level of policy development, can evidently reach agreement more readily on a specific problem than on a general area of related problems.

What kinds of problems or problem areas are most salient to city councils? And is such salience related to policy development? Although we do not pro-

Table 15.8. Problems and Problem Areas Perceived as Pressing by City Councils

	POLICY DEVELOPMENT					
Types of Problems Perceived	*Retarded* $N = 9$	*Emergent* $N = 12$	*Transitional* $N = 25$	*Maturing* $N = 15$	*Advanced* $N = 16$	*Total* $N = 77$
Services & Utilities						
Sewerage & drainage	1	1	5	2	—	9
Sanitation & disposal	—	1	—	—	—	1
Water sources	1	—	1	—	1	3
Financing services	—	1	2	4	3	10
Total in Area	2	3	8	6	4	23
Per cent in Area	22%	25%	32%	40%	25%	30%
Amenities						
Total in Area	—	—	—	—	—	—
Promotion & Development						
Planning, master plan	—	1	—	—	3	4
Zoning & maintenance	2	1	4	—	—	7
Transportation & traffic	—	1	5	2	3	11
Attract business & industry	—	1	2	—	—	3
Urban renewal & development	—	1	—	—	3	4
Assessment and taxes	—	—	—	2	—	2
Total in Area	2	5	11	4	9	31
Per cent in Area	22%	42%	44%	27%	57%	40%
Social & Remedial						
Water pollution	—	—	—	—	1	1
Race & ethnic problems	—	—	—	—	1	1
Educational problems	—	—	—	1	—	1
Housing	1	—	—	—	—	1
Total in Area	1	—	—	1	2	4
Per cent in Area	11%	0%	0%	7%	12%	5%
Government & Intergovernmental						
Annexation	1	—	—	—	—	1
Local government personnel	—	1	—	—	—	1
Citizen participation	—	—	—	—	1	1
Total in Area	1	1	—	—	1	3
Per cent in Area	11%	8%	0%	0%	6%	4%
Not Classifiable	3	3	6	4	0	16
	34%	25%	24%	26%	0%	21%
Grand total	100%	100%	100%	100%	100%	100%

pose to introduce a formal hypothesis, we are altogether unprepared for the results obtained. Taking all those councils where at least three councilmen had named the same problem, we obtain the findings reported in Table 15.8.

As Table 15.8 shows, no three councilmen in any council, whatever the city's stage or phase of development, articulated problems relating to amenities; and only a few councils on various levels of development mustered enough members who considered planning or zoning as especially pressing problems. We shall leave it to another occasion to interpret the full implications of the results reported in Table 15.8. Suffice it to say here that problems involving provisions for amenities clearly do not rank high on the agenda of problems considered pressing. Put differently, amenities appear to be luxuries that councils are willing to indulge in only after other urban problems, notably sewerage and drainage, financing of services and transportation, have been solved. But planning and zoning also do not stand out as pressing problems. Either these matters are being satisfactorily handled already, so that they are perceived as problems by only a few councils, or they are not recognized as viable means for coping with environmental challenges.[21]

When asked why they considered a problem to be a problem, a variety of reasons were given by councilmen that could be coded into three categories—operational and financial, political, and inevitable or uncontrollable. Councils were characterized in terms of the dominant set of reasons that were given.[22] We do not entertain any particular hypothesis about how councils on various levels of development are likely to rationalize their city's problems. But we note two results in Table 15.9. First, great majorities of councils in all cities, regardless of level of policy development, attribute community problems to circumstances beyond their control. This is to say that a substantial number of problems, as we have speculated all along, have their roots in environmental conditions. But we also note that "political" reasons are given by more councils as we move from the retarded to the advanced stage of development. The linearity of the data suggests that politicization of the decision-making milieu in these cities may well be related to policy development. The more politicized

21. Our measure of salience, as mentioned in the text, was whether a problem or problem area was mentioned by at least three respondents. We shall not try to interpret the proportions obtained for the services and utilities as well as promotion and development areas across the developmental continuum because the results may be an artifact of council size. As five councils in the transitional stage, three in the maturing phase and seven in the advanced stage had more than five members (usually seven), and as no retarded or emergent council had more than five members, clearly any one problem had more of a chance to be named by at least three respondents in the more developed cities. But as, for instance, nine of the advanced councils had only five members, yet all advanced councils are accounted for in naming at least one problem, the council size factor does not seem to have too much of a distorting effect. But we note it as interesting that the more developed a city's policy, the more councils tend to mention problems related to utilities and services and to promotion and development.

22. The dominant set of reasons was simply defined as that set which included the most responses among all sets, regardless of absolute number.

Table 15.9. Reasons Given for Problems and Policy Development

	POLICY DEVELOPMENT				
Type of Reasons	*Retarded* $N = 9$	*Emergent* $N = 12$	*Transitional* $N = 25$	*Maturing* $N = 15$	*Advanced* $N = 16$
Operational-financial	22%	8%	36%	20%	25%
Inevitable-uncontrollable	78	92	84	73	62
Political	11	17	12	27	38

*Percentages total more than 100 since any one council could give sets of reasons that are numerically tied.

the social environment, the more likely it seems to be that policy development takes place.

4. *Policy positions and policy development.*

Once problems have been identified and agreed upon as agenda items, the legislature or council will seek to evolve a policy position. A policy position by the council, whether held by all members or only a majority, is of course an emergent property of the council following upon interaction, deliberation and possibly compromise, and it is not simply the addition of individual members' policy preferences. What we are tapping, then, when we ask individual councilmen to suggest the "most needed" community-wide improvement and then aggregate these recommendations, is not the council's policy as it emerges in the voting situation, but rather the initial state of a council position before the legislative process has had an opportunity to affect the decisional outcome.[23] But as actual council policy is reflected in the policy outcomes out of which the typology of policy development is constructed, inquiry into the hypothetical initial state of the policy process can shed light on the dynamics of policy-making. We shall first explore the diversity and visibility of improvement recommendations made by councils in varying stages and phases of policy development. Again we stipulate:

Hypothesis 7: The more diverse improvements recommended in a council, the more developed is city policy likely to be.

And again, as with problem perceptions, we find the diversity hypothesis falsified by the data.[24] As Table 15.10 shows, highly diverse improvement

23. We could argue our case more liberally on statistical grounds and possibly test it if we had more and numerically more diverse legislative bodies available for analysis: the larger a legislative body, the more likely it is that averaged individual preferences will approximate, if not correspond to, the preference of the collectivity.

24. The improvement diversity measure was constructed in the same way as the problem diversity measure. See fn. 18, above.

Table 15.10 Relationship Between Improvement Diversity and Policy Development

Improvement Score Quartile	POLICY DEVELOPMENT Retarded N = 9	Emergent N = 12	Transitional N = 25	Maturing N = 15	Advanced N = 16
I. (Most)	33%	50%	20%	13%	31%
II.	33	17	36	33	0
III.	11	8	16	27	57
IV. (Least)	22	25	28	27	12
	99%	100%	100%	100%	100%
Index	+11	+25	−8	−14	+19

proposals are just as likely to be made in the less developed as in the most developed councils. However, though problem and improvement proposal diversity is low in the more developed cities, and perhaps because of it, we expect that the improvement recommendations that are made are highly visible in these cities. Hence:

Hypothesis 8: The more visible the improvement recommended in a council, the more developed is city policy likely to be.

Table 15.11. Relationship Between Improvement Visibility and Policy Development

Improvement Score Quartile	POLICY DEVELOPMENT Retarded N = 9	Emergent N = 12	Transitional N = 25	Maturing N = 15	Advanced N = 16
I. (High)	11%	25%	28%	7%	31%
II.	22	17	16	46	31
III.	33	25	24	40	13
IV. (Low)	33	33	32	7	25
	99%	100%	100%	100%	100%
Index	−22	−8	−4	0	+6

Table 15.11 supports the hypothesis.[25] Recommendations for improvements are more visible in the developed than the less developed cities, and only in maturing and advanced cities do a majority of councils fall into the two upper visibility quartiles.

25. The improvement visibility measure was constructed in the same manner as the problem visibility measure. See fn. 19, above.

We expect on the basis of this finding that councils in the more developed cities are more agreed on what specific improvements or what general improvement areas are needed than councils in the less developed cities:

Hypothesis 9: The more agreement there is in a council on the single most needed improvement, the more developed is city policy likely to be.

Hypothesis 10: The more agreement there is in a council on a general improvement area, the more developed is city policy likely to be.

Table 15.12. Relationship Between Agreement on Specific Improvement and General Improvement Area and Policy Development

	POLICY DEVELOPMENT				
Single Improvement Agreement	*Retarded* $N = 9$	*Emergent* $N = 11$*	*Transitional* $N = 25$	*Maturing* $N = 15$	*Advanced* $N = 16$
67–100%	11%	0%	12%	7%	6%
51–66%	0	36	20	33	19
0–50%	89	64	68	60	75
	100%	100%	100%	100%	100%
Index	−78	−64	−56	−53	−69
Improvement Area Agreement					
67–100%	22%	45%	40%	60%	37%
51–66%	45	45	28	33	44
0–50%	33	10	32	7	19
	100%	100%	100%	100%	100%
Index	−11	+35	+8	+53	+18

*One council in this type could not be properly measured and had to be dropped from the tabulation.

Table 15.12 presents the data.[26] They represent some interesting findings. In the first place, with respect to agreement on the single most visible improvement proposal made, there is a very low level of agreement regardless of a city's location on the policy development continuum. Only few councils are highly agreed, and only a few more manage to achieve better than simple majority agreement. In all types of city policy development, majorities of the councils fall below the majority criterion needed for agreement. Interestingly, and though the percentage differences are small, fewer councils in both types

26. The improvement agreement measures are the same as those used in connection with problem agreement. See fn. 20, above.

of "phase" cities are in the non-agreement category than councils in the "stage" cities. But, in general, we must consider Hypothesis 9 as being falsified by the data.

If we turn to the less demanding Hypothesis 10–less demanding because agreement is needed only on a general area rather than on a specific case of improvement–the data give only weak support to the hypothesis. Although few of the retarded councils are high on improvement area agreement and the more developed councils tend in the expected direction, the significant aspect of the table is that only one council in each of the two types of "phase" cities is unable to achieve a minimal level of agreement. The tendency already noted in connection with single improvement agreement is exaggerated under the less demanding condition of general improvement area agreement.

What are we to make of these unexpected findings? Are they merely due to random fluctuations in the data, or are they of theoretical significance? We must seek an explanation in the nature of the emergent and maturing phases of policy development as these were defined. Cities in these phases undergo sudden bursts of activity, reflected in policy outcomes, that move them from one stage into another. It would seem that this unfolding of policy-making "energy" is greatly aided by *pre-decisional* agreement or at least by relatively little disagreement in councils as to what improvements or areas of improvement are most needed. This finding and our interpretation suggest that we are tapping a very real component of the policy process by aggregating individual responses into a group response.[27]

What types of improvement were recommended by the councils that are agreed? Because of the dispersion of single improvement recommendations, we shall present only the data on improvement areas.[28] What is of interest in the data presented in Table 15.13 is, first of all, that the improvement areas are quite different from the comparable problem areas of Table 15.8. Only one council in a maturing city suggested services and utilities as an area needing improvements. But while no council had perceived amenities as a *problem,* a fourth of the councils in each of the developmental types, except the retarded, reported that amenities constitute an area where improvements are needed.

This discontinuity in council policy maps from problem perceptions to policy positions requires explanation. Does it mean that councils do not behave rationally? One might be inclined to think so, but discontinuity is not necessarily the same thing as inconsistency. Because amenities are not recognized as "problems," it does not follow that councils may not wish to pursue policies to obtain amenities for their cities. For policies, we argued, are not simple condi-

27. We would like to point out here that we had very similar results in the earlier study in which we used a *closed* agree-disagree scale measuring attitudes concerning the scope of government activity and in which we used *individual* councilmen as our units of analysis: see Eyestone and Eulau, in Wilson, (Ed.), *op. cit.*

28. An improvement area was assumed to be salient in council preferences if at least three respondents articulated problems in the area.

Table 15.13. Relationship Between Needed Improvement Areas and Policy Development

	POLICY DEVELOPMENT				
Improvement Area	*Retarded* $N = 9$	*Emergent* $N = 11$	*Transitional* $N = 25$	*Maturing* $N = 15$	*Advanced* $N = 16$
Services and utilities	0%	0%	0%	7%	0%
Promotion and development	0	8	4	14	25
Amenities	11	25	28	26	25
Less than 3 informants	89	67	68	53	50
	100%	100%	100%	100%	100%

tioned responses to environmental challenges; they are also the products of those ends-in-view, values or images of the future that policy-makers carry with them into the policy-making situation. While the policy positions articulated in response to the question about needed improvements may not be relevant to the problems that councils perceived and articulated, they are certainly not inconsistent with them. The results suggest that policy images are important components of the council's policy map as a whole.

5. *Policy images and policy development.* What kind of future a legislative body envisages is likely to color its perceptions of environmental challenges and its current policy preferences. But images of the future are also likely to be projections of current trends in a city's policy development. They tend to orient the council toward the future and may influence future development, but they are not independent of present tendencies. Moreover, the more limited the legislature's jurisdiction, the better-defined its image is likely to be. In the case of municipal councils whose tasks are well set by statutory requirements and limitations we can expect that long-range goals are well-defined.

Because we know that policy development varies with demographic indicators of environmental challenges such as size, density and growth, and because we also can assume that these indicators are highly related to ecological factors such as residential patterns or level of industrialization, we hypothesize:

Hypothesis 11a: The more developed a city's policy, the more will councils tend to envisage the city's future as "balanced" or industrial.

Hypothesis 11b: The less developed a city's policy, the more will councils tend to envisage the city's future as residential and/or recreational.

The ease with which it was possible to classify responses into the categories of "residential" or "recreational," on the one hand, and of "balanced" or "industrial," on the other hand, supports our speculation that long-range images or goals are likely to be well-defined in legislative bodies with limited scopes of action.[29] As Table 15.14 shows, the reciprocal Hypotheses 11a and 11b are well supported by the data.

Table 15.14. Relationship Between Policy Image and Policy Development

Content of Image	POLICY DEVELOPMENT				
	Retarded $N = 9$	*Emergent* $N = 12$	*Transitional* $N = 25$	*Maturing* $N = 15$	*Advanced* $N = 16$
Residential-recreational	56%	50%	25%	27%	13%
Split or non-classifiable	22	8	12	7	19
Balanced and/or industrial	22	42	36	66	68
	100%	100%	100%	100%	100%

Because policy images are well-defined, we hypothesize that there is a great deal of agreement within the councils on policy goals. But as, by definition, the less developed cities are engaged in a more limited range of activities than the more developed ones, we can expect the difference to be reflected in the level of agreement:

Hypothesis 12: The less developed a city's policy, the greater the proportion of councils reaching high agreement on the image of city future.

Table 15.15 supports the hypothesis. It not only support it but reveals an extraordinarily high level of agreement, especially in the retarded and emergent cities where two-thirds and more of the councils are unanimously agreed on the policy image. But in the transitional, maturing and advanced cities, too, most councils agree on long-range goals by overwhelming majorities. We are dealing here, it seems, with that substantive consensus on values that facilitates the democratic process of bargaining, compromise and adjustment. It is within this consensus that disagreements over particular policies can be resolved and lasting community conflicts be reduced to manageable format. However, the fact that agreement on future goals is inversely related to policy development represents a profound dilemma for democratic theory.

29. Because an "industrial" future was envisaged in only a handful of councils, we combined this category with the "balanced" category which implies that the council envisages a balance in residential, commercial and industrial development.

Table 15.15 Relationship Between Agreement on Policy Image and Policy Development

Policy Image Agreement	POLICY DEVELOPMENT *Retarded* N = 9	*Emergent* N = 12	*Transitional* N = 25	*Maturing* N = 15	*Advanced* N = 16
100%	78%	67%	52%	53%	50%
67–99%	0	25	32	27	31
51–66%	0	0	4	13	0
Split or non-classifiable	22	8	12	7	19
	100%	100%	100%	100%	100%

CONCLUSION

A metropolitan city's development toward distinct and differentiated styles of social life is powerfully shaped by policies that are responses to challenges from the metropolitan environment. Wether a city stands still, moves forward to reach a new level of development or reverts to an earlier state depends on the strength of such challenges as can be measured by city size, density or growth rate. In general, development involves the adoption of policies that either adapt the city to the changing environment or control the environment. In this process of adjustment and control through appropriate policies the city's resource capabilities seem to play only a limited part. It appears that policy-makers' willingness to tap city resources in order to adopt appropriate policies is a critical component of the policy development process.

Policy-makers' willingness to set their city on a course of development depends on the content of their policy maps—how they perceive the problems facing the city, what preferences they entertain with regard to policy alternatives, and how they envisage the city's future. In general, it seems that municipal decision-makers' policy maps constitute a consistent whole, although there may be discontinuities and deviations. It also appears, in general, that the various components of the policy map are meaningfully related to the stage or phase of city policy development. There is in the councils of a metropolitan region such as that around the San Francisco Bay a satisfactory level of agreement on what the problems are that cities in different stages of development face, and there is very high agreement on what the city's future should be like. There is less agreement, as one might expect, on the specific policies that should be adopted to obtain the goals that are envisaged, but there is sufficient agreement on the general area of issues that needs attention.

It has been the burden of our argument that the systematic study of public policy cannot be content with correlating indicators of environmental challenges or indicators of resource capability to policy outcomes. Rather, it was our assumption that policy development is greatly influenced by the predilections, preferences, orientations and expectations of policy-makers—in short, by the political process itself. The data presented in the analysis, though limited, confirm the validity of this assumption. Yet, as we noted, the fact that level of agreement on policy goals seems to be inversely related to policy development raises many problems for the policy-maker. Not the least important is the question of how a developed community can maintain a sufficient consensus on public goals. In the city councils of the San Francisco Bay metropolitan region a high level of agreement on policy goals still exists. Whether it will continue to exist in the face of increasing differentiation of areas within the city challenges the urban political process.

Chapter 16

Political Matrix and Political Representation

Scholars interested in theorizing about political representation in terms relevant to democratic governance in mid-twentieth-century America find themselves in a quandary. We are surrounded by functioning representative institutions, or at least by institutions formally described as representative. Individuals who presumably "represent" other citizens govern some ninety thousand different political units—they sit on school and special district boards, on township and city councils, on county directorates, on state and national assemblies, and so forth. But the flourishing activity of representation has not yet been matched by a sustained effort to explain what makes the representational process tick.

Despite the proliferation of representative governments over the past century, *theory* about representation has not moved much beyond the eighteenth-century formulation of Edmund Burke. Certainly most empirical research has been cast in the Burkean vocabulary.[1] But in order to think in novel ways about representative government in the twentieth century, we may have to admit that present conceptions guiding empirical research may be obsolete.

Originally published, with Kenneth Prewitt, in *The American Political Science Review*, Vol. 63 (June, 1969), pp. 427–441. Reprinted by permission.

The larger project of which this analysis is a part, the City Council Research Project, is sponsored by the Institute of Political Studies, Stanford University, and is supported by the National Science Foundation under grants GS 496 and GS 1898.

1. See, for instance, Heinz Eulau, John C. Wahlke, William Buchanan, and LeRoy C. Ferguson, "The Role of the Representative: Some Empirical Observations on the Theory of Edmund Burke," *American Political Science Review*, Vol. 53 (September, 1959), 742–56; or Warren E. Miller and Donald E. Stokes, "Constituency Influence in Congress," *American Political Science Review*, Vol. 57 (March, 1963), 45–56.

This in turn means that the spell of Burke's vocabulary over scientific work on representation must be broken.[2]

To look afresh at representation, it is necessary to be sensitive to the unresolved tension between the two main currents of contemporary thinking about representational relationships. On the one hand, representation is treated as a relationship between any one individual, the represented, and another individual, the representative—an *interindividual* relationship. On the other hand, representatives are treated as a group, brought together in the assembly, to represent the interest of the community as a whole—an *intergroup* relationship. Most theoretical formulations since Burke are cast in one or the other of these terms.

Current empirical studies of representation by and large make individualistic assumptions. Partly these presuppositions are rooted in the individualistic culture of democratic politics; but they are also eminently congenial to the methodology of survey research that takes the individual as the empirical unit of analysis. In concentrating on the individual, be he representative or represented, contemporary research has gained much insight into the ideology of representation and possibly into representational behavior. We know, for instance, that the representative may see himself as a "trustee" or "delegate" (or some mixture) and that such self-images serve the public official in defining political situations, in guiding his actions, or in justifying his decisions.[3] But research into the rationalizations of the representatives has not led to an adequate theory that would explain the functioning of contemporary representative government. Other investigations are less "individualistic" in their presuppositions. In particular the theoretical discussions of "public interest" or "general will" suggest an understanding of representation as a relationship between collectivities. These investigations, however, have not provided the empirically grounded theory of representation we feel is needed.

A viable theory of representation, it seems to us, cannot be constructed from individualistic assumptions alone. It must be constructed out of an understanding of representation as a relationship between two collectives—the representative assembly and the represented citizenry. However, neither can a viable theory be advanced in the absence of empirical investigation into the

2. For a fuller discussion of this point of view, see Heinz Eulau, "Changing Views of Representation," in Ithiel de Sola Pool, Ed., *Contemporary Political Science: Toward Empirical Theory* (New York: McGraw-Hill, 1967), 53–85.

3. We may note, in making this statement, that of 474 state legislators interviewed in the late fifties, 38 per cent *failed* to articulate any kind of representational role in response to an open question about how they would describe the job of being a legislator. See John C. Wahlke, Heinz Eulau, et al. *The Legislative System* (New York: Wiley, 1962), p. 281. Ten years later, of 435 city councilmen interviewed in connection with this study, as many as 59 per cent failed to make any spontaneous mention of their putative representational role in response to the same question. As far as we know, no student of representational behavior has as yet examined the implications of the evidently *low salience* of thinking about representation among political practitioners. The matter will be treated in a forthcoming monograph by Katherine Hinckley.

thinking and the acting of the individuals in the collectives. What we grope toward, then, is a theoretically adequate treatment of representation as a property of the political system, but a treatment tutored by systematic data.

A FRESH LOOK AT REPRESENTATION

Our beginning point is a highly suggestive passage in Professor Pitkin's recently published explication of the concept of representation. She elaborates on representation as something that "must be understood at the public level":

> The representative system must look after the public interest and be responsive to public opinion, except insofar as non-responsiveness can be justified in terms of the public interest. At both ends, the process is public and institutional. The individual legislator does not act alone, but as a member of a representative body.[4]

By elevating representation from the level of individual relationships to the level of the political system, Pitkin suggests that representation is, in her own words,

> primarily a public, institutional arrangement involving many people and groups, and operating in the complex ways of large-scale social arrangements. What makes it representation is not any single action by any one participant, but the overall structure and functioning of the system, the patterns emerging from the multiple atcivities of many people.[5]

Having pointed out that representation is a systemic phenomenon, Pitkin goes on to note that representation *may or may not emerge* from whatever is the relationship between citizens and public officials. "I am not suggesting," she writes, that representation "must emerge from any particular system; there is no guarantee that it will. But it may emerge, and to the extent that it does we consider that system as being a representative government."[6]

If, as Pitkin suggests, representation is a collective and public phenomenon that may or may not emerge in a political community, and if emergence of a representative relationship is conditioned by the "over-all structure and functioning of the system," our attention should be directed to properties of the political system that either facilitate or impede representation. This we propose to do.

Some Methodological Considerations.

In describing representation as an emergent property of the political system, Pitkin anticipates a course of methodological inquiry that has engaged us

4. Hanna Fenichel Pitkin, *The Concept of Representation* (Berkeley: University of California Press, 1967), 224.

5. *Ibid.*, pp. 221–2.

6. *Ibid.*, p. 224.

for a number of years and that underlies the procedures adopted in present research on the governance of cities. First, our analysis assumes that representation as well as other variables we consider are group rather than individual properties; thus we make statements about governing bodies and not individual public officials. Second, although we study 82 governments formally defined as "representative," we see representation not as something existing by definition but as something which emerges in the relationship between governing assemblies and governed citizens. Third, whether the particular relationship we might call representation does emerge is affected by the political matrix within which representatives and represented act. Finally, the analysis is configurative, not causal; we want to determine how a particular configuration of system properties, including representation, are linked together.

Of course not all properties of the political community are likely to be equally relevant to the emergence of representation. Our reading of the theoretical literature about American politics directed us to four variables usually considered germane to representation: the degree of social pluralism, the effectiveness of elections as sanctioning mechanisms, the support available to the governing group, and the recruitment processes that select public officials. For present purposes, we consider these four variables—taken together—to constitute a political matrix. The configuration of the political matrix, then, should be critical to how the governing group responds to social pressures and political demands.

Two of these properties—degree of social pluralism and election effectiveness—are first-order system variables that can be directly measured with relevant indicators. The other two properties—recruitment and support—in addition to representation, are *constructed* into group properties from individual data. The data base for our measures of these three variables are interviews with 423 city councilmen in 82 cities of the San Francisco Bay metropolitan region. In order to make the relevant information appropriate for systemic analysis it was necessary to convert the responses of individuals into group properties. This we did in one of two ways. In the case of representation and support we treated the councilmen as informants. We read appropriate questions in the interview schedule for the council *as a whole* and assigned the council to a code category. Because in this analysis we use only one measure of representation, no further index construction was necessary. Our measure of support is constructed from five separate indicators that are sufficiently cumulative to permit a simple summation index. Recruitment as a systemic property, on the other hand, was measured by aggregating the codings of each individual councilman's recruitment pattern into a single council measure. We describe the procedures more fully as we introduce the measures in the analysis.

To employ these coding procedures, of course, is to take certain liberties. For example, although we sometimes speak of community support for the council, we actually are inferring level of support from responses of the councilmen themselves. This is not the place to engage in a complicated defense of whether "definitions of the situation" do indeed serve as the "reality" for those who see it as such. Our intent is to explore in a tentative fashion the relationship among several variables; level of community support being one of these variables, we sought the best measure possible within the confines of our data. A second methodological assumption made is that single group measures can be constructed from the individual responses of those who belong to the group without doing violence to the data. Again, this is not the time to present an extended discussion of "group properties" and how to construct them. Our general strategy is to pursue certain theoretical questions as vigorously as possible, but to report specific findings in a tentative way, paying full heed to the data difficulties.

REPRESENTATION AS RESPONSE

Whether the relationship between the governing few and the governed many can be said to be a representative one depends of course on how the term is defined. Representation has been subject to a variety of definitions. Some studies have described a legislative assembly as representative when the social and economic characteristics of the constituency were fairly well mirrored in the assembly. Other studies, pursuing the logic of "mirror representation", have been less concerned with demographic representation and instead have examined whether in ideology or general values the assembly reflected the constituents. Yet other studies, dropping the mirror analogy, have defined representation in terms of equal access to the assembly by all members of the constituency.

The definition of representation which guides the theoretical endeavors in this paper differs from these formulations. In coding the interviews we made what to us was a surprising discovery; of the 82 councils, as many as 36 did not in any discernible manner seem to act in response to any politically organized views in the public. These 36 councils seemed to rely on their own sense of what the community needs were. This finding alerted us to Pitkin's observation that representation is an emergent property whose appearance cannot be taken for granted. The finding further suggested the importance of looking at the representative relationship in terms of whether the elected assembly acts in response to public views, especially views as delivered in some identifiable manner.

Pitkin left no stone unturned in her effort to salvage the concept of representation as a viable tool for theorizing about problems of democratic governance. After reviewing and interpreting almost any conceivable formulation of the concept's meaning, she settles for this definition: "representing here means acting in the interests of the represented, in a manner responsive to them." [7] We

7. *Ibid.*, p. 209.

find this definition useful because it seems to conceive of representation in two related ways: first, the representative assembly defines *what* it should do—"acting in the interest of the represented"; that is, it decides on the political agenda and, in so doing, formulates community goals. Second, the assembly does so in a manner *responsive* to the sentiments of the constituents.[8]

In studying the protocols from the councils, it became clear that, as they govern, councils can act in response to two types of politically organized and publicly voiced opinions. First, councils can consider the views and wishes of attentive publics, of fairly well-defined and permanent interest clusters in the community. These attentive publics may have differing views of how the community should be governed, in which case the council must compromise and adjust. Or the attentive publics may be more or less of the same view, in which case the council need only determine what this view is and act upon it. In either case, we say that the council, by acting in response to the viewpoints and thinking of attentive publics represents these publics. Second, the council may not concern itself with cohesive attentive publics but may, instead, act in response to *ad hoc* pressures and petitions. Neighborhood groups, for instance, may organize on a sporadic basis, make a claim on the council for some service or benefit, and expect to be listened to by "their representatives." Under these conditions, councils placate or respond to specialized and transitory citizen groups. If in the first case the council represents attentive publics, in this case it represents issue-specific groups of citizens.

There is a third type of representative relationship with the public. As previously noted, some councils appear to be altogether immune from external pressures; no identifiable groups of citizens, permanently or sporadically organized, appear to intrude on council deliberations about community affairs. In such cases, councils may or may not be acting *in the interest* of the represented (an issue we do not explore here); they are not, however, acting *in response to* the represented. Rather, these councils entertain a self-defined image of what community needs are. It is in terms of its own image that the council tackles the problems which come to its attention.

The 82 councils divided into the three categories as follows:[9]

Councils responsive to attentive publics	20	24%
Councils responsive to *ad hoc* issue groups	26	32%
Councils entertaining self-defined image	36	44%

8. Pitkin's treatment of responsiveness appears to stress the condition in which the representative assembly stands ready to be responsive when the constituents do have something to say. An assembly may, therefore, be responsive whether or not there are specific instances of response. Our analysis, as will be clearer shortly, stresses the actual act of response rather than simply the potential for it. The difficulties of empirically working with a concept stressing the possibility of an act rather than the act itself dictated our decision to modify Pitkin's theoretically suggestive definition.

9. The coding procedure used was as follows: Both investigators, reading jointly, read through all parts of the interview schedules pertinent to how councilman defined their

The distribution of the councils into this three-category classification essentially sets the question. For present analytic purposes, representation is taken to mean a relationship between governed and governors wherein the governing group responds to ("represents") politically organized viewpoints among citizens, that is, responds to something *other* than its own image of what the community needs. With representation so understood, we ask: under what political conditions is a representative relationship between governors and governed likely to emerge in a community? Our analysis examines the patterns among the four variables that we have singled out as relevant for representation and examines the connections between the political matrix, as constructed from these four indicators, and the emergence of representation.

REPRESENTATIONAL RESPONSE STYLE AND SOCIAL PLURALISM

An assumption which frequently appears in discussions of representation and modern society might be stated as follows: increasing complexity and differentiation in modern societies makes it more and more difficult for representative bodies to respond to the variety of interests which constitute the political community. Persons who make such observations usually assume representation to be a relationship between individuals. We were interested to see if representation, treated at the systemic level, was indeed less likely to emerge in larger and more complex communities. Table 16.1 presents relevant data.

Using population size as an indicator of a community's social pluralism,[10] it is clear that responding to interests voiced from the community is *facilitated*

---

relations with the public for all members of any given council. If the councilmen seldom mentioned any groups or groupings in the public or if they failed to describe an actual case where they had been responsive to public pressures or if they simply asserted (a not unusual occurrence) that they knew what was best for the community and acted upon it, the council was placed in the "self-defined image" code. If the councilmen made references to neighborhood groups or to transitory groups wanting, say, a stoplight at a given corner, or to election groups and if the councilmen indicated that they responded to pressures from such groups and attempted to placate them, then the council was coded in the "responsive to issue-groups" category. If the councilmen defined for us a fairly well organized public, attentive to what the council was doing, and if the councilmen indicated (usually by citing an illustrative case) that they were responsive to these attentive publics, the council was placed in the "responsive to attentive publics" code. The procedure, then, used the councilmen as individual informants about the responsive style of the council. It is quite possible, though not a frequent occurrence, for a given individual councilman to not feel responsive to, say, attentive publics but to describe the council as acting in that way.

10. That size is an adequate indicator of "social pluralism" may not be self-evident. We refer the reader to Jeffrey K. Hadden and Edgar F. Borgatta, *American Cities: Their Social Characteristics* (Chicago: Rand McNally, 1965) for evidence of the correlative power of size as an indicator of a city's demographic and ecological diversity and pluralism.

in the more pluralistic communities. How are we to reconcile this finding with the assumption that social complexity impedes the exercise of the representational function? It may be correct that the larger and more complex a social system, the more difficult it is for any *one* citizen to make his wishes known or for any *one* representative to respond to individual constituents. The data in Table 16.1 emphasize why an individualistic conception of representation is obsolete. Representation as a relationship between two collectivities—the represented and the representatives—appears to emerge more easily in the larger, more complex communities than in the smaller, more homogeneous communities. To understand representation as a systemic property we may have to rethink many of our conventional assumptions. Indeed, the responsiveness of the representative assembly is facilitated under just those conditions assumed to impede individual responsiveness.

Table 16.1. City Size as Indicator of Social Pluralism and Council Response Style

Representational Response Style	CITY SIZE <10,000 $N = 32$	10–50,000 $N = 33$	>50,000 $N = 17$
Self-defined Image	56%	39%	29%
Ad hoc Issue Groups	31	36	24
Attentive Publics	13	25	47
	100%	100%	100%

$$\frac{x^2}{d.f.} = \frac{8.10}{4} = 2.03$$

Gamma = +.38

The pattern in Table 16.1 makes considerable sense. It may well be that in the smaller and more homogeneous communities, the social structure is such that there is simply little opportunity for the council to respond to stable, attentive publics or to *ad hoc,* spontaneous issue groups. Unlike in larger and heterogeneous cities, where various social groups are present and likely to make their demands known to the city council, in the smaller, more homogeneous settings, the group life is likely to be less developed and the public pressures brought on the council are probably less frequent or urgent. If this is so, councils in small cities are unable to identify groups to which they might *wish* to respond, if they only could, and will have to rely on their own images of what is in the best interest of the represented. As Table 16.1 shows, this is in fact the case: the smaller the city, the more councils act in their self-images;

the larger the city, the more councils are responsive to groups that articulate interests.[11]

REPRESENTATIONAL RESPONSE STYLE AND ELECTORAL TOLERANCE

It is customary to entertain many assumptions, which often remain untested, about the consequences of elections for representation. Different nominating procedures (primaries vs. conventions), voting rules (list vs. transferable vote), electoral arrangements (at-large, multimember vs. single-member constituencies), counting procedures (majority vs. proportional), election types (partisan vs. nonpartisan), and so on, are said to produce very different types of elected representatives.

Even more to the point, assumptions about elections are very central in writings that consider such issues as "accountability" and "responsiveness." As Dahl has written, elections "are crucial processes for insuring that political leaders will be somewhat *responsive to the preferences of some ordinary citizens.*"[12] The assumption made by Dahl and by many other writers on democratic politics is that public officials choose policies in anticipation of likely electorate response at the next election. Schlesinger employs similar reasoning and states the point even more strongly: "The desire for election and, more important, for reelection becomes the electorate's restraint upon its public officials."[13] In democratic theory, then, elections are viewed as the sanction available to the public. In the absence of this sanction, office-holders would not be accountable. And, if the governors are not accountable, it is difficult to imagine them being responsive. "The point of holding [the elected official] to

11. In Table 16.1 and all following tables our interpretation of the data is largely based on comparison of the distributions in "high" and "low" categories of the "independent" (column) variable. However, we are attaching to each table two statistics: the raw χ^2 score adjusted for degree of freedom which can tell us something about the relative order of the data; that is, by dividing chi square by the table's degree of freedom, it is possible to compare tables of different numbers of cells as long as the "*N*" remains the same or nearly so. Because we are not essentially dealing with a sample but with a universe (82 out of 90 cases in the defined universe), we are not concerned with the sampling problem of whether the distribution in any table is due to chance or not at some set level of confidence. Gamma is introduced as a measure of relationship because it seems especially suitable to data ordered by ordinal or weak ordinal scales.

12. Robert A. Dahl, *A Preface to Democratic Theory* (Chicago: University of Chicago Press, 1956), p. 131, italics added. At another point Dahl argues, "The effective political elites, then, operate within limits often vague and broad, although occasionally narrow and well defined, set by their expectations as to the reactions of the group of politically active citizens who go to the polls." *Ibid.*, p. 72.

13. Joseph Schlesinger, *Ambition and Politics* (Chicago: Rand, McNally, 1966), p. 2. Schlesinger's study is a very careful and ingenious examination of how the political opportunity structure in the U.S. might facilitate or impede political ambitions and thus affect the workings of democracy. He does not, however, consider the consequences for democratic politics if men in public office are not ambitious.

account after he acts is to make him act in a certain way—look after his constituents, or do what they want."[14]

The difficulty with these assumptions about representative democracy is that they, in turn, make the assumption that elections do indeed remove or threaten to remove men from public office. We have serious doubts that this is the case. For one thing, and a fact too often overlooked by theorists who emphasize elections as a sanction, a very sizable group of office-holders retire from office voluntarily. As Charles Hyneman sharply pointed out three decades ago, turnover in legislatures is due not to election defeats, or even to fear of same, but because men simply decide to leave public office. The real task, Hyneman wrote in 1938, "is to find out why so many legislators, senators and representatives alike, choose not to run again."[15] In his analysis of eight states covering the period 1925–33 he found that *more than 60 per cent* of the retirements from both lower houses and Senates were due to failure to seek reelection.[16]

Alerted by Hyneman to the question of voluntary retirement, we checked to see how frequently city councilmen retired from office for reasons other than election defeat. In 82 cities over a ten-year period (approximately five elections per city), more than half of the councilmen retired voluntarily from office. Although a few leave the council to seek higher office, survey data indicate this number is not large. And though a few might retire out of threat of election defeat, survey data indicate that this occurs very infrequently.[17]

This high and persistent rate of voluntary retirement from elected office certainly should caution us against the easy assumption that "elections make public officials responsive" and thus guarantee representative government. For if the representative body plans to depart from office in any case, why should it

14. Pitkin, *op. cit.*, p. 57.

15. Charles S. Hyneman, "Tenure and Turnover of Legislative Personnel," *Annals of the American Academy of Political and Social Science,* Vol. 195 (1938), p. 30. Hyneman also remarks that his finding "completely knocks out the supposition that the transiency of legislative personnel is due to the fickleness of the voter at the polls . . . Only 16.1 per cent of the 1,965 House members and 14.7 per cent of the 511 senators who quit service during this period were eliminated by defeat in the general election" (pp. 25–27).

16. Possibly one of the reasons Hyneman's findings have had such little impact on theories about elections is that he was concerned with the implications of turnover for questions of legislative experience. Students who followed Hyneman's lead also addressed themselves to this qusetion. As far as we have discovered, no political scientist has yet considered how the high rates of voluntary retirement might affect the attention of lawmakers to voter preferences.

17. The mean per cent of voluntary retirements is .53; the standard deviation is .18. The rate of voluntary retirement is not related to any major demographic characteristic of the city, not to size, population density, per cent of the working force in manufacturing occupations, nor to median income. The stability of this rate across all types of cities suggests that it is a very permanent, even institutionalized, feature of nonpartisan city politics in the Bay Area. By the way, only 3 of the 82 cities studied have limitations on tenure. The survey data which help us understand the reasons for the high rates of voluntary retirement are presented and analyzed in Kenneth Prewitt, *The Citizen-Politician: A Study of Leadership Selection* (Indianapolis: Bobbs-Merrill, forthcoming).

be concerned with voter approval of its policies? To explore the relationship between elections and representative response style, we need to determine whether the voting public does indeed ever remove incumbents from office.

We constructed an index of "forced turnover" based on the number of incumbents who won, divided by the number of incumbents who sought reelection over a ten-year period (five elections). (The index does not include incumbents who were appointed to office in the expired term.)[18] In 21 cities no incumbent seeking reelection was defeated. On the other hand, in only four cities did as many as half of the incumbents suffer defeat. The distribution, therefore, is highly skewed toward success in being reelected. Nevertheless the spread of election defeats is sufficient to permit us to classify cities into three theoretically useful groups: those in which a bid for reelection never failed, those in which it sometimes failed but less often than twenty-five per cent of the time, and those in which it failed for at least one of every four incumbents.

Table 16.2. Forced Turnover and Representational Response Style

	PER CENT OF FORCED TURNOVER		
Representational Response Style	None $N = 21$	1 – 24 $N = 39$	25 + $N = 22$
To self-defined image	71%	41%	23%
To *ad hoc* issue groups	19	31	45
To attentive publics	10	28	32
	100%	100%	100%

$$\frac{\chi^2}{d.f.} = \frac{10.96}{4} = 2.74$$

Gamma = +.44

We derive from general democratic theory a simple hypothesis. Cities with the highest rate of forced turnover, where electoral tolerance is relatively low, should have councils tending to act in response to public pressures and petitions. Conversely, councils which govern in a milieu where elections never force anyone from office will act in response only to their own image of what the community needs. This, as Table 16.2 shows, is the case.

18. Appointed incumbents were excluded because of the high rate of appointment to the councils–24 per cent for all cities averaged over the ten year period. Appointment can be a strategy designed, in this context, to assure election. Omitting these appointed incumbents therefore strengthens the index of forced turnover. The aggregate election data which were used in constructing these analyses were initially collected by Gordon Black, now at the University of Rochester, in collaboration with William Hawley, Institute of Governmental Studies, Berkeley. We are indebted to both Black and Hawley for their help.

Thus, on the one hand, conventional democratic theory appears to be confirmed. The presence of an electorate which removes men from office leads to more acts of response by the representative body. On the other hand, conventional theory also holds that councils not responding to political groups would be ousted from office. If we read Table 16.2 in reverse it is evident that this does not happen; elections do not necessarily remove councils which respond only to their own image of community needs. The inability of conventional theorizing about elections to help us explain Table 16.2 is due to an oversight in much of the contemporary literature about representative democracy. Nowhere that we could find have scholars systematically examined the implications for representation *if elections are not used to force turnover* on representative bodies. But the reluctance, or inability, of the electorate to remove public officials is something we must take into account if our theory of representation is not to make unfounded empirical assumptions. Just why nonresponsive councils are seldom removed from office is a question to which we turn momentarily, but first we take a quick look at the relationship between social pluralism and electoral tolerance.

Table 16.3. City Size and Forced Turnover

	CITY SIZE		
Per Cent of Forced Turnover	<10,000 $N = 32$	10–50,000 $N = 33$	>50,000 $N = 17$
None of incumbents	37%	25%	7%
1–24	41	45	64
25 or more	22	30	29
	100%	100%	100%

$$\frac{\chi^2}{d.f.} = \frac{6.26}{4} = 1.57$$

Gamma = +.28

We expect that the electorate uses its voting powers to force turnover more often in larger cities, where pressures on the governing bodies are diverse and frequent, than in the more homogeneous and politically quiet environment of the smaller community. Table 16.3 shows this to be the case. The medium-sized and larger cities are characterized by higher rates of forced turnover than are the smaller cities, though even in the latter election defeats are not uncommon. Interpreting Tables 16.2 and 16.3 together, it seems that electoral tolerance is negatively related to the degree of representational response. Where councils need not fear the vote of the people, they are also less likely to act in response to the voice of the people.

REPRESENTATIONAL RESPONSE STYLE AND COMMUNITY SUPPORT

For purposes of our theoretical exploration, let us assume that the first three tables provide findings on which we can build. Governing bodies with self-defined images of the public interest are found in smaller communities and are less subject to electoral sanctions than councils which act in response to public pressures. This is a paradox for representational theory. In order to solve the paradox, it is necessary to consider another aspect of the political matrix that may be related to a council's representational response style–a system property we characterize as "community support." We expect, for instance, that where a council is generally supported in what it does by the citizenry, it is relatively free to define the community interest in its own image. And if this is so, it helps explain why a council, though nonresponsive, faces little risk in being ousted from office.

In order to characterize the citizenry of the 82 cities as more or less supportive of the council, we assumed that support was forthcoming if, according to council reports, any one or all of the following conditions were met: (1) that the public held a favorable and respectful image of the council; (2) that the public was generally agreed with the council on its duties; (3) that the public did not include disruptive elements; (4) that there were not many groups steadily critical of the council; and (5) that the public seemed appreciative of the council's policies. We combined these items into a single index of community support.[19]

The measure of community support allows us to investigate the paradox that councils acting on the basis of their own images are less exposed to electoral sanctioning than councils which placate *ad hoc* issue groups or are attentive to more stable interest groups. As Table 16.4 shows, communities in which the electorate does not force incumbents from office are seen as overwhelmingly supportive of their councils; in communities where some or relatively many incumbents are forced from office, the citizens are seen as almost evenly split in the support they are giving their councils.

In communities, then, in which the citizenry is on the whole satisfied with council operations and policies and is apparently giving the council its support,

19. Four of the five items used in the support index were coded by using the informant procedure describeed in footnote 9. Councils were classified according to whether they reported (1) the public to have a respectful view toward councilmen, (2) the public to be in agreement with the council's definition of its duties, (3) the public to include disruptive and unfriendly elements, and (4) the public to be generally supportive in its behavior toward the council. The fifth item, whether there are critical groups in the community, was initially an aggregate measure of individual responses to a question about the number of critical groups. Councils were ranked in terms of this aggregate measure and those above the median were said to have supportive publics, those below, to be operating in a non-supportive environment. Each council was given a score of 1 for each plus on the five items. The support scores were then dichotomized to provide the "relatively high" and "relatively low" classifications used in the analysis.

Table 16.4. Forced Turnover and Community Support

Level of Community Support	PER CENT OF FORCED TURNOVER None $N = 21$	1 – 24 $N = 39$	25 + $N = 22$
Relatively high	81%	49%	45%
Relatively low	19	51	55
	100%	100%	100%

$$\frac{\chi^2}{d.f.} = \frac{7.14}{2} = 3.57$$

Gamma = –.42

we can assume that citizens do feel "represented" by the council even though the council follows its own definition of what is in the best interests of the governed. If this inference is sound, it helps explain why councils which do not act in response to community groups are yet free of threats of election defeats. It is precisely because it does not hear from the public that the council is able to rely on its own judgment. As Table 16.5 indicates, there is a very significant difference in councils' representational response styles between the more and less supportive political milieux, and the relationship is exceptionally strong. The table and our analysis suggest that, in dealing with representation as a system property, we must at all times keep in mind that it is embedded, as Pitkin so well put it, "in the complex ways of large social arrangements." It remains, therefore, to ascertain in what type of community support is forth-

Table 16.5. Community Support and Representational Response Style

Representational Response Style	COMMUNITY SUPPORT *Relatively High* $N = 46$	*Relatively Low* $N = 36$
To self-defined image	63%	19%
To *ad hoc* issue groups	17	50
To attentive publics	20	31
	100%	100%

$$\frac{\chi^2}{d.f.} = \frac{16.52}{2} = 8.26$$

Gamma = .54

coming. From all that we know about small, relatively homogeneous cities we expect that they are more likely to have a supportive citizenry than will larger, more heterogeneous cities. Table 16.6 shows that our expectations are met: the relationship between support and social pluralism is as strong as between support and response style. Small communities, it appears, generate relatively high levels of political support that, in turn, leave the governing body free to pursue community interests as it sees fit.

Table 16.6. City Size and Community Support

	CITY SIZE		
Level of Community Support	<10,000 $N = 32$	10–50,000 $N = 33$	>50,000 $N = 17$
Relatively high	72%	58%	23%
Relatively low	28	42	77
	100%	100%	100%

$$\frac{\chi^2}{d.f.} = \frac{10.59}{2} = 5.30$$

Gamma = −.53

RECRUITMENT AND REPRESENTATION

The study of political representation must, at some time, confront the naked fact that in any political community a handful of men are chosen to govern over a very large number of citizens. As Lord Bryce observed:

> In all assemblies and groups and organized bodies of men, from a nation down to a committee of a club, direction and decision rest in the hands of a small percentage, less and less in proportion to larger size of the body, till in a great population it becomes an infinitesimally small proportion of the whole number. This is and always has been true of all forms of government, though in different degrees.[20]

The phenomenon that so impressed Bryce alerts us to the fascinating research problem of linking political recruitment and political representation. Since it is clear that a few men are chosen to govern the many and since, at least under democratic rules, the few are charged to "represent" the many, it is important for a theory of representation that we investigate how the few are chosen. This directs our attention to political recruitment–the process or set of processes by which in a city of, say, 30,000 inhabitants, the population is

20. J. Bryce, *Modern Democracies* (New York: Macmillan, 1924), p. 542.

narrowed to only 5 men who, as councillors, assume formal authority to govern the remaining 29,995 citizens.

In spite of the obvious logical connection between how the governors are recruited from the people and how they represent the people, the linkage has received little attention in empirical political studies. Some years ago, one of us had occasion to point out that "the relationship between the process of selection of legislators and the modes and consequences of legislative behavior . . . offer wide and fertile fields for empirical research,"[21] but the relevant questions were not pursued in *The Legislative System* or, as far as we can tell, in any other subsequent work.

One of the main reasons for this inattention to the link between recruitment and representation is the tendency of scholars to treat recruitment as an individual characteristic. There are studies of the political career, of the selective effect of personality on political success, of nominations of candidates, of the ascent and descent of political leaders, and so on.[22] Although these studies are productive in their own right, the preoccupation with recruitment at the individual level blocks theorizing activity and empirical research which could connect recruitment and representation. If the position taken in this paper that representation is a systemic property be accepted, however, it is evident that recruitment must also be conceptualized at that level.

We should note that there are studies which treat recruitment and representation at least as aggregate variables. These are the studies which examine the socioeconomic attributes of elected officials and compare them with a demographic profile of their constituents.[23] The difficulty with this research design is that it locks the analyst into a very narrow definition of both recruitment and representation. As to recruitment, it means studying who is selected but not the processes by which this happens. For representation it means that the analysis is limited to a "mirror theory" wherein the very complex process of representation is reduced to a very simple formula of statistical "representativeness." This approach can yield only limited understanding.

Our own conception of recruitment centers in the problem of "sponsorship" —the degree to which the recruitment process is open or unsponsored and the degree to which it is closed or sponsored. Where sponsorship is highly developed, persons already in established political positions exercise considerable control over who will sit on the council. Sponsorship implies that there are fairly determined or even institutionalized pathways to office. The route to the

21. Wahlke, Eulau, *et al.*, op. cit., p. 269.

22. The literature, of course, is quite large. Representative studies are reviewed in Prewitt, "Political Socialization and Leadership Selection," *Annals of the American Academy of Political and Social Science*, Vol. 361 (September, 1965), pp. 96–111.

23. See, for instance, the collection of articles in Dwaine Marvick, (ed.), *Political Decision-Makers* (Glencoe: Free Press, 1961); Donald R. Matthews, *The Social Background of Political Decision-Makers* (Garden City: Doubleday, 1954); and the chapter by Thomas R. Dye in Herbert Jacob and Kenneth N. Vines, (Eds.), *Politics in the American States* (Boston: Little, Brown, 1965). This issue is explored with the city council data in chapter 2 of the book by Prewitt cited in footnote 17.

council might be through an apprenticeship on the planning commission or by being an officer of the Chamber of Commerce or by being active in the local ethnic association. For a man to gain a council seat in a community where sponsorship dominates political recruitment, it is important and maybe even necessary for him to first join the inner circles. Sponsorship does not mean, however, that restrictive criteria are being applied, at least as we normally think of restriction in political recruitment. Our analysis is not concerned with whether persons with the "wrong" social traits are eliminated from consideration. In addition, sponsorship is not a notion which masks some conspiracy theory. A community can rely heavily on sponsorship as a means for recruiting political talent without there being manipulation by powerful persons behind the scene.

Sponsorship is an issue of considerable theoretical interest to students of political recruitment. A problem for most elected governing groups is how to maintain some policy continuity despite personnel turnover. This is an especially difficult problem for city councils where, as we have seen, the rate of voluntary retirement is high and where the average tenure is fairly low. (The average number of years of service is 6.5). Continuity of policy viewpoint can be maintained despite turnover if control can be exercised over successive recruits. A procession of like-minded men through office is equally as effective in stabilizing city policies as is low turnover. If indeed sponsorship aids a governing group to maintain control over both its members and its policies, sponsorship should also relate to how the group defines its representational function. A reasonable hypothesis is that sponsored recruitment insulates the council from certain political experiences and that this insulation will in turn lead to a representational response style that minimizes the impact of organized demands from the public on council thinking.

The measure of sponsorship used here was derived by aggregating individual recruitment patterns at the council level. Just as any one councilman could, on the one extreme, be an "outside challenger" who initiated his own career and attained a council seat with minimum prior contact between himself and those already in office, so the council group as a whole could have followed this career line. At the other extreme, just as an individual might have been asked to run for office by current incumbents or even appointed to office, so the council as a group could have had this experience. Between these extremes more or less prior involvement with city affairs could be characteristics of individual councilmen or the council as a whole. Sponsorship is admittedly a highly multidimensional measure as it pertains to the council, but it undoubtedly captures at the group level something of the rich variety of recruitment patterns that are possible.[24]

24. The measure of sponsorship is particularly problematic since we are summing not just individual experiences to get a group score but individual experiences which took place over a considerable span of time in some cases. It may be that the aggregation of individual career experiences into a council recruitment measure disguises more variance in the origi-

Recruitment patterns, of course, are part of the political matrix and are likely to be related to other system properties. In communities where elections are not a sanctioning mechanism and where there is, as a result, little or no forced turnover, the recruitment pattern is likely to be characterized by considerable sponsorship, while in politically volatile systems relatively little sponsorship is likely to be practiced. As Table 16.7 reveals, these expectations are reasonably well substantiated by the data.

Table 16.7. Forced Turnover and Political Recruitment

	PER CENT OF FORCED TURNOVER		
Amount of Sponsorship	None $N = 21$	1 – 24 $N = 39$	25 + $N = 22$
Little	5%	36%	27%
Some	38	51	59
Much	57	13	14
	100%	100%	100%

$$\frac{\chi^2}{d.f.} = \frac{18.59}{4} = 4.65$$

Gamma = –.44

Similarly, we expect that sponsorship is more likely to appear in a supportive political environment than in a critical one. In a community seen as supportive, where the council is relatively free to do as it pleases precisely because what the council does pleases the citizenry, incumbents are likely to bring into the council men who have already had experience in local community affairs and who can be counted on to continue the policies which seem so satisfactory.

nal data than the index should be burdened with. Councilmen enter the council at very different points in time and recruitment, as a system property, may have undergone major changes since the entry experiences of the older members. For the present, however, we are trapped by our own data; when we began the study we still were thinking of recruitment as an individual attribute and thus mainly collected data about individual careers. Despite the relatively weaker nature of our sponsorship measure, we are reluctant to give up our theoretical posture. We simply note, then, that the weaker relationships in tables using the sponsorship measure may be traced to these methodological difficulties. A council was given a sponsorship measure by computing the mean of six alternate paths to office. The "sponsorship continuum" ranged from the case in which an outside challenger initiates his own career and attains a council seat with minimum contact between himself and those already in established positions, to the case in which a councilman was deliberately selected—either asked to run or appointed to the council—by those already in office. The means were then ranked and, for present purposes, the lowest quartile in the rank constitutes the low sponsorship councils; the highest quartile constitutes the high sponsorship councils; the remainder we assigned to the middle group.

On the other hand, and the relatively weaker relationships shown in Table 16.8 underline the point, a council more exposed to criticism and social pressures may *also* seek to perpetuate its policy views by bringing like-minded and trusted members into the council fold. On balance, then, either alternative is possible. Support as a system property and recruitment through sponsorship are moderately related.

Table 16.8. Community Support and Political Recruitment

	COMMUNITY SUPPORT	
Amount of Sponsorship	*Relatively High* $N = 46$	*Relatively Low* $N = 36$
Little	19%	33%
Some	48	53
Much	33	14
	100%	100%

$$\frac{\chi^2}{d.f.} = \frac{4.50}{2} = 2.25$$

Gamma = +.38

Recruitment practices might also be related to the degree of social heterogeneity or homogeneity of a community. In small communities where men are more likely to share each other's characteristics, know each other better and are more likely to be of similar mind, sponsorship should be practiced more frequently than in more pluralistic settings. Again the data suggest, as Table

Table 16.9. City Size and Political Recruitment

	CITY SIZE		
Amount of Sponsorship	<10,000 $N = 32$	10–50,000 $N = 33$	>50,000 $N = 17$
Little	19%	30%	29%
Some	37	61	53
Much	44	9	18
	100%	100%	100%

$$\frac{\chi^2}{d.f.} = \frac{11.14}{4} = 2.79$$

Gamma = −.34

16.9 shows, that this seems to be the case, though a good deal of sponsorship is evidently also practiced in the larger and medium-sized cities.

We noted in connection with Table 16.1 that the response style of a council depends in some important measure on the actual presence of groups or publics to which the representative group can respond. We assumed that the same reasoning would hold for recruitment practices; a socially diverse community would sustain a relatively open recruitment process. Although the reasoning is not incorrect, Table 16.9 indicates that recruitment practices may be less affected than response style by community characteristics. This being the case, the relationship between recruitment and representation is perhaps more problematical than our initial theoretical reasoning might suggest.

Table 16.10. Political Recruitment and Representational Response Style

	AMOUNT OF SPONSORSHIP		
Representational Response Style	*Little* $N = 21$	*Some* $N = 41$	*Much* $N = 20$
To self-defined image	38%	37%	65%
To *ad hoc* issue groups	33	36	20
To attentive publics	29	27	15
	100%	100%	100%

$$\frac{\chi^2}{d.f.} = \frac{4.85}{4} = 1.21$$

Gamma = −.25

Where a council is free to recruit its own successors, with a view toward maintaining continuity in policy leadership by like-minded and trusted men, it should also be free from those public pressures which would force it to consider views other than its own when selecting policies. But, it seems, sponsorship is practiced to some degree in the larger, more pluralistic cities where councils are exposed to a politically more active environment. It is not surprising, therefore, that, as Table 16.10 shows, the relationship between recruitment and representation is relatively weak. Although the data point in the theoretically expected direction–councils practicing "much" sponsorship seem more likely to follow their own image of the community interest, while councils characterized by "little" sponsorship are more likely to respond in one way or another–the relationship between the two variables is lower than that between any other unveiled in the total configuration of the analysis.

Because of the small number of cases, we are generally reluctant to subject the data to a multivariate analysis which would permit us to untangle the relationship between recruitment and representation. However, since councils in the larger cities reported more sponsorship than expected, we decided to control the relationship between recruitment and representation by city size, collapsing however both the size and the representation variables. Table 16.11 reports the results.

Table 16.11. Political Recruitment and Representational Response Style, Controlled by City Size

	CITY SIZE					
	<25,000			>25,000		
Sponsorship	*Little* $N = 10$	*Some* $N = 27$	*Much* $N = 15$	*Little* $N = 11$	*Some* $N = 14$	*Much* $N = 5$
Representational Response Style						
To self-defined image	50%	41%	67%	27%	29%	60%
To issue groups and publics	50	59	33	73	71	40
	100%	100%	100%	100%	100%	100%
	Gamma = −.25			Gamma = −.32		

It appears that where *much* sponsorship is practiced in a city's recruitment process, size does not have an independent effect on representational style. In large and small cities, councils practicing a great deal of sponsorship tend to follow their own image of community interests. But where sponsorship is less frequently practiced, councils in large cities are more responsive to issue groups or attentive publics than councils in the smaller cities. In the latter, one half of the ten councils with open recruitment practices yet are able to pursue their own conceptions of the community interest. This may be due, of course, to the fact, suggested in regard to Table 16.1, that in smaller cities there may just not be any groups or publics sufficiently active to be paid attention to by the council. In general, we can conclude that the uncontrolled results of Table 16.10 do not give too distorted a picture of the relationship between recruitment and representation.

Because community support seems strongly related to the kind of representation that emerges, whereas recruitment seems less critical, we controlled the recruitment-representation relationship by our support variable. Table 16.12 shows some interesting outcomes. Where the community is supportive, sponsorship has no effect at all on representational style. Regardless of whether much or little sponsorship occurs, councils in supportive communities are pursuing their own notions of the public interest. There is, of course, one very plausible interpretation of why sponsorship is so unrelated to response style in such communities. In small cities, recruitment processes need not be controlled to insure a succession of like-minded men through office. In the socially homogeneous and politically satisfied community, anyone who presents himself for office is acceptable. Selection of public leadership by some random method is as likely to produce men with roughly the same views as does selection by sponsorship. Thus the high-support but low-sponsorship communities do not present an anomaly at all.

Table 16.12. Political Recruitment and Representational Response Style, Controlled by Community Support

	COMMUNITY SUPPORT					
	Relatively High			*Relatively Low*		
Sponsorship	*Little* $N = 9$	*Some* $N = 22$	*Much* $N = 15$	*Little* $N = 12$	*Some* $N = 19$	*Much* $N = 5$
Representational Response Style						
To self-defined image	78%	50%	73%	8%	21%	40%
To issue groups and publics	22	50	27	92	79	60
	100%	100%	100%	100%	100%	100%
	Gamma = .00			Gamma = −.52		

In communities where support from the citizenry is relatively low, however, sponsorship has the expected consequences for representational behavior. Councils with little sponsorship are almost always those which respond to public pressures, while those with more sponsorship apparently are those less likely to respond (but the small number of cases does not permit us to be confident that this result is sufficiently stable to allow a firm inference). While recruitment does seem to play a role in representation, the degree of support that a community is willing to give is clearly a more important factor in shaping representational style.

Support in turn is attenuated by the political system's electoral tolerance. As Table 16.13 indicates, in a relatively supportive environment where retirement is forced upon incumbents by electoral defeat, councils tend to be attentive rather than self-sufficient in their representational behavior. In less supportive communities forced turnover accentuates the tendency for councils to act in response to community groups. Eleven of twelve councils with high forced-

Table 16.13. Forced Turnover and Representational Response, Controlled by Community Support

	COMMUNITY SUPPORT					
	Relatively High			*Relatively Low*		
Percent Forced Turnover	*None* N = 17	*1–24* N = 19	*25+* N = 10	*None* N = 4	*1–24* N + 20	*25+* N = 12
Representational Response Style						
To self-defined image	82%	58%	40%	25%	25%	8%
To issue groups and publics	18	42	60	75	75	92
	100%	100%	100%	100%	100%	100%
	Gamma = +.55			Gamma = +.42		

turnover rates indicated responsiveness to issue groups or attentive publics, fifteen per cent more than reported in the original Table 16.2. The fact that our measure of forced turnover is truly independent of our representational style and support measures makes this result all the more significant.

SUMMARY AND CONCLUSIONS

The analysis suggests that the four components of the political matrix–the complexity of the social environment, the impact of elections in forcing incumbents from office, the degree of public support perceived by the council, and the amount of sponsorship in political recruitment–may explain a great deal about whether a responsive relationship between governors and governed will emerge. Since the analysis has been configurative, on the assumption that representational "responding to" emerges, if it does, in the context of the "overall structure and functioning of the system," we do not assess the relative impact of any given variable. Rather we stress two things: first, there seems to be a theoretically meaningful cluster of political phenomena that is strongly related to the response style adopted by the governing body; and second, under certain, very identifiable political conditions the governing body may remain indifferent to any views of the public good except its own and yet not suffer at the hands of an antagonistic electorate. What then do we make of these findings for a theory of representation?

In order to pursue a theory of representation we have chosen a particular concept of representation. The concept with which we work stresses that political representation is a relationship between two collectivities–i.e., representation occurs when the few who are chosen to govern respond to some organized demands or preferences of the many who permit themselves to be governed. The theory to which this concept directs us is one which emphasizes that a politically responsive relationship may or may not emerge, and that the type of community in which it does emerge is characterized by an identifiable matrix of properties.

The analysis led to some unexpected findings; we summarize them here, but remind the reader that they are tentative. What we have attempted is to break new ground in theorizing about representation in modern society; the specific findings to which our theorizing activity give rise will undoubtedly be modified as additional empirical work along these lines takes place. The findings, then, are presented as suggestive of what we may expect from a rethinking of "representation" rather than as confirmed facts about the political world.

1. By the definition we introduced, an elected assembly is representative when it acts in response to publicly expressed and more or less organized viewpoints from the citizenry. We found that the governing councils most often act in response to interest groups or attentive publics in the larger, more diverse communities. In the smaller, homogeneous cities, councils tend to rely on their own image of what the community requires. Thus, as an initial observation, we suggest that as a system property representation is more likely to emerge under just those conditions often presumed to impede responsiveness at the individual level.

2. A theory of representation as an emergent property may have to be adjusted in the light of certain facts about elections too long ignored. We are not sure, as one author has recently stated it, that "elections are thought of as providing the great sanction for assuring representative behavior."[25] The patterns uncovered in our analysis suggest a considerably more complex relationship between elections and representative government. Where an aroused electorate does, from time to time, unseat incumbents, the governing groups do tend to be attentive. However, it does not follow that elected assemblies concerned only with their own definition of the political situation will be turned out of office, for such self-images may indeed coincide with public preferences.

3. A council tends not to be responsive, as we use the term, where the public is viewed as being most supportive. This finding suggests a major qualification to the assumption that "elections force representativeness." Representative government can function quite independently of elections, though only under certain conditions. A politically satisfied community is apparently unconcerned about whether the council acts in response. If the job is being done, the citizens would just as soon not be bothered. It appears then not to be the inattentive council which is thrown out of office but only the council whose performance is suspect.

4. A fourth finding is one which validates the observations just made; commu-

25. J. Roland Pennock, "Political Representation: An Overview," in Pennock and John W. Chapman, (Eds.), *Representation: Nomos X* (New York: Atherton Press, 1968), p. 8.

nities in which the council sees itself as generally supported tend to leave to the council itself the selection of its successors. The pattern of sponsored recruitment, in which candidates are insulated from the competitive struggle for a council seat, tends to be associated with a representational style also suggesting a certain insulation from public pressures.

Students of democratic politics are deeply interested in the processes available to the public for controlling and holding accountable the political leadership. The analysis presented here is closely related to an understanding of these processes. It appears that members of the public dissatisfied with their representative assembly can intrude into its deliberations and force attentiveness in two ways at least, (1) by playing a role in determining who is selected to the representative body, and (2) by defeating incumbents when they stand for reelection. Put differently, when members of the public control the constituting of the representative assembly, they also influence how that assembly will define its representational role. When, however, citizens do not exercise that control, allowing the assembly more or less to determine its own members and seldom unseating an incumbent, they thereby permit the representative group the privilege of defining for itself the goals and programs of the community.

Part V

Accent on Interpretation

Chapter 17

Notes on Power and Personality

What would politics in America be like without lobbies and lobbyists? A silly and fanciful question, the realist will say. Why not take for granted what is so self-evident? What is to be gained from being absurd? Lobbies are as obviously part of the political landscape as parties are. No parties, no politics; no lobbies, no politics.

Of course. American politics, as we know it, could probably not function without lobbies. The tricky item is "as we know it." But just what do we know about lobbying? Positivism can dry up the imagination. If we look at things only "as we know them," there is a good chance of ending up in a tautological limbo where, *mirabile dictu,* things are as they are. Yet most talk about politics ends up just there: American politics is inconceivable without interest groups, and interest groups are inconceivable without lobbying. Without lobbying, interest groups could not perform the function of interest articulation that is required for the maintenance of the American political system as we know it—a tautological discovery. I am not prepared to controvert the argument. For I would look like a fool if I did.

Yet I hope to show that my initial question is not so absurd after all. It may have an intellectual nuisance value—or, as we say in the language of science, a heuristic value. It may serve to orient inquiry. Even historians, whose imagination rarely moves from the concrete to the abstract, sometimes ask: How would we have explained the course of history if it had culminated in X rather than in Y? In scientific work, the null hypothesis often saves us from grievous error.

These reflections are occasioned by the publication of what I believe is the

Section I of this chapter was originally published as "Lobbyists: The Wasted Profession," in *Public Opinion Quarterly,* Vol. 28 (Spring, 1964), pp. 27–38. Reprinted by permission.

first systematic interview survey of the lobbying profession, if profession it can be called, by Professor Lester W. Milbrath of Northwestern University.[1] The appearance of *The Washington Lobbyists* is, therefore, something of an event —an opportunity, I hope, for cerebration as much as for celebration. Before the publication of this book, information on lobbying came largely from three sources: the not altogether unprejudiced investigations of Congress,[2] the not altogether dispassionate revelations of journalists,[3] and the not altogether coherent studies of political scientists.[4] After reading the book, full of facts and figures though it is, I am appalled by how little we know about the politics of lobbying—if by knowledge we mean a set of verified propositions about reality.

What recommends Milbrath's book as a peg for cerebration beyond its own limits is that it points up the limitations of the traditional studies of interest-group politics. These studies, descriptive rather than systematically explanatory or theoretical, and focused on institutions or organizations rather than on individual actors, commonly take the form of case studies—sometimes of a particular group or set of groups in a particular political system or culture, sometimes of a particular decision or cluster of decisions, and sometimes of group activity in general in a particular system.[5] Milbrath's book represents, therefore, a new departure. Once again, as it was first in the study of electoral politics and more recently in the study of legislative politics, the sample survey turns out to be an innovating tool in the study of a political phenomenon.

The Washington Lobbyists is, above all, a book about lobbyists—who they are, whom they represent, how they work, what they seek, and how they try to influence the governmental decision-making process. To find these things out, Milbrath interviewed 101 lobbyists who came from a random sample of 114 lobbyists drawn from the list of 614 persons with a Washington address who had registered during the first two quarters of 1956 under the Federal Regulation of Lobbying Act of 1946. In addition, to assess the evidence about lobbying provided by the lobbyists themselves and to penetrate somewhat more fully

1. Lester W. Milbrath, *The Washington Lobbyists,* Chicago, Rand McNally & Company, 1963.

2. See *Final Report,* U.S. Senate, Special Committee to Investigate Political Activities, Lobbying and Campaign Contributions, Government Printing Office, May 31, 1957. This report of the McClellan Committee can serve as a guide to past congressional investigations of lobbying.

3. Among the best known are Kenneth G. Crawford, *The Pressure Boys: The Inside Story of Lobbying in America,* New York, Messner, 1939, and Karl Schriftgiesser, *The Lobbyists: The Art and Business of Influencing Lawmakers,* Boston, Little, Brown, 1951.

4. The best and fullest bibliography may be found in Milbrath, *op. cit.,* pp. 399–421. A critical survey is Samuel J. Eldersveld, "American Interest Groups: A Survey of Research and Some Implications for Theory and Method," in Henry W. Ehrmann, editor, *Interest Groups on Four Continents,* Pittsburgh, University of Pittsburgh Press, 1958, pp. 173–196.

5. I am indebted in this connection to an unpublished working paper on pressure groups by Professor John C. Wahlke of the University of Iowa, who first made me aware of the flaws of the literature on interest groups.

the interactional process of lobbying, interviews were conducted with thirty-eight "significant others" in Congress–Senators, Representatives, chiefs of committee staffs, and staff assistants. The material provided by these interviews represents the richest source of information now available about lobbying and lobbyists.

The wealth of data is such that no simple summary is feasible, and I can only recommend careful perusal of the book. For, I am sure, different things will be of interest to different readers. The book as a whole consists of four parts. In Part One lobbying is defined, various approaches to the study of interest-group activities are assessed, and the characteristics of the groups whose lobbyists constitute the sample are described. In Part Two Milbrath deals with the lobbyist as a political actor. The various chapters are concerned with the recruitment of lobbyists, their personal attributes, lobbying as an occupation, lobbyists' relations with their employers and with governmental decision makers. In Part Three Milbrath introduces a model of government as a communication network and deals with patterns of communication within and among lobbies, approaches used by lobbyists in contacting public officials, and the problem of keeping communication channels open. In Part Four Milbrath addresses himself to ethical and practical questions about lobbying in the American democracy.

The presentation of the material is such that one can be of two minds about it. On the one hand, because it is tedious and pedantic, it is almost a matter of chance if one gets to interesting findings. In fact, the author's occasional summaries are so barren that one sometimes wonders whether they could not have been written without access to the rich body of data that preceded them. On the other hand, precisely because the data are described in dreary detail and because there is little flight of the imagination from the data, the reader is in a position to make interesting discoveries of his own or at least come up with hypotheses that he may wish to test. Hopefully, Milbrath's IBM cards will be made available for secondary analyses through the Inter-University Consortium for Political Research.

Milbrath also attempts a new theoretical departure in the study of what has conventionally been called "pressure politics"–whether a successful departure I will postpone for later discussion. The point to be made here simply is that in self-consciously theorizing about the lobbying process, Milbrath at least *tries* not to commit the *faux pas* of taking for granted whatever is to be discovered and tested. This, it seems to me, has been the error of many who have written on group politics, from Arthur F. Bentley to E. E. Schattschneider.[6] The result of the error has been lack of a cumulative research tradition. Bentley took a stance toward the group process with which nobody seemed to be able to disagree, precisely because it seemed so realistic, yet which was insuffi-

6. Arthur F. Bentley, *The Process of Government,* Chicago, University of Chicago Press, 1908; E. E. Schattschneider, *The Semi-sovereign People,* New York, Holt, Rinehart & Winston, 1961.

cient to generate careful, microscopic research that could disprove or support his propositions. For to say, as Bentley did, that politics is nothing more and nothing less than the activities and relationships of social groups, whose unending interactions constitute the political order, represents a realism that only points to a seamless web. The metaphor is mine, not Bentley's, but I think it symbolizes the approach that has been dominant ever since. If one makes the assumption—whether explicitly or implicitly—of the social process as a seamless web, research, if any, is not likely to lead anywhere.

In fact, when, in the twenties and early thirties, scholars began to pay empirical attention to interest-group politics, their descriptive case studies or global generalizations did not acknowledge any indebtedness to Bentley, and there is no internal evidence in their writings that they were aware of Bentley's sometimes subtle theoretical formulations.[7] Interest groups and their activities were simply taken for granted.

When, in due time, the attempt at closing the gap was made—for example by Herring in more or less impressionistic fashion, or by Bailey in the form of an empirical case study—the political process appears yet again as a seamless web. Herring defined the policy-making process as "a working union of interests, ideas, institutions, and individuals." [8] Bailey, in what I believe is still the best case study of legislative policy making, tried to bring order out of the chaos of Herring's four interacting I's in a particular historical context in relation to a particular economic issue.[9] But his "attempt to make a vector analysis of legislative policy-making"—the vectors presumably being the four I's—did not really come off. Vector analysis, whatever it was meant to mean, yielded to minute description and suggestive interpretation. No hypotheses were formulated about just how the four I's interact, and the solution of the problem was left to the reader's imagination. The boundaries of the political process involved in the "story behind the Employment Act of 1946" were set by the study's context and scope, not by a coherent conceptual schema. As far as I know, no systematic research has ever been conducted along these lines.

Truman's *The Governmental Process* remains as "seminal" as it was when it appeared in 1951.[10] It represented an intellectual tour de force that no other political scientist had previously dared to undertake. The work remains seminal because, though quoted often and widely and, on occasion, the target of polemics, it has not produced the research renaissance that might have been

7. I have in mind studies such as Peter H. Odegard, *Pressure Politics: The Story of the Anti-saloon League,* Boulder, University of Colorado Press, 1928; E. Pendleton Herring, *Group Representation before Congress,* Baltimore, The Johns Hopkins University Press, 1929; Harwood L. Childs, *Labor and Capital in National Politics,* Columbus, Ohio State University Press, 1930; or E. E. Schattschneider, *Politics, Pressures and the Tariff,* New York, Prentice-Hall, 1935.

8. E. Pendleton Herring, *The Politics of Democracy,* New York, Rinehart, 1940, p. 421.

9. Stephen K. Bailey, *Congress Makes a Law: The Story behind the Employment Act of 1946,* New York, Columbia University Press, 1950, p. x.

10. David B. Truman, *The Governmental Process,* New York, Knopf, 1951.

expected—at least not in the field of interest-group politics as such. Just why this is so I cannot say with certainty. For one thing, perhaps because *The Governmental Process* built a grand structure, it was necessarily full of ambiguities. It seemed to fill out, often through brilliant intellectual construction, what were really deep lacunae in research. It tended to give the impression that more was known about interest-group politics than actually was. For another thing, the book was a symptom of what Truman himself later called "the impact on political science of the revolution in the behavioral sciences."[11] While the book represented a heroic effort to link the microcosmic concerns of analysis at the level of the individual actor with the macrocosmic concerns of analysis at the level of the political system, it evidently fell between two stools: it was equally praised by the behavior-minded "young Turks" at war with the formalistic institutionalists and the antiquarian theorists, and by the "old guard," of whatever hue, who felt rewarded by Truman's adroit use of their work, even if they distrusted his theorizing. Let me emphasize that I am not saying all this—about Truman or Herring or Bailey—because I want to take the kind of polemical pot shots that have been aimed all too often at group theorists. My concern is solely that group theories have yielded so little empirical research of a systematic character. On the other hand, I cannot conceive of hard-boiled empirical research that might have brought Truman's grand design to fruition. Truman himself went off to the apparently happier hunting ground of congressional politics.[12]

Perhaps the best proof of what I have said about group theorists is that once a scholar like Milbrath descended into the empirical arena, concentrating on the individual actor as the unit of analysis and using the systematic sample survey as his tool, he did not find much in the group-theoretical literature on which to build in his own work—some mild genuflections in his footnotes notwithstanding. I find in *The Washington Lobbyists* few of the notions that so dominated the literature from Bentley to Truman. The reason for this is, I think, that these notions did not yield propositions sufficiently valid to satisfy the requirements of operational definition, on the one hand, and of syncretistic treatment, on the other hand. Either these notions were too diffuse, as in the work of Bentley and Herring, or they were too universal, as in the work of Latham, who translated governmental institutions into "official groups" and obliterated the distinction between hunter and hunted,[13] or they were too constricted, as in the work of Gross, who treated the group process in terms of a single, limited model—that of conflict.[14] Apparently, once the individual

11. David B. Truman, "The Impact on Political Science of the Revolution in the Behavioral Sciences," in *Research Frontiers in Politics and Government*, Brookings Lectures, Washington, D.C., The Brookings Institution, 1955, pp. 202–231.

12. David B. Truman, *The Congressional Party: A Case Study*, New York, Wiley, 1959.

13. Earl Latham, *The Group Basis of Politics: A Study in Basing Point Legislation*, Ithaca, Cornell University Press, 1952.

14. Bertram M. Gross, *The Legislative Struggle: A Study in Social Combat*, New York, McGraw-Hill, 1953.

actor, rather than the group as a whole or the political process as a whole, becomes the unit of research, the problem of translating macro- into micro-formulations turns out to be extraordinarily difficult. At least, I assume that Milbrath made the effort but despaired.

That it took so long for a political scientist to go out and talk to people about whom so much had been written so authoritatively itself sheds some light on the theoretical and methodological problems involved. Apparently, it is not only more convenient to talk about politics in the real world without data than with them, but it is also more reassuring to do so if one feels that one's task is to illuminate a thesis rather than test a hypothesis. It is pertinent to compare the approach of the muckrakers, much preoccupied with interest groups, with that of the group theorists, for their modes of analysis, in spite of different predispositions, are much alike. The muckraking view (which also influenced a good deal of the early literature in political science) was that "special interests" are a threat to democracy and the "public interest." The view of the "realistic" group theorists was that interest groups are legitimate channels of private demand making on government, and that "pressure," so-called, is a "natural" phenomenon. The "public interest," therefore, can never be more, or less, than the product, however computed–through aggregation, combat, or compromise–of private pressures as potent as the "forces" that fascinated a Newton. Truman had called a halt to this analogical naïveté:

> The politician-legislator is not equivalent to the steel ball in a pinball game, bumping passively from post to post down an inclined plane. He is a human being involved in a variety of relationships with other human beings. In his role as legislator his accessibility to various groups is affected by the whole series of relationships that define him as a person.[15]

Interestingly, Truman's injunction paid off in the study of legislative politics, though not in the study of interest-group politics. As behavioral research penetrated the study of legislative institutions by studying legislators, it became increasingly clear that he was right. Garceau and Silverman,[16] Matthews,[17] and Wahlke and his associates[18] came to disenchant the proponents of the view that the universe of politics is a multiverse of quasi-mechanical forces.

Milbrath's interviews with lobbyists and with some of the targets of their activities–Congressmen and congressional staffers–open up new theoretical

15. Truman, *The Governmental Process,* pp. 332–333.

16. Oliver Garceau and Corinne Silverman, "A Pressure Group and the Pressured: A Case Report," *American Political Science Review,* Vol. 48, September 1954, pp. 672–691.

17. Donald R. Matthews, *U.S. Senators and Their World,* Chapel Hill, University of North Carolina Press, 1960, pp. 176–196.

18. John C. Wahlke, Heinz Eulau, William Buchanan, and LeRoy C. Ferguson, *The Legislative System: Explorations in Legislative Behavior,* New York, Wiley, 1962, pp. 311–342.

possibilities. I am by no means satisfied that his formulations do his material justice. I am saying only that his theorizing is in the right direction, because, on reading what lobbyists and others told him and what he did statistically with what they told him, one gets a more human view of the lobbying process than the mechanical metaphor of "pressure" can ever possibly convey. We are back, again, in the world of *social* relations, out of a world of mechanical relations. Lobbyists no longer appear to be the kind of superman—shady or not—that the image of power associated with the mechanical model seemed to impart. And the world of social relations, as Einstein once suggested, is much more difficult to study than the world of physical relations.

To handle the relations in which he is interested—between lobbyists and their clienteles, between lobbyists and officials, betwen lobbyists and lobbyists—Milbrath introduces a model of government as a communication system. Lobbying conceived as communication seems to meet the requirements of a science that purports to explain human behavior. Nevertheless, I do not find the communication model very persuasive as a tool for explaining lobbying. If the mechanical model of "pressure politics" is much too strong to accommodate the realities of lobbying, the communication model is too weak. This is not to say that the communication model does not make for more researchable questions than the mechanical model, nor that it does not "fit" at least some aspects of interest-group politics. It seems to be "weak" in the sense that it does not tell us much more than what the data, in their stark nakedness and unclothed by conceptual garment, can tell us. In fact, as I have suggested already, I find the raw data more palatable than the uses to which they were put.

"Communication" is so built into all social relations that a communication model does not really explain a highly specific social process like lobbying. In the end, all social relations are communication: learning is communication, praying is communication, loving is communication, selling is communication. And lobbying is communication. Just because lobbying, like everything else human beings do, involves communication (in the concrete sense of exchanging verbal or nonverbal symbols whose meaning is mutually understood), it does not follow that a model of communication is the best tool to explain lobbying, as it does not follow that, because selling involves communication, a communication model contributes much to explaining what goes on in the market place.

If lobbying had been picked as an empirical arena in which to test some hypotheses derived from communication theory, relevant behavioral patterns of the lobbying process could well have served the purpose. But Milbrath did not set out to test communication hypotheses, but to study and explain lobbying. In fact, his approach is much more eclectic than the introduction of the communication model as an explanatory tool would suggest. And I am by no means discounting the possibility that communication theory may be useful in bringing a great number of apparently heterogeneous social processes under a common theoretical roof—the master schema that has been the dream of theorists from Plato to Parsons. But this also is not the task at hand.

It seems to me that at this stage in the scientific study of human behavior, special theories and special models present a more fruitful research strategy. While, in the long run, these partial models may fall by the wayside, perhaps only after having led us on a wild-goose chase, they should be more useful in the short run in leading us to a few viable propositions that can withstand empirical refutation and can serve the purpose of theory construction. Immortality as a theorist is, after all, a commodity not easy to come by.

Now, I doubt that Professor Milbrath aspires to immortality. And I would not deny that notions derived from communication theory can be useful in organizing and presenting relevant data. But three things should be pointed out. First, Milbrath overstates his case when he writes: "Communication is the only means of influencing or changing a perception; the lobbying process, therefore, is totally a communication process" (p. 185). Second, the theoretical underpinnings presumably derived from communication theory are not utilized very extensively in the *analysis* of the research findings. They are used for purposes of global interpretation, when convenient, rather than for specific explanation. And, third, the analysis of the data is permeated by concepts derived, more or less explicitly, from other theoretical formulations. In fact, concepts derived from role analysis and personality theory are more prominent in the data analysis than concepts derived from communication theory. This is all to the good, but it suggests strongly to me that Milbrath's theoretical formulations were an afterthought rather than a forethought. I may be dead wrong in this, but many of the data presented in the bulk of the book and the ways in which they are handled analytically lead me to this conclusion.

If lobbying as a political process was Milbrath's central concern, I think he could have made better use of his data by addressing himself at the very outset, rather than at the end of his book, to the critical problems of the impact of lobbying on governmental decisions. To deal with it successfully would seem to require a model more immediately relevant to lobbying in the context of other factors that influence the decision-making process. The way in which Milbrath deals with this problem pinpoints the weakness of the communication model. But it is Milbrath who says: "We want to evaluate the effectiveness of lobbying tactics. Finally, we want to form a general estimate of the influence of lobbying on the policy-making process." Having stated these objectives, the burden of proof in terms of the communication model becomes extraordinarily heavy.

How does Milbrath deal with the questions that arise in this connection? First of all, he deals with them not in terms of the roles and functions of lobbyists, but in terms of the responses that are given by the recipients of lobby communications. In other words, the focus of evidence shifts from lobbying to its context, and it is the context that circumscribes the lobbying function. One would have expected that the proof of influence or lack of it would consist in demonstrating the degree to which lobbying as a political activity affects the context. For, presumably, without lobbying the context would be different. Let me illustrate this by way of some propositions that I derive from Milbrath's discussion. The effectiveness of lobbying varies with (1) the decision maker's degree of freedom from those expectations of his constituents that define his role; (2) the decision maker's personal convictions about an issue; (3) the degree of conformity that a legislative working majority can achieve through discipline or compromise; (4) the degree of need a decision maker has for information about some problem; (5) the degree to which informal relations within the decision-making group make for mutual respect and trust; (6) the degree to which decision makers rely for advice on staff assistants. If these hypotheses are valid, it appears that there is relatively little room for lobbying to be effective. The task of research would be to measure, if measurement were possible, the contribution lobbying makes to whatever variance in decision-making behavior is yet to be accounted for.

What do we learn about the contribution that lobbying makes? Here the research focus shifts back to the lobbyists themselves, who were asked how often their views had been solicited. We learn that "no more than 10 per cent of the lobbyists achieve this [i.e. solicitation of their views] with even one official; only 9 per cent are consulted frequently on a wide range of policy issues. There is no evidence . . . that lobbying messages are widely sought after by decision-makers" (p. 340). And so it goes. Milbrath suggests that lobbyists "do have a kind of nuisance impact," and there are situations—as when legislation is specialized and affects only a small segment of the population—in which lobbyists may be more effective. But "on broad political issues commanding considerable public attention, the major determinant is the desire of the public. Lobbyists can do very little to affect the outcome, though they may influence the details of a bill or the specific language of small sections" (p. 343). Finally, Milbrath rejects the contention that lobbyists are most influential in closely contested decisions. He feels that it is rather superficial to give lobbyists credit for the outcome if they have switched a few votes in a close contest: "It ignores all the factors that originally made the contest close, the influences that created the firm stands of the persons lined up on both sides of the issue" (p. 345). This conclusion is surprising indeed. For it appears that lobbyists cannot even be credited with a small contribution to the total variance in decision making. One wonders what the shouting was all about.

Yet, having come to these conclusions, Milbrath does not bury the corpse. Instead, he addresses himself to something he calls "the balance of power in lobbying." And he comes up with the old mechanistic model:

> An important factor attenuating the impact of lobbying on governmental decisions is the fact that nearly every vigorous push in one direction stimulates an opponent or coalition of opponents to push in the opposite direction. This natural self-balancing factor comes into play so often that it almost amounts to a law [p. 345].

I find it rather incredible, after all that has been said about the contribution lobbying makes, that presumably lobbying tends toward zero, except on details, on specialized matters, or where it involves only a small clientele. To bolster up this model of "countervailing power" (which, Milbrath admits, "is criticized vigorously by some persons"), the author footnotes Banfield's study of influence processes in Chicago:[19]

> In each of the six case studies of decisions in Chicago, described by Banfield, one group or coalition was opposed by another. . . . Subsequently, he searched for an "underlying logic" for the decisions and felt that there must have been some "invisible hand" at work. . . . These notions are not far from the concept of a natural self-balancing factor [p. 345, footnote 4].

The ghost of Adam Smith, reincarnated. And we are not much wiser than before. Even if the "pushes" exerted by lobbyists, weak as they seem to be, were "balancing," making for a situation in which "officials can more freely exercise their judgment than when the groups push on only one side" (p. 345), I do not for the world of me see what is "natural" or "self-balancing" about the process. And being something of a nonbeliever in matters scientific, I am at a loss to see just what an "invisible hand" has to do with it. If anything, and if I may be permitted use of the metaphor, it seems to me that in just these situations it is the decision maker, caught between two sets of group demands, who acts as the "balancer" or "broker" among conflicting interests.

But all this is really beside the point. The point is that I do not find any indication of what the communication model contributes to our understanding of lobby impact on decision making, and I miss any reference to the model in this central matter. It is as if all that has been presented in the bulk of the book is for naught. There we learned about the relative effectiveness of direct and indirect communication tactics, about attempts to locate key people, about the uses of research, about hearings and testimony, about collaborative relations between lobbyists and decision makers, about the use of intermediaries such as constituents or friends, about lobby-inspired letter and telegram campaigns, about publicizing voting records, and so on. Why, one wonders, do interest groups expend so much time, money, and effort to influence the decision-making process if the payoff of lobbying is so minimal?

Milbrath's answer is largely a *non sequitur*. He invokes Eckstein, who, in the postscript of his fine study of the British Medical Association, had raised certain questions of a "structural-functional" sort. Eckstein's questions referred to pressure groups, but Milbrath considers them relevant to lobbies. Eckstein had asked: "What contributions do pressure groups make to the political system as a whole, and do these contributions tend to make the system more or less viable (stable, effective)? Are their consequences 'dys-

19. See Edward C. Banfield, *Political Influence,* New York, Free Press of Glencoe, 1961. The reference to the "invisible hand" is on pages 327–328.

functional' or 'eufunctional' for the larger systems in which they operate?" [20] I find it interesting that Milbrath fails to note Eckstein's sensitivity to his own questions. For, having stated the question, Eckstein goes on: "These questions, as I have said, are not my principal theoretical concerns here. Moreover, one hesitates to comment on them in passing, for anyone can see that they are very difficult and not to be taken lightly." Milbrath is less reticent. Let me quote the paragraph immediately following his quotation of Eckstein's questions:

> In this context it is relevant to point out again that lobbying is inevitable and is likely to grow in scope. One lobbyist says it is analogous to automobile drivers: there are a few bad drivers, but people continue to drive, and more cars are added to the road each year. Lobbying is protected by the First Amendment to the Constitution, and government officials are not disposed to hamper its growth or activities [p. 356].

I must confess to puzzlement. If the structural-functional approach has virtue, it is that it presumably leads us to appraise the functions performed by a given structure in the political system not from the perspective of that structure alone, but from the perspective of alternate–whether real or hypothetical–structures. Otherwise, the conclusion is foregone. But Milbrath does not ask: If lobbies are not quite what they are made out to be, and the evidence suggests they are not, what alternate structures are there for performing the functions that lobbying presumably performs? Only the discovery of functionally equivalent, though structurally different, units of action is likely to satisfy our thirst for "explanation." I am not sure if the structural-functional approach makes for explanation, as explanation is commonly understood in science. But it surely makes for some interesting and possibly fruitful research questions. At least it does not take for granted whatever it is that should be discovered. Those devoted to the Constitution, including the First Amendment, are likely to smell subversion, but unless we ask questions about functions in terms of alternate structures, we are led into a cul-de-sac. And that, precisely, is where Professor Milbrath ends up.

II

The practice of law, like that of medicine, ministry or pedagogy, is in the care of skilled specialists who, because of prolonged training, continued commitment to expertise and social responsibility, are called "professionals." This characterization does not exhaust the catalogue of criteria that distinguish a professional from members of other occupations, but it is sufficient to pinpoint a central problem of professional life. The problem is essentially this: precise-

Section II of this chapter was originally published in *Washington Law Review,* Vol. 41 (January, 1966), pp. 187–97. Reprinted by permission.

20. Harry Eckstein, *Pressure Group Politics: The Case of The British Medical Association,* Stanford, Calif., Stanford University Press, 1960, p. 152.

ly because he has had the advantage of specialized training and experience, the doctor, the pastor, the teacher or the lawyer is the stronger partner in the relationship with patient, communicant, student or client. He controls the interpersonal situation with regard to the person who comes to him for help. Our conventional use of the word "help" seems to confirm the asymmetrical nature of the relationship, and out of recognition of this asymmetry arises the particular obligation of the professional not to exploit the relationship for his own purposes. To harness the problem, the professions have developed codes of ethics which define, among other things, what is to be considered proper conduct in the practitioner's relationship with his clientele.

But are the social restraints imposed on the professional sufficient to offset the power imbalance in the relationship between himself and his client? A great deal of the variance in professional conduct can be explained on the level of social analysis, that is, in terms of professional roles and rules. But there remains an area of conduct which cannot be explained in terms of social roles alone, and where analysis on the deeper level of personality is in order. If the professional's relationship with his client is to be successful—successful in the sense that the client derives from the contact those satisfactions which it is reasonable for him to expect—it is also likely to depend on the degree of self-awareness and self-knowledge which the practitioner brings into the situation. Such self-awareness and self-knowledge, in turn, are likely to be functions of what is loosely called a man's personality.

While some practitioners in any profession seem to have a personality especially suited to the performance of professional tasks, others may only approximate desirable personality characteristics, and still others may be altogether devoid of them. Of course, if every member of a profession had just the right personality, there would be little reason for concern and even less incentive for personality study. But as many practitioners may not have and probably do not have suitable personality traits, the study of the personalities of professionals should be high on the agenda of a profession's self-scrutiny. Admittedly, there are persons with personality characteristics that make them palpably unfit for a given type of professional work, but these people are—hopefully—eliminated early in the course of their educational preparation. In any case, there undoubtedly remain enough practitioners whose effectiveness could be greatly improved by self-conscious insight into and control over personality characteristics which interfere with professional functions.

If I understand the intent of Professor Weyrauch's study[21] of the personalities of (German) lawyers correctly, it has two major objectives: first, to discover just what the personalities of his subjects are—a diagnostic objective; and second, to formulate desirable traits which, if internalized, would contribute to shaping the lawyer's personality in support of a "wide distribution of democratic values among all persons" (p. 279)—a prescriptive objective.

21. Walter O. Weyrauch, *The Personality of Lawyers: A Comparative Study of Subjective Factors in Law*. New Haven: Yale University Press, 1964.

In some respects, these two objectives are interdependent. For the evaluation of *given* personality characteristics is predicated on a standard which would define *desirable* characteristics. If such a standard were agreed upon, the task of diagnosis would be greatly facilitated. But it is not. In particular, there seem to be two viewpoints that are diametrically opposed. On the one hand, there are those–I would think they are the vast majority of practicing psychiatrists or psychoanalysts–whose standard of the normal personality is defined for them by the culture in which they live, or, more correctly, by the culture as they perceive and interpret it. On the other hand, there are those who take the view that the culture itself may be or is sick, and that it cannot provide, therefore, a desirable standard for assessing personality traits. The task of this second group, then, is twofold: first, to postulate a set of desirable cultural values, and second, to construct an image of the healthy personality, that is, the kind of personality conducive to the creation and maintenance of the preferred cultural value system.

The main difficulty with the first viewpoint is that it is largely tautological. The construct of an ongoing culture, whatever it is (authoritarian, democratic, anomic, anal, etc.), is derived from some distribution (mean, median, mode) of the personalities found in the culture and becomes an empirical type. The normal personality is the personality that comes closest to the culture construct. Pathology is defined as deviation from the construct. But as the culture construct is itself a distributive or exaggerated model, it is self-fulfilling. Normal persons are those whom the culture defines as normal.

The difficulty with the second viewpoint–and Professor Weyrauch's study falls into this category–is that in postulating a desirable set of values to be internalized before a personality can be described as healthy, an almost unbridgeable gap occurs between what is real and what is preferred in personality. If one inspects–from the perspective of what a healthy person should be–what one finds in reality, the resultant picture looks grim indeed, and if the picture is drawn as a collective profile by methods which tend to select and exaggerate particular traits, the picture looks not just grim but dismal.

Now, the negative picture itself, as it emerges from Professor Weyrauch's study, for instance, does not bother me as such and as much as it may be bothering others, especially members of the legal fraternity. What bothers me is the implicit process of infinite regression to which *any* criticism of the profile must necessarily lead. If the criticism comes from the legal profession, it *must* be interpreted as some sort of irrational defense mechanism–lawyers are not willing (or able?) to see the culture for what it is; they are not willing (or able?) to see themselves for what they really are; or they distort (unconsciously?) their self-images to make themselves comfortable in what is really a detestable cultural environment.

This is not to say that I reject the notion, quite well articulated by Professor Weyrauch, that professionals seem particularly resistant to analysis of the relationship between their institutional roles and their personalities. But it cannot be simply ascribed to psychological defensiveness. Rather, it is probably due in large part to the institutional role requirement that the professional, in his interpersonal relations, maintain sufficient social distance from the client, lest his objectivity be impaired and his impartiality in dealing with clients be jeopardized. Why, indeed, should personality have anything to do with the doctor's technical skills, the minister's oratorical clarity, or the lawyer's knowledge of the law and court procedure? I am not defending these questions (for they are ill-conceived, though often asked). I merely want to suggest that while much human behavior is personality-related and should certainly be studied from the perspective of personality, a much greater variance in behavior can be explained (and more economically) by reference to institutionally-prescribed roles and rules which are followed quite irrespective of particular personality dynamics.

It is necessary, at this point, to say something more than the problem perhaps warrants about Professor Weyrauch's methods of inquiry and interpretation, largely because he himself devotes 63 out of 282 pages to methodology. And I shall not touch on methodological matters that are not immediately germane. Professor Weyrauch went to Germany and talked with some 130 persons, including 34 attorneys, 32 judges, 19 law professors, 18 government lawyers and state attorneys, 6 house counsels or business lawyers, 4 law students, and 17 laymen. The latter included two legislators and four housewives married to lawyers. The rest of the laymen are not clearly identified. In choosing the sample, Professor Weyrauch sought to avoid the "common danger of distortion resulting from a one-sided selection of an elite sample" as well as the danger of selecting "eccentric lawyers and cranks" which might "facilitate a manufactured conclusion of the emotional instability of lawyers" (p. 35). He continues: "To counteract these dangers lawyers were frequently chosen by chance. The interviewer accidentally met an acquaintance on the streets or at some social occasion and engaged him in a conversation that eventually led to the interview. In other instances, mere chance led to a spontaneous interview with a stranger" (p. 35).

Of the total sample, 63 were subjected to longer interviews than the rest. As to the length of the interviews, we learn that "intensity and content of the interviews varied from case to case. Some subjects were interviewed for hours, in a few instances for days, others for shorter periods. Sometimes a casual conversation of a few minutes was incorporated in the research because it was pertinent" (p. 35). The interviews are said to have been conducted by the method of free association: "The line of associations was left to the subjects, the interviewer merely encouraging their flow of thoughts. This process proved capable of yielding data of surprising content and depth. Indeed, the method of stimulating free association was later adopted as the main strategy of interviewing" (p. 41).

This must suffice as a summary of the author's methods, though he makes a great many other observations. Now, the issue I want to discuss is whether, given the goal of constructing a collective profile of the legal profession, these methods are adequate and appropriate. First, the sample. As quantitative evaluation was not the object of the research, the smallness of the sample is not objectionable as such. What is objectionable, however, is the way in which respondents and informants were chosen (and, moreover, it is never clear just who is quoted, and whether the quotations come from a conversation of a "few minutes" or from interviews carried on "for days"). We are told they were selected "by chance" or "accidentally." But, in fact, the sample was anything but random. Evidently anticipating this criticism, Professor Weyrauch writes:

> Of course this method does not preclude distortion by the unconscious preferences of the author, for instance, because of his choices of contacts and the type of his past law practice. However, the numerous professional contacts of the author while practicing law in Germany did not always depend on his volition. They were frequently initiated in the compulsory context of threatened or pending litigation. These diversified past contacts were sufficiently alive to be utilized in the interview situation (p. 35).

This may all be true, but it does not make the sample any more acceptable for the purpose of a collective profile. Combined with the author's loose use of quasi-quantitative terms like "few," "some," "many," "frequently," "often," and so on, we are left guessing about the size and quality of the bricks out of which the house is constructed.

The arbitrariness of the sample and the evidently equally arbitrary length of the interviews are confounded by the method of interviewing. Since writing the book, Professor Weyrauch has conceded, in a reply to a review by Professor Max Rheinstein, that "in the present research the interviews were not entirely non-directive. I think this would have been almost impossible in conversations which extended over hours, and which were often carried on in a friendly and relaxed atmosphere." [22] This, I daresay, is something of an understatement. From what I can reconstruct out of the bits and pieces of conversation reported in the book, Professor Weyrauch played an active, in fact often aggressive, part in the interviews, a part that is counter to the benevolent, supportive role of the psychiatrist in the therapeutic situation.

Possibly, the technique of "adversary interviewing," if it can be called so, can produce some interesting material that more passive interviewing might not elicit. But if it is useful in research on the psychology or sociology of the legal profession or on legal behavior, it deserves careful scrutiny. It may well be an appropriate method of conversing with lawyers, accustomed as they are to the discovery of truth through adversary procedures. Whether "truth" comes out of this system is not the issue here, but it might well tell us something

22. Weyrauch, *Some Comments on Professor Max Rheinstein's Review*, 74 Yale L.J. 1335, 1337 (1965).

about the mental stance and the behavioral style—I purposefully avoid using the term personality—of lawyers.

Finally, Professor Weyrauch goes to great length in defending his interviewing method by rejecting the method of more structured interviewing as inappropriate in the case of an elite not conditioned, as Americans are, to polling. German lawyers, he believes, would react with hostility to questionnaires and object "because it puts lawyers on a level with other persons and exposes them to comparison with anonymous individuals with whom they may not wish to be identified, even in the most indirect form" (p. 52). I can only refer to my own experience. In the past year I interviewed, with the aid of local assistants, 97 Austrian politicians. The interview averaged an hour and a half and consisted of open-ended, though structured, questions. Not only did we have the full cooperation of the respondents who did not object to being interviewed in a standardized manner, but their cooperation was facilitated by their knowing that all other respondents were interviewed in exactly the same manner. In fact, we were complimented for our objective approach to the interview situation. The group, by the way, included lawyers and other professionals with law degrees. I cannot believe that German lawyers would be very different from this Austrian sample.

I mention all of these methodological problems because they are relevant to the question of just how a collective profile can be constructed. I would argue that even if one had a genuinely random sample of lawyers, and even if the respondents were interviewed in a systematic fashion—in other words, if one would impose rather stringent conditions on research—the construction of a collective profile is a most hazardous enterprise, as the more grotesque descriptions of "national character" a few years back have shown. In short, if this kind of research is worthwhile, and I think it is, I would plead for distributive data which permit us to inspect the raw materials before some kind of summary statement is attempted.

Just as it is of questionable scientific merit to characterize a whole people as "authoritarian" or "democratic," so it is rather dubious to characterize a whole profession as "obsessional" or "compulsive." Yet, this is just what Professor Weyrauch does. Let me quote from his evaluation in the chapter entitled "The Mental Health of Lawyers." After admitting the difficulty of sorting out compulsive from normal individuals and leaving unanswered the question of the positive functions of compulsiveness, Professor Weyrauch continues:

> It appears, though, that lawyers *as a group* show signs of anxiety and compulsiveness with high frequency. . . . Contrary to their professional manner, many of the subjects were inhibited and timid in private contacts. It is probable that they had made efforts since their early years to cope with a felt inadequancy. From the various alternatives originally available to them, at least as far as German conditions were concerned, the one of asserting their manhood by founding a family early and standing on their own feet was evidently thought to be least desirable.

Instead, they may have attempted to solve their problems by choosing law as a profession, the immediate consequence of which was to prolong adolescence. The many years of study gave, for instance, excuses not to marry and to stay with the parents or with a widowed mother (p. 265). (Emphasis added and footnote omitted.)

I am sure that many readers will consider this statement as absurd. But even if we take Professor Weyrauch at his word that the study is "hypothesis-forming rather than hypothesis-testing" (pp. 4–5), one may question the validity of an evaluation such as this, given the methods of inquiry that were employed. I doubt very much that the *kind* of interviews conducted in this study can produce the *kind* of materials which are needed for the *kind* of interpretation that is sought. I am all the more flabbergasted because, in a moment of perhaps uncalled-for methodological candor, Professor Weyrauch informs us that:

Stereotyped answers, parochial attitudes, and techniques of evasion soon accumulated to a surprising extent. After about fifteen intensive interviews little new material was uncovered, although most subjects continued to be convinced of the uniqueness of their statements. The repetitive flavor in many interviews and the resulting danger of boredom might have been fatal to the research but for the stimulation provided by a small circle of persons who showed genuine interest (p. 41). (Footnote omitted.)

In other words, Professor Weyrauch's technique of interviewing was evidently not more successful than the technique of structured interviewing. What he complains about here is a common experience in more standardized interviewing, and we do not have any distributive data at all to judge for ourselves. But if Professor Weyrauch's subjects behaved this way, one wonders just what the merits of his interview technique are, and one has even more reason to wonder about the elaborate and intricate interpretation put on what, from a psychoanalytic viewpoint, are obviously poor results. If, after 15 interviews, the method of free association cannot produce more and new materials, it is hardly worth the time it takes to employ it. The point to be made is, of course, that Professor Weyrauch's method, as suggested earlier, was psychoanalytic in a very special sense, though it did not keep him from coming to rather extravagant conclusions about the psychic life of lawyers.

It is difficult to say something substantial about the substance of this book rather than about its methods, for one's appraisal of substance depends on one's appraisal of method. Another methodological observation must, therefore, be made. In order to protect the anonymity of his respondents, to "de-identify" them, Professor Weyrauch breaks his interviews down into isolated quotations. The quotations are organized according to certain value categories, such as enlightenment, skill, respect, affection, rectitude, well-being, wealth and power, derived from the work of Professor Harold D. Lasswell of the Yale Law School. This is quite skillfully done for the purposes of description and classification, but it is unfortunate for the purposes of interpretation and evaluation. Though the study claims to be "contextual" (p. 34), the quotations are presented out of the context from which they come. This may be legitimate to illustrate particular hypotheses, but it severely limits the substantive usefulness of the book. From the perspective of a collective profile, this extreme type of de-identification does not permit the reader to appraise either the incidence or quality of a given type of statement. Certainly, the study of personality involves more than the stringing together of out-of-context quotations from a set of very diverse conversations with a variety of persons quite differently connected with the legal process. When, many years ago, Professor Lasswell suggested certain "political types" on the basis of depth materials of a psychoanalytic sort, he presented his data in context, that is, he summarized the material on any one individual *in toto*.[23] This is necessary because psychoanalysis permits a great variety of interpretations. In Lasswell's reports, the reader was in a position to judge for himself whether the analyst's interpretation was adequate and appropriate or not. This is quite impossible in the presentation of material by Professor Weyrauch.

Finally, a methodological comment about the comparisons between German and American lawyers to which Professor Weyrauch aspires. For anyone who takes comparison seriously as the single, most relevant approximation to the experimental design of natural science, Professor Weyrauch's comparisons are unacceptable. Take a statement like this:

> An American psychiatrist with teaching experience in medical and law schools, after seeing the data, was struck by a similarity in the attitudes of lawyers in Germany and United States and their use of similar psychological defenses. The interviewer's personal observations of American law students, lawyers, and law professors over a period of more than ten years seem to bear this out (p. 278). (Footnote omitted.)

I don't think I need to comment on this use of comparison. Professor Weyrauch has conceded its inadequacy in his reply to Professor Rheinstein: "The comparisons with the American scene are, of course, unsupported by my data, and are not meant to be more than mere suggestions in my book."[24]

All this is not to say that this is not a very suggestive book, even if it does not really say anything valid about "the personality of lawyers," as its title claims, or anything reliable about "a comparative study of subjective factors in law," as its subtitle alleges. For recorded here are the fragments of conversations with German lawyers about a great variety of topics, from legal education, legal practice, legal procedure, legal ethics, and so on, to observations about the status and prestige of lawyers, the differences between the systems of Anglo-American and Roman law, the economics of the legal profession, and sundry other matters. And it provides some insights into certain opinions,

23. Lasswell, *Power and Personality* (1948); Lasswell, *Psychopathology and Politics* (1930).

24. Weyrauch, *supra* note 22, at 1336.

attitudes, orientations, perceptions, taboos, preferences, identifications, expectations and behavioral styles of *some* German lawyers. Unfortunately, because of its inadequate comparative framework, it is impossible to say whether these things are expressions of the German culture in particular or of the culture of the legal profession across national boundaries in general. In short, the question whether there is a culture of the legal profession transcending the frontiers of nation or legal system remains unanswered.

As a political scientist, I was particularly interested in Professor Weyrauch's evaluation of the lawyer's role in politics. As is well known, lawyers do play a highly visible role in American politics.[25] But again, because I think Professor Weyrauch is more intent on making a case for his psychoanalytic interpretation than on evaluating the role of the legal profession in politics, he is the prisoner of his approach. In a critical paragraph he writes, for instance: "Although in every power process lawyers will be found on both sides of the fence, it is likely that the more highly qualified will adhere to the side holding and defending an already existing power position" (pp. 280–81). This may be so, but Professor Weyrauch's estimate here is not based on inference from empirical data, but derived from his almost axiomatic position that lawyers, as a group, are characterized by compulsive personality traits. He writes:

> Correspondingly on the American domestic level, lawyers will be prominent in the battle for states' rights, frequently resisting federal interference, stalling projects of wider than local scope, and advocating the status quo, irrespective of whether the matter is one of racial, religious, or social discrimination (p. 283).

The issue is not whether this conclusion is true or false in an empirical sense, but whether the data support the axiom that lawyers behave as they do because they have certain (obsessional or compulsive) personalities. I am not in a position to contradict Professor Weyrauch's diagnosis. I would only argue that, until all the facts are in, or at least more facts than we now have, it is hazardous to make such statements. Indeed, because they are familiar presuppositions about the behavior of lawyers, they deserve empirical investigation. It is my impression that lawyers have played equally prominent roles in the forefronts of revolutionary movements, from the French to the recent Cuban Revolution. What is needed, clearly, are comparative historical and sociological studies of lawyers in different societies.

In particular, we need studies of the legal profession that are cast in more sophisticated research designs, including, for purposes of scientific control, lawyers in politics, lawyers out of politics, and politicians who are not lawyers. Otherwise the data that are collected do not permit the falsification of hypotheses, regardless of whether these hypotheses are derived from psychoanalytic or any other set of axiomatic presuppositions.

25. See Eulau and Sprague, *Lawyers in Politics: A Study in Professional Convergence* (1964).

III

Some books are written to be read; others to be consulted; and still others to be studied. This research report of decision-making in four American communities, involving the scope of their governmental activities, requires intensive study.[26] It deals with the emergence and resolution of diverse substantive issues that faced the four communities in the period between the end of the second World War and the termination of the research in 1961. It investigates the questions of how and why public issues were articulated as they were in the preferences, demands and expectations of both community leaders and ordinary citizens. It is equally concerned with the problem of how the decisions made were patterned by relatively stable, but also shifting, influence relations among ideologically and otherwise opposed sides, and by the prevailing as well as changing power structures and regimes of the four communities. Its central focus, therefore, is the problem of stability and change as functions of convergent and divergent tendencies in the political process.

Of course, this rather skeleton characterization of the book does not come close to describing its total content. No review of a few hundred words can satisfactorily describe or do critical justice to a research report of almost 800 pages. It can, at most, serve as a guide to a report that must be studied and cannot simply be read. Moreover, this is a book whose study requires an open mind. For it contains much with which one can readily quarrel. Nevertheless, I shall deny myself the privilege of dissent, for I feel that the virtues of the research far exceed the vices of the report.

An unbiased study of this research requires that one accept, at least initially and however tentatively, the set of conceptual formulations that direct the analysis. This is no easy assignment. For the authors, intent on giving empirically viable definitions to such traditionally ambiguous concepts as influence, power, status, regime, consensus and so on, make few concessions to conventional terminology. One is continuously challenged to avoid giving these terms one's own parataxic meanings.

First of all, this is a fresh contribution to the cumulative study of community politics. It is self-consciously geared, in both text and footnotes, to the debate about community power between those who, following Hunter, proceed from the assumptions of stratification theory and rely chiefly on sociometric methods, and those who, like Dahl and his associates, make pluralistic assumptions and stress concrete decision-making situations as objects of inquiry. I doubt that the warring camps will be happy with the theoretically often novel formulations and the methodologically quite eclectic procedures that Agger

Section III of this chapter was originally published in *The American Political Science Review,* Vol. 58 (December, 1964), pp. 972–73. Reprinted by permission.

26. Robert A. Agger, Daniel Goldrich, and Bert E. Swanson, *The Rulers and the Ruled—Political Power and Impotence in American Communities.* New York: John Wiley & Sons, 1964.

and his coworkers have adopted. But as the debate between stratification theorists and pluralists went on throughout the period during which their research was in various stages of development, it is quite clear that the authors profited from it. They succeeded in avoiding some of the difficulties and in harnessing some of the advantages of either approach. Indeed, though many problems remain, they demonstrate that rapprochement is not beyond the range of possibility, and that there need not be conflict between the analysis of the actual roles which actors take in decision-making situations and the analysis of their place in the social structure. Both types of analysis can be complementary, just as the reputational method of sociometry, if not overburdened by undue inferences, need not yield results that are at odds with the emphasis on events preferred by the pluralists.

Second, this is a study in comparative politics. From this perspective, of interest is not so much the comparison of the substantive politics that transpired in the four research locations, as is the use made of these locations for the purpose of testing the adequacy of certain typologies of political structure within which the political process takes place, and without which genuine comparison is impossible in the first place. Agger and associates developed two typologies—of "power structure" and "regime"—in order to come to comparative grips with the otherwise highly diverse-seeming political systems which they encountered in the four communities. The power structure is conceived as a function of two variables: (1) the extent of the distribution of political power among the citizenry, and (2) the degree of ideological convergence or divergence among the leadership. Dichotomization of the variables yields four types of power structure called Consensual Mass, Competitive Mass, Consensual Elite, and Competitive Elite. Political regime, on the other hand, is seen as a function of two other variables: (1) citizens' sense of electoral potency, and (2) the probability that efforts to shift or maintain the scope of government will be stymied by the use of illegitimate sanctions. Again, dichotomization of the variables results in four types of regime termed Developed Democracy, Underdeveloped Democracy, Guided Democracy, and Oligarchy. These typologies help to facilitate comparison of otherwise noncomparable political processes and to pinpoint the direction of political change. While these typologies serve the authors, their theoretical validity requires careful scrutiny and their utility calls for application in still other research arenas.

This is, third, a study of change through time. One of the well-known weaknesses of behavioral research has long been its synchronic character. While synchronic analysis need not be static, it is clearly unable to control the critical factor of time that is so important for the purpose of generalization. Agger and coworkers have developed an ingenious technique for coping with the problem of comparing the developmental stages of political change. Because the field research in the four communities was conducted at different points in time, yet because the political situation in each community at the time of field work was of particular interest, this period was characterized as "Time E to M"–i.e., the period between the occurrence of the Event at the researcher's focus of attention and the moment of Measurement. In the case of Farmdale this was 1950–52; in the case of Oretown 1952–53; and in the cases of Petropolis and Metroville it was 1957 and 1958. Another period, "Time M to M + 1 or M + 2" could then serve as the period in which "natural experiments" in the various locations were observed for the purpose of testing hypotheses suggested by previous observations conducted during Time E to M. The periods following this "experimental" stage, of varying length because the research had to be brought to a close (in Farmdale M + 3 to M + 9, in Metroville M + 3 only, for instance), could be utilized as a further check on the validity of the observations made during E to M. Finally, the periods prior to E to M, in each case going back to 1946, could be characterized as E – 1 and so on and could serve the purpose of systematically reviewing alternate community backgrounds. In other words, the research has a high degree of historical depth without being "historical," an accomplishment probably unmatched so far by behavioral inquiry in any other substantive area of investigation.

Last, but not least, this is a clear example of the possibility of exploiting data concerning the political behavior of individuals for global analysis. The book moves from formal to operational definitions; from the latter to observations and measurement of behavior; from there to both aggregated and group properties of the structures and processes that are described; and from such molar description to the testing of rather global hypotheses. Indeed, the hypotheses presented and tested in the last chapter constitute the high point of the entire enterprise. They deal with the emergence and existence of Developed Democracy, the relationship between regimes and power structures, the dynamics of power structure, the formation of political leadership groups, shifts in the scope of government, the impact of governmental structure on type of power structure, and so on. In testing relevant hypotheses, the authors could not only make use of the four communities as their units of analysis, but also of the four communities in different time periods–that is, they had four times fifteen or sixty units of analysis available for this purpose. For instance, with regard to the hypothesis–"a Competitive Mass type of power structure is sufficient but not necessary for the existence of a Developed Democratic type of regime"–it was found that, without exception, during 31 periods of Competitive Mass power structure the prevalent type of regime was Developed Democracy, but that during 29 periods of other types of power structure, fourteen were also characterized by Developed Democracy.

As I suggested, a brief review of this intensive research report is necessarily a troublesome affair. All I dared to do here, therefore, was to suggest some aspects of the book that interested me, that (I think) interested the authors, and that (I hope) will be of interest to political scientists. It is my conviction that Agger, Goldrich and Swanson are to be congratulated on *The Rulers and the Ruled*. That it is a major empirical undertaking in the field of community power structures is only one of its virtues. But it is also a sophisticated venture in modern political theory and, in its comparative aspects, an important contribution to the methodology of political science.

IV

There is something majestic in the analysis of human societies across time and space. It is the splendor of global and historical perspective that makes the works of a Comte, a Spencer, a Pareto or a Weber lasting and ever stimulating monuments of inquiry into the social ways of mankind. Their daring willingness and exemplary ability to mobilize contemporary knowledge of history and geography, of politics and economics, for sociological synthesis and endow it with theoretical significance made for a genre of writing at once truly civilized and truly scientific. Its shortcomings notwithstanding, this genre still awes the modern social scientist who aspires to being civilized and scientific. But it is a genre that few modern social scientists care to practice. The explosion of social science knowledge, both cause and consequence of the scientific division of labor in the modern university, seems to have an intimidating effect on the contemporary analyst of human societies who seeks universal validity for his theoretical constructions. The few who are still inclined to practice the art of global analysis do not really offer a rich intellectual fare. What they provide is largely a kind of empirically disembodied theoretical framework, global in aspiration, to be sure, but grossly neglectful of the rich diversity of human experience. I do not wish to minimize their efforts or achievements. But I prefer something else.

Although it is modestly subtitled "A Theory of Social Stratification," Gerhard Lenski's *Power and Privilege*[27] is a far-ranging and profound inquiry into the causes and effects of human inequality as well as into the foundations and consequences of political and economic power. Of the book's thirteen chapters, eight are devoted to the structure and dynamics of distributive systems in hunting and gathering societies, in simple and advanced horticultural societies, in agrarian societies and in industrial societies. In a *tour de force* of sweeping scholarship Lenski guides us through the centuries to the most remote corners of the earth. The Northern Maidu Indians of California, the Siriono of eastern Bolivia, the Arunta of Australia, the Roro of New Guinea, the Yoruba of Nigeria, the Ankole of Uganda, the Mayas, the Aztecs and the Incas, the Greeks and the Romans, the Chinese and the Japanese, Ottoman Turkey, Czarist Russia, medieval and modern Europe, the Soviet Union and the United States—all of these and many more societies provide the data for Lenski's analysis of stratification around the world. If, in what follows, I sound unduly abstract, it is because I must limit myself to a discussion of

Section IV of this chapter was originally published in *The American Political Science Review*, Vol. 61 (June, 1967), pp. 482–85. Reprinted by permission.

27. New York: McGraw-Hill Book Company, 1966.

Lenski's theory and method of inquiry. It is all the more important to emphasize, therefore, that even if one were to find fault with his theory and method, the great bulk of Lenski's book is a fascinating empirical account of human experience concerning the classical question of "who gets what and why?"

There are two theories in Lenski's book—the theory with which he began and the theory which evolved in the course of his investigations. Not that they are totally different. Rather, the "final" theory is largely a modification of the initial theory. This is as it should be. Lenski's candor is admirable:

> The high degree of support for the theory was not completely unexpected because of the manner in which the theory was constructed. Despite some appearances to the contrary, the theory presented in the early chapters was not a simple exercise in deductive logic. Rather, it represented the end product of an already extensive process of both induction and deduction. In a sense, the theory was designed to fit the facts, or at least those facts with which I was familiar when I began writing this volume. However, the theory with which I began writing was not the same that I had taught ten years previously. On the contrary, over the course of that decade I constantly shifted and modified my theoretical position to try to get a better fit between theory and data. In the process I found myself shifting from what was basically a functionalist position to what I have called a synthetic or synthesizing position. In other words, I found an increasing need to incorporate hypotheses and postulates which had little or no part in the functionalist tradition, yet without wholly abandoning the latter (p. 435).

Methodological absolutists will undoubtedly dissent from this mode of theory construction. But I am quite convinced that in the present state of the social sciences premature (and often pretentious) theoretical closure is the surest way to some sort of neo-scholasticism. The social scientist, it seems to me, is at his best if he is sensitive to the open-endedness of all current theories and maintains a healthy respect for those facts that do not fit his particular working theory of the moment. Lenski's work exemplifies the soundness of this position. It takes the kind of truly cross-cultural analysis that he undertook to abuse us of the intellectual Olympianism implicit in much current "pure" theory.

The central problem of Lenski's theory is the phenomenon of human inequality. What moved him to tackle the problem, apart from its intrinsic importance, was the diversity of "explanations" that have been offered for social inequality through the ages, and especially his dissatisfaction with those two major contemporary approaches which go under the name of "functionalist" and "conflict" theories. Behind these alternate formulations lie more basic issues predicated on differing behavioral assumptions about the nature of man and society as well as their interrelations. Although Lenski accepts, for working purposes, the assumption that "societies, like individuals, are basically self-seeking units" (p. 42), the assumption does not become an ideological straitjacket. But more about the basic issues later on.

What of the initial theory itself? It consists of two postulates, two derivative "laws," two major hypotheses and a central proposition, as well as of a variety of auxiliary hypotheses and a good deal of supportive explication. Assuming the self-seeking nature of man, the first postulate states that "power alone governs the distribution of rewards." But as selfish interests can only be satisfied through cooperation, it is a second postulate that "men's selfish interests compel them to remain members of society and to share in the division of labor." The first law of distribution follows: "men will share the product of their labors to the extent required to insure the survival and continued productivity of those others whose actions are necessary or beneficial to themselves." But this law says nothing about the distribution of societal surplus goods and services. Again assuming self-interest and short supply of surplus values, there will be conflict over control of the surplus. Defining power, with Weber, "as the probability of persons or groups carrying out their will even when opposed by others," the second law of distribution follows: "power will determine the distribution of nearly all of the surplus possessed by a society" (all quotes on p. 44). This second law, in turn, points to the critical relationship between the two chief variables, power and privilege:

If privilege is defined as possession or control of a portion of the surplus produced by a society, then it follows that *privilege is largely a function of power, and to a very limited degree, a function of altruism.* This means that to explain most of the distribution of privilege in a society, we have but to determine the distribution of power (p. 45).

Lenski then introduces two hypotheses: first, "in the simplest societies, or those which are technologically most primitive, the goods and services available will be distributed wholly, or largely, on the basis of need"; and second, "with technological advance, an increasing proportion of the goods and services available to a society will be distributed on the basis of power" (p. 46).

At this point Lenski warns against a general theory of distribution or stratification that would be universally applicable. Just as the economist eschews a single general theory of market behavior and takes account of the existence of different kinds of market (perfect competition, monopoly, duopoly, oligopoly, and so on), Lenski recommends the same approach for a theory of stratification. He argues, therefore, that if the two laws of distribution and the two hypotheses are valid, then "the nature of distributive systems will vary greatly, depending on the degree of technological advance in the societies involved" (p. 47).

I cannot possibly summarize here the whole of Lenski's explication of his theory. Suffice it to say that by classifying societies in terms of their technologies, he is in fact controlling, wholly or partly, many other relevant variables. Moreover, he frankly acknowledges the possibility of second-order variations that may be due to the physical environment, the "military participation ratio," within-society technological variations, or "political cycles" that make for different degrees of constitutional legitimacy. To deal with these, Lenski is prepared to rely on inductive logic in order to formulate both causal and descriptive generalizations. In further explicating his theory, he has also much to say about force and its transformation into social power, the rule of right, the varieties of institutionalized power and the reactions of classes to the on-going system of distribution.

Lenski's view of stratification is multidimensional—that is, there may be a political class system, a property class system, an occupational class system, or an ethnic class system, and so on, all of which may constitute a particular distributive system. Class systems differ in importance, complexity, span, shape, degree of mobility, degree of hostility and degree of institutionalization. In view of the great variety of class systems in different societies, Lenski does not underestimate the difficulties involved in comparing highly diverse distributive systems. But he does not hesitate to propose meaningful, if rough, comparisons between distributive systems in terms of their degree of inequality, their rate of vertical mobility and their degree of class hostility. In summary, then, Lenski's theory predicts that "variations in technology will be the most important single determinant of variations in distributive systems" (p. 90). But this does not preclude other factors from also being considered as possible sources of variations in stratification. Indeed, "one of the most important concerns in the analysis which follows will be the identification of these factors and the determination of the magnitude of their influence" (p. 90).

In this summary of Lenski's initial theory I have neglected to mention the great care taken in the definition of the concepts that represent the variables in the hypotheses whose interrelations constitute the theory. In many respects, Lenski's book is a model of theory construction that is highly instructive. In reformulating problems and concepts for empirical inquiry, he demonstrates the utility of two techniques: first, the technique of transforming categorical concepts into variable concepts; and second, the technique of breaking down compound concepts into their constituent elements. This strategy of theorizing is mandatory, it seems to me, if comparative analysis of dozens of societies is to have the theoretical payoffs that one hopes for in the crucible of empirical research.

Where does Lenski's test of his initial theory come out? In general, theory and evidence corresponded reasonably well, but modifications and changes were necessary. In the first place, the study of advanced horticultural and agrarian societies showed that the relationship between technology and political organization is more complex than expected:

> In these societies one finds significant variations in level of political development associated with apparently limited variations in technology. This suggests that we must think of the level of technological advance either as a *necessary,* but not sufficient, cause of political advance, or as the generator of a "threshold effect,"

whereby a limited advance in technology causes (or makes possible) a major advance in political organization. Perhaps both apply. . . . This has significant consequences for the distributive process because the level of political development is clearly a major determinant of the character of distributive systems (pp. 435–36).

Second, Lenski came to the conclusion that a sharper analytic distinction must be made between the concepts of "technology" and "economy." He found that "economic variations which occur independently of technological variations appear to have effects on distributive systems comparable to those produced by political variations" (p. 436), possibly as a result of the influence of different environmental factors.

Third, especially in the more advanced societies, ideology seems to have more of an impact than anticipated: "The importance of ideology was seen most clearly in the somewhat unexpected halting, and possible reversal, of the trend toward increasing social inequality, so pronounced in the evolution from hunting and gathering to agrarian societies." It had been predicted that the degree of inequality would vary directly with the size of a society's surplus, though the hypothesis had been qualified for democratic societies with an egalitarian or socialistic ideology. The evidence "strongly suggests that the average level of inequality in the most advanced industrial societies is no greater than that in the average advanced agrarian society, and probably less" (p. 437).

Fourth, Lenski found that in the more advanced societies variations in the personal attributes of political leaders have a greater impact on distribution than expected, particularly when constitutional government is at low ebb: "Though there are obviously limits to the influence which the personal factor can exert, they are not so narrow as to make it trivial. Though the variable involved is essentially nonsociological in character, sociological theories must find a place for it" (p. 438).

There are other modifications of the original theory. For instance, type of polity seems to have an effect on the size of the surplus: "The creation and preservation of an economic surplus in agrarian societies would probably have been impossible without an authoritarian, undemocratic, and exploitative political system" (p. 440). Other changes of the initial model involved the separation of certain variables from a cluster of factors originally labeled "constitutionalism," such as "degree of external threat," which was found to be linked with variations in type of polity, at least in advanced horticultural societies. Similarly, "rate of economic development" seems to be linked with variations in distribution: "Specifically, a high rate of economic development appeared to be linked with a greater willingness on the part of the dominant classes to make sacrifices in *relative* terms, i.e., in their share of the gross national product, in order to insure increases in absolute terms" (p. 440).

Finally, Lenski returns to the eight issues that have divided functional and conflict theorists, "conservatives" and "radicals." He finds that on three of the eight issues (the nature of man, the inevitability of inequality, and the conception of class) his final theory leans heavily in the conservative direction; on two issues (the nature of society and the degree to which inequality makes for conflict) it leans heavily in the radical direction. On the three remaining issues (the degree to which inequality is maintained by coercion, the question of how rights and privileges are acquired, and the nature of the state and the law), the final theory "involves a complex mixture of elements in both traditions: strongly conservative with respect to economically and technologically backward societies, and radical with respect to more advanced societies. In summary, it is *an extremely complex mixture of elements from these two older traditions, yet at the same time unique and different*" (p. 443).

In conclusion, I cannot do better than quote Lenski's own assessment of what I think is a masterpiece of comparative social analysis. Referring to the transformation of his theory from its initial to its final formulation, he writes:

> These changes direct attention to what has proven a highly rewarding feature of the methodology of our analysis: the practice of constantly alternating the processes of induction and deduction. . . . This is not done often enough in contemporary sociology, with the result that the fit between theory and data is often poor or unclear. By constantly comparing theory and data, and, when necessary, modifying the theory to conform to the data, cumulative growth and development are achieved. The possibility of this is further enhanced by working with an open theoretical system which permits the addition of new variables and the elimination or modification of old ones. As a consequence, a considerable number of important insights have emerged which were by no means obvious at the start of the analysis (p. 440).

Chapter 18

From Utopia to Probability: Liberalism and Recent Science

Every age, every epoch, every period has its own peculiar, if not always unique, style of thought, mode of perception, and method of expression. Call it, with the Greeks, *"ethos,"* or call it, with the Germans, *"Zeitgeist,"* what it all adds up to are the pervasive patterns of sensing and thinking, of believing and orienting, that are characteristic of human behavior in a particular place at a particular time. One need not assume, with Hegel, that they are the true forces which underlie and shape the course of social events; just as one need not assume, with Marx, that they are mere epiphenomena determined by inexorable forces of economic production. Indeed, such assumptions, being prejudgments, tend to preclude disinterested inquiry into the engaging problem of the relationship between ideas and action. It is sufficient to assume, without evading the puzzle of cause and effect, that man's broad and deep patterns of thought and belief are instrumental in his quest to make himself at home in a world which is only in part of his own making.

Self-conscious sensitivity to the relationship between ideas and action is the peculiar mark of our time. Our time, we are told by some, is characterized by the "end of ideology." Whatever the validity of this characterization, it cannot and does not mean that our time is lacking in certain clearly structured and discernible patterns of thought. Perhaps, instead of speaking of the "end of ideology," it would be more appropriate to say that whatever modes of thinking are involved in most traditional ideologies—be they conservatism, socialism or communism, nationalism or pacifism—have lost their instrumental

Originally published in *Antioch Review*, Vol. 26 (Spring, 1966), pp. 5–16. Reprinted by permission.

value, that these modes no longer serve the task of adjusting man to his environment and of shaping the environment to man's needs.

Our beliefs can be analyzed from a dual perspective: their substantive content or their form—the patterns in which ideas are expressed. But, to be effective instruments of adjustment, the form and content of ideas need not constitute a unity. Failure to recognize this possibility, it seems to me, has hampered both Marxism and conservatism. Marx, in trying to make socialism "scientific," only succeeded in imposing upon it the empty rationalism of the Enlightenment whose intellectual heir he was despite his emotional commitments. The conservatives, on the other hand, chiding reason and rejecting scientific method as a tool of social analysis, have never been able to catch up either with themselves or with the changing times. If, as far as Marxism or conservatism are concerned, the "end of ideology" is a fact, it is due to their failure to adopt a viable strategy of cognition that can serve the purpose of directing social and political action.

What of liberalism? Its strength as a "belief system," it seems to me, has been the strength of its "thought system." For, from its beginnings, the liberal *way* of thinking, whatever the content of its thought, was firmly anchored in the methods of modern science. The late Morris R. Cohen expressed it well when he wrote, in *The Faith of a Liberal:*

> Liberalism is an attitude rather than a set of dogmas—an attitude that insists upon questioning all plausible and self-evident propositions, seeking not to reject them but to find out what evidence there is to support them rather than their possible alternatives. This open eye for possible alternatives which need to be scrutinized before we can determine which is the best grounded is profoundly disconcerting to all conservatives and to all revolutionaries.
>
> Liberalism can move forward, like science, because it embraces self-correcting principles which permit the correction of error and partial truth without an overthrow of the system that makes such correction possible. Like science, liberalism is based on the faith that other human beings can carry forward, by rational methods, the gains that we have won in human understanding.

Yet, though science is triumphant, more so in our time than ever before, liberalism is in crisis. How can one explain this paradox? It is due, I think, to certain changes in the modes of scientific thinking to which liberalism has failed to adapt. The key terms characterizing these changes are "indeterminacy" and "probability." There are others, but these are critical. For they are symptomatic of the transformation of scientific ways of thinking from causal determinism to probabilism. Regardless of whether the model was mechanistic, as in post-Newtonian political theory (of which the American Constitution is still the prime example), or whether it was organic, as in post-Darwinian social theory, liberalism's dominant mode of thinking was deterministic. It was deterministic not only in the sense that every effect was assumed to have an identifiable cause, but it was deterministic also in assuming that, if certain conditions were satisfied, certain consequences were sure to follow.

The determinism implicit in eighteenth- and nineteenth-century scientific thinking was not altogether harmful for liberal social thought as an ideology or for liberalism as a political movement. It gave the impetus and drive that made liberalism an agent of societal fermentation; that gave it, time and again, that zest for change and reform which became its hallmark; that led it to bold social and political experimentation; and that, last but not least, endowed it with a spirit of optimism and hope for a better future that testified to its fundamental humanism.

But there were dysfunctional consequences as well. Two of these, closely linked, are particularly noteworthy. One of them is liberalism's utopian component; the other a failure of imagination. Lionel Trilling once put it well:

> Surely if liberalism has a single desperate weakness, it is an inadequacy of imagination: liberalism is always being surprised. There is always the liberal work to do over again because disillusionment and fatigue follow hard upon surprise, and reaction is always ready for that moment of liberal disillusionment and fatigue— reaction never hopes, despairs or suffers amazement. Liberalism likes to suggest its affinity with science, pragmatism and the method of hypothesis, but in actual conduct it requires "ideals" and absolutes; it prefers to make its alliances only when it thinks it catches the scent of Utopia in parties and governments, the odor of sanctity in men; and if neither is actually present, liberalism makes sure to supply it. When liberalism must act with some degree of anomaly—and much necessary action is anomalous—it insists that it is acting on perfect theory and is astonished when anomaly then appears.

Trilling's indictment is severe, but to the point. Its utopianism and lack of imagination in the face of unexpected events were not disturbing as long as liberalism was on the march—when it drove out the Inquisition, dethroned despotic monarchs, abolished censorship and human oppression; in retreat, the tensions arising out of liberalism's scientific and utopian components often made for ambivalence or even impotence in social and political action.

Liberalism's failures were undoubtedly due to its utopianism, itself an expression of bondage to the deterministic view of the universe characteristic of Newtonian and Darwinian science. If cherished goals, whatever they were—a free market, the rights of man, regulation of competition, social security, or any other, depending on time and place—were not achieved as programmatically specified, the tendency was to blame the opposition (which one had to tolerate and live with) rather than the program. The program itself was beyond reproach. That it might be unrealistic, ill-timed or unwise were considerations which, if they did arise, could not be admitted. Even though God may not have been a liberal when he created the world, liberals had to talk like gods when they announced their plans. For men of good will—and liberals could well pride themselves on being such—the liberal program was so obvious, so self-evident, so desirable, and, above all, so inevitable, that only fools or knaves would not see its virtues. Because liberalism was modern and permeated by the spirit of science, its dream would surely come true. Utopia was always just around the corner.

But utopia proved elusive. Many plans did not jell at all. Others, that jelled, did so only piecemeal. Still others, as the French Revolution or the Weimar Republic showed, were aborted for ends never contemplated. Democracy, perhaps the most glorious item on the agenda of liberalism, could deteriorate into mass apathy and dictatorship. A free market might mean unfettered competition. Civil rights on paper were not civil rights in practice. Free speech could be abused to abolish free speech. Liberalism's response to these frustrations was surprise and disappointment. In the face of uncertainty, hope would yield to ambiguity. Indeed, "tolerance of ambiguity" came to be celebrated as the true characteristic that set the liberal off from the doctrinaires on the Left and on the Right. And liberal man, the utopian, became a man of inaction.

The dilemma that I have been delineating stems, it seems to me, from an unresolved problem in the method of classical science, with which liberalism has so long been allied. The problem centers in the discrepancy between the concern of science with uniformities and regularities, on the one hand, and, on the other, its lack of concern with unique events. Science, in seeking to discover and account for uniformities and regularities in nature, developed laws or principles which, by definition, left unique events outside its system of explanation. Being eminently interested in the world of macrophenomena, where unique events are relatively rare, science could easily enough live with the unique events that it could not explain. They were treated as "deviant cases," and insofar as they were felt as problematic at all, it was assumed that, in due course, what appeared to be unique events would turn out to be less unique than they appeared. They would, sooner or later, take their rightful place in the regular order of the universe.

But in the world of human affairs where liberalism sought to serve as a guide to action, the same assumption could only be made at great cost. For in this world unique events not only were more frequent than in nature, but they could also less easily be suspected of being deviations from underlying regular patterns of behavior that would be identifiable if only enough events were observed. Unique events had a way of intruding in social affairs with a suddenness and intensity that tended to give them an authority of their own quite independent of whatever more inclusive set of events might be assumed to exist. In human affairs, it seems, science and its method deserted liberalism in its most fateful hours. The sense of surprise and disillusionment, nourished by its utopian component and mobilized by unique events, was the necessary consequence of liberalism's commitment to a mode of thinking only secondarily interested, if interested at all, in the unique.

No wonder that critics of liberalism, and also some liberals themselves, saw in its failure to cope with unique events the weakest link in the liberal alliance with science. If the methods of science could not serve as guides to action in crisis, what justification was there for assuming their viability under normal conditions? Some critics went further and denied the possibility of a science of human affairs, because unique events would forever escape the magnet of scientific calculation.

As long as science was predicated on deterministic presuppositions that could only cope with uniformities and regularities, these arguments did, indeed, represent a case against a science of human affairs. And they represented a case also against liberalism as an ideology that, because its modes of thought had an affinity to the methods of science, seemed to be the most suitable system of beliefs with which to make oneself comfortable in a rapidly changing world. But, I shall argue, unique events are no longer immune to scientific calculation. And if they are calculable, as more regular events are calculable, there is much hope for the future of a science of man and his works, as there is for the future of liberalism as a viable ideology. What is needed, clearly, is an accurate view of the changed focus of recent science, on the one hand, and a corresponding awareness of the implications of this focus for liberalism as an ideology.

Because liberalism has always been, in its modes of thought and orientation to the world, closely akin to science, it is necessary to appreciate those changes in recent science that have so drastically revised the scientific outlook itself. For we can assume that, after some time lag which is required to let an outlook become a part of the consciousness of a period, these changes will also be absorbed into the cognitive patterns of liberalism.

Not the least significant aspect of the transformation in the scientific view of things is the possibility of reconciling those parts of the liberal ideology that involve knowledge with those parts that involve belief. Probabilistic thinking conceives of knowledge and belief as being interrelated in a complex chain of assumption, hypothesis, and proof. In this chain there are the strong links of knowledge and the weak ones of belief. The task of science is to replace the weak links by reducing ignorance on which belief thrives. But while the older, deterministic outlook of science assumed that ignorance could be so totally abolished that belief would give way to knowledge, the probabilistic outlook assumes that there will always be an area of ignorance where action—whether that of the scientist in the laboratory or that of the decision-maker in the real world—is bound to be based on belief rather than on knowledge. By attaching the calculus of probability to its assertions of truth, modern science acknowledges the necessity of belief as a basis of behavior in those areas of inquiry where the truth value of scientific assertions remains shaded by ignorance.

This is not to say that I agree with those who find in probability a justification for a belief in "free will" as a basis of moral action. As the future is always a combination of causal influences from the past with unpredictable elements, one might well argue that there must be a field of action where "free will" has, as it were, a free rein. But this argument makes the rather fragile assumption that something called "will" can and does fill the void left by the unexplained variances of probability statements. Moreover, "will" is a rather mythical concept, and whether what it refers to is "free" or not is largely a matter of arbitrary assignment. I think it is simply a more attractive way of saying that action in an area where variances remain unexplained is largely based on belief with a rather low truth value.

Paradoxically, the modern doctrine of "free will," opposed as it is to causal determinism, claims to be supported by the Heisenberg principle of indeterminacy—the notion that the act of observation disturbs the relationships that are observed. For if, so the reasoning goes, no distinction can be made between the observer and the observed, and if the observer changes the world through his act of observation, then the observer's "will" must be paramount. But this, it seems to me, is to make improper use of the indeterminacy principle. Indeterminacy refers only to the transition from macro- to micro-phenomena; it does not refer to the transition from observations of our environment to unobserved, and therefore postulated, macro-objects. In fact, indeterminacy in quantum mechanics does not pertain to the relationship between the scientific observer and his environment. Rather, it is relevant only when the existence of micro-phenomena is to be inferred from the observed existence of macro-phenomena.

Moreover, the advocates of "free will" neglect another important aspect of the indeterminacy principle that is critical for the contemporary view of science as an exercise in probability. For though the principle asserts the existence of "uncertainty relations" because it is impossible to measure simultaneously the momentum and the position of sub-atomic elements, so that a unique correspondence might be established between them, quantum theory is able to calculate the probability with which an electron, for instance, has a certain momentum when it has a given position, and vice versa. This inherently statistical nature of atomic processes cannot be simply ignored, as it is by those who set determinism against "free will." Because the new physics is not deterministic, it does not follow that it justifies an assumption of "free will." On the contrary, Heisenberg simply held that in the measurement of large scale phenomena the effects of disturbances are sufficiently small to make the effects of observation also negligible. On the other hand, in subatomic phenomena, because of the discontinuous character of the processes involved, the relationship between the observer and the observed causes uncontrollable and sizable fluctuations in the system that make knowledge something less than certain. And because it is not certain, it calls for statistical interpretation, and its predictions must be based on a calculus of probability.

But the significant point to be made is that quantum mechanics, in shaping the new view of what science is all about, answered the question that had escaped nineteenth-century science: whether causality is an ultimate principle or whether it is only an expression of statistical regularity, perhaps applicable to macro-phenomena but not micro-objects. Quantum mechanics discovered that individual atomic events are not causally interpretable but are subject to the laws of probability. Once this was recognized, as in Heisenberg's principle, causality could only be conceived of as an idealization of the regularities evident in the macro-world of the senses. Contemporary liberalism cannot ignore this shift in the scientific outlook from causal to statistical analysis. And even if the new "if–then at certain level of confidence" does not seem to differ radically from the straight "if–then" of classical causal theory, the reformulation seems to have far-ranging consequences for how we perceive and interpret the world in which we live.

Nevertheless, there is a profound difference between the two types of thinking, and that difference lies in their varying orientation toward unique or nonrecurring events. To appreciate the difference, one must keep in mind that the statistical theory of probability is only one among several theories, and that the statistical methods of probability must be distinguished from probabilistic modes of thought in general. And while there is a good deal of disagreement among philosophers of science about the validity of various theories of probability, the pervasiveness of probabilistic thinking is the most significant fact of current orientations to reality. While the "relative frequency" or "limiting frequency" approach of statistical probability is especially useful in empirical research, in both the natural and social sciences, it leaves open the question of whether an explanation must be statistical in order to be probabilistic, or whether some event to be explained cannot be probable in a nonstatistical sense. This, of course, is a critical question in regard to the problem of a probabilistic explanation of unique events. And unique events, as I have suggested, are of particular interest because of their consequences for social and political behavior.

Just how pervasive probabilistic thinking is in our time appears from the variety of conceptions that are current in the disciplines that surround empirical science. Mathematicians have formulated what they call the "set-theoretical" approach; philosophers are concerned with "logical probability"; and, in recent years, game theorists and statistical-decision theorists have employed the notion of "subjective probability." But these different uses should not disguise the basic unity of the probabilistic mode of thought.

For an understanding of statistical probability, it is important to realize that statistical statements do not simply say that an event is invariably accompanied by the occurrence of another event. Statistical laws merely assert that, in a great number of similar situations, an event is accompanied by another with an invariable relative frequency. This means, quite simply, that though statistical and causal statements are not necessarily independent of each other, there may yet be statistical relationships that escape causal explanation. Statistical probability statements, then, are assertions that acknowledge exceptions —deviant cases—but the exceptions themselves are assumed to occur in a regular percentage of cases. While this approach has freed causality from its deterministic chains, it still leaves unanswered the problem of unique or non-recurring events.

Just what is the problem? An event is unique if it cannot be classified in a series of similar observations, a condition necessary to determine statistical probability. Especially in human affairs, both the number of known factors affecting an event and the number of unknown factors is likely to be so great that an appropriate classification of comparable events is extremely difficult, if not impossible. It is largely an act of faith to argue that, with enough ingenuity, such events can be classified. It may be possible on a sufficiently high level of abstraction, but one must ask how high this level must be in order to permit statistical treatment of the relevant events. So we are left with the vague feeling that even in spite of high levels of abstraction some events may be non-comparable and therefore unique. And if this is so, does it make sense to think of a unique event in probabilistic terms?

It is futile to argue that events, and especially human events, are either always unique or never unique. Only bitter-end historians, on the one extreme, and out-and-out "counters," on the other, might do so. It is more sensible to assume that while most events are probably not *sui generis,* some may well be. For the assumption that an event can be unique implies the corollary assumption that most events are not. The unique event derives its meaning from being located in a frame of reference that is generic. It is for just this reason that, if one wishes to keep an open mind, one cannot but assign some measure of probability, however small, to unique events. For otherwise one would have to attribute unique events to pure chance, a procedure which would mean that the idea of probability as a practical approach to action would have to be surrendered in favor of fatalism and superstition.

But how can one assign a probability number to a unique event? Can it be anything but an altogether arbitrary procedure? The answer can be found, I think, in the idea of personal or subjective probability. This conception of probability does not involve arbitrary application, because it is subject to modification as a "degree of rational belief," suggested by John Maynard Keynes in his *Treatise on Probability*. If I understand this use of the probability concept correctly, it refers to the degree of confidence that one can have in the truth of a hypothesis as a guide to action, provided some very important conditions are met. In the first place, the probability estimate is rational if one's preferences concerning alternative courses of action can be meaningfully ordered. (Such preference-ordering creates problems of its own, but we can ignore them here.) Secondly, the estimate must be sufficiently stable through time; that is, it must not be whimsical or hysterical. Finally, the estimate must be subject to change as new evidence becomes available and makes revision necessary.

If we conceive of probability in these terms, the probabilistic mode of thought does not assure the inevitable success of an action or a decision. It merely guarantees their reasonableness. The hypothesis under which decisions are made or actions are taken is not absolutely true or false, to be accepted or rejected out of hand. Though it may turn out to be correct, there remains the realization that events might have falsified the hypothesis. If it turns out to have been wrong, the failure need not be ascribed to faulty thinking, for the action was taken as rationally as was possible under given circumstances. In either case, the door is left open for new directions.

It remains to appraise the implications of probabilistic modes of thought for the cognitive stance of contemporary liberalism. It seems to me that in assigning a probability estimate to actions and events, whether repetitive or unique, the modern liberal has an opportunity to free himself from the deterministic chains of the older science. His expectations concerning the future need no longer catch the "scent of Utopia" that, perhaps more than anything else, left him ill prepared to cope with events that defied his utopian dreams. He might still assign the wrong probabilities to the hypotheses under which he must choose and act. But—and this is crucial—in freeing himself from the deterministic mood of the earlier science and in accepting the notion of probability as a degree of rational belief, he not only maintains the affinity of the liberal ideology with science, but he also reasserts the linkage of liberalism with the tradition of human rationality.

In fact, I believe that liberalism has already undergone, in the last decade or so, a subtle and profound transformation in its modes of thinking along these lines. This transformation has been so slow, so imperceptible, that even most liberals, though acting in terms of probabilistic calculations, have not realized it. It has been my intention to bring this transformation into the liberal consciousness, for I think that it augurs well for liberalism as an ideology with which one can live in facing the hazards of the future.

Chapter 19

Values and Behavioral Science: Neutrality Revisited

Contemporary behavioral science, and especially the behavioral study of politics, finds itself in a peculiarly polemical situation in regard to its relationship to values. It is being attacked, from without, by some who see in the methods and discoveries of behavioral science a threat to traditional human values, and who consider it their sacred mission to protect these values from the pernicious consequences of behavioral inquiry. Indeed, they would destroy behavioral science, if they could, and hand the study of human affairs back to speculative philosophy. On the other hand, an attack is mounted, from within, by some who criticize their fellow behavioral scientists for not orienting their work more purposefully towards curing the world's personal and social ills, and who demand that behavioral science be placed unequivocally in the service of human needs and aspirations—at least as they conceive them. In fact, they would transform behavioral science into an ideology—a program for social and political action.

That, decades after Dewey, Lynd, and Geiger,[1] the problem of the place of values in behavioral science and the function of behavioral science in the realization of human values should still be discussed in *these* terms is, if I am to be charitable, a sign of our continued intellectual immaturity in the study of man and society. If I were to be cynical, I might speak of a case of academic featherbedding. As I hope to be enlightening, I want to suggest that, to judge by the current polemics, behavioral scientists themselves have failed to articulate with sufficient candor some of the dilemmas in regard to the relationship

Originally published in *Antioch Review,* Vol. 28 (Summer, 1968), pp. 160–67. Reprinted by permission.

1. George Geiger's sensible discussion of "Values and the Social Sciences" can be found in chapter 8 of his *Philosophy and the Social Order* (Boston: Houghton Mifflin, 1947).

between values and behavioral science for which, at least at present, no ready solutions exist, but which, for just this reason, seem to disturb the equanimity of the critics.

Paradoxically, though they come to quite opposite conclusions and offer quite different remedies for what they diagnose as the disease, both types of critic share the same mistaken conception of the "value problem" in behavioral science. In a nutshell, both allege that behavioral scientists are insensitive to values, and both attribute this alleged insensitivity to what they declare to be the commitment of behavioral scientists to "value neutrality." This conception is so far off the mark that one's first inclination is to ignore it and go on with one's work. And the huge majority of behavioral scientists are doing just that —and thereby heightening the furor, and the frustration, of the critics. But, on second thought, some comment seems to be called for, on two accounts. First, even though the various criticisms, in the terms in which they are voiced, fail to draw blood, they convey an altogether erroneous image of behavioral science. And second, silence in the matter would undoubtedly be interpreted as confirming the critics' claim of ethical pussyfooting and social irresponsibility on the part of behavioral scientists.

It is my contention that the real situation in which behavioral science finds itself vis-à-vis values is just the contrary of what its critics perceive it to be. Granted, for argument's sake, that the relationship between values and behavioral science is a problem, it is so not because behavioral scientists are insensitive to values, but because, on being increasingly involved in questions of social and public policy, they have become hypersensitive to values. As behavioral scientists have been ever more frequently called upon for advice and recommendations in practical affairs, they have also learned that it is quite easy to burn their scientific fingers in the cauldron of social and political controversies.

Because behavioral scientists are hypersensitive rather than insensitive to values in their work, the relationship between values and behavioral science is, indeed, a live issue; but it is so in a sense quite different from that experienced during the earlier "pragmatic revolt" in the social sciences. The issue, clearly, is not "value neutrality" in the traditional meaning of the term. I doubt that today even the most positivistic of positivists—say a pure mathematician—would take the position that science is or can be "value-free." That science, and behavioral science in particular, no matter how remote apparently from immediate actualities, must serve some socially useful purpose is no longer denied; and such denial is not the issue, even though the critics of behavioral science talk as if it were.

It is agreed, therefore, that values enter behavioral inquiry at many points and in many forms: in the selection and formulation of problems for research, in the choice of what are deemed to be the significant variables, in the interpretation of research findings, in the application of behavioral knowledge to questions of public policy, as cultural determinants of meanings, as standards of professional conduct and as professional goals, as substantive topics worthy of inquiry in their own right and, last but not least, as biases. It seems to me, therefore, that the critics of behavioral science, in once again demanding the abandonment of the notion of "value neutrality," are in pursuit of a ghost, for the notion of "value neutrality" does not refer to anything that exists or, for that matter, ever existed in the social sciences.

Yet, after all this has been said and acknowledged, it does not follow that problems do not exist. And it does not follow that these problems can be simply thought away—as the speculative philosopher would have it—or that they can be turned into virtue—as the behavioral ideologue would like to do. Take, for instance, "value bias" which remains a perennial danger in scientific work on human behavior. It refers to those decisional premises that orient scientific research. Of course, only a scientist not devoted to truth and objectivity as professional standards or goals would consciously and purposefully cultivate biases stemming from prior commitment to the interests of race, class, religion, ideology, tribe or nation. But such biases have a way of entering scientific work as latent and often unconscious forces. I would think it utopian to assume, as some earlier positivists did assume, that value bias can be easily eliminated by some act of scientific will. But I do believe that if "value neutrality" is construed not as an absolute end but as an instrument of observation, it may be useful because it calls attention to just that function which the term "neutrality" conveys: that we seek to "neutralize" our biases by bringing them as much as possible into the open or, if they remain latent, by treating them as "errors" which can be isolated and discounted in very much the same way as we allow for other errors of observation, sampling, measurement or inference characteristic of all scientific work. In this functional sense, then, "value neutrality" does not mean self-deception that value biases do not exist or can be easily banned from the scientific process, but it suggests the discovery of techniques which make possible the self-conscious neutralization of biases and an increase of the level of confidence in the results of behavioral science.

Value neutralization must not be confused with value neutralism. If by the latter one means scientific indifference to values, it is not only impossible, but also undesirable. For such value neutralism would be the very opposite of the kind of judiciousness in regard to values which the quest for neutralization, as I have sketched it, implies. If fact, indifference to values, as the term "value neutralism" suggests, is counter to the ideals of science. On the other hand, rejection of neutralism can also not mean that behavioral science is, or must be, somehow subservient to values. The problem of the relationship between values and behavioral science is such, it seems to me, that balanced judgment—what I have just referred to as judiciousness—be desirable. This judiciousness may be activated as a norm of conduct to guide the scientist's behavior in the research process and, as I shall indicate, in what follows the research.

It is important to remember that there are many other such norms in the culture of science. Truth, objectivity, honesty or integrity are values that serve as norms of conduct that the scientist seeks to live by, just as he must insist on freedom of inquiry if he wishes to function effectively as a scientist. No one has ever believed that these norms are self-fulfilling, and though their observance has been enforced with considerable success by the scientific community, their violation is by no means an impossibility. I would argue, therefore, that judiciousness vis-à-vis values can also serve as a standard of conduct, provided its meaning is clarified and the conditions of its activation are specified. To treat it otherwise—to label it "value neutrality" and then invoke all the familiar arguments against that notion—would be to prejudge what is as yet to be defined.

Perhaps we should ask, at this point, why it is that such values as truth or objectivity have proved to be so acceptable to the scientific community as norms of professional conduct. My answer is that they proved useful, and were therefore acceptable. For they permitted the scientist to move ahead with the task of conquering the unknown. In other words, while often treated as if they were some absolute ends in themselves, they never were. Perhaps no better example exists of the pragmatic contention that values are instrumental, that they make sense not as articles of faith, but only as links in a chain of means and ends that is a continuum and has no ultimate end—links that are interchangeable as means are treated, for some purposes, as ends, and as ends are treated, for other purposes, as means. For the scientist, then, truth and objectivity are instruments in his quest for knowledge.

It seems to me that the notion of "value neutrality," understood as the cultivation of a judicious attitude towards values, has never been given a chance. Put differently, its instrumental character has never been properly explored. The battle once waged over the place of values in the social sciences, and the battle which some critics of modern behavioral science are once again trying to wage, has treated "value neutrality" as if it were some ultimate, absolute end which either had to be embraced altogether or rejected altogether. But if it is so treated, it is only an abstraction—an abstraction, I agree, that can serve no good purpose and should be banned from discourse about the ethics of science. On the other hand, if it conceived instrumentally as a norm of scientific behavior, even if honored in the breach as much as in the practice, it will no longer be necessary to make the problem of the relationship between values and behavioral science a matter of faith. It is, I think, the methodological virtue of the instrumental standpoint that it provides for just those intellectual operations that allow us to clarify the relationship. For if values are treated instrumentally, our attention is focused on their functions, and their functions point to the context in which values guide behavior.

What, then, is the context in which "value neutrality," as a norm of judicious conduct with regard to values, may be activated? I think it is just that point in the process of inquiry where that process reaches its (always tentative) termination—the point, in other words, at which the findings of behavioral research come within the purview of the public, indeed become "public property." At this point, the behavioral scientist faces two dilemmas at once. First, he may come to realize that the findings of his research contravene the values that guided his inquiry, and possibly even values which are widely cherished by the public. And second, he may discover that there is nothing in his work that prevents its being used for social purposes of which he disapproves. He may voice his disapproval, and he must do so if his conscience dicates it. But in neither case does he have easy options. He cannot maintain that his scientific findings invalidate values, nor can he object to misuse of his findings, on the ground that his science has at its disposal a knowledge of good and evil, of right and wrong, of justice and injustice. To make this claim would violate the norm of value judiciousness. He can only seek to balance as judiciously as possible what his scientific work reveals and what his value position demands.

Yet, those critics who speak of "value neutrality" as an absolute ignore the fact that such dilemmas exist in the relationship between values and behavioral science, and they ignore the context in which these dilemmas arise. And not only do they ignore the dilemmas, but they deny them out of existence by a kind of preventive mental therapy of good intentions which assumes that "right" values can somehow be derived from the very processes of behavior which behavioral science investigates. Once derived, these values would have such compelling force that they cannot but be accepted by all men—at least by all men of "good will." Non-acceptance would have to be ascribed to sheer perversion, or at least blindness to the benign benefits which behavioral science as the new dispensation can bring to all mankind. To buttress the argument, these advocates of behavioral science as the cure-all of personal and social ills usually rest their case on one or another catalogue of "fundamental human needs," discoverable, if not discovered already, by behavioral science. The satisfaction of these needs becomes a self-evident proposition, and the "scientific ideology of human behavior," as one might label it, is born.

A lengthy discussion of this argument would lead us too far afield. Suffice it to say, therefore, that even if the epistemological and methodological problems involved in deriving values from human needs could be solved, there is at present little agreement among behavioral scientists as to just what human needs are "fundamental." And there is a good deal of disagreement as to the priority of needs which a catalogue of needs might list. The difficulty is, of course, that any ordering of needs is impossible without an ordering of preferences—which brings us back to where we started from, namely the non-instrumental, absolutist position that values constitute a hierarchy rather than a chain of means and ends.

To express all this by way of the medical analogy, the diagnosis (of which behavioral science is quite capable) is one thing, but the therapy is another. Even if there were consensus on the nature of "social diseases" (which is difficult to obtain, but possible), there is unlikely to be a similar consensus on the steps that should be taken to remedy these diseases or on the order in which such steps might be taken. The notion that behavioral science can provide the criteria for a program of social or political therapy is, at most, an article of faith in a catechism of Utopia; but it has very little to do with contemporary reality.

In the reality with which behavioral science is concerned—the context in which a psychology of mental processes may be abused for the purposes of political manipulation, a sociology of small-group functioning may serve the purpose of union busting, a political science of legislative operations may be exploited to thwart majority rule, or an anthropology of kinship structures may be employed to justify demagogic leadership, and so on—the scientist's dilemmas cannot be solved by magic formulas. This is the context from which there is, at least at present, no escape. But it is also the context in which the notion of "value neutrality"—meaning judiciousness in the matter of balancing the findings of behavioral science and values—must be explicated.

I can only hint at what "value neutrality" in this specific sense of the term implies. I think that it serves to sensitize the behavioral scientist to the fact that he serves two masters: social values and scientific values. His science demands of him a maximum of truth and objectivity as means to scientific knowledge. Social purpose demands of him that he see to it that the consumers of his knowledge use it with a maximum of realism and rationality. One cannot expect more of him. My point is that these two masters are not at loggerheads, that they need not make mutually contradictory demands on the scientist. For I believe that the scientist's commitment to social purposes can best be implemented if he serves well the demands of science, and he can best serve the demands of science if he demonstrates judiciousness in regard to the multiple uses to which his scientific knowledge may be put.

While behavioral science is mute as to the values which policy may seek to implement, the behavioral scientist can bring to bear on these policy problems those insights of conditions and consequences which are the proper domain of his science. Those who find this muteness disturbing—though, let me emphasize, it has nothing to do with "value neutralism" as I have used the term—are mistaken if they attack behavioral science for being insensitive to values. For this muteness, in the post-pragmatic era, does and cannot mean what "value neutrality" was once meant to mean, but it is only evidence of the behavioral scientist's sensitivity to the mutual implications of the dual quest for scientific knowledge and social utility, and to the dilemmas that arise out of this quest. It is the peculiar function of behavioral science as a "policy science," to borrow Harold D. Lasswell's term, that it mediates, through judicious efforts of valuation, the tensions which occur only all too often in the two-way passage from science to values and from values to science. If anything, then, "value neutrality" can only mean today that there are dilemmas to be solved that the two-way passage occasions, not that solutions are to be prejudged.

Chapter 20

The Behavioral Movement in Political Science: A Personal Document

To those who in the years immediately following World War II were dissatisfied with the state of political science and groping for a new beginning in the study of politics, the future was all promises although the present looked dim indeed. Today it is fashionable to speak of the "behavioral revolution" as if there had been some kind of well-organized plan, if not plot, to remake the established order, or at least spontaneous and widespread discontent at the grass roots of the discipline. Nothing could be further from reality. On the contrary, the movers and shakers of those years were lonely and isolated young men in quest of something that they vaguely felt was needed, perhaps more cocky than their accomplishments-to-date warranted, and confident that things could not possibly get worse. But they were lonely and isolated, surrounded by colleagues who were mostly indifferent. The hostility came later.

They were lonely and isolated, but they were not alienated. This, in retrospect, is probably the main reason why this generation finally succeeded in changing and shaping the outlook of the discipline, in creating and producing something new in the study of politics. Had they been alienated, they could have found refuge in the neighboring disciplines of sociology or social psychology where the contemporary discontent seemed to have more opportunity

Originally published in *Social Research,* Vol. 35 (Spring, 1968), pp. 1–29. Reprinted by permission.

for fermentation. Some, in fact, deserted political science. But most stuck to the discipline and brought about not so much a revolution as a renaissance.[1]

Adding just another article of the formal and impersonal kind to the already long list of articles describing, analyzing, praising or denouncing the behavioral movement in political science, would give little satisfaction, and the reader would be little served. For what might be said has been said elsewhere and perhaps said better.[2] Because this is a rather dull prospect, I want to bring back to life what it meant to have experienced the renaissance in political science. There is good reason for doing this. That, in due time, the "new men" found some common ground, that there was a convergence, was less of their own making than due to the situation they all encountered. Most articles tend to look back on the intellectual ferment of the post-war years from the perspective of the common ground that finally emerged. Much more interesting, however, is the intellectual odyssey of any one of us who lived through these years. For all of us had not only similar but also very different experiences. We had different intellectual backgrounds, we went to different schools, we were in different fields, we eventually belonged to different "circles," we had different temperaments—in short, we were a quite heterogeneous lot.

There is a memorable passage in a young intellectual rebel's recollection about the teaching of politics at Harvard *circa* 1908. This is what Walter Lippmann wrote:[3]

> When I first attended college lectures on politics it was not considered necessary to discuss the politician. Occasionally he was mentioned in a dim sort of way, but always as if he were an intruder who did not fit in and was soon destined to disappear. The boss and the district leader, the caucus and the conference, spoils and deals were regarded as belonging to the pathology of politics. There was no place for these perversions. We studied the unperverted political system as it was presumed to exist in a platonic heaven before it fell to earth and was embodied in such gross and unmentionable persons as Charles Murphy and Honey Fitz.

1. This theme is more fully developed in an essay entitled "Tradition and Innovation: On the Tension between Ancient and Modern Ways in the Study of Politics," in Heinz Eulau, Ed., *Behavioralism in Political Science* (New York: Atherton Press, 1969).

2. See David B. Truman, "The Impact on Political Science of the Revolution in the Behavioral Sciences," in *Research Frontiers in Politics and Government* (Washington, D.C.: Brookings Institution, 1955), pp. 202–231; Robert A. Dahl, "The Behavioral Approach in Political Science: Epitaph for a Monument to a Successful Protest," *American Political Science Review*, 55 (December, 1961), pp. 763–772; Evron M. Kirkpatrick, "The Impact of the Behaviroral Approach on Traditional Political Science," in Austin Ranney, Ed., *Essays on the Behavioral Study of Politics* (Urbana: University of Illinois Press, 1962), pp. 1–29; David Easton, "The Current Meaning of 'Behavioralism' in Political Science," in James C. Charlesworth, Ed., *Contemporary Political Analysis* (New York: Free Press, 1967), pp. 11–31; Albert Somit and Joseph Tanenhaus, "Political Science as a Learned Discipline: Behavioralism," in *The Development of American Political Science* (Boston: Allyn and Bacon, 1967), pp. 173–194; Heinz Eulau, "Political Behavior," *International Encyclopaedia of the Social Sciences* (New York: Macmillan and Free Press, 1968).

3. Walter Lippmann, "Politics for Politicians," *New Republic*, 32 (October 25, 1922), pp. 17–18.

Our textbooks on politics maintained a splendid isolation from the haunts and manners of the politician. They were written by men who believed that the undifferentiated voter was the center of the political system because it had been said at the beginning that this was a government founded on the consent of the governed. But this undifferentiated voter, like his cousin, the economic man, was an excessively inhuman creature. He was pure brain. He was reason incarnate. He was a universal robot, deduced mechanically from the Theory of Party Function in a Democracy.

I cannot remember whether I came across this passage while still in college or graduate school, but it does not matter. For what Lippmann had written of Harvard in the first decade was pretty much what I found as a student in the fourth decade. What brings most young students to the study of politics is a passion for politics. To find out that political science is often remote from the vital controversies and urgent needs of the day is an experience that every generation is likely to have. But this is only one part of the story. The other part has to do with the discovery of why this is the case. And this discovery is that political science, if taken seriously as a science, has no easy answers that might cure the world's social and political ills, and that there are reasons inherent in the scientific enterprise that make it appear remote from the burning issues of the times.

The undergraduate years did not have much of a direct impact on my later discontent with the discipline, though they prepared the ground. Like most young men in the 'thirties I read Marx, and though I was not untouched by what he had to say, especially about the importance of social class relations in politics and economics, I was not impressed by the scientific pretensions of the Marxian analysis. It was clear enough that Marx's "science of society" was a perversion of what I had learned science to be all about. Nevertheless, it would be quite dishonest to deny that Marx sensitized me to the significance of social structure, and years later I wrote a book about voting behavior in which social class served as the critical variable.[4] That I did not swallow the dialectic hook, line and sinker prevented all kinds of intellectual and personal unpleasantries that some others encountered in due time. I never had to live Marx down, and I, therefore, never had to regret my interest in the phenomenon of social class in politics.

Having been exposed to Marx made it all the more surprising, when I became a graduate student, that political science seemed so little concerned with problems of scientific method—at least at my university. That there was more concern elsewhere—at Chicago, for instance, where Charles Merriam had called attention to "new aspects of politics"—I did not know.[5] In any case, I

4. See Heinz Eulau, *Class and Party in the Eisenhower Years* (New York: The Free Press, 1962).

5. See Charles E. Merriam, *New Aspects of Politics* (Chicago: University of Chicago Press, 1925).

cannot remember one seminar where problems of scientific method were raised, and I suppose that this omission was not atypical of the situation in most universities. In politics, American or comparative, the accent was on accurate historical description of institutions; in public law it was on the logic of legal discourse; and in international relations it was on gut reactions to current events which were mostly deplored as unfortunate, or on dreams of world order.

Political science seemed dead and dull. Yet some thoughts had come to crystallize. One was that political science should be true to life, but that life was not to be had by reading Plato or St. Augustine. The funny thing was that we never read Plato or St. Augustine. Rather, what we read were summary regurgitations of the classical texts. It made little difference anyhow. Political theory, as history of political ideas, was an autonomous field that had little to do with what went on in the other fields, and no effort was made to make it relevant. How delighted I was many years later when I came to read the first book of *Leviathan!* Or when I first actually read *The Prince*, which radically changed my view of Machiavelli! As Robert Lane made clear to me then, the systems of the classical theorists were "peopled"—an insight now commonplace but certainly not self-evident in all the talk about "sovereignty" or "social contract" that we had in college.[6]

The other thought was that even though political science might never rival the physical sciences in exactitude, it deserved a better fate than it was doomed to have if nothing was done about its status as a science. Just what precipitated this line of thinking is hard to recall, but I vividly remember looking one day at the list of new acquisitions posted in the library and noticing a book called *The Structure of Social Action* by Talcott Parsons. This was in 1937. The title sounded intriguing, for "social action" was much in the air. Little did I suspect what the book was all about, but I remember reading it and nothing else for a week. Although I did not come out of this experience as either an actionist or a Parsonian, I was suddenly aware of names I had never heard of in the political science courses—Durkheim, Pareto and Weber, above all Weber. Actually, I had heard of Weber in an undergraduate ethics course where the professor had talked about his *The Protestant Ethic and the Spirit of Capitalism*. But that was in philosophy; in political science Weber was unknown.[7] I was much impressed by the notion of "ideal types" as a tool of analysis, and when I came to write my doctoral dissertation, Weber's concept of "ideal types," though I misunderstood it, was very much with me and caused some concern to the dissertation readers.

6. Robert E. Lane, "Political Character and Political Analysis," *Psychiatry*, 16 (November, 1953), pp. 387–398.

7. I am not certain about Weber's influence on the other social sciences in this country, but in political science his work was not widely known before 1946 when H. H. Gerth and C. Wright Mills published *From Max Weber: Essays in Sociology* (New York: Oxford University Press, 1946).

Marx, Weber–and Dewey. I had come across his *Liberalism and Social Action* when it was published in 1935. While it was not his best book, it was provocative enough to search for more. I read *The Public and Its Problems* (1927) and *The Quest for Certainty* (1930). And so a vaguely felt positivism was married in my mind to pragmatism–an unholy wedlock, to be sure, and a source of intellectual tension to this day, but a happening, to use a fashionable phrase, that kept me from being either an extremist positivist or an extremist pragmatist in the debate over values and science.[8] When, in 1939, Robert Lynd published his *Knowledge for What?*, it struck home. Lynd articulated what I had come to feel all along: that social science should deal with life, that it should deal with problems, and that it should be scientific. I did not realize then how difficult it would be to be true to these three commandments at once. One has to learn that the pursuit of one objective might, for a time, preclude the pursuit of another. But the general direction toward the behavioral study of politics was set in these prewar years in the way I have described.

There were, of course, other intellectual events as well. Harold Lasswell had come to lecture, and though I was not sure as to what he was all about, he made an impression. Surely, I had to find out about psychology. In Egon Brunswik I found a truly stimulating teacher. I audited two of his courses as a graduate student–one on "The History of Psychology," the other on "Modern Theories of Psychology." I learned about Freud, and though I did not pursue his writings until later, I recognized his relevance to political science. Of more immediate impact was Kurt Lewin whose essay on "The Conflict between Aristotelian and Galileian Modes of Thought in Contemporary Psychology" has influenced my thinking ever since.[9] I still recommend it to students in search of certainty.

The other major influence was Frederick J. Teggart, the sociological historian, something of an iconoclast and academic *enfant terrible* at the university, but a wonderful antidote to the sterile historicism of political science. The notion that it is the task of history as a discipline to explain "how things have come to be what they are," struck me as eminently sensible, and I have always found it more interesting to read history backward rather than forward. Later, after I had read Karl Mannheim and become familiar with the sociology of knowledge, the exposure to Teggart's approach to history made even more sense.[10]

The point, in recounting this early intellectual development, is not to sug-

8. I have tried to articulate the distinction between value neutrality, value neutralism and value neutralization in the Introduction to *Political Behavior in America: New Directions* (New York: Random House, 1966), pp. 9–13.

9. The essay is most easily available in Kurt Lewin, *A Dynamic Theory of Personality* (New York: McGraw-Hill, 1935), pp. 1–42.

10. Teggart's work is now accessible in a paperback, *Theory and Processes of History* (Berkeley: University of California Press, 1960), which includes two books published in 1918 and 1925. For Mannheim, see *Ideology and Utopia* (New York: Harcourt, Brace, 1946).

gest that the behavioral approaches are rooted exclusively in Marx, Weber, Dewey or Lewin, or any other particular social theorist. On the contrary, it is to emphasize that this was my route and that, undoubtedly, other political behaviorists came to the common enterprise by other intellectual routes. At Chicago, I know from Harold Lasswell, philosophers like George Herbert Mead or Alfred North Whitehead loomed large in theoretical thinking about politics.[11] At Illinois, the name and work of Arthur F. Bentley were honored and more influential than elsewhere.[12] When, years later, my colleagues and I wrote that "in general, the political behavior approach has been essentially catholic and eclectic," we meant just that.[13] To speak of the "behavioral movement" as if it had been or were an intellectually homogeneous or ideologically disciplined undertaking is simply wrong.[14] There were, in due time, convergences; but there were many divergences that, in fact, made for the vitality of the developments after the second world war.

II

The direction had been set in graduate school, if without the benefit of much guidance from my teachers in political science. I am grateful to some of them, for though they may have looked askance at my deviant ways, they did not actively discourage them. But it was Harold Lasswell who became the decisive influence.

In June, 1941, when I was issued my walking papers by the university, properly certified as a Ph.D., there were no teaching jobs to be had—at least none of the kind I might have cared for. By that time, Herbert Simon had arrived from Chicago, full of revolutionary ideas about the study of public administration and fuller still of the ideas of Chester I. Barnard whose *The Functions of the Executive* (1938) had only recently been published. I could not guess then that, several years later, Simon's *Administrative Behavior* (1947) would so forcefully challenge the public administration fraternity. Simon was the first Chicagoan I had come to know reasonably well; and in short order he wrote to Lasswell, Lasswell wrote to me, and four weeks later I was a research associate (at a salary better than that of an assistant professor and not to be sneezed at after the many lean depression years) at Lasswell's "Experimental Division for the Study of War Time Communications" which he had set up at the Library of Congress.

11. See Heinz Eulau, "The Maddening Methods of Harold D. Lasswell," *Journal of Politics,* 30 (February, 1968).

12. Arthur F. Bentley, *The Process of Government—A Study of Social Pressures* (Chicago: Univerisity of Chicago Press, 1908).

13. Heinz Eulau, Samuel J. Eldersveld and Morris Janowitz, Eds., *Political Behavior: A Reader in Theory and Research* (Glencoe: The Free Press, 1956), p. 4.

14. This is the main reason, I think, why the attack on political behavior research by Leo Strauss and his students has so totally failed to be convincing. See Herbert J. Storing, Ed., *Essays on the Scientific Study of Politics* (New York: Holt, Rinehart and Winston, 1962).

What we did, in essence, was apply the Lasswellian "value categories" to content analyses of international communications in the world press.[15] For reasons not quite clear to me, I found myself reading Latin American newspapers and trying to make sense of the Lasswellian vocabulary, which was all new to me. It meant lonely evenings reading Lasswell's *Psychopathology and Politics* (1930), *World Politics and Personal Insecurity* (1935), *Politics, Who Gets What, When, How* (1936), and whatever else was recommended to me. During the day, fed up with content analysis, I often escaped to the nearby Congress and Supreme Court (in seven university years I had never been inside a legislature, a court room or even a party rally; nobody had told me at school that such exposure might be of some interest or use to a budding political scientist). But doing Lasswell's work by day and reading his stuff at night for about six months had a profound effect on my thinking and doing. The thinking had to do with understanding Lasswell's extraordinarily subtle and complex formulations of the political process; the doing involved a commitment to empirical research from which I never recovered.

Moreover, the seemingly endless coding, all the pluses for strength and the minuses for weakness in the flow of symbols, and the poring over Lasswellian prose were richly rewarded by the company that Lasswell was keeping at the Library of Congress. He had assembled a research team of young men, including anthropologists, psychologists, sociologists and political scientists, almost all of whom were to influence the course of behavioral science after the war. Among the political scientists and political sociologists were David Truman, Ithiel Pool, Alexander George, Edward Shils, Nathan Leites, Bruce Lannes Smith, Morris Janowitz, Sebastian de Grazia and others. From Shils, walking me under an inevitable umbrella down Pennsylvania Avenue, I heard about Toennies, Simmel, Mannheim and other European sociologists I had never heard of. From Leites, giving a seminar in a language that combined Freud and Lasswell and was at first quite incomprehensible, I heard about the relevance of culture and personality for political science. From Janowitz, then and later, I learned all kinds of things, but above all that social organizations and institutions need not be the disembodied things I had studied in college.

It is always idle to speculate about what would have happened if . . . . For instance, what my intellectual development would have been if I had not been in Washington during those war years? But whatever, being forced to and being gradually able to talk in the language of social science rather than of political science certainly made a difference. The Lasswell set was of course not the only group of social scientists in Washington. One met economists from OPA or WPB (at dinner in the old Brookings building on Jackson Square), sociologists and social psychologists from FCC, OWI or OSS (at cocktail parties, of course). It was a strange and exciting world that had

15. For the work of Lasswell's "Experimental Division," see Harold D. Lasswell, Nathan Leites and Associates, *Language of Politics: Studies in Quantitative Semantics* (New York: George W. Stewart, 1949).

opened up, a period of eye-opening for those who had come from the universities. What academic compartmentalization had made difficult in the university was a matter of ease in wartime Washington. Individual scholarship yielded to team research and disciplinary isolation to interdisciplinary collaboration. These were years of liberation from the strait jacket that was called "discipline." We stopped defining ourselves and worked on problems. In a book published after the war, *Human Relations in a Changing World: Observations on the Use of the Social Sciences* (1949), Alexander H. Leighton wrote the postscript to the common experience.

Harold Lasswell had anticipated the interdisciplinary thrust of the Washington years in the prewar essay entitled "General Framework: Person, Personality, Group, Culture," which appeared in a 1939 issue of *Psychiatry*.[16] Here, it seemed then as it does now, was a bold and imaginative design for integrating social science knowledge about individual, society and culture. At the time I did not appreciate the enormous theoretical and methodological difficulties that stand in the way of linking micro and macro units, just as I did not appreciate the problems of reduction and construction that are involved in moving from one level of analysis to another. What I did understand was Lasswell's sensitivity to the problem of the "standpoint of the observer." Many years later, when I came to write a little book on political behavior, Lasswell's essay still served as guide, and I acknowledged my indebtedness by dedicating the book to him.[17]

It was impossible to move in the Lasswellian environment without having to come to grips with Freud, and I was soon immersed in Freudian psychology. Much has been made of the early Lasswell's orthodox Freudian approach, but Lasswell was too much of a pragmatist to be genuinely orthodox for very long. Pragmatism as a philosophy of action is so deeply rooted in the American milieu that one becomes a pragmatist even without having read Peirce, James or Dewey. Lasswell had read them, and their pluralistic, empirical, experimental and tolerant mood of pragmatism not even the persuasiveness of the Freudian argument could overcome.[18] Confronted with the pragmatic paradigm, the Freudian psychology is both too simple and too complex. Its simple components are so common-sensical as to discourage empirical research; and its complex components are empirically not researchable, especially where mass behavior rather than individual behavior is concerned. As political science is more concerned with the former than with the latter, Freudian psychology has never been as influential in the study of politics as more socially oriented psychological theories. Nevertheless, I came to be quite convinced that, at

16. This essay was reprinted in Harold D. Lasswell, *The Analysis of Political Behavior* (New York: Oxford University Press, 1948), pp. 195–234.

17. See Heinz Eulau, *The Behavioral Persuasion in Politics* (New York: Random House, 1963).

18. See Lasswell's "Afterthoughts: Thirty Years Later," in the new edition of *Psychopathology and Politics* (New York: Viking Press, 1960), pp. 269–319.

least in the early stages of research, free-associational thought is just as significant for social science as is logic. Years later, after reading Jacques Hadamard's *The Psychology of Invention in the Mathematical Field,*[19] I appreciated the Freudian technique of thinking all the more.

III

When, after the war, I found a teaching job at a small liberal arts college, I inherited courses with the conventional labels–American Government, Public Administration, Political Theory, Comparative Government, and so on. But what was I really to teach? I could not possibly teach what I had been taught. I was on my own. Fortunately, the college was "progressive" and "experimental." This meant I could do what I wanted to do; but wanting to do something is one thing, doing it another. This was in 1947, and there were hardly any materials in the literature of political science that could be of help. The obstacles to teaching politics from a behavioral perspective seemed almost insurmountable. In fact, should I teach political science at all? What was political science anyway? I could make a case for social science, but I was quite sure that political science, as it had come down in the old textbooks, would not "send" the group of superb veterans, many of my own age, who had returned to college asking for more than the same.

I still marvel today at the fare that I offered in those first few years of teaching. It was a most incredible potpourri of readings. We read Abram Kardiner's *The Psychological Frontiers of Society* (1945), Erich Fromm's *Escape from Freedom* (1941), Alexander Leighton's *The Governing of Men* (1946), J. C. Flugel's *Man, Morals and Society* (1945), Ruth Benedict's *The Chrysanthemum and the Sword* (1946), the Lynds' *Middletown in Transition* (1937), F. S. C. Northrop's *The Logic of the Sciences and the Humanities* (1947), Laura Thompson's *Culture in Crisis: A Study of the Hopi Indians* (1950), W. Lloyd Warner's *Democracy in Jonesville* (1949), and of course, Lasswell. It was not a consistent fare, but it was a stimulating one. Some of my students wandered off into sociology, social psychology and anthropology in graduate school, but some stuck to political science and became innovators in the discipline–among them David Apter, Fred Greenstein and Daniel Goldrich. I cannot claim having taught them anything, for I was learning as they were learning. But I think the reading made a difference and had some impact on later developments.

These were busy years of teaching, and there was little time for research. I talked empiricism in the class room but did scarcely anything concrete. In part this was because, like most of our generation, I had not been trained to do anything other than "library research." I had only the vaguest notions about sampling and statistics; I had never written a questionnaire nor done a system-

19. (Princeton: Princeton University Press, 1945).

atic interview. The time had come to catch up and retool as all of our generation had to do if we were to undertake behavioral research in politics. In 1951-1952 a grant from the recently established Ford Foundation made possible a year of stocktaking and new learning. I settled down to statistics and survey research. I went to Chicago, Ann Arbor, Berkeley and elsewhere to find out what was going on. Things were going on–what David Truman later called "the impact on political science of the revolution in the behavioral sciences" was in full swing.

When I returned to teaching in 1952-1953, some wonderful things seemed to have happened in political science. For once there were books written by political scientists that one did not have to be ashamed of. Gabriel Almond had written *The American People and Foreign Policy* (1950), and Lasswell had published, in collaboration with Abraham Kaplan, *Power and Society* (1950). David Truman's *The Governmental Process* had come out in 1951 and was soon followed by David Easton's *The Political System* (1953) and Robert A. Dahl's and Charles E. Lindblom's *Politics, Economics and Welfare* (1953). Most of these books did not report hard-nosed empirical research, but they breathed fresh theoretical air into the discipline. The political sociologists had also become active, and one could now use such "readers" as *Public Opinion and Communication* (1950) by Bernard Berelson and Morris Janowitz, or *Class, Status and Power* (1953) by Reinhard Bendix and S. M. Lipset. And there were some manifestoes in the journals. Oliver Garceau made recommendations on "Research in the Political Process." [20] Morton Grodzins surveyed the changing focus in "Public Administration and the Science of Human Relations." [21] A Committee on Political Behavior set up by the Social Science Research Council issued its first report on "Research in Political Behavior." [22] Avery Leiserson added his voice with "Problems of Methodology in Political Research." [23] All of these books and articles found their way into the classroom.

It was about this time that most of the profession's indifference turned into hostility. In retrospect, it was not what the behaviorists were doing but rather what they were thought to be threatening that occasioned ridicule or rebuff. It was also the mystery of numbers ("mere counters" was a favorite expression of the opponents), the new language with its strange concepts, and the more generous research funds in support of behavioral research that aroused opposition. The behaviorists, it was said, were dealing in trivialities (like "voting behavior"); they were alleged to be unconcerned with "values"; they ignored "institutions." Most of these charges were silly, and most of the lament was uninformed, diffuse or suspicious. It caused all kinds of unnecessary confusion.

20. *American Political Science Review,* 45 (March, 1951), pp. 69–85.
21. *Public Administration Review,* 9 (Spring, 1951), pp. 88–102.
22. *American Political Science Review,* 46 (December, 1952), pp. 1003–1032.
23. *Political Science Quarterly,* 68 (December, 1953), pp. 558–584.

I remember a man coming up to me at a publisher's cocktail party with the aggressive question—"now, in one clean sentence, tell me what this behaviorism is all about?"—and then telling me what it was all about.

Groups of like-minded scholars, often united by bonds of personal friendship, began to emerge. Whether the "Chicagoans" like V. O. Key, Almond, Truman, Simon, Pool, Leiserson or the de Grazias saw themselves as collective carriers of the creed I cannot tell, but they were perceived as a "group" by others. The SSRC Committee on Political Behavior had been purposefully instituted and provided research leadership. The SSRC Committee on Comparative Politics, established somewhat later and chaired by Almond, developed its own research programs and came to have an enormous influence on the study of the new nations. I found myself in contact with men who, at one time or another, were connected with the Survey Research Center at Michigan—including Samuel J. Eldersveld, Dwaine Marvick, Morris Janowitz, Warren Miller, Robert Lane, James C. Davies and others. Going to professional meetings and conferences increasingly meant having contact and conversation with those moving and shaking the discipline.

But the "renaissance" was intellectual and not organizational. In fact, if there was a "policy," it was non-political. I never heard talk about "taking over the establishment" or secession from the American Political Science Association. I remember a conversation with the late Morton Grodzins in the early 'fifties in which he emphatically argued against separatism and advised us to do our empirical work and not let ourselves be derailed from research by time-consuming organizational shenanigans. The burden of proof would be on the work accomplished; if it turned out to be good, it would find acceptance on its merits.

The pattern of acceptance was strange, however. It began in the mid-'fifties. Perhaps seeing the handwriting on the wall, several university departments decided to have their "own" behaviorist. Harold Lasswell would undoubtedly call this strategy "restriction by partial incorporation." It was apparently thought that having a single behaviorist around would (a) show the intellectual tolerance of the department and its "progressive" spirit, and (b) effectively protect the department from further inroads of dangerous thoughts. In short, an attempt was made to make a "field" out of political behavior, and by making it a field restrict its spread to the older fields. Sometimes the local behaviorist, usually hired after much argument, played along, largely because the situation did not seem propitious for doing otherwise. More often than not he was an "Americanist," for it was on American data that political behavior research was initially nurtured and nourished. But, whatever else it may have been, it was not a field—it was an approach, a method, an orientation, a "mood," as Dahl has called it, or a "persuasion," as I have called it. But a method, mood or approach does not make an academic field, and it does not allow itself to be restricted to a single field. Soon comparative politics, international politics and public law would be permeated by the new methods and ideas. Departments discovered that there were more behaviorists around than they had bargained for.

Name-calling was of little help, for the new men had many different methodological and substantive axes to grind. Some, like Herbert McClosky or Robert Lane, worked in the intellectual tradition of social and clinical psychology; some, like Sebastian de Grazia or Morton Grodzins, were closer to cultural anthropology; and others, like Sam Eldersveld or myself, were more drawn to political sociology and institutional analysis. Some were empirical theorists, like David Easton or Richard C. Snyder, and others were theoretical empiricists, like Karl Deutsch or Robert Dahl. Some were functionalists, like Gabriel Almond, and others were organization theorists, like Herbert Simon. Some dealt in aggregate statistics, like V. O. Key; some in roll calls, like David Truman; some in opinions, like Bernard C. Cohen; some in attitudes, like Warren Miller; and some in roles, like John Wahlke. By the second half of the 'fifties, and whatever their substantive interests or methodological stances, the postwar generation of "Young Turks" had proved itself. Harold D. Lasswell became President of the American Political Science Association in 1955–1956, twenty years after he had done his most original work.

IV

The road led to Michigan's Survey Research Center, to the State Legislative Research Project, and to the Center for Advanced Study in the Behavioral Sciences. Each of these experiences had its unique impact on the work I was doing. I came to the Survey Research Center to learn the new techniques of survey analysis, to the Legislative Project to apply them, and to the Center at Stanford to review and set new goals.

The 1954 summer seminar on political behavior held at the SRC under the auspices of the Committee on Political Behavior differed from the earlier seminar held at Chicago in 1951—and the difference points up the development that was taking place. The 1951 seminar had programmatic objectives and its outcomes were a series of research designs for work yet to be done (and some of it never done). The 1954 seminar was a training seminar and its immediate results were a number of empirical studies that used the SRC's election surveys. Not only did I learn a great deal about sampling and machine work during that hot summer in Ann Arbor, but the need to reconceptualize the original data for the kind of secondary analysis I had in mind forced me to read a great deal about "social role" and related matters. I was acquainted with role concepts from earlier reading of Ralph Linton's *The Cultural Background of Personality* (1947) and Theodore M. Newcomb's *Social Psychology* (1950), but I had never read the classical statements of Charles H.

Cooley, *Social Organization* (1902) and *Human Nature and the Social Order* (1909),[24] or of George Herbert Mead, *Mind, Self and Society* (1934).[25]

Mead's work, in particular, proved highly suggestive. His emphasis on the social mechanisms that made for such psychological phenomena as identification, role-taking and other forms of symbolic behavior seemed to make more sense than Freud's unconscious or subconscious processes, for Mead's ideas could be more readily operationalized for research. This is not to say that I deny the importance of the unconscious. But, from a practical standpoint, Freudian psychology requires the intensive study of individual personality which is impossible in the study of the behavior of large aggregates or institutionalized elites. In Mead I found concepts and suggestions that could guide the analysis of the kind of data that survey research produces, and that could be used to make sense of data that otherwise might have escaped analysis. What astounded me at the time was that though he had so little to work with by way of empirical knowledge, for the prevailing social psychology was still quite underdeveloped, Mead seemed so eminently contempoary. The explanation is, I believe, that Mead the psychologist-philosopher was a man of great common sense, sensitive to the common things of life.[26]

A year later, in the summer of 1955, the State Legislative Research Project was founded and funded, and it occupied me for the next seven years until its final report was published in 1962.[27] The story of the project has been told elsewhere.[28] Here I must acknowledge the dual and sometimes dualistic influence of my colleagues, John Wahlke who gave the study much of its theoretical orientation, and William Buchanan who brought to it more technical research know-how than the rest of us had. And so we lived the wholesome tension between theory and research for seven years, designing the study, interviewing, coding, analyzing and finally writing. At long last being a behavioral political scientist had become a way of life. It is difficult to be so deeply involved in a research project and continue to read at the rate I had been used to before becoming immersed in the tedious little things, often the simplest clerical things, that one cannot avoid—even with the help of research assistants.

24. Cooley's two books are now available in a single volume published by The Free Press in 1956.

25. Although published in 1934 by the University of Chicago Press, the volume consists largely of lectures delivered in the 'twenties that had been recorded by some of Mead's students and were edited by Charles W. Morris.

26. Other members of the 1954 seminar, at times quite critical of my devotion to role analysis, were Robert Agger, Robert Lane and Allan Sindler.

27. See John C. Wahlke, Heinz Eulau, William Buchanan and LeRoy C. Ferguson, *The Legislative System: Explorations in Legislative Behavior* (New York: John Wiley & Sons, 1962).

28. See John C. Wahlke et al., "The Annals of Research: A Case of Collaboration in Comparative Study of Legislative Behavior," *The American Behavioral Scientist*, 4 (May, 1961), pp. 3–9.

One work stands out, S. F. Nadel's *The Theory of Social Structure* (1957). It came to our attention just as we were readying the data for analysis. Nadel, an English anthropologist, suggested to us the notion of "role system" which, in many respects, became the conceptual base of our explorations into legislative behavior. Not that we slavishly followed his formulations. If one learns one thing in doing empirical research, it is that the gap between theory and data is never fully closed, and that the data, no matter how carefully chosen to accommodate one's theoretical notions, have a way of being stubborn and resistant to what one may wish to do with them along theoretical lines.

In *Totem and Taboo* (1918) Freud discusses "animism, magic and the omnipotence of thought." I sometimes feel that much of what we are talking about in social science is not too far removed from the primitive's confusion of wishes and reality. There was, at the time, much talk of "functions" in political science, and as self-conscious avant-gardists we were not immune to the functional bug that was *au courant*. If someone saved us from making the kind of functional statements that are more reminiscent of the "omnipotence of thought" than of scientific method, it was Robert K. Merton in his discussion of functionalism.[29] The irritating thing about "functions," however conceived, is that they are so plausible in thought and yet so elusive in research. Because we assume functions to be there ("they *must* be there"), although we may not find them, we continue to speak in functional language. Our own work was not free of functional statements that I now consider of dubious merit. But we were quite innocent at the time.[30]

It was Max Weber, I think, who once wrote that ideas come when they please and not when it pleases us. This is probably true, but I found that being at the right place at the right time can help a great deal in one's thinking. I spent the year 1957-1958 at the Center for Advanced Study in the Behavioral Sciences, located on a hill overlooking Stanford University and a good part of San Francisco Bay. Of all the opportunities ever dreamed of by a social scientist, the Center is the social scientist's dream come true. Here, in an atmosphere of complete freedom where not academic status or past accomplishment but only intellectual fellowship mattered, we could take a long look backward as well as forward. Only three of us that year–David Easton, Ithiel Pool and I–were political scientists, but we probably learned a great deal from the seminars on child socialization, finite mathematics and other esoteric subjects. The world of the behavioral sciences appeared a booming, blooming

29. See Robert K. Merton, "Manifest and Latent Functions," in *Social Theory and Social Structure* (Glencoe, Ill.: The Free Press, 1957), pp. 19–84.

30. We had not come across, for instance, Carl G. Hempel's severe critique, "The Logic of Functional Analysis," in Llewellyn Gross, Ed., *Symposium on Sociological Theory* (Evanston, Ill.: Row, Peterson, 1959), pp. 271–307. Intellectural honesty suggests this: even if we had read Hempel, I doubt that we could or would have changed the functional statements we made in some places. Functionalism was too much the fashion in political science *circa* 1960.

and buzzing universe that can yet make sense if one surmounts the parochialisms of one's own field. In the Center's atmosphere of tolerance one learned that today's verities may be tomorrow's falsehoods, that social and political science must be lived and cannot just be learned. Paradoxical though it may be, living with it distinguishes our generation from the generation before us. The generation before us was largely afraid of the new developments; our generation welcomes them, even though they may make our own work obsolete. And if there is today so much receptiveness to new ideas, new concepts, new tools and techniques in political science, it is due to the leavening influence of the behavioral movement that from 1954 on found in the Center for Advanced Studies a hospitable and stimulating institutional environment.

V

Even though few of us were intellectual missionaries, there were missions to be performed, and missions in the modern world invariably lean on institutional crutches. The Center for Advanced Studies in the Behavioral Sciences was only the most splendid of the crutches. The first institutional crutch had been, of course, the Department of Political Science at the University of Chicago where, in the late 'twenties and 'thirties, a "first generation" of behavior-oriented scholars had been trained. But this I only know from hearsay, and in the spirit of this essay I must leave it to Chicagoans to talk about the influence that Charles Merriam, Leonard White, Quincy Wright, Harold Gosnell or Harold Lasswell may have had on them. In the early years I sometimes thought of myself as an "imaginary Chicagoan," which was a nice game to play but no substitute for the real thing.

Similarly, I must leave it to others to tell the story of the two Social Science Research Council committees—the Committee on Political Behavior and the Committee on Comparative Politics—that in the 'fifties did so much to advance behavioral and systematic political science. Both committees, I daresay, were greatly aided by the fortunate circumstance that the SSRC's President in those years was E. Pendleton Herring, a distinguished political scientist, who gave support and encouragement. His own books, and especially *The Politics of Democracy* (1940), had done a great deal to break down the formalism of an earlier political science. I remember swiping whole chapters from this book when I had to prepare my first lectures on American politics.

As far as I was concerned, the most important institutional crutch was the political behavior program organized at Michigan's Survey Research Center under the leadership of Angus Campbell, a social psychologist, to whom our whole profession must feel deeply indebted. Not that the relationship between the SRC and political science was all unidirectional: political scientists like V. O. Key, David Truman or Sam Eldersveld gave the Center perhaps as much as they received. But the Center's studies of American elections, beginning in 1948, had and still have great impact on political science.[31]

More important yet, out of the Center's work came the Inter-University Consortium for Political Research under the indefatigable leadership of Warren Miller. The original idea had been to make available, through pooled effort, the SRC's election data, either for secondary analyses by individual scholars or as teaching materials. If, it was thought, six or ten political science departments would join up, the Consortium idea could be considered a success. In fact, nineteen departments joined in the first year, 1962, and five years later over one hundred colleges and universities were affiliated in the common enterprise. Today, the Consortium is the single most important institutional vehicle for the study of political behavior. Not only does it distribute the SRC election surveys, but it is the major depository of data from many research projects in the political field. Through its summer programs, now attended by some three hundred graduate students and young professors, the Consortium has become a major training center. Through its conferences on particular topics at the frontiers of political science it has become the main stimulator of behavioral research. Through its contacts with scholars and research organizations abroad it has aided in making research there more empirical and scientific as well as in making research at home less parochial. All of these developments were aided, of course, by the rapid advances in computer technology which made data storage, retrieval and distribution a fact of research life. But, in the end, it was Warren Miller's skill and energy that built the Consortium and made possible the phenomenal growth of political behavior research in the 'sixties. Having followed this growth closely from the beginning, I am still amazed by what Miller and his associates, Philip Converse and Donald Stokes, have accomplished.

Long before the founding of the Consortium, some of us were concerned about the state of publications in political science. In the 'forties and early 'fifties the professional journals were largely edited by men suspicious of or hostile to the behavioral approaches. Although some behavioral research was gradually reported in these journals, there clearly was a publication gap. Most commercial publishers did not dare to venture beyond the traditional, and it was only in the 'sixties that they began to vie with each other for behavior-oriented books and authors. When, in 1955, Eldersveld, Janowitz and I tried

31. See, especially, Angus Campbell, Philip E. Converse, Warren E. Miller and Donald E. Stokes, *The American Voter* (New York: John Wiley & Sons, 1960), and *Elections and the Political Order* (New York: John Wiley & Sons, 1966). I should mention, in this connection, that of perhaps equal immediate impact was the work on voting behavior done at the Bureau of Applied Social Research of Columbia University by Paul F. Lazarsfeld and his associates. In fact, I was greatly influenced by all of Lazarsfeld's work and that of some of his students like S. M. Lipset, James S. Coleman, Charles Y. Glock and others of the "Young Turks" at Columbia. But I did not come to know them until later. See Paul F. Lazarsfeld, Bernard Berelson and Hazel Gaudet, *The People's Choice* (New York: Columbia University Press, 1948); and Bernard R. Berelson, Paul F. Lazarsfeld and William N. McPhee, *Voting* (Chicago: University of Chicago Press, 1954).

to put out a first "reader" on political behavior, two or three of the conventional publishers, advised by equally conventional consultants, turned us down. The Free Press of Glencoe, a courageous outfit more attuned to present needs and future demands, published the book without much ado. Out of this association came, a few years later, *The International Yearbook of Political Behavior Research,* a set of seven volumes reporting new research at the cutting edges of the discipline.[32] By 1968 it was no longer necessary to continue the series. The journals had by now been opened up to behavioral research, and the publishers were competing for contracts with behavioral political scientists.

I know next to nothing about the origins of Alfred de Grazia's magazine PROD (Political Research Organization and Design), later called *The American Behavioral Scientist,* which cheered us up in the late 'fifties. But I knew something in advance of the series called *Handbooks for Research in Political Behavior* that James A. Robinson began editing in 1963.[33] Interestingly, by the middle 'sixties, the problem was no longer one of finding outlets for research. On the contrary, the flood of behavioral books, monographs, research reports and articles called for a medium that would critically summarize and evaluate the flow of publications. Again it was James Robinson's energy and imagination that produced *Political Science Annual: An International Review.*[34]

I am not pretending or aspiring to write a history of all the developments that made for institutionalization of behavioral theory and research in political science. I am merely recalling those events in which I was personally involved or that had personal meaning for me at the time they happened. I am sure that others saw the developments differently, for all of us occupied quite different points from which to observe and participate.

And I hope it will not be inferred from all this that the behavioral movement has taken over political science. It would be false as a statement of fact or as a prediction. On the contrary, I believe that other approaches—historical, juridical or normative—will continue to be practiced in the foreseeable future. In fact, I think that rather than having displaced these approaches, the behavioral penetration of political science has had the effect of vitalizing and improving the older forms of writing and research. This is not to say that no excellent work was done in the past but that, even though the behavioral persuasion may not have persuaded all political scientists, it has had a salutary influence on the quality of all of political science.

32. All of these volumes were published by the Free Press. They include Morris Janowitz, Ed., *Community Political Systems* (1961); Dwaine Marvick, Ed., *Political Decision-Makers* (1961); Samuel P. Huntington, Ed., *Changing Patterns of Military Politics* (1962); Glendon Schubert, Ed., *Judicial Decision-Making* (1963); David E. Apter, Ed., *Ideology and Discontent* (1964); J. David Singer, Ed., *Quantitative International Politics* (1967); and Seymour M. Lipset and Stein Rokkan, Eds., *Party Systems and Voter Alignments* (1967).

33. The volumes in this series are published by the Northwestern University Press.

34. Published by The Bobbs-Merrill Company of Indianapolis. The first volume appeared in 1966.

This interpretation of what has been and is happening in political science largely guided my work between 1961 and 1967 as associate editor for political science of the *International Encyclopaedia of the Social Sciences*.[35] Had I been what at times I have been accused of being, "an intolerant behavioral imperialist," I could have assigned the three hundred and fifty odd political science articles exclusively to political behaviorists or their fellow travelers. I did not do so because I viewed the encyclopaedia as a document that should be true to the state of affairs and not as a propaganda instrument for a future that I personally might prefer. We therefore solicited contributions from all kinds of scholars, behavioral or not–from Leo Strauss, the most persistent and severe critic of behavioralism, to William Riker, one of the most advanced of the mathematical behaviorists. What mattered to us was to get the best possible articles. But this is not really the point I want to make. The point is that political science has not been conquered by the behaviorists, and there is no reason to believe that it will be in the future, if one means by conquest the annihilation of all approaches that are not behavioral. Behavioral theory and research have come to occupy an important and perhaps the central place in political science as a whole, but it is not an intellectual dispensation that all political scientists will want to embrace with equal fervor.

VI

To a participant observer the behavioral movement in political science is truly "movement," for it never stands still. There were fads, fashions, fantasies and fallacies that at times seemed to make the movement fall apart, but they also prevented the behavioral persuasion from becoming an ideology. And foibles, fumbles and failings have their own way of fertilizing the scientific enterprise.

Most of the problems that arose were at the soft under-belly of theory rather than at the hard bones of empirical research. This is not to minimize the work of those who were venturesome enough to stick their theoretical necks out, or to deny their influence. I variously and vicariously shared the enthusiasms of those who sought salvation in one kind or another of systems theory, decision theory, communication theory, functional theory, group theory and so on. There was no escape from these formulations that were all components of the behavioral persuasion. But I do not believe that, in the long run, the behavioral movement will be judged by these theoretical perishables; it will be and must be judged by its more empirical staples.[36] It is in the tedious cruci-

35. David L. Sills, a sociologist, was editor in chief; Peter Bock served as staff editor for political science, and I am deeply indebted to him for his perseverance and help. The work, in seventeen volumes, was published in 1968 jointly by the Macmillan Company and Free Press.

36. Some of the works I have in mind have already been cited; see footnotes 15, 27, 31 and 32. I might add the following: Robert A. Dahl, *Who Governs?* (New Haven: Yale University Press, 1961); Edward C. Banfield, *Political Influence* (New York: Free Press, 1961); Robert E. Agger et al., *The Rulers and the Ruled* (New York: John Wiley & Sons,

ble of empirical research that the political behavior approaches encounter their critical tests.

If one juxtaposes the theoretical enthusiasms and the empirical work that was done in the same period, one is struck by their basic dissociation. That, in the wake of the interdisciplinary awakening, political scientists had become sensitive to the enormous complexity of social affairs is understandable; and that they would be attracted by theoretical formulas seeking to comprehend the "total situation" or "whole configuration of events" is equally comprehensible. At the same time, the notorious failure of political science to develop methods of inquiry adequate to cope with the complexity of politics encouraged theoretical fancy. "Concern with methodology," I wrote in 1958, "has not been a hallmark of political science. One seeks in vain in the vast literature of politics for the kind and degree of methodological awareness easily found in the work of economists, sociologists, or psychologists."[37] And a few years later I noted the paradox that "there seems to be an inverse relationship between theorizing as an independently creative activity and the empirical accessibility of the phenomena theorized about." [38]

As a result, at the very time when political scientists seemed to advance their science by novel theoretical ventures, they may have actually moved away from the scientific enterprise. If I greeted the new theoretical efforts with joy, I maintained a measured skepticism nevertheless. For it was quite clear that political science, to be a science, would have to meet the problem of causation. And this the new theories failed to do. "The defense, or better, the rationalization," I wrote in 1963, "has been that, in any case, the task of behavioral research is to establish functional rather than causal relations between variables. This is a rather disingenuous avoidance of the causal challenge." [39]

1964); V. O. Key, Jr., *Public Opinion and American Democracy* (New York: Knopf, 1961); Robert E. Lane, *Political Ideology* (New York: Free Press 1962); Morton Grodzins, *The American System* (Chicago: Rand McNally, 1966); David B. Truman, *The Congressional Party* (New York: John Wiley and Sons, 1959); Donald R. Matthews, *U.S. Senators and Their World* (Chapel Hill: University of North Carolina Press, 1960); Raymond A. Bauer et al., *American Business and Public Policy* (New York: Atherton Press, 1963); James D. Barber, *The Lawmakers* (New Haven: Yale University Press, 1965); Richard F. Fenno, Jr., *The Power of the Purse* (Boston: Little Brown, 1966); Morris Janowitz, *The Professional Soldier* (Glencoe: The Free Press, 1960); Gabriel A. Almond and Sidney Verba, *The Civic Culture* (Princeton: Princeton University Press, 1963); Samuel J. Eldersveld, *Political Parties: A Behavioral Analysis* (Chicago: Rand McNally 1964); Donald R. Matthews and James W. Prothro, *Negroes and the New Southern Politics* (New York: Harcourt, Brace & World, 1966).

37. "H. D. Lasswell's Developmental Analysis," *Western Political Quarterly,* 11 (June, 1958), p. 229.

38. "Segments of Political Science Most Susceptible to Behavioristic Treatment" (1962), in James C. Charlesworth, Ed., *Contemporary Political Analysis* (New York: Free Press, 1967), p. 40.

39. *The Behavioral Persuasion in Politics,* p. 128.

The work that critically influenced my thinking about the "causal challenge" had been Robert M. MacIver's *Social Causation* (1942), a much neglected book that I first encountered in the late 'forties. "Too often," MacIver had written, "the attempt is made to investigate the causes of undelimited phenomena . . . and when the investigator is baffled by the hopeless task of finding specific causes for manifestations that appear in endlessly variant conjunctures he is apt to abjure the quest for causes altogether and even to deny its scientific validity." [40] Political scientists were in a hurry, and they often forgot that "an empirical science is built by the slow, modest, and piecemeal cumulation of theory, methods, and data." [41] As MacIver put it, "the goal of causal knowledge is never attained, though our endeavors can bring us always nearer." [42]

The neglect of MacIver's book on causation was probably due to the fact that it appeared at a time when political scientists had little opportunity for reading; but it was probably also due to the fact that the technology of social science was insufficiently developed to confront the causal challenge. It was brilliant Herbert Simon who among political scientists first picked up the challenge although there is no indication in his work that he was acquainted with MacIver's vindication of causal analysis. Simon evidently arrived quite independently at the realization that unless the problem of "power" as "a central problem of political science" is solved, "political science, defined as the study of power, cannot be said to exist." [43] And it had been his discovery that in referring to an asymmetrical relationship the problem of power "was identical with the general problem of defining a *causal relation* between two variables." [44]

Simon tackled the problems involved by mathematical means that were largely beyond the comprehension of most political scientists, and for a time Simon was a lonely pioneer, at least as far as this aspect of his work is concerned. His revival today, largely due to Hubert M. Blalock's important work, *Causal Inferences in Nonexperimental Research* (1964), suggests that a new generation of political scientists is prepared to abandon the hasty search for "global" understanding and settle down to the difficult task of empirical causal analysis.

Yet, as I survey the scene, new difficulties are on the horizon. Paradoxically, the new computer technology which makes more sophisticated and complex analysis possible also seems to bring with it a new version of a rather brute empiricism. The concepts that are used have a modern ring and the canons of scientific procedure are scrupulously observed, but disillusionment with theory

40. Robert M. MacIver, *Social Causation* (New York: Harper Torchbooks, 1964), p. 375.

41. *The Behavioral Persuasion in Politics*, p. 116.

42. MacIver, *op cit.*, p. 392.

43. Herbert A. Simon, *Models of Man* (New York: John Wiley and Sons, 1957), p. 4. See especially "Notes on the Observation and Measurement of Political Power" (1953), *ibid.*, pp. 62–78.

44. *Ibid.*, p. 5.

and preoccupation with technology seem to make for a new untheoretical approach. For instance, there is much interest in the relationship between structural and contextual properties of political systems and policy outputs or outcomes. But the studies reported so far are largely descriptive and devoid of theoretically interesting hypotheses. Because one can dump all kinds of data into the computer, scale them, factor-analyze them or correlate them, what comes out of the computer is not *ipso facto* of theoretical merit.

I am of course perfectly aware of the manifold problems and dilemmas involved in the continued tension between theory and empirical research. What I am pleading for is simply that we keep these problems and dilemmas at the forefront of attention rather than shove them aside as if they did not exist. Blindness is dogma's first cousin. The behavioral persuasion in the study of politics can remain true to itself only if it remains true to that liberal spirit that through the centuries has fostered the advance of science. As Morris Cohen, the philosopher, put it many years ago, science can move forward "because it embraces self-correcting principles which permit the correction of error and partial truth without an overthrow of the system that makes such correction possible." [45]

45. Morris R. Cohen, *The Faith of a Liberal* (New York: Henry Holt, 1946), p. 452.

Index

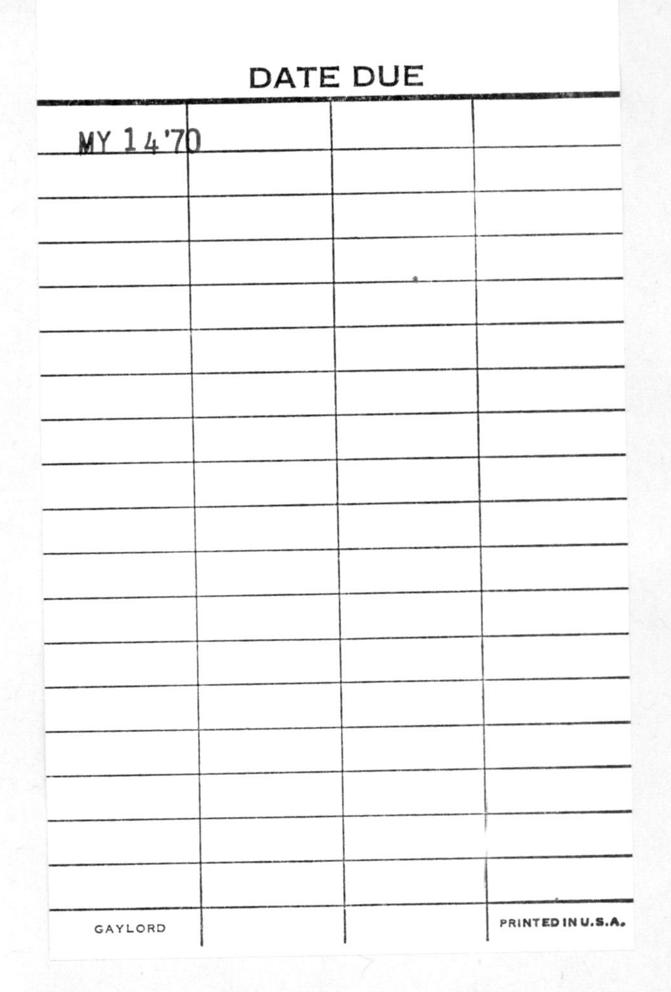